CRIME FICTION

ALSO BY BARRY FORSHAW

Nordic Noir
Italian Cinema
American Noir
British Crime Film
Sex and Film
British Gothic Cinema
Euro Noir
Historical Noir
BFI War of the Worlds
British Crime Writing: An Encyclopedia
Brit Noir

CRIME FICTION

A Reader's Guide

Barry Forshaw

Oldcastle Books

This edition published in 2019 by Oldcastle Books,
Harpenden, UK
oldcastlebooks.co.uk

Copyeditor: Judith Forshaw

First edition published by Rough Guides in 2007

© Barry Forshaw, 2007, 2019

The right of Barry Forshaw to be identified as the author of this work has been asserted in accordance with the Copyright, Designs and Patents Act 1988.

All rights reserved. No part of this book may be reproduced, stored in or introduced into a retrieval system, or transmitted, in any form or by any means (electronic, mechanical, photocopying, recording or otherwise) without the written permission of the publishers.

Any person who does any unauthorised act in relation to this publication may be liable to criminal prosecution and civil claims for damages.

A CIP catalogue record for this book is available from the British Library.

ISBN
978-0-85730-335-6 (print)
978-0-85730-336-3 (ebook)

2 4 6 8 10 9 7 5 3 1

Typeset by Elsa Mathern

Printed and bound in Great Britain by Clays Ltd, Elcograf S.p.A.

For more information about Crime Fiction go to @crimetimeuk

CONTENTS

Foreword: Ian Rankin 7
A note on locating authors in *Crime Fiction: A Reader's Guide* 9

CHAPTER 1
Reading the entrails: origins, motives, sources 11

CHAPTER 2
The Golden Age: classic mysteries 25

CHAPTER 3
Hardboiled and pulp: tough guys and tough talk 43

CHAPTER 4
Private eyes: sleuths and gumshoes 59

CHAPTER 5
Cops: police procedurals and mavericks 83

CHAPTER 6
Professionals:
lawyers, doctors, forensic scientists and others 136

CHAPTER 7
Amateur investigators:
journalists, other professionals and self-styled sleuths 155

CHAPTER 8
Dark psychology: external – and internal – pressure 174

CHAPTER 9
Psychopaths and serial killers 202

CHAPTER 10
In the belly of the beast: criminal protagonists 217

CHAPTER 11
Organised crime: wise guys and godfathers 234

CHAPTER 12
Crime and society: class, ethnicity and politics 244

CHAPTER 13
Espionage: spooks and betrayals **265**

CHAPTER 14
Domestic noir: lies and murder in the family **293**

CHAPTER 15
Cosy crime: dialling down the sex and violence **301**

CHAPTER 16
Blockbusters: crime on a grand scale **312**

CHAPTER 17
Comic crime: tongue-in-cheek mayhem **323**

CHAPTER 18
Through a glass darkly: historical crime **336**

CHAPTER 19
Foreign bloodshed: crime in translation **371**

Appendix 1: Six key Scandinavian thrillers **410**
Appendix 2: Top political thrillers **412**
Appendix 3: Five favourites **413**
Appendix 4: Addenda: J Kingston Pierce **415**
Appendix 5: Addenda: Craig Sisterson **417**

Acknowledgements **419**
About the author **421**
Index of authors and directors **423**
Index of titles **435**

FOREWORD
Ian Rankin

Has crime fiction finally achieved the literary respectability that has long been its due? Certainly, crime novels are covered in the books pages of newspapers far more often than they were. But when a famous prize-winning literary novelist turned his hand in recent years to crime fiction, he felt obliged to put it out under another name. Is there still something disreputable about the genre?

While I have written in a variety of genres, I continue to find the crime novel the perfect vehicle for a discussion of contemporary issues in the most unflinching terms. After all, the detective has an 'all areas pass' to every aspect of the contemporary urban scene, and this is a way for the crime writer to take the reader into forbidden territory; for instance, it was always my mission in the Rebus books to show people an Edinburgh that the tourist doesn't see. And crime fiction has always been good at articulating the fears that society has harboured at all moments of history – such as the stranger who will casually take your life. Equally, the genre is able to deal with high moral purpose in quite as rigorous a fashion as Dostoyevsky did in *Crime and Punishment* and Dickens did in *Bleak House*.

It's difficult these days to write about contemporary life in a crime context and not have violence. Mind you, I don't think that is just an issue for the crime novel – it is a problem for all contemporary fiction.

Violence fascinates us because it is deemed unacceptable by society and therefore the people who commit violence are breaking our self-imposed rules, rules that underpin the very notion of civilisation. Rule breakers make us curious: why don't they want to be like us? Why do they make the choice not to conform? Do they actually make a choice, or is it made for them (by their genetic coding, their circumstances, etc.)? The crime novel should tackle the question of violence whether we reach any answers or not, shouldn't it?

People are interested in crime fiction because they are fascinated by the margins of the world, those places where society's rules break down. They wonder what they would do in similar situations, how they would cope. They learn how to deal with fear and the unknown. And at the end, they have the sense that a certain justice has been seen to be done.

Barry Forshaw has tackled these issues (and many others) in a book that covers crime fiction from every part of the world – it's a daunting task.

Ian Rankin, Edinburgh

A note on locating authors in *Crime Fiction: A Reader's Guide*

As you will see, this study is divided into various sections and categories – sometimes, I admit, a touch arbitrarily, but I felt I needed to give a coherent shape to the whole book. If you are seeking a particular author, my advice is not to second-guess what category I've placed them in – apart from anything else, several authors appear in multiple categories – but to turn straight to the indexes at the end of the book. And if I've missed a favourite author, I trust you will cut me some slack. I've tried to be as inclusive as possible, but in a book of this size it was inevitable that there would be many omissions. Not that this caveat will get me off the hook – I tried to be as comprehensive as I could with my arm-straining two-volume, 900-page encyclopaedia, *British Crime Writing*, but over the years people have relished pointing out to me who is missing…

CHAPTER 1

READING THE ENTRAILS
Origins, motives, sources

Is it possible to predict the direction crime fiction will take now that we are well into a new century? Initially, the auguries are bad: many classic genres (notably the police procedural) have undergone a distinct hardening of the arteries, as inspiration gives way to cliché and innovation to repetition. As all hard-pressed crime writers know, it becomes increasingly tough to come up with something new. Editing *Crime Time* magazine, most of the letters I received lamented the difficulties of tracking down that one fresh and inventive novel among much that is – shall we say – warmed over. And yet crime fiction remains (*pace* books about witches, wizards, dragons and spurious codes) one of the few evergreen areas of modern publishing, with fresh trends continually appearing, including the Nordic noir wave (still healthy) and domestic noir, both covered herein.

While a case can be made for the origins of the crime novel lying in the 19th century, equally plausible cases can be made for antecedents even further back. It is cold comfort that, according to the Bible, when Cain slew Abel, the third human ever created had managed to murder the fourth. A little later, **Sophocles**' *Oedipus Rex*, a search for the truth about himself, has all the classic ingredients of the psychological mystery, even down to the final painful acquisition of knowledge leading to the destruction of the protagonist, and most of his family. Noir territory, indeed. No less dark are

William Shakespeare's pivotal assassination dramas *Julius Caesar* (think conspiracy theories) and the malign 'Scottish play' (for Lady Macbeth read almost every femme fatale to glower from the silver screen). But, while we can possibly shoehorn the Bible, Sophocles and Shakespeare into the genre as progenitors of crime fiction, the concept of the cliffhanger mystery novel took off in the 19th century almost equally and simultaneously in gothic, Romantic and realist writing. Where the gothic writers preferred a darkly supernatural sense of suspense and denouement, horribly real cops, secret agents and villains occur regularly in the work of **Honoré de Balzac**, while the world's first dogged detective (albeit also a blackguard) trails **Victor Hugo**'s Jean Valjean through almost every page of *Les Misérables* (1862).

An obsession with crime, the dark, nefarious underworld and just retribution was revealed in the popularity of publications such as *The Newgate Calendar*, and by the end of the century lurid 'penny dreadfuls' and 'shilling shockers' vied for bookstand space with **Bram Stoker**'s comparatively respectable parlour-piece *Dracula* (1897), just as the world's first serial killer, Jack the Ripper, was stalking the streets of Whitechapel, and canny film producers were seeking sensational stories to project onto the minds of a willing and hungry public huddled in circus tents.

But the most significant innovation of the 19th century was that of American polymath **Edgar Allan Poe**'s C Auguste Dupin, who first displayed the requisite cool ratiocination and ability to marshal facts that were to become the *sine qua non* of the investigative detective. Poe even created the less brilliant follower for his detective (in order that the hero's mental pyrotechnics might be displayed more satisfyingly). Poe was greatly admired in France, and translation of his work by Baudelaire (among others) was to spread his influence far beyond the provincial Stateside streets of Baltimore and Richmond.

Leaving aside **Charles Dickens**' Inspector Bucket and Mr Nadgett (who certainly deserve namechecks in any overview of crime fiction) and the master's unfinished murder novel *The Mystery of Edwin Drood* (1870), it is tidier to settle on his friend **Wilkie Collins**, with *The Woman in White* (1859) and *The Moonstone* (1868) as the first instances of great crime novels. A reacquaintance with these two most readable books demonstrates that many of the key elements we recognise so well (notably the hyper-intelligent, hyper-ingenious villain, the slightly dim hero whom we follow piecing together the mystery, and a narrative crammed full of delicious obfuscation)

Edgar Allan Poe
(1809–49)

Orphaned, a failed soldier, a bankrupt gambler and an alcoholic incapable of holding down a job, forced to live with his child wife's mother, and eventually dead in a gutter aged 40. How could this man become an outstanding poet, essayist and progenitor of at least five literary genres: the short story (or tale), horror, science fiction, psychological fiction and the crime novel? Probably his background predisposed him to introspection, gloom and despond, but the elegance of his style and intricate intellectual curiosity give even his darkest works a burnished gleam. The obsessive protagonists of many of his tales prefigure both the criminals and sleuths of later writers: 'The Tell-Tale Heart' (1843) deals explicitly with a murderer's guilt, as does 'The Cask of Amontillado' (1846). But it is the three tales featuring the detective C Auguste Dupin (massively influential on Conan Doyle), who uses observation, logic and lateral thinking to solve crimes, that claim primacy for crime enthusiasts. 'The Murders in the Rue Morgue' (1841) is the prototypical locked-room mystery; 'The Mystery of Marie Rogêt' (1842) was based on an actual case in New York and introduces the problem of reconstructing what happened to a murder victim in the last days of her life; 'The Purloined Letter' (1845) involves a psychological game to reveal a blackmail trophy.

The Mystery Writers of America award, the Edgar, is named in his memory.

---

are firmly in place. But it is also salutary to note that one element – the elegance and polish of the prose – has become less common since those distant days. Whenever the diehard crime reader picks up a modern novel as well written as Collins' were, it's a cause for some celebration. Of course, eventually the genre had to accommodate lean, pared-down prose as much as Collins' more intricately orchestrated language. It was a matter of economics, cut-and-thrust suspense, and popular appeal.

And it was another writer, from the next generation, who was to bring the concept to its greatest fruition – a marriage of author and character that few have achieved since.

Arthur Conan Doyle's creation of the master detective Sherlock Holmes – as noted above – owed much to Poe's Dupin (the latter is even discussed in the stories), but his extension of the concept into a considerable canon of work that stretched over 40 years demonstrates a craftsmanship that simply beggars belief. His masterstroke, of course, was to take the relationship between the unconventional, brilliant investigator and his assistant and develop it into something rich and resonant. Again and again, the sheer pleasure of the stories comes from the nuances of the relation between Holmes and Watson as much as from the plot revelations (some of which, as Conan Doyle well knew, were outrageously implausible), and the way in which details of Holmes's character were freighted in (the violin, the depression caused by inactivity, the '7 per cent solution', etc.) ensured that Conan Doyle's detective became probably the best-known Englishman in fiction, and one of the first truly international bestsellers. His influence is felt to this day, with writers such as **Joe Ide** providing contemporary spins on Holmes-like detectives.

At about the same time as Conan Doyle was concocting Holmes, other criminal currents were stirring. In Russia, **Fyodor Dostoyevsky** was creating a template for the existential psycho-killer (*Crime and Punishment*, 1866) and the familial destruction novel (*The Brothers Karamazov*, 1880). And a French realist dealt with a range of shady lowlife scenarios and godfathered the domestic *ménage à trois* that results in murder. Two lovers who can't keep their hands off each other and who have sex on the floor; an inconvenient and unattractive husband who has to be removed. I know – you're thinking of **James M Cain**'s *The Postman Always Rings Twice* (1934)? Or one of its many imitators? No, another writer got there earlier... **Émile Zola**, with his carnal and edgy *Thérèse Raquin* in 1867. Who can write about sex like Zola these days, with authors all flinching in advance at the thought of nomination for the Bad Sex Award or political correctness? What about this passage:

> Then, in a single violent motion, Laurent stooped and caught the young woman against his chest. He thrust her head back, crushing her lips against his own. She made a fierce, passionate gesture of revolt, and

then, all of a sudden, she surrendered herself, sliding to the floor, on to the tiles. Not a word passed between them. The act was silent and brutal.

The Vintage Classics translation by Adam Thorpe makes one realise why Zola was so shocking in his day.

The inherent brutality (as well as the concupiscence and violence) of Zola's work found expression in another infernal triangle in the blunt and excoriating *La Bête Humaine* of 1890 (the Oxford World's Classics version is translated by Roger Pearson), a richer, more complex experience than *Thérèse*. The unlucky trio here are the eponymous 'human beast' Lantier, gripped by a hereditary madness and a desire to murder; Séverine, an object of lust for men, yet someone who retains an unsullied centre; and Roubaud, her brutal husband who cuts the throat of one of her ex-lovers. American paperback editions emphasised the steaminess (calling it *The Human Beast* and adorning the jackets with copious cleavage); English editions tended to stick to the original French title. The book, though, is about far more than a sordid homicide: Zola's targets include the French judicial system (which he was to excoriate during the Dreyfus affair) and there is a brilliant realisation of the world of railways and railwaymen. My advice to crime writers looking to re-energise their batteries when writing about murder and sex? Pick up two visceral novels written well over a century ago and learn from a master.

By the turn of the century, the Polish exile **Joseph Conrad** was writing (in English) about terrorism and subterfuge in a pair of mirror novels concerning anarchists: tragically incompetent ones in England in *The Secret Agent* (1907), and doomed but heroic ones in Tsarist Russia in *Under Western Eyes* (1911). Notions of international conspiracy featured in **Rudyard Kipling**'s Indian Great Game masterpiece *Kim* (1901), but soon focused on Germany and were epitomised by two seminal spy novels: *The Riddle of the Sands* (1903) by the Irish Republican gunrunner **Erskine Childers**, and **John Buchan**'s *The Thirty-Nine Steps* (1915), which he followed up with skulduggery in the Middle East in *Greenmantle* (1916). While the emancipated inter-war world of the Jazz Age saw an exponential rise in popular fiction of all sorts, headlined by a crime sector ranging from the roughhouse of **Sapper**'s Bulldog Drummond to the elegant amateur detective work of **Agatha Christie**'s protagonists, it would be a later English writer, **Eric Ambler**, who almost single-handedly created the sensibility that lies behind the modern thriller: the layers of psychological complexity that inform the

Fantômas

Fantômas is the master criminal created by **Pierre Souvestre** and **Marcel Allain** in 1911. The duo were the French equivalent of later American pulp writers who churned out bloody and sensational fare to order – and Fantômas was designed to inaugurate a series of five novels. But the immense success of the character (a ruthless, megalomaniac master of disguise who always eludes capture) meant that he went on to enjoy a lengthy literary life, with other authors taking over to chronicle his adventures. The first novel (entitled simply *Fantômas*) was written in the crudest of styles, but its canny use of crowd-pleasing elements (violence, horror and a bracing amorality) guaranteed some high-minded disapproval – and healthy sales as a result. Intriguingly, the character was taken up by the artistic avant-garde, and the poet **Guillaume Apollinaire** was a devoted follower. But when **Louis Feuillade** began his series of Fantômas films, the character's place in the firmament of popular culture was assured (not least because the films were far more accomplished than the novels). By the late 20th century, the novels were only fitfully reprinted; for those who read French, however, Fantômas novels can still be found on the bookstalls along the Seine.

work of **Graham Greene** and **John le Carré** clearly owe as much to Ambler as they do to **Joseph Conrad** or **Fyodor Dostoyevsky**. But before Greene and le Carré brought the thriller to this level of literary *gravitas*, another significant movement had transformed the genre. And this revolution had begun in the despised medium of the American pulp magazine.

In its day, the writing in such gaudily illustrated American pulp magazines as *Black Mask* and its stablemates had enjoyed a considerable readership, even though the writers who turned out a massive wordcount for modest returns had little thought of literary respectability. That was to come much later – and despite such trenchant practitioners as **Cornell Woolrich** and **James M Cain**, two men came to personify the tough, witty and exuberant writing that became known as the American hardboiled school: **Dashiell Hammett** and **Raymond Chandler**. Between them, they created a landscape that continues to resonate in the crime genre today, and the crackling one-liners of Chandler still inspire writers, even those whose 'mean streets' are the Home Counties. Chandler had a particular dislike of the classic English detective story and famously praised Hammett for giving murder back to those who 'had a reason for it, rather than just to provide a body'. The heirs apparent of Chandler included such accomplished and powerful writers as **Ross Macdonald**, and Chandler also lived to see **Mickey Spillane** take the tough private eye downmarket and way over to the right politically, while upping the ante in the sex and violence stakes.

As what might be defined as the modern era dawned, it seemed that the possibilities of crime fiction were limitless. Readers were less concerned with the arbitrarily drawn battle lines between genres and were happy to investigate the best writing in any area of the crime novel. In Britain, by the 1980s two women writers had been established as the twin queens of crime: **PD James** and **Ruth Rendell**. Taking the police procedural and classic crime novel, both writers deepened and enriched existing formulas, mining them for their narrative possibilities while adding new levels of invention and psychology. The crime-consuming public took to its heart the tough Scottish novels of **Ian Rankin** on the one hand and, on the other, the laconic, nigh-comic, post-hardboiled dialogue of American novelists such as **Carl Hiaasen**, **James Lee Burke** and **Elmore Leonard**. And today, the field is so rich in idiosyncratic and individual practitioners (covering the spectrum from **Robert Wilson** to **Abir Mukherjee**, from **Attica Locke** to **Pierre Lemaitre**, and from **Harlan Coben** to **Val McDermid**) that jeremiads about the future of the genre might seem to be unnecessary. Only a handful of crime writers might be considered to have reached 'the edge', where future invention seems inconceivable – **James Ellroy** and **Thomas Harris** among them – but more of that later.

This book presents a selection of the best in crime writing from the last century or so, organised by subject (or subgenre). Often, the books selected are simply the best of an author's writing, or at least a useful introduction to often extensive bodies of work. Along the way, brief sections on the more popular authors are added, as are profiles of those writers whose contribution to the evolution of crime writing is irrefutable. Notes on significant screen adaptations are included, along with a selection of sideways glances at the subject.

But, to begin with, a few classics that definitively established the genre and its various strands.

Trent's Last Case   1913
EC BENTLEY

One of the most celebrated of murder mysteries that preceded the Golden Age is also one of the most unusual in terms of its unorthodox structure. While the detective protagonist presented to us by Bentley (amateur sleuth Philip Trent) initially appears to conform to the standard requirements for such characters (resourceful, tenacious, cracking a baffling murder case through the steady accumulation of facts), the author has quite a surprise for us in the latter half of the book – a surprise that, at a stroke, makes *Trent's Last Case* a rather postmodern novel. The eponymous investigator is employed by a London paper to file pieces of investigative journalism, and he is sent to Marlstone to look into the murder of an American moneyman named Manderson who has been shot in his garden shed. Trent, in somewhat unconventional fashion, begins to dig beneath the surface of the mystery and discovers that the attractive widow of the murdered man, Mabel, was suffering in a loveless marriage to the ruthless financier. Ill-advisedly, Trent finds himself falling in love with the seductive widow, but he is still able to solve the murder – albeit in a rather vague fashion that irritated, among others, **Raymond Chandler**. But now comes the surprise that Bentley has up his sleeve: the narrative continues, with Trent relocated to Germany and struggling to shake free from the *amour fou* that has blighted his life. It's this radical shaking up of the standard narrative procedure (almost before the rules of the genre had been set in stone) that now seems postmodern – as if Bentley was uncomfortable with what he perceived to be the demands of the detective story. Bentley, basically a humourist, and inventor of the clerihew verse form, followed up with *Trent's Own Case* in 1936.

The Thirty-Nine Steps   1915
JOHN BUCHAN

Without *The Thirty-Nine Steps*, the world would be missing such classic novels as **Geoffrey Household**'s *Rogue Male*. And **Alfred Hitchcock**'s matchless British film of Buchan's novel. And, for that matter, the spy thriller in the **Ian Fleming** vein – although the latter adds a libido and relative classlessness to John Buchan's upper-crust English hero. The most famous novel by Buchan remains as much of a delight as when it first appeared – and it is one of the greatest espionage thrillers ever written, its dated aspects part of its charm. Concise and eventful, Buchan's story has his mining engineer Richard Hannay at a loose end after returning from Rhodesia, as conflict bubbles away in Europe in the years before the Great War. After an American spy is killed in his flat, Hannay goes on the run (across a brilliantly realised Scotland – this is the ultimate picaresque thriller) from both the police and enemy agents. Those who feel they know Buchan's tale too well from the numerous adaptations should really go back to the irresistible source novel.

THE 39 STEPS   1935
Director: Alfred Hitchcock

The blueprint for many of Hitchcock's subsequent films (*North by Northwest*, *Saboteur*, *Torn Curtain*), this is one of that rare breed of films (like **Michael Curtiz**'s *Casablanca*) in which absolutely every element (screenplay, direction, cinematography, playing) is balanced to perfection. Robert Donat is perfectly cast as the very British hero, and the customary Hitchcock cocktail of suspense and dry humour gets its most adroit workout in the director's English period before he was tempted by Hollywood. Subsequent remakes (with Kenneth More in 1959 and Robert Powell in 1978) were efficient enough, but not remotely in the league of Hitchcock's original.

The Man Who Was Thursday   1908
GK CHESTERTON

Chesterton was born in London in 1874 and made his mark speaking out against the Boer War. In many ways, he was the quintessential Edwardian writer, hobnobbing with the likes of **HG Wells** and **George Bernard Shaw**. From his large range of writing, he is best remembered these days for his Father Brown stories, in which the gentle ecclesiastical sleuth solves problems after the fashion of the ratiocinator of 221b Baker Street. Admirers, however, rate *The Man Who Was Thursday* as his finest work in the crime field. It's a cutting analysis of anarchism (much as **Joseph Conrad** had undertaken in *The Secret Agent* the year before). Chesterton's protagonists

Sir Arthur Conan Doyle
(1859–1930)

Sir Arthur Conan Doyle's imperishable creation – Sherlock Holmes – is one of the best-known characters in world fiction, with current iterations (such as Benedict Cumberbatch's modern-day version) still captivating admirers. However, a famous *Punch* cartoon of the day showed the author shackled to his celebrated pipe-smoking creation, and Conan Doyle often voiced his exasperated desire to be remembered for something other than his cocaine-using protagonist (whom he unsuccessfully tried to kill off with a plunge down the Reichenbach Falls). But it was Holmes rather than the author's own preferred historical fiction that made Conan Doyle (along with **HG Wells**) the most celebrated popular writer of his age – even though he seemed to lack the rigorous deductive reasoning of his hero. The most famous incident in the author's non-literary life – dramatised in both the cinema and on TV – involved Conan Doyle's credulous belief in doctored pictures of fairies produced by two schoolgirls. To modern eyes, Conan Doyle's acceptance of this ludicrous hoax seems astonishing, but the author's personal losses (as so often) predisposed him towards a desire to believe in the supernatural (surprisingly, not reflected in his fiction), and he famously espoused several very suspect causes – Conan Doyle was, in fact, something of a target for charlatans.

While the four novels featuring Holmes and Watson (most notably *The Hound of the Baskervilles*) have their virtues, none is as completely successful as the many perfectly proportioned short stories, originally

are Lucian Gregory and Gabriel Syme, who wear the apparel of poets. One, however, is an anarchist, and the other a policeman. In the dark counter-world in which they both move, personality and function are defined by a code word, and one of the duo becomes 'Thursday'. But their universe is not just a place of vaguely surrealistic posing; it is also a world of madness and fear. The London locales here are conjured with a disorientating eye (as are the settings for a chase in northern France), and the narrative functions both as a thriller and as a complex symbolist nightmare. The Father Brown books may be the author's most popular work, but this is his best.

published in *The Strand* magazine (1859–1930). Holmes first appeared in *A Study in Scarlet*, published in *Beeton's Christmas Annual* in 1887, and was an immediate hit. But by 1891 Conan Doyle was already talking of killing him off. He attempted to do so in 1893, but public and financial pressure meant that, in total, some 56 Holmes stories were eventually published.

Conan Doyle's legacy is quite as tangled – and death-fraught – as any cases the writer created for his Baker Street mastermind and the faithful Dr Watson, and his collection of manuscripts has been the source of quite as much plotting and counter-plotting as the 'Naval Treaty' that Sherlock Holmes retrieved. From the 1930s onwards, the disputes began, with Conan Doyle's sons Adrian and Denis spending their legacy in profligate fashion, before both dying at surprisingly early ages (Adrian had tried – with a conspicuous lack of success – to continue the Great Detective's adventures in his own series).

Conan Doyle was a prolific writer, covering historical romances (*The Exploits of Brigadier Gérard*) and even science fiction (the Professor Challenger stories, including the prototype dinosaur urtext *The Lost World*), but Holmes remains his most enduring creation.

The Riddle of the Sands 1903
ERSKINE CHILDERS

Highly regarded as an account of small sailing boat cruising, this was also one of the first of many books that rang alarm bells about German preparations for aggressive warfare against her neighbours. Two gentlemen facing the prospect of an idle London summer take off on a sailing holiday along the East Frisian shore. Various encounters lead them to suspect the build-up of German military and naval resources destined to form an invasion force aimed at Britain, and the race is on to alert the British authorities. In no way naive, the book was not only prescient in historical terms but also laid the foundations for many of the basic formulae of spy novels to follow, notably those of **John Buchan**. Winston Churchill took it seriously enough to instigate the Admiralty's fortification of England's east coast defences and the creation of naval bases at Scapa Flow, the Firth of Forth and Invergordon. Childers himself, an experienced soldier and sailor, was later executed as a traitor by the newly formed Irish Free State, despite having supported them after the Easter Uprising.

THE RIDDLE OF THE SANDS — 1979
Director: Tony Maylam

Taking advantage of the maritime setting and slow pace of the novel, the perfectly cast gung-ho British actors Michael York and Simon MacCorkindale do a fair job of bringing a slightly edited version of **Erskine Childers'** novel to life, as does Howard Blake's fitting score. Both Hans Meyer and Alan Badel bring suitable menace to their roles as devious Germans Grimm and Dollmann respectively, while Jenny Agutter once again dons an Edwardian costume to bring a feminine element to what is the essential Boy's Own adventure.

The Case-Book of Sherlock Holmes — 1927
SIR ARTHUR CONAN DOYLE

This volume features the final 12 stories published in *The Strand* magazine that Conan Doyle was to write about the detective, and in many ways they crystallised the universal appeal of the character. The stories are particularly interesting in their willingness to take on subjects that must have been uncomfortable to a less tolerant readership than that of the present century. In many of them, a dark and destructive secret lies at the heart of rigidly maintained Victorian propriety, and Conan Doyle's dispassionate unearthing of these undercurrents gives the stories a peculiarly subversive charge. But then again, they were written several years after the turn of the 20th century. Many of the great Conan Doyle classics are to be found here, such as 'The Adventure of the Creeping Man' and 'The Adventure of the Mazarin Stone'. Conan Doyle had tried to kill off the detective in the

Reichenbach Falls struggle with his nemesis, Professor Moriarty, but the writer's affectionate farewell to his greatest creation in the introduction to the stories is genuinely touching.

SHERLOCK HOLMES 1984–94
Producers: Michael Cox and June Wyndham Davies

For many years, the urbane Hollywood expatriate Basil Rathbone remained the perfect incarnation of the Great Detective (not least for his Holmesian profile and ability to wear a deerstalker without looking absurd), but his otherwise splendid series of adaptations for Universal Studios in the 1940s were compromised by a fluctuating sense of period, and a doltish (if lovable) Dr Watson. The BBC ran a successful series in the 1960s, with the lugubrious Douglas Wilmer in the lead, stolidly supported by Nigel Stock, also slightly parodic, as the doctor. But two decades later, and at a stroke, the brilliant and neurasthenic performance of Jeremy Brett established itself as definitive, aided by his impeccable accent, fastidious attention to detail and two excellent – and intelligent – Watsons (first David Burke, later to be succeeded by Edward Hardwicke). Granada's cleverly written series of adaptations consolidated their appeal with period atmosphere and a supporting cast that drew from the cream of the British acting profession. Brett's bipolar depression is thought to have contributed significantly to his interpretation of Holmes's character.

SHERLOCK 2010–17
Producers: Sue Vertue and Elaine Cameron

The success of *Sherlock*, a postmodern, self-referential, modern-day riff on Conan Doyle by **Steven Moffat** and **Mark Gatiss**, established a pre-*Doctor Strange* Benedict Cumberbatch as a world-class star, his arrogant Holmes addressing the detective's borderline autistic personality more directly than in earlier incarnations (Martin Freeman's bemused Watson was another factor in the show's success). After 13 episodes had been broadcast (with four three-part series airing from 2010 to 2017, and a one-off special set in the canonical Victorian period), the show became a tad too self-congratulatory – while still maintaining its audacity and imagination. Andrew Scott's antic Moriarty echoed Batman's nemesis the Joker.

The Amateur Cracksman 1899
EW HORNUNG

While Hornung's debonair criminal protagonist Raffles is more remembered than read these days, the author's influence on the genre is still notable. A badge of intellectual respectability was conferred on Raffles in the 1930s, when **George Orwell** wrote a celebrated essay praising the old-fashioned charm of Hornung's well-turned caper novels at the expense of what he (rather old maidishly) perceived as the depraved brutality of such then modern crime novels as **James Hadley Chase**'s *No Orchids for Miss Blandish*. This slightly sentimental view of Hornung's amiable thief is perhaps the best way to approach him. Raffles, however, remains an important prototype of many latter-day crook heroes (not least **Louis Joseph Vance**'s *The Lone Wolf*, the Falcon movies of the 1940s, and **Leslie Charteris**'s *The Saint*), and, along with his partner Bunny, moves in a charmingly realised English period universe. Raffles (who excelled at cricket) carries his non-professional professionalism through the picaresque adventures here (with a colourful dramatis personae of character types), even though modern readers may look askance at the relationship between Raffles and his adoring ex-fag Bunny. The plotting is loose and discursive, but the gallery of effects remains diverting. Intriguingly, this book and later adventures such as *The Black Mask* (1901) and *A Thief in the Night* (1905) could be seen as a refracted critique of British society – after all, Raffles' quintessential English diligence is entirely at the service of crime.

RAFFLES 1930
Directors: Harry d'Arrast and George Fitzmaurice

Although previous silent incarnations exist, notably by John Barrymore in 1917, Ronald Colman's smooth charm is absolutely perfect for the gentleman thief who spins circles around the duffers at Scotland Yard. Today, age gives the film a perfect period feel. Based on *The Amateur Cracksman*, a Sam Wood 1939 scene-for-scene remake featured the only other conceivable actor seemingly born to play the part – David Niven.

CHAPTER 2

THE GOLDEN AGE
Classic mysteries

Crime fiction came of age in the years between the World Wars, a period that produced a plenitude of writers who gained enormous popularity. Many continued to publish new work well into the 1950s and 1960s, and still sell in substantial numbers today. The most celebrated writer of the period, which many regard as the 'Golden Age' of detective fiction, was **Agatha Christie**. She was canny enough to appropriate several of Conan Doyle's Sherlock Holmes concepts for her Belgian detective Hercule Poirot, but while we remain ready to plunge into the fogbound streets of Victorian London with our sense of irony firmly held in check despite the occasional Holmes parody, Poirot seems to suffer much more often from being played in tongue-in-cheek fashion. Why this distinction between the two eccentric sleuths? Possibly it lies in the genius of one author as against the craftsmanship of the other. The pleasure of Christie's work doesn't really depend on Poirot's character (or, for that matter, that of her equally distinctive and brilliantly conceived detective, elderly spinster Jane Marple); it's those wonderfully engineered plots that remain as diverting as ever. There are, of course, two diametrically opposed schools of thought on Christie, mainly concerning social attitudes. If you hate the often patronising view of the working classes and the socially stratified never-never land Britain she nostalgically creates, then nothing will persuade you to open a Christie novel. But (as **Minette Walters** has pointed out), Christie was able to take on board social change, albeit peripherally – there is an acknowledgement in later books that real life is lived outside the privileged circle in which the majority of her characters move, and that people can reside in inner cities as well as in quaint English villages. And, if we can still read **John Buchan**, happily ignoring those aspects of his work that aren't consonant with current tastes, why not Christie?

Taking a step on from the 'locked room' mystery, this was the period that gave birth to the 'whodunnit', in which the 'who' was often the least likely protagonist. Beneath Christie's burgeoning skirts, there are the other giants of the Golden Age: **Dorothy L Sayers**, **Ngaio Marsh** et al. And what about **John Dickson Carr**? Although such writers as **Freeman Wills Crofts**, **Gladys Mitchell**, **Cyril Hare**, **Patricia Wentworth**, **Leslie Charteris** and Crime Writers' Association founder **John Creasey** are well known only by cognoscenti these days, there are many rediscoveries to be made (such as the late-flowering Golden-Ager **Robert Barnard**), and it's a field richer in mystery and imagination than one might think at first glance...

The Tiger in the Smoke 1952

MARGERY ALLINGHAM

While many writers of the classic British crime novel fought shy of psychopathic killers in their work (or were unaware of such aberrant behaviour), Margery Allingham's signature novel produced one of the most memorable murderers in fiction. The book's reputation has grown over the years since publication in the 1950s, although the eccentric picture of the underworld now seems a touch quaint. In the teeming streets of a foggy London, a man with a knife is carving a bloody path. Meg is about to be married to Geoffrey Levitt, but other things are preying on her mind. She has been under the impression that her unlovable first husband Martin died during the war, but then she receives a photograph which appears to prove that he is in fact alive. Meg's life is about to change – and very much for the worse. At the same time, the brutal Jack Havoc is summarily dispensing with anyone who gets in his way, including members of his old gang. A wide variety of characters (including Allingham's long-term detective, Albert Campion) and plots intersect in what is the darkest of the author's many books. While writers such as Agatha Christie largely dealt with death in sedate villages or country houses, Allingham bravely took on the depiction of the urban criminal underworld, and it is here (for the modern reader) that the book comes a little unstuck, with the argot and descriptions now seeming a little unrealistic. However, several things in *The Tiger in the Smoke* date not a whit, among them the brilliantly evoked post-war setting and the chilling portrait of pure evil incarnated in the murderous Jack Havoc.

TIGER IN THE SMOKE — 1956
Director: Roy Ward Baker

Roy Ward Baker's creditable stab at **Margery Allingham**'s novel is, to date, the only film of one of her books. It effectively utilises the Rank Organisation's 1950s facility for capturing the London milieu; the gritty settings (as crucial here as in the Boulting Brothers' adaptation of Graham Greene's *Brighton Rock*) make up for any inadequacies in the casting. The novel's sense of barely repressed psychosis, however, is only fitfully achieved, which vitiates Allingham's rigorously maintained tension.

The Oaken Heart — 1941
MARGERY ALLINGHAM

Perhaps this isn't a crime novel, but there are only so many times you can enter Margery Allingham's menacing world by re-reading her most distinguished books – *The Tiger in the Smoke*, for example. If your taste for Allinghamiana remains unslaked, then perhaps you should pick up the quirky and involving *The Oaken Heart*, the book the author wrote during the winter of 1940–41. Allingham was living in the Essex village of Tolleshunt D'Arcy and taking a full part in the local voluntary activity – first aid and so forth – and her record of the events and people of this fraught wartime period is rendered with the skill found in the best of her crime writing.

The Beast Must Die — 1938
NICHOLAS BLAKE

Nicholas Blake is not much read these days – a fact that would surprise his enthusiastic following in his mid-20th-century heyday. But are the Blake novels as good as their reputations, or has memory lent enchantment? This most famous of Poet Laureate's **Cecil Day-Lewis**'s thrillers (written under his Blake nom de plume) still reads in the 21st century as one of the most distinctive crime novels ever written. The plot involves a writer of detective fiction who plots a perfect murder, one that he himself will eventually commit. When a personal tragedy (the death of a close relative) destroys writer Frank Cairns' life, his tracking down of the man responsible achieves a pathological intensity, with inevitable death at the conclusion. But the final confrontation is not what the reader expects. With Blake's famous investigator Nigel Strangeways on hand, the sheer pleasure afforded by this book is guaranteed.

QUE LA BÊTE MEURE/KILLER! 1969
Director: Claude Chabrol

The brilliant use of Brahms' *Four Serious Songs* (with their death-directed philosophy) in the score establishes Chabrol's remarkable thriller as an art-house take on **Nicholas Blake**'s novel; the richness of the subtexts, the flat Gallic tone, and the understated performances make for a memorable adaptation, and the translation of the novel's setting into that of a bleached-looking autumnal France is completely successful. As ever, Chabrol freights in his very individual take on **Alfred Hitchcock**'s patented 'transference of guilt' concept.

Green for Danger 1944
CHRISTIANNA BRAND

Set in a British military hospital in Kent during World War II, Brand's beautifully turned novel is celebrated as much for its perfectly realised milieu (rarely has wartime Britain been so well evoked) as for its unorthodox plotting. If the motivation of the killer hardly stands up to rigorous examination, this does not ruin the spell the book casts. As German air raids pound the country, a group of nurses and doctors carry on as best they can – with all the accoutrements of everyday life (including sex and jealousy). When an air raid warden dies a day after an operation, it becomes clear that a killer is at work – and those who discover the murderer's identity die. As well as the tensely handled plot elements, the characters – all subtly damaged or disappointed in life – are beautifully drawn.

GREEN FOR DANGER   1946
Director: Sidney Gilliat

Cast the larger-than-life Alastair Sim in a movie (as any producer would have known) and you watch him walk away with the film. Fine, if it's a Sim vehicle, and that's what the audience is paying for. But what about a tightly contrived conversation piece like this adaptation of **Christianna Brand**'s novel? In fact, the actor shows that he is perfectly capable of reining in his mannerisms and not drawing attention away from the matchless ensemble playing required here (while still affording us the trademark humour). Undervalued for years, this is now seen as a very cherishable miniature in suspense.

Crime: a publishing phenomenon

The rise of literacy and popular culture inaugurated by the Great War provided a robust platform for the flowering of crime fiction. Many authors emerged and flourished in the 1920s – the now largely unread **Edgar Wallace, HC McNeile ('Sapper'), Sax Rohmer** and, in the States, **SS Van Dine** and **Edgar Rice Burroughs** became international celebrities. Part of their success was due to a change in the publishing industry, most notably the advent of the paperback – and, even more significantly, the paperback 'original'. For a few pence (or cents), a gripping piece of fiction was available in its entirety, for the first time, replacing the old magazine serialisation marketing methods that Dickens, Poe, Collins and Conan Doyle had to deal with. Although Allen Lane's Penguin imprint is frequently credited with inventing the paperback concept (and books by Sayers, Christie and Hammett were among the first 20 Penguin titles), publishers such as Hodder and Stoughton and Collins had built substantial popular crime lists before Penguin launched its distinctive green crime livery. But it was the royalties from popular paperback publishing in America, and from the sale of film rights, that created the first millionaire crime writers.

The Hollow Man/The Three Coffins   1935
JOHN DICKSON CARR

The tradition of American writers who opt to set their books in Britain (so strong is their love of the country and its traditions) continues to this day with Elizabeth George, but the most distinguished member of this club remains the wonderful John Dickson Carr, a writer who is firmly on the top ten list of many a crime fiction connoisseur. His long-term protagonist,

---

Agatha Christie
(1890–1976)

Despite her place at the top of the pantheon as Britain's queen of crime, there are those who will simply never read an Agatha Christie novel. Endless TV and film adaptations of her crime novels have created a series of ineluctable images in the public mind: picture-postcard English villages; meddling spinsters whose attempts at sleuthing are welcomed by the police (rather than rebutted as they would be in real life); and Belgian detectives with waxed moustaches and absurd accents. Most damning of all (for many enthusiasts of the crime novel) is the belief that Christie simply didn't move in the real world. She was, after all, in reality Lady Mallowan, and also penned romances under the nom de plume Mary Westmacott. This litany of complaints is a touch unfair: Christie, after all, is not to blame for the glossy patina that film and TV have added to her work, and the 'real world' of, say, **Raymond Chandler**'s novels is scarcely more realistic (Chandler once pointed out that, in real life, Marlowe would simply have been eliminated by the gangsters he so annoyed).

Despite these caveats, *Guinness World Records* cites Christie as the bestselling fiction writer ever, with an estimated two billion crime novels sold in over 40 languages. Her novels reflect the not uncommon problem confronting crime writers: how to introduce novelty to a well-worn formula? She solved this by becoming increasingly exotic in her settings, especially after her second marriage to archaeologist Sir Max

the cultivated sybarite Dr Gideon Fell, is one of the most individual sleuths in the field, and the perfectly judged soupçons of characterisation (always economical) that Carr affords Dr Fell are one of the pleasures of the books – along with the impeccable plotting. Those who know Carr's name (but not his books) are usually aware that the 'locked room' mystery is his *chef-d'œuvre*. And the perfect entry point for the author is *The Hollow Man* (retitled *The Three Coffins* in the US), with its nigh-supernatural killer, impenetrable mystery, and skilfully conjured atmosphere.

Mallowan (*Murder in Mesopotamia*, *Death on the Nile*, *Murder on the Orient Express*), although she rarely strayed from the basic principle of the 'country house' mystery.

In 1926, she became the subject of her own mystery when she disappeared for 11 days (actually, it was not that mysterious – her retreat to a hotel in Harrogate appears to have been a desperate response to a crisis in her marriage; she checked in using the name of her husband's mistress). The incident dominated the tabloid headlines, and **Michael Apted**'s 1979 film *Agatha* (with Vanessa Redgrave in the title role) proposed an explanation.

She was created Dame Commander of the Order of the British Empire in 1971, but, unlike latter British crime dames **PD James** and **Ruth Rendell**, she took little active part in parliamentary matters.

A recent trend in adaptations of her work has been to stress its darker, less 'cosy' aspects – the dramatist **Sarah Phelps** has been at the heart of this astringent, bracing new vision with her versions of *And Then There Were None* (2015), *The Witness for the Prosecution* (2016), *Ordeal by Innocence* (2018) and *The ABC Murders* (2018).

Murder on the Orient Express 1934
AGATHA CHRISTIE

Murder on the Orient Express is the perfect entry point for those wishing to see why the Christie name is such a copper-bottomed franchise. Christie's favourite sleuth, Hercule Poirot, has solved a case and is taking the Orient Express home when it becomes stuck in the snow, and a variation on the 'country house' scenario sets in with the icy conditions. Poirot's fellow travellers include an unpleasant millionaire, Samuel Ratchett, along with his secretary, MacQueen, and valet, Masterman. During the night, Ratchett is stabbed to death in what seems like a frenzied attack, and it's up to Poirot and the train's director, Monsieur Bouc, to track down the murderer from among the wide variety of suspects. The measure of Christie's achievement is that, even though the solution to the mystery is well known to most readers these days (not least because of the many rip-offs of her seminal novel), the impeccable storytelling still grips.

MURDER ON THE ORIENT EXPRESS 1974
Director: Sidney Lumet

Albert Finney's performance as Poirot may be something of a music hall turn, but (unlike Peter Ustinov in other films) it is at least this side of caricature, and sets the scene for David Suchet's slightly more sober outings behind the waxed moustache (though ridicule of the character is also present here). The star-studded cast incarnate **Agatha Christie**'s clearly differentiated characters with aplomb, while director Lumet maximises one of his key assets: the romance of steam, as embodied in the glittering Orient Express itself (and charmingly enhanced by Richard Rodney Bennett's celebrated orchestral score).

MURDER ON THE ORIENT EXPRESS 2017
Director: Kenneth Branagh

News of this Kenneth Branagh remake of Christie's train-set classic was met with a mixture of anticipation and trepidation. The suggestion that Poirot would (for once) not be played as a parody was welcome, but the sight of the actor's ludicrous walrus moustache somewhat undercut this resolve to treat the character seriously. With impressive production values and a judicious use of CGI, the film looks sumptuous, but – on balance – Branagh's all-star cast did not displace memories of Lumet's similarly stellar assembly of actors. The most recent Poirot is the American actor John Malkovich, discreetly goateed in *The ABC Murders* for the BBC.

Murder is Easy 1939
AGATHA CHRISTIE

Murder is Easy isn't one of Agatha Christie's best-known titles – and it doesn't feature Miss Marple or Hercule Poirot – but, like many of her books, it is set in a 1930s English village with a cast of eccentric, and rather unlikely, characters. The plot follows the usual Christie course, and the murderer comes up with some quite imaginative ways of dispatching the victims. As always, there's a nice sense of period. This is one of many Christie novels whose gentle pleasure can be found in its polished surface, impeccable plotting and powerful nostalgic tug – the lack of social reality matters not a jot.

Crime on stage and on the air

The fact that Agatha Christie's *The Mousetrap* has outlived any stage play on any continent in any era is not news. It opened in London in November 1952, and over 27,000 performances later the audience is still encouraged not to reveal exactly whodunnit. Nevertheless, it was a late entry to popular culture. **JB Priestley**'s slightly parodic *An Inspector Calls* was an enormous hit in London in the 1940s, while the adventures of Dick Barton and the darker noir of *The Man in Black*, not to mention **Francis Durbridge**'s amateur sleuth Paul Temple, dominated the British airwaves in the 1940s and 1950s. Meanwhile, Stateside, Dick Tracy felt the collars of innumerable wireless villains on a weekly basis from 1934 onwards. But once again it was Christie who raked in the royalties, with stage adaptations of conversation pieces such as *And Then There Were None* (originally titled *Ten Little Niggers*) and *Appointment with Death* providing staple food for repertory theatre companies worldwide. Other items on the popular playlist included the classic 'body in the box' mystery *Ladies in Retirement* (by **Reginald Denham** and **Edward Percy**) and **Joseph Kesselring**'s evergreen *Arsenic and Old Lace*, while **Susan Hill**'s *The Woman in Black* has proved that all is not dead (or is it?) behind the stage curtain.

The Mysterious Mr Quin 1930
AGATHA CHRISTIE

Christie had a particular skill in the short literary form – her primary speciality was, of course, plotting – and the short story allowed her to distil her inspiration in its most unadulterated form. *The Mysterious Mr Quin* is a collection of intricately plotted and atmospheric mysteries, with the marvellously beguiling conundrum in each one centred on the shadowy presence of Mr Harley Quin. Who is this mysterious Mr Quin? And why does his presence have such a strong effect on Eleanor Portal, the woman with the dyed black hair? Characterisation is basic but absolutely perfect for this kind of page-turning yarn.

The Case of the Turning Tide 1941
ERLE STANLEY GARDNER

While renowned for his *Perry Mason* series (at least by those who can divorce his memory from the long-running, often by-the-numbers, US TV series featuring *Rear Window* killer Raymond Burr), with this book – one of his non-series titles – Gardner set out to fracture the standardised forms into which he felt the mystery novel had fallen (even as early as 1941). Instead of following a mechanically placed series of clues, he attempted to emulate a natural flow of events. Salesman Ted Shale is walking along a beach, hoping to sell paper products to a millionaire aboard his yacht. But he sees a young women fall from the vessel into the ocean, seemingly unconscious. Going on board, he comes across two bodies – one of them the man he had hoped to do business with. While still utilising the intimate knowledge of legal loopholes that was his stock-in-trade in the *Perry Mason* books, the spread of interest among a larger cast of characters – all equally strong – pays dividends here.

Hangover Square 1941
PATRICK HAMILTON

Patrick Hamilton came from a family of novelists, and this fertile ground produced one of the most individualistic of British writers in any field, let alone crime. His 1929 play *Rope* (filmed by **Alfred Hitchcock** with James Stewart in 1948) demonstrated his interest in malformed psychology, with the real-life

Leopold and Loeb case (involving two young murderers) transformed into an intelligent thriller, while his masterpiece, the trilogy *Twenty Thousand Streets under the Sky* (1929–34), has emerged from a period of neglect. But his most celebrated novel, *Hangover Square*, remains his calling card book in the crime genre. George Harvey Bone is a schizophrenic, obsessed with the calculating Netta. Bone moves from inertia to murder under the influence of a dark mental compulsion. While the take on mental health is hardly a rounded one to modern eyes, it remains a novel of great power.

HANGOVER SQUARE 1945
Director: John Brahm

Laird Cregar was a heavyweight character actor who always played older than his age – and, regrettably, died young after a crash diet. But among his all-too-brief film legacy is his memorably charismatic turn in this highly professional adaptation of **Patrick Hamilton**'s novel. And Bernard Herrmann's sinister Lisztian piano-led score complements a dark picture of an off-kilter mind and ratchets up the tension considerably.

Rogue Male 1939
GEOFFREY HOUSEHOLD

'I cannot blame them. After all, one doesn't need a telescope sight to shoot boar and bear; so that when they came on me watching the terrace at a range of five hundred and fifty yards, it was natural enough that they should jump to conclusions...' From the first sentences of Geoffrey Household's lean and powerful novel, the reader is held in the proverbial iron grip. The premise is simple enough: an Englishman (from the hunting set) decides to utilise his shooting skills in a way that will affect (for the better, he hopes) the course of world events: he will assassinate a European dictator. The dictator, unnamed in the novel, is clearly Hitler, and this high-concept premise is an early example of a marketing tool that would be used again. But Household's wonderfully detailed, high-tension offering remains nonpareil. The unnamed narrator is viciously tortured, then ruthlessly tracked by secret agents and the police, until he is finally obliged to live like a beast in order to survive. He goes to ground, living beneath the earth. And growing ever closer is his sinister nemesis Quive-Smith. John Buchan was a clear influence on the novel, and the chase across the countryside owes something to *The Thirty-Nine Steps*, as does the upper-crust background of the narrator. The book, however, is more than a simple adventure story, thanks to its strongly drawn psychological underpinnings.

ROGUE MALE   1976
Director: Clive Donner

A strong, unmannered performance by Peter O'Toole as the English sniper and an intelligent script by novelist **Frederic Raphael** ensure that this pulse-racing TV adaptation of **Geoffrey Household**'s novel keeps much closer to the original than Fritz Lang's creditable 1941 version (retitled *Man Hunt*, with the American Walter Pidgeon as Household's very British protagonist). Donner's film is a much more faithful take on the novel and retains the quintessential Englishness of Household's original – and Donner evokes far more of the sense of menace beneath the bucolic setting. Lang opts for expressionist menace, his métier – fine, but some distance from Household.

Malice Aforethought   1931
FRANCIS ILES

The rediscovery of this well-loved jewel in the crown of crime novels – and a book that reinvented the form – began with a sympathetic TV adaptation some years ago. But Francis Iles (**Anthony Berkeley Cox**) despite being a consummate plot creator, had a writer's tone of voice that is only present in the novel. When the book first appeared, the then radical concept of announcing to the reader the identity of the murderer at the very beginning of the novel created a storm; we know from the first line that Dr Bickleigh has decided to murder his wife in the small but exclusive Devonshire hamlet of Wyvern's Cross. Amazingly, despite many imitators over the years, the device still functions as persuasively in the present as when the novel was written. The beleaguered Bickleigh (with his mounting passion for Gwynfryd Rattery) is one of the best-remembered protagonists of crime fiction, and there are few who will regret acquainting themselves with this beautifully crafted piece of work.

MALICE AFORETHOUGHT 2005
Director: David Blair for Granada Television

An earlier TV adaptation (with Hywel Bennett as Bickleigh) may have had a harder edge, but this version (with Ben Miller sympathetically assuming the henpecked mantle of Bickleigh) has its quiet virtues – although the conspicuous production values (always foregrounded, in the manner of many period adaptations on television these days) tend to draw attention away from the central story. Nevertheless, the sense of lower middle-class orthodoxies destabilised by a single, egotistical act committed by its central character is nicely captured.

The List of Adrian Messenger 1959
PHILIP MACDONALD

A late entry in the Golden Age category, but fully in the spirit of the period, *The List of Adrian Messenger* presents a stylised picture of England that nevertheless has a ring of truth about it. The story is set in stuffy cabinet rooms in Whitehall; ancient offices in the City with antediluvian lifts (easily rigged for purposes of murder); and liveried hunts where the 'blooding' of a new hunt member is an important ritual. Canny sleuth Anthony Gethryn tracks down a highly ingenious and utterly ruthless murderer – a murderer who, in fact, is prepared to kill a great many innocent people to conceal the death of one individual target.

Philip MacDonald (who also wrote as Oliver Fleming, Anthony Lawless, Martin Porlock and Warren Stuart) is now a neglected name in the crime field, but he enjoyed some popularity for his ability to create an entirely different narrative style and subject matter for each novel. In 1931, a year in which he wrote some eight novels, MacDonald took a significant trip to Hollywood where he wrote several screenplays (perhaps making the cinematic potential of his most famous novel no surprise). He worked with **Alfred Hitchcock** and also toiled on the long-running *Charlie Chan* and *Mr Moto* series. His most often used protagonist was the intuitive Colonel Anthony Gethryn, who advised Scotland Yard and first appeared in *The Rasp* (1924), an undistinguished novel with a country house setting. The much later *The List of Adrian Messenger* was nominated for the prestigious US Edgar award.

THE LIST OF ADRIAN MESSENGER 1963

Director: John Huston

John Huston's film of **Philip MacDonald**'s novel was generally dismissed on release as a lightweight, gimmicky *jeu d'esprit*, but under the diverting surface, it's actually something more. However, the pleasures that the film affords today are precisely those that brought down much critical wrath on the head of its director when the film was released: that is, its extremely contrived nature (now perhaps a touch postmodern), whereby a slew of major Hollywood stars (Kirk Douglas, Burt Lancaster, Frank Sinatra, Robert Mitchum, Tony Curtis), masquerade under several pounds of latex as a variety of suspects (or murder victims) in an investigation that wends its way from gloomy pubs to aristocratic hunt meets. Ironically, although the information was kept secret at the time, it has subsequently been revealed that several of the Hollywood stars we think we are seeing – all apparently looking stunningly grotesque in their makeup – are often not the performers themselves. The journeyman actor Jan Merlin stood in for much of the filming (though not for Kirk Douglas or an unmistakable Robert Mitchum) and the real stars mainly limited their appearance to the final sequence in which they strip off their makeup (an image as eerie and grotesque as in any horror film).

What makes the film deeply enjoyable is the pitch-perfect performance as the English sleuth Gethryn by the American actor George C Scott, who most audiences would have been happy to have seen in a whole series of Gethryn films, so winning was his understated acting. Similarly, Kirk Douglas, as the only one of the American 'stars' given something substantial to do, proved yet again that he was prepared to play fast and loose with his heroic image. At the time, some in literary quarters applauded the return of the English detective to the big-budget feature film, with all the accoutrements of country houses and familiarity with the less intelligent detectives at Scotland Yard – there is even a French Watson (played by Jacques Roux), who survives one of the murderer's more outlandish acts of carnage. But the response at the time was marked by dismay at what was felt to be John Huston's tongue-in-cheek disregard for the hallmarks of the genre, and most critics thought that the director's glory days were well in the past. What is clear, however, is that Huston is enjoying himself, appearing in a cameo as a red-coated foxhunting type – exactly the sort of role the director adopted at home in his Irish mansion (hence the film's largely uncritical view of some of its blue-blooded hunting/shooting/fishing characters) – and that sheer filmmaking acumen never deserts him. Apart from its impeccable casting, including such actors as Clive Brook and Gladys Cooper, the film is finessed by a highly atmospheric Kurt Weill-esque score by Jerry Goldsmith, one of the many incidental pleasures that this unfairly dismissed movie affords the viewer.

Surfeit of Lampreys 1941
NGAIO MARSH

The Roderick Alleyn books of Ngaio Marsh are among the most enjoyable relics of the Golden Age of British crime. Despite Marsh's New Zealand nationality (her Christian name means 'reflections on the water' in Maori), her 32 novels are perfect examples of the genre, and the 1960s Fontana editions of her books remain (like Fontana's editions of **Eric Ambler**) a wonderfully collectable series of beautiful paperbacks. Museum pieces perhaps, but with a vitality that belies their period trappings. Her most celebrated novel – a book that has rarely been out of print since its first publication – begins with the murder of an English aristocrat, pierced through the eye. Alleyn makes heavy weather with a group of English eccentrics, all drawn with Marsh's characteristic humour and affection. The characters may be writ large for some tastes, but this is civilised and ingenious fun. Marsh is less read these days than she should be, but those who pick up *Surfeit of Lampreys* will find it reaching across the years with a vividness that still surprises and still dazzles.

Margery Allingham's Mr Campion's Farewell 2014/1969
MIKE RIPLEY

The slightly wordy legend on the jacket reads 'Margery Allingham's Albert Campion Returns in Mr Campion's Farewell Completed by Mike Ripley', but this is the only example of prolixity in this truly civilised and entertaining read. Mike Ripley (with the cooperation of the Margery Allingham Society) has completed an untitled novel left unfinished by the writer's widower, Pip Youngman Carter, when he died in 1969. It's hard to imagine a contemporary writer with a more instinctual feel for the correct idiom here, and if we are to have Allingham at several removes, Mr Ripley is the perfect conduit. Eschewing the customary sardonic wit of his Angel novels (or – to be more precise – holding it in check), Ripley provides us with another diverting case for Albert Campion, dragooning several other characters from the Allingham canon. Whether or not you are a worshipper at the shrine of one of the greatest writers of Britain's Golden Age of crime fiction, you would be doing yourself a favour by picking this one up.

Gaudy Night

1935

DOROTHY L SAYERS

The affection with which the work of Sayers is greeted by crime admirers remains surprising to the non-initiated. And many would choose this novel as her signature work. Sayers was a far better writer than her contemporary Agatha Christie, and her academic background allowed her to freight in serious literary conceits along with the more populist concerns of the crime thriller. Her protagonist, Lord Peter Wimsey, with his aristocratic manners and mien, may seem precious in an era of alcoholic, working-class coppers with fractured marriages, but the books chronicling Wimsey's adventures

Whodunnit? The legacy

The Golden Age crime scenario, in which one of a limited range of seemingly innocent protagonists turns out to be a murderous monster, has an irresistible allure. But quite how the guilty party – normally the least likely suspect – is tracked down is key to the genre's appeal. The influence of Christie, Marsh, Sayers and Carr is both inescapable and endurable, and the long-running US television series *Murder, She Wrote* (1984–96), featuring English actress Angela Lansbury as Jessica Fletcher, a crime-novel-writing update of Christie's Miss Marple, provided a weirdly postmodern twist on an ongoing phenomenon. American TV seemed to be uniquely fuelled during the 1970s and 1980s by an imaginative array of eccentric detectives: the urban cowboy *McCloud*, lollipop-sucking hard-ass cop *Kojak*, and various crimefighting duos such as *Starsky and Hutch* and *Dempsey and Makepeace* sleuthed their way across our screens with what became monotonous regularity. But the most enduring was Peter Falk's *Columbo*, an endearingly shabby and boss-eyed cigar-smoking modern-day version of **Fyodor Dostoyevsky**'s Porfiry Petrovich, whose ability to ask the key question just as he was leaving the crime scene, having lulled the suspect into a sense of false security, became a legendary problem for the teams of scriptwriters. More recently, a slew of forensic scientists have moved in with the coppers, notably in *CSI* and its offshoots.

remain models of their kind. Sayers also showcases her other long-term character, Harriet Vane, in *Gaudy Night*, and her tantalising relationship with Wimsey approaches resolution here. Harriet returns to Oxford after a decade in which she has become a novelist, has lived with a man, and has got over being accused of his murder (in *Strong Poison*). She becomes involved in the case of a prankster, a seemingly unstable individual who is making life hell for an entire Oxford college. Inevitably, Lord Peter also gets involved and forms a powerful team with Harriet to crack the mystery. The setting of Shrewsbury College is as cannily conjured as anything in the campus novels of **David Lodge** and **Malcolm Bradbury**, and while the central mystery remains the focus, Sayers is able to address such issues as identity and the worth of people's jobs (notably the idea of women's professions in the 1930s). The relationship between Harriet and Lord Peter is handled with immense assurance, and it's not hard to see why, for many, this remains the great Sayers novel.

The Franchise Affair   1948

JOSEPHINE TEY

It's comforting to say that a particular book is an author's best – particularly when few well-read people are likely to gainsay you. So, without hesitation, *The Franchise Affair* is Josephine Tey's best book – and that in a career studded with many literary triumphs. Interestingly, this much-loved crime novel doesn't actually contain a murder – although Tey gets away with the omission swimmingly. Based on a real-life story of abuse and kidnap, the plot (in which a young girl is humiliated and turned into a household slave) seems ever more topical when such events seem to come to light every few months. A solicitor in a respected firm, a bachelor of mature years, finds his ordered existence disturbed by the appearance of Marion Sharpe, who moves, with her mother, into the eponymous The Franchise, a local manor house that has seen better times. The couple is accused of kidnapping and abusing a schoolgirl – and all their lives are changed by what ensues. As much a subtle meditation on the nature of appearance and reality as a brilliantly written genre novel, this is a startling product of the Golden Age and looks forward with unnerving prescience to the darker, psychological obsessions of the next generation of crime writers. Tey herself, as an unlikely sleuth, is foregrounded in a civilised series of novels by **Nicola Upson**.

THE FRANCHISE AFFAIR 1950

Director: Lawrence Huntington

This adaptation of **Josephine Tey**'s novel firmly belongs to the era of buttoned-up, emotionally-repressed cinema in the UK – an era that was soon to be violently swept away by the British 'New Wave' of such films as *Saturday Night and Sunday Morning*. But that very repressed manner perfectly meshes with the ethos of Tey's original, suggesting dark undercurrents kept ruthlessly in check. The film's structure is as carefully modulated as the novel on which it is based.

CHAPTER 3

HARDBOILED AND PULP

Tough guys and tough talk

It is the most beloved – and respected – of crime genres. While the Golden Age of British crime writing is held in high esteem (and America had some similarly classic Golden Age writers, such as **John Dickson Carr**), the real heavyweight – in terms of literary standing – is the American pulp tradition, forged in the bloodstained pages of post-World War I magazines such as *Black Mask* and boasting the two patron saints of American crime writing: **Dashiell Hammett** and **Raymond Chandler**.

The iconographic elements of the hardboiled world (private eye with a whisky bottle in a filing cabinet, femme fatale, rich – and usually corrupt – clients) remain as sure-fire a combination today as when they were freshly minted, despite a million parodies. And the image of the lone investigator cutting through the polished surface of society to reveal the decay beneath has an existential force that makes most crime fiction seem trivial. This is a world in which female sexuality is often a snare and a delusion, plunging the hapless hero into a hazardous world of carnality and danger; and while the structure of society (manipulative politicians, brutal police) may seem callously efficient, the classic pulp novels present a world in which all is illusion – and fate can randomly destroy the protagonist.

The superficial ease of churning out potboilers attracted many hacks, such as the prolific but now little read **Ellery Queen**. But more literary sophistication was built into the genre by **Ross Macdonald**, with his private eye Lew Archer often investigating the dark secrets of families with forensic skill, and by **Jim Thompson**, whose chilling, amoral characters earned him the soubriquet the 'Dimestore Dostoyevsky'. And, while the sexual politics of the genre may seem less than enlightened today, the treatment of violence and the erotic is as intoxicating as when these novels were written.

The Asphalt Jungle 1949
WR BURNETT

Burnett was particularly prolific as a screenwriter in the Hollywood of the 1930s and 1940s, and his literary production didn't lag far behind, with over 50 novels to his credit (in crime and other genres). He was one of the progenitors of the gangster genre, and the Edward G Robinson/Mervyn

---

Pulp crime: from *Black Mask* to EC Comics

Pulp magazines, avidly consumed in America between the World Wars (and equally enthusiastically received in Great Britain), were cheap and accessible sources of fiction for non-literary readers, utilising genres that were then considered to be unsophisticated and meretricious (crime, horror and science fiction). Tempted by the lurid and eye-catching covers of the crime pulps (including the celebrated *Detective Story* and the daddy of them all, *Black Mask*, co-founded by the legendary high-end journalist **HL Mencken** and edited by **Joseph T Shaw**), with their half-naked blondes, corpses and blazing guns, readers encountered sensational fiction that ranged from the crudely written to some of the most brilliant and inventive prose produced in the States at that time, from such masters as Chandler, Hammett, Cain and Woolrich. While their writers may now be seen as consummate stylists, they were then admired for the adroit fashion in which they handled all the crucial sensational elements of the genre they were effectively inventing. Others who got their start in the pulps included **Erle Stanley Gardner** and **John D MacDonald**.

LeRoy film of his novel *Little Caesar* (1930) made a considerable impact, inaugurating the famous Warner Brothers cycle of mobster movies. Burnett went on to script both *Scarface* (1932) and *High Sierra* (1941). *The Asphalt Jungle* was one of the first novels to describe a heist – in commanding detail – and remains (with *High Sierra*) one of the author's best-regarded books. His protagonist, Riemenschneider, is fresh out of prison and keen to get back to the activities that put him there in the first place. Planning a new heist, his financial backer is the corrupt lawyer Emmerich, whose complicated private life has forced him to hire a bent private eye. Other members of the ill-assorted team include the brutal Dix and his girlfriend, the latter yearning for an Arcadian escape from her dispiriting life. The conflicts within the gang are described with a mordant voice that places the reader firmly in the centre of these preparations and the subsequent robbery. When things (inevitably) go wrong, the self-detonation of the group is as fascinating as anything in crime fiction.

Even before the death of the pulps (brought about by a saturated market, the growth of the paperback novel, and the burgeoning medium of television), a sophisticated form of crime fiction was quietly flourishing in another despised genre: the comic book. Often produced by the men behind the pulps (such as publisher Martin Goodman), comics – like pulps – contained a considerable level of dross. But at the offices of Entertaining Comics (EC Comics) in New York, publisher **William M Gaines** and editor **Al Feldstein** inaugurated a cottage industry producing illustrated crime stories quite as ingenious, ruthless and adult as anything in their prose equivalents (and, in many cases, considerably more accomplished). From 1950 to 1954, in such titles as *Crime SuspenStories* and *Shock SuspenStories* (note the missing 'e's), the duo (aided by the astonishing graphic skills of such illustrators as Johnny Craig, George Evans and Reed Crandall) produced a series of perfectly formed *contes cruels*, unabashedly adult in their depiction of violence and (to a lesser degree) sex. Massive disapproval on the part of the self-styled moral guardians ultimately crushed the company's books in a wave of media hysteria in the 1950s. However, the EC crime comics (often Cain-inspired) – like the best stories in *Black Mask* – have rarely been out of print, appearing again and again in increasingly deluxe editions.

THE ASPHALT JUNGLE — 1950
Director: John Huston

Huston's first film, a remake of **Dashiell Hammett**'s *The Maltese Falcon* (1941), marked him out as a forceful director of crime movies, and his reputation was consolidated by this classic adaptation, shot in a pseudo-documentary style. The script matches the terseness and force of the novel, and the casting (notably Sterling Hayden and Louis Calhern) does full justice to Huston's vision. Oh, yes – and there's a scene-stealing early performance by Marilyn Monroe.

The Postman Always Rings Twice — 1934
JAMES M CAIN

This is simply one of the most influential crime novels ever written. The relatively straightforward plot (after a passionate affair, a young woman persuades her lover to kill her older husband, with disastrous consequences) has been ripped off time and again, and at least three classic movies have been adapted from James M Cain's slim and acerbic novel (two American and one Italian). A stage production in London drew large audiences, and the celebrated EC Comics used the concept so often it became the standard house plot. One would have thought that all the above might lead to overfamiliarity, but coming back to *The Postman Always Rings Twice* in its original form is salutary. To call this book seminal is to underestimate its importance: in the relatively few pages of *Postman*, the author burns out a passionate and searing tale of adultery and murder that still manages to make some cogent

THE POSTMAN ALWAYS RINGS TWICE — 1981
Director: Bob Rafelson

An earlier version with Lana Turner and John Garfield (**Tay Garnett**, 1946) managed to catch some of the eroticism of **James M Cain**'s novel but censorship restrictions of the day meant that most of the sensuality had to be conveyed by indirect means. No such restrictions applied when Rafelson made this steamy version, with Jack Nicholson and Jessica Lange having clothes-tearing sex on the kitchen table. The Italian director **Luchino Visconti** made a strong Neorealist version of the novel in *Ossessione* (1943), again more unbuttoned in its graphic sexuality.

points about the despair and striving towards hope that are part of the human condition. Frank Chambers is a drifter, deposited after a truck ride at a grimy diner in the country. The café is run by an unsympathetic older man, Nick, whose young wife, the seductive Cora, is clearly chafing at the bit in this dead relationship. Frank and Cora begin an all-enveloping carnal affair, and decide to murder her husband. But their actions finally spell catastrophe for them. In its day, Cain's novel was considered to be scandalous stuff; even today its heady eroticism and tensile strength make for a pungent read.

The Big Sleep 1939

RAYMOND CHANDLER

Chandler is the master. Dashiell Hammett may have been the original progenitor of the hardboiled private eye novel, and many of the elements (tough loner detective, sexually available female clients, uneasy relationship with the police) were present in the soup of the pulp magazines to which both men contributed gritty work, but Chandler refined the form to its nth degree – and the fact that Chandler was able to write a series of novels featuring his private detective Philip Marlowe (as opposed to Hammett's single novel-length Sam Spade story, *The Maltese Falcon*) allowed him to introduce refinements that Hammett simply didn't have time to do. *The Big Sleep* is a coruscating diamond of a novel: mordant, fiercely plotted and boasting a matchless cast of characters. In the confines of a stifling hothouse, the insubordinate Marlowe is hired by the paralysed General Sternwood, who is being blackmailed by a pornographer – and the problem lies with his daughters, one of whom is running wild. Marlowe is soon up against murderous gangsters in a plot so tortuous that **Howard Hawks** barely understood it when he filmed the novel. Reading all the Marlowe novels in succession will make it perfectly clear that the first book is the best, despite a subsequent enriching of characterisation.

The genius of the Marlowe books lies in two elements: the evocative picture of a sun-baked Los Angeles (from its down-at-heel 'negro bars' to the grandest of wealthy estates) and the impeccable whip-crack dialogue, a yardstick for the genre ever since Chandler refined it. Written the following year, *Farewell, My Lovely* already displays signs of the richness of character and psychology that was to appear in Chandler's later books. Here, Marlowe finds himself intimidated by the mountainous ex-con Moose Malloy, who hires him to track down the latter's mistress. Soon, other cases crowd in involving blackmail, sudden death and precious jewels.

As his correspondence with fellow thriller writer **Ian Fleming** indicated, Raymond Chandler grew tired of his gumshoe, notably so by the time the penultimate Marlowe novel, *The Long Goodbye*, appeared in 1953. Nevertheless, he wanted to invest his writing with more texture and truthful characterisation. In many ways, *The Long Goodbye* is his richest book in terms of literary achievement, although its extra gravitas saps some of the earlier vitality. While *The Big Sleep* is the most integrated of the Marlowe novels, there are some who would claim *The Long Goodbye* as his most profound book. After its powerful beginning, with Marlowe encountering the drunken Terry Lennox, the detective lands in jail when it is thought that he helped Lennox escape a murder charge. But then Lennox's body is found, and Marlowe is the only person prepared to investigate the death. The narrative process here is far less rigorous than before, with the messiness of real life replacing the tighter structure of the earlier books.

Raymond Chandler
(1888–1959)

Raymond Chandler was born in the 19th century but remains a modern writer for both the 20th century and beyond. While the superficial elements of the sultry 1930s Los Angeles that was his stamping ground are very specifically of their period, the penetrating sensibility of his tough but principled protagonist, Philip Marlowe, remains contemporary even today. Chandler was born in the States but, upon his parents' divorce, he was moved to England, and his education was at the prestigious Dulwich College (in light of this, his friendship and literary discussions with the very English **Ian Fleming** do not seem quite so surreal). His first literary outings were as a journalist and poet in the UK and created little interest, but after

THE BIG SLEEP 1946

Director: Howard Hawks

Along with **John Huston's** *The Maltese Falcon*, this is the definitive private eye movie. Hawks' inimitable direction wrings every ounce from the flintily witty script by William Faulkner, Jules Furthman and Leigh Brackett, and the impeccable pairing of Humphrey Bogart and Lauren Bacall is *sui generis* (the film was in fact made in 1944, the same year Bogart and Bacall first appeared together in another Hawks movie, *To Have and Have Not*). This is famously the film that freighted in some wonderful sexual double entendres (such as the discussion of horse racing: 'A lot depends on who's in the saddle') that slipped past an uncomprehending censor. A leaden 1978 remake by **Michael Winner**, set in England, is best avoided, despite an extraordinary performance by Robert Mitchum and a truly bizarre cast.

---

serving in the Canadian army in France in the Great War, he went back to his native country. A spell as an oil executive was abortive, mainly due to the author's increasing alcoholism (later to become a professionally crippling addiction), but this resulted in a piece of great good fortune for crime readers everywhere, as Chandler began to make a living turning out tough crime stories for such phenomenally popular pulp outlets as *Black Mask* magazine.

These early stories now read as fascinating prototypes for later novels such as *The Long Goodbye* (1953), but the richness of characterisation that was to make him the best of all hardboiled writers was some time in the future. In addition to the immense achievement of his Marlowe novels, Chandler did some sterling work in Hollywood producing an original script for **George Marshall's** *The Blue Dahlia* (1946) and notably working with **Billy Wilder** on **James M Cain's** *Double Indemnity* (1944) and (fractiously) with **Alfred Hitchcock** on **Patricia Highsmith's** *Strangers on a Train* (1951). Nevertheless, it is his literary achievement that makes him second to none in the annals of crime writing – and Philip Marlowe remains the key prototype for Chandler's legion of followers, even to this day.

No Orchids for Miss Blandish 1939
JAMES HADLEY CHASE

Many people have picked up this most notorious of pulp crime novels because of **George Orwell**'s celebrated essay 'Raffles and Miss Blandish'. In this piece, Orwell (in the old-maidish tone he sometimes adopted) had tut-tutted at the immoral sex and violence of James Hadley Chase's (pseudonym of **René Brabazon Raymond**) racy tale of kidnapping, rape and murder, extolling in its place the anodyne charms of the classic British crime novel as encapsulated by the gentleman thief Raffles. But those who subsequently read *No Orchids for Miss Blandish* in search of illicit thrills would be dismayed. And even Orwell would have been deeply disappointed by later editions of the book, in which Chase, obviously stung by this moral outrage, toned down the more extreme elements of the novel (no orgasms from the act of murder now). Read today, Blandish is something of a period piece, but it still has a crude energy that sustains the reader's attention. Rural gangs in 1930s Kansas plot to steal the valuable diamonds of the heiress to the Blandish fortune, but her boyfriend is killed in the robbery and they kidnap her. As the ransom demands are delivered, the young woman is subjected to a horrendous sexual ordeal at the hands of the depraved gang, which was modelled on the real-life Ma Barker gang. Chase was no stylist, but the uncomplicated, raw appeal of his books made his name a byword for sexually inflected crime writing for many years. Time has not been kind to his massive output – only *Miss Blandish* remains consistently in print, although he published well over a hundred novels, including others written

NO ORCHIDS FOR MISS BLANDISH 1948
Director: St John Legh Clowes

This quaint British film was once excoriated for its immorality in the same way that **George Orwell** had condemned the original novel. The banning of the film for many years created an underground interest that simply is not repaid by this crude, badly acted farrago (the American accents of the largely British cast are particularly ludicrous, notably an uncredited Sid James as a Chicago denizen). **Robert Aldrich**'s later stab at the novel (as *The Grissom Gang*, 1971) was much more successful: operatically violent, unsubtle, darkly humorous, and acted with panache.

under the pseudonyms James L Docherty, Ambrose Grant and Raymond Marshall, many set in an America recreated with the help of maps and an American slang dictionary (the English Chase barely even visited the US).

The Moon in the Gutter 1953
DAVID GOODIS

If writers such as David Goodis could look back from the beyond at the esteem in which their work is now held, they would be bemused indeed. Goodis (and such fellow pulp scribes as **Cornell Woolrich**) regarded themselves as professionals, turning out saleable material by the yard for a tough and demanding market. They didn't write for posterity – but posterity has been kind to Goodis, whose reputation has grown and grown. His big break came in 1947 when his second full-length novel, *Dark Passage,* was filmed by Delmer Daves, with Humphrey Bogart. *The Moon in the Gutter* was published in 1953, and is proof of the author's stature, with its economical and assertive prose. The anti-hero, William Kerrigan, becomes obsessed by the fact that his sister took her own life. Why did she kill herself? Drinking in a rundown bar, Kerrigan meets the seductive Lorretta Channing, a woman from a very different social class. And soon Kerrigan finds out that she may be a key to his sister's death, as well as providing him with a tempting opportunity to change his own unsatisfactory life. The descriptive writing of this sordid world is brilliantly sustained, with the tenements, bars and lost men and women who populate them conjured in transparent

TIREZ SUR LE PIANISTE/SHOOT THE PIANIST 1960
Director: François Truffaut

The jokey, facetious tone of Truffaut's seminal *nouvelle vague* film gives little hint of the dark, psychologically bleak universe of **David Goodis'** source novel – French directors of this era may have liked American pulp novels, but the genre's influence in films is usually refracted through a distancing, parodic approach (as in **Jean-Luc Godard's** highly referential *A Bout de Souffle/Breathless*, 1960). Pleasure here is to be had from the exuberance of a New Wave take on Goodis' book rather than it being a serious attempt to deal with the material. Two decades later, cult whizz-kid **Jean-Jacques Beineix** tried to pull the same stunt but, despite the presence of Gérard Depardieu, his 1983 take on *The Moon in the Gutter (La Lune dans le Caniveau)* fell flat.

prose. Goodis revisited the lowlife mien in *Down There* (aka *Shoot the Piano Player*, 1956), the tale of a concert pianist whose career nosedives after his wife's suicide. This is among the most penetrating self-examinations in the writer's body of work, mirroring his own psychological conflicts – conflicts that torpedoed his career as a writer in Hollywood – and foreshadowing his own early death. Of all writers of noir fiction, Goodis comes closest to the existential angst of **Albert Camus** and **Jean-Paul Sartre**.

Red Harvest 1929
DASHIELL HAMMETT

If left-wing politics have recently crept back into the crime novel, they'll have some way to go to match the hard-edged commitment of the first great US pulp master, Dashiell Hammett. The hard-drinking writer's streetwise Marxism informed his work in the blistering *Red Harvest*, a groundbreaking work that remains unmatched in cold-eyed cynicism. The novel is crammed with information gleaned from the author's time as a Pinkerton detective, and the edgy authenticity extends to locale: 'The city wasn't pretty... set in an ugly notch between two ugly mountains that had been all dirtied up by mining.' Sam Spade in Hammett's *The Maltese Falcon* may be the quintessential private eye, but it is *Red Harvest* that presents his bleakest and most existential vision of a corrupt society. The shadowy protagonist

Film noir

Refugee filmmakers from Nazi Europe had a huge impact on Hollywood in the 1940s. Directors such as **Fritz Lang**, **Billy Wilder**, **Robert Siodmak** and **Douglas Sirk** brought with them much of the German Expressionist style, and a darkly imaginative *mise-en-scène*, European panache and the often politically driven concerns of their homeland. These sensibilities dovetailed perfectly with the increasing popularity of pulp crime fiction, producing a smoky, shadowy, tersely written style dubbed 'noir' by the later French critics and *nouvelle vague* filmmakers of *Cahiers du Cinéma*, among them **François Truffaut** and **Jean-Luc Godard**. The comparison is the middle-aged, overweight Continental Op, hired by the only honest man in the blighted town of Personville (called 'Poisonville' by one of the characters), who is subsequently murdered. The Op opts to hang around and stick it to the killers, which essentially means taking on the entire town. He finds himself playing equally irredeemable rival gangs against each other, and as they bloodily slaughter each other, the Op finds the police force as corrupt as the gang leaders. Hammett's take on a society that is scoured clean only when the Op wipes out every remaining member of the gangs is uncompromising; life is shown as a series of brutal encounters that are played out among interchangeable opponents. The lean, pared-down prose is timelessly modern, even in the 21st century.

YOJIMBO 1961

Director: Akira Kurosawa

This astonishing reworking of **Dashiell Hammett**'s hardboiled classic sees the cynical anti-hero recast as a masterless samurai in a lawless village in medieval Japan. The only other worthwhile film adaptation is another radical take on Hammett's original: **Sergio Leone**'s *A Fistful of Dollars* (1964) has Poisonville relocated to an Italianate American West. Leone keeps the body count high, and transforms the overweight protagonist into a grizzled (but prettier) Clint Eastwood.

with the homegrown Hollywood crime movies of the 1930s – the Warner Brothers mobster cycle and the jokey William Powell/Myrna Loy *Thin Man* series – makes the impact clear. The *émigrés* also had an immediate influence on many of their American peers – **Howard Hawks**, **Val Lewton** and **William Wellman** among them.

This new style demanded snappy dialogue-driven writers. Not only were **Chandler** and **Hammett** signed up by Hollywood studios, but big guns such as **William Faulkner,** playwright **Clifford Odets** and the remarkable female writer **Leigh Brackett** dallied under LA palms, while pulpists such as **David Goodis, Kenneth Fearing** and **Jonathan Latimer** were suddenly earning pay cheques way beyond their most fevered dreams.

Build My Gallows High 1946
GEOFFREY HOMES

This is the last novel **Daniel Mainwaring** wrote under this pen name (the first being the intriguingly titled *The Man Who Murdered Himself*, 1936) and tells the tale of Red Bailey, ex-New York private eye with shady connections, now retired to hopeful anonymity in the countryside. Then he is blackmailed back for one last job, but it's a setup, revenge for a nasty episode involving the fickle dame Mumsie McGonigle – an episode that has funded his retirement. Her current squeeze, mobster Guy Parker, is behind it, and soon Red is caught up in a game of bluff and double-bluff to save his skin. Doom-laden and paranoid, it is no coincidence that Mainwaring went on to write screenplays for **Joseph Losey**'s *The Lawless* (1949) and **Don Siegel**'s *Invasion of the Body Snatchers* (1956).

OUT OF THE PAST/BUILD MY GALLOWS HIGH 1947
Director: Jacques Tourneur

Jeff Bailey – played by noir veteran Robert Mitchum (of whom David Thomson said: 'How can I offer this hunk as one of the best actors in the movies?') – is forced to abandon his idyllic, rural existence, dallying with the girl next door, when his past, in the form of a brilliantly ruthless Kirk Douglas, calls in a debt. The debt, in the form of double-crossing femme fatale Jane Greer, is related in classic flashback and leads the three protagonists to inevitable doom. The contrasts between good life and bad, between now and then, are brilliantly realised in day and night sequences, bridged by Mitchum's extraordinary range of mood and conviction. An uncommon instance of the film being better than the book, with Mitchum endowing Jeff/Red Bailey with a tragic nobility scarcely present in the original text.

Kiss Me, Deadly 1952
MICKEY SPILLANE

Chandler loathed the brutal Mike Hammer, perceiving him as a coarse caricature of his trench-coated knight errant Marlowe, and critics delighted in execrating the graphic brutality, blatant sexuality and fervent red-baiting of Spillane's gumshoe. But there are few aficionados of the detective story who won't (privately) admit to having avidly consumed a Mike Hammer novel or two. While the brutal Hammer is the least PC of protagonists, that very factor alone makes him perversely attractive. In Spillane's private eye thrillers, the action explodes in a blood-spurting, cartilage-destroying opera of mayhem. Mike and a bevy of instantly available broads don't make love – they screw. With their instantly accessible, fevered prose and helter-skelter pacing, Spillane's Hammer books, beginning with *I, The Jury* (1947), rapidly became one of the great runaway successes of publishing history – a visceral cocktail that went for the reader's killer instinct. And their influence on the American public was incalculable: the private eye parody in **Vincente Minnelli**'s classic 1953 musical *The Band Wagon* is a riff on Spillane, not Chandler.

One of the truly iconic titles of the thick-ear school of private eye novels, it's hard (in the 21st century) to disentangle the resonances of this novel from the (far superior) film made of the book. Here, Mike is alternately seduced and beaten to a pulp in a plot involving drug trafficking, with the usual assortment of available females and sinister heavies. The novel, of course, starts with one of the most famous images in the Hammer canon: Mike encounters a girl, naked under a trench coat, while driving on a nighttime highway. She's been tortured – and Mike is soon driven off the road by the hoods responsible. This time, the luckless woman is killed. Mike finds out that she was working for the FBI, and a bloody reckoning is in the offing. Everything is relatively one-dimensional, but the page-turning quality is undeniable – if you can take Mike Hammer, that is.

KISS ME DEADLY   1955
Director: Robert Aldrich

At a National Film Theatre audience with **Mickey Spillane,** the author was clearly dismayed that everyone present regarded Aldrich's adaptation as a classic – and, although no one said it, far superior to its source novel. This is one of the key movies of the age of paranoia: Aldrich ditched the drugs McGuffin and substituted a far more allusive nuclear theme, incorporated in a 'Pandora's box'. Significantly, Aldrich loathed Spillane's thuggish hero and encouraged an unsympathetic performance from Ralph Meeker.

Jim Thompson
(1906–77)

The 30 or so novels produced by Thompson, usually as paperback originals, were little regarded during his lifetime, despite a highly refined literary sense and a peculiar mix of raw lowlife realism, incisive and often brutal characterisation, unusual narrative structures, and a psychological insight second to none in the pulp tradition. Often narrated in the first person, this technique allowed him to develop the 'unreliable narrator', a theme popular among postmodern novelists.

Much of his work was biographical and drew on direct experience. Born in Oklahoma, his father was a county sheriff who was caught up in a corruption scandal. The family later moved to Texas, and most of Thompson's novels are set in a drab Southwest. Nearly always on the breadline, and a hardened alcoholic, he worked variously in hotels (as a procurer) and in the oilfields, began writing up true crime stories for pulp magazines, and became head of the Oklahoma Federal Writers Project, a New Deal initiative in the 1930s. His first crime novel, *Heed the Thunder*

The Grifters   1963

JIM THOMPSON

One would hardly turn to crime writers of the pulp and post-pulp era (even the best of them) for a balanced and percipient examination of gender issues. After all, everyone behaves badly in noir fiction – and if women seem just that much more duplicitous, that's almost a back-handed compliment: the scheming, treacherous femmes fatales of crime fiction are usually that bit smarter than the gullible males they put through the wringer. But certain writers were able to present a more nuanced picture of the relationship between the sexes, even within the imperatives of dark-hued novels – such as the gifted Jim Thompson, whose examination of both the male and female psyche was complex and unpredictable. In *The Grifters*, a novel about deception on every possible level, Roy Dillon is a charming and attractive con artist, whose mother, Lilly, is involved with the Mob, while

(1946), inaugurated an extraordinary series of very varied books, united only in their concentration on losers, chancers, nymphomaniacs and psychopaths. The nether world he portrays is comparable to that of **William Burroughs** in his more lucid moments (*Junky*, 1953) or **Nelson Algren** on a particularly bad day. What fame he achieved in his lifetime was established by *The Killer Inside Me* (1952), which remains a masterpiece by any standards.

In 1955 he moved to Hollywood, where he adapted the screenplay for **Stanley Kubrick**'s *The Killing* (1956) and *Paths of Glory* (1957) while drinking his fees in the bars on Sunset Boulevard. His later books lost some of his inventive and literary verve and, although popular in France by the time of his death, none of his books were in print in the US. Interestingly, he made a brief appearance in **Dick Richards'** 1975 film *Farewell, My Lovely*. His critical reputation revived in the 1980s and, in addition to *The Getaway*, several notable films have been made of his novels: *Pop. 1280* (as *Coup de Torchon* by **Bertrand Tavernier**, 1981), *The Kill-Off* (**Maggie Greenwald**, 1989), *After Dark, My Sweet* (**James Foley**, 1990) and *The Killer Inside Me* (**Michael Winterbottom**, 2010), as well as *The Grifters*. Many of his books, however, remain unfilmable.

THE GRIFTERS 1990
Director: Stephen Frears

A fearsome array of talent, including Anjelica Huston, John Cusack and Annette Bening playing the versatile but troubled con artists, and a script by **Donald E Westlake**, helped British director Frears capture a genuinely stark feel for the seamy side on the fringes of American society and, in addition, garner a cluster of Oscar nominations. Huston brings a classical Greek tragic quality to her role as the stoic failed mother in hock to the Mob, but Westlake dodges the typically Stygian finale of **Jim Thompson**'s novel.

his girlfriend Moira has a similarly slippery moral compass. After a con job goes wrong and Roy is left injured, his nurse, Carol, seems to inhabit a different, more innocent universe. However, Roy's largely successful attempts to avoid arraignment for his scams are threatened when Carol

– who is not quite what she seems – is stirred into the heady brew that is Roy, his mother and his mistress. Reading *The Grifters* is like being cast into a world where every value is up for grabs, not least sexuality: by the end of the novel, the reader (whatever their gender) will be questioning all assumptions about what might constitute fixed male and female verities.

The Bride Wore Black 1940
CORNELL WOOLRICH

The first of Woolrich's full-length novels, and the first of six written in the 1940s featuring 'black' in the title (which in turn inspired the French *Série Noire*), this is a classic revenge story with, as usual, a twist. The novel opens with a quote from **Guy de Maupassant**: 'For to kill is the great law set by nature at the heart of existence. There is nothing more beautiful and honourable than killing!'

Julie Killeen sees her husband mown down outside the church moments after her wedding. She vows to track down the drunk driver and his four passengers, and does so by wooing each of them before settling their hash, and her debt. However, over the years she spends stalking and dispatching her prey she is in turn tracked by a homicide cop, Lew Wanger, who finally reveals that her sanguineous trail of revenge was based on a misreading of the facts. All five men were in fact – if not in spirit – innocent. To reveal the reason would be a spoiler, but this outrageous murder novel is a great 'six for the price of one' bargain.

THE BRIDE WORE BLACK/ LA MARIÉE ÉTAIT EN NOIR 1968
Director: François Truffaut

Of course, having Jeanne Moreau in the lead always helps, as does a Bernard Herrmann score. And for once the self-confessed noir/pulp enthusiast Truffaut actually plays along with the qualities of **Cornell Woolrich's** original novel, albeit injecting a strong vein of sangfroid Gallic humour. **Quentin Tarantino** was to reference the movie in his *Kill Bill* volumes.

CHAPTER 4

PRIVATE EYES
Sleuths and gumshoes

The crime genre has several elements that are absolutely emblematic, but few would deny that the private detective is perhaps the single most important – certainly where American crime fiction is concerned, although several writers have attempted to translate the necessary accoutrements (guns, seductive clients, caustic wit) to a British milieu (and beyond), including, for instance, **Mark Timlin**, with his hyper-violent Nick Sharman series. An early prototype of the investigator for hire was **Carroll John Daly**'s Race Williams in the pages of *Black Mask* in the 1920s, while, of course, **Dashiell Hammett**'s Sam Spade and **Raymond Chandler**'s Philip Marlowe (also born in the pulps) remain the *locus classicus* of the figure. Later proponents, such as **Ross Macdonald** (with his well-read Lew Archer), added extra dimensions of psychological acuity – although the irreverent wisecracking was revived in **Robert B Parker**'s studiedly brilliant Spenser novels. And the genre has continued to offer the possibility for fine writing, quite as accomplished as more overtly 'literary' models – as in the novels of **James Lee Burke** featuring Cajun detective Dave Robicheaux. One of the most interesting developments of the form has been the introduction of female private investigators (notably **Sue Grafton**'s Kinsey Millhone and **Sara Paretsky**'s VI Warshawski). Wisely realising that too thorough a feminisation of the private eye parameters would be counterproductive,

Grafton and Paretsky invested their heroines with a notable toughness – and the reader is persuaded of the unlikely premise that these distaff gumshoes could survive for as long as they have in a dangerous world. And while current authors are ringing the changes on the professions of their protagonists (from **Steph Broadribb** and **Janet Evanovich**'s bounty hunters to **Liza Marklund** and **Julia Dahl**'s journalists), the private eye will no doubt be pounding those mean streets as long as the crime genre is around.

Case Histories 2004
KATE ATKINSON

Is this a crime novel? Or something more 'literary'? Since the award-winning *Behind the Scenes at the Museum* (1995), Kate Atkinson has demonstrated a reluctance to conform to the expectations readers may have of her work – and this hybrid novel (utilising crime novel tropes to more ambitious, non-genre ends) is typical of the surprises that each new book by the author springs on the reader, each one delivered with the same cool and effortless prose. Part of the pleasure with each succeeding book is that anticipation: what has she come up with this time? *Case Histories*, the first in the Jackson Brodie series – which is still running in 2019 – is couched in the form of an investigation. The central character is ex-copper Brodie, who now earns his crust away from the force, tackling small cases privately. His life is in something of a mess (with a dead marriage not the least of his problems), and thoughts of mortality haunt him. The novel deals with three cases he is struggling with, involving a disappearance, a murder and a reunion. The plotting here is deliberately amorphous, and Atkinson is more concerned with the emotional chasms between people than with the mechanics of the crime genre, although she plays fair by the latter. *Case Histories* is a truly unusual and intriguing crime outing.

Cross 2009
KEN BRUEN

Ken Bruen has long been a writer spoken about by both his fellow scribes and his devoted readers with great affection. Among his many skills, perhaps his most notable is the astonishing consistency he has shown over his series of books. The Galway-born author's Jack Taylor private eye novels have bagged both Shamus and Crime Writers' Association awards, and *Cross*, the sixth in the series, is a first-rate entry, played out against a slowly – and sometimes reluctantly – modernising Ireland and Galway city. The author's PhD in metaphysics is reflected in the mental processes of Taylor, whose frequently alienated state is one of the many unusual aspects of these very individual novels.

Purple Cane Road 2000
JAMES LEE BURKE

When it comes to literate American crime writing, Burke has few peers. And the writing has a forceful yet poetic quality that differentiates it from anything else around. His protagonist Dave Robicheaux, too, had something new: flawed, yes, and given to some moralising observations that at times sound like the American Religious Right (surprising from an author who clearly regarded Reaganite USA as a very dark place to be, as he now sees the Trump regime), but Robicheaux is the most fully rounded protagonist in modern American crime fiction. *Purple Cane Road* really vaulted Burke beyond genre and into the general bestseller charts, possibly because it is one of his most idiomatic and mature novels. Dave Robicheaux's mother Mae is dead, murdered by bent policemen. The detective undertakes his most personal journey when he discovers that Mae worked as a prostitute, and her involvement with the Mob may have led to her death. His subsequent quest is concerned as much with his own identity and antecedents (in flux after his unsettling discovery) as it is with settling old scores. Burke's strategy here is to subtly subvert the standard detective narrative, creating an atmospheric picture of the underbelly of American life.

Feast Day of Fools 2011
JAMES LEE BURKE

There are those who have problems with the religious underpinnings of one of the great American crime novelists, James Lee Burke. In the novels featuring his troubled private investigator Dave Robicheaux (not this book), there is an element that gives Burke naysayers ammunition: the detective's ex-nun partner who provides (simultaneously) raunchy sex and a strong sense of the spiritual – a phoney attempt (it's claimed) to have the best of all possible worlds from a sensualist/believer such as Burke. Faith

James Lee Burke
(1936–)

One of the most distinctive crime-cracking protagonists on the scene is James Lee Burke's quick-witted gumshoe Dave Robicheaux, and *The Neon Rain* (1987) was a perfect calling card for an accomplished new writer. Burke had enjoyed only small success as a writer of non-crime novels, but his time had come once he fell into the genre that he quickly made his own.

Burke's novels are set on the Gulf Coast, where he grew up. Born in Texas, James Lee Burke ensured that the New Orleans and Bayou backgrounds of his books were crammed full of authentic detail about Cajun culture.

is at the heart of his *Feast Day of Fools*, but this time there is no attempt at proselytising; religion here, largely speaking, is of the gun-toting, unnuanced kind that has hijacked Republican politics in the US.

As with another American writer who combines extreme violence with poetic lyricism, Cormac McCarthy, Burke's stamping ground is deep southwest Texas, and the locales fairly leap off the page in pungency and bitter vigour. We are once again in the company of Sherriff Hackberry Holland, a veteran of the Korean War, dispensing his precarious line of law enforcement near the border with Mexico. As in earlier Holland books (notably *Rain Gods*, the previous title in the series), the universe he moves in is surrealistic and minatory. We are given another monstrous villain in the psychotic Preacher Jack Collins, along with the equally terrifying mercenary Krill. And Burke is even audacious enough to up the ante with another psychopath, the illiterate Negrito, along with the psychologically troubled Reverend Cody Daniels (who enforces the power of the Scriptures with the barrel of a gun). Holland struggles to deal with all these antisocial characters, along with gunrunners, drug smugglers and an enigmatic Chinese woman, 'La Magdalena', who is engaged in smuggling Mexicans into the United States.

His books have also taken on board some cogent social issues: in *Heaven's Prisoners* (1988), a priest involved in the sanctuary movement is killed when a private plane crashes, and the narrative touches on US involvement in Central American terrorism. But *The Neon Rain* is Burke's most cogent example of narrative and setting being married with consummate precision.

Dave Robicheaux finds himself caught in a morass of violence in this darkest of Burke novels, while the cast of characters he encounters (including drug pushers who target children and CIA agents prepared to provide weapons for foreign death squads) is drawn with particular richness and rigour. The truly interesting thing about these books is the level of ambition, with such themes as redemption and the horror of the human condition treated with a surprising degree of seriousness in the context of popular novels. But James Lee Burke remains primarily an entertainer, and subsequent books in the series have continued to redefine the genre.

Even more than in previous James Lee Burke novels, this is a heavily loaded, overwrought narrative, and it's a measure of the author's skill that he always succeeds in persuading us of the reality of this crazed world. His efforts are couched here in the customary poetic prose (aromatic, but never purple) and – Burke detractors should note – there is no attempt to freight in propaganda for the benefit of God's grace. Religion here – as in most of the best thrillers – is a dangerously destabilising force rather than a source of salvation.

The Final Detail 1999

HARLAN COBEN

Harlan Coben's reputation among discerning crime readers is unassailable (even if it's sometimes hard to give a damn about the references to American sports). A key book by this American crime maestro is *The Final Detail*, in which the author delivers a rich essay in human malevolence. Coben's novel features sports agent-cum-detective Myron Bolitar, who is looking into the murder of Clu Haid, a New York Yankees baseball player. Haid (to

Myron's dismay) appears to have been shot by Myron's friend and partner in his sports agency, Esperanza Diaz. Was she the one to pull the trigger – or is the answer closer to home for Myron, with his own murky past at the heart of the killing? Coben, as ever, takes us on a gritty journey into some of the less savoury byways of human behaviour, but it's a journey shot through with wry humour and acute observation.

City of Bones 2002
MICHAEL CONNELLY

Admirers of Michael Connelly are fiercely loyal, and there was much rejoicing at the return of detective Harry Bosch (retired for several books) in this outstanding thriller. *City of Bones* rings some changes on previous Bosch outings, and demonstrates a welcome reluctance to repeat a successful formula. Harry opens up a 20-year-old murder case, with devastating consequences (not least for himself). A gruesome discovery is made in Los Angeles: the bones of a 12-year-old boy are found scattered in the Hollywood Hills. The case conjures for Harry dark memories from his past. Seeking to unearth hidden mysteries, he is able to find out who the child was and reconstruct his sad, abused life. Harry determines that the boy will not be forgotten, but a burgeoning affair with a policewoman distracts him. And (as so often in crime novels) murders in the distant past have an ineluctable way of bursting to light in the present. Connelly's background as a police reporter gives his books the powerful verisimilitude that few in the field possess. Harry and his new amour are characterised as sharply as ever, and the balance between such detail and the demands of machine-tooled plotting are adroitly choreographed. When so many crime writers are all too happy to repeat themselves, it's refreshing that Connelly clearly rejects such easy options.

The Gods of Guilt 2013
MICHAEL CONNELLY

There is a danger with prolific authors: we might see just a little too much of their signature characters, so that the novelty – and appeal – wears a little thin. So far, there is absolutely no danger of that with the ever reliable

Michael Connelly, who alternates his two protagonists, low-rent lawyer Mickey Haller and tough cop Harry Bosch, and sometimes (to the delight of his fans) sets them against each other in the same book. *The Gods of Guilt* is an outing for Haller, and within just a few pages establishes itself as one of the most sheerly readable entries in the series, effortlessly gripping us for the whole of its 400-odd pages.

Mickey receives a text saying 'Call me ASAP – 187.' He is familiar with the California penal code and the numbers that represent murder. Such cases are inevitably attractive to him, as the remuneration is always the most generous. Needless to say, though, he has to deliver the goods. Mickey discovers that the victim is an ex-client of his, a prostitute whose life he had tried to turn around. But it seems his efforts have been in vain – she has been plying her old trade again. Mickey, despite his slippery moral standards, is at heart a man of conscience and knows that he has tried his best – but he learns to his horror that his attempts to get her life on an even keel may be precisely what led to her death. In trying to unearth the facts behind the murder, he comes up against some very dangerous and ruthless people – but, more importantly, he also has to confront (not for the first time) some crushing levels of personal guilt. For Mickey, redemption becomes the name of the game.

Of the quartet of American crime novelists whose speciality is ironclad storytelling (the others are Linwood Barclay, Harlan Coben and Robert Crais; James Lee Burke is a different kettle of fish), Michael Connelly is perhaps the most interested in the conflicted character of his protagonists, and the always beleaguered Mickey Haller is his masterstroke. *The Lincoln Lawyer* was the book that put Mickey on readers' radars, and if this doesn't quite have the panache of that book, it's still an immensely assured piece of writing – and will be catnip for Michael Connelly fans.

The Last Detective 2003

ROBERT CRAIS

Former TV cop-show scriptwriter Robert Crais – he honed his craft on seminal American series, notably *Hill Street Blues* and *Miami Vice* – reversed the usual trajectory by leaving Hollywood for his typewriter, producing well-turned thrillers such as *LA Requiem* (1999), *Demolition Angel* (2000) and *Hostage* (2001). Like his inspiration, **Raymond Chandler**, he utilises the delirious panoply of Los Angeles as a backdrop for his writing, and his sardonic private eye Elvis Cole is securely fixed in the constellation of literary detectives, as is his other recurring character, the hard-as-nails Joe Pike. Often accused of being formulaic, Crais's cinematic approach moves the action along.

The Last Detective is quite his most accomplished novel – even if the first few chapters don't initially exert the customary grip, despite a high-octane opening. The excellent *Hostage* began with a bungled raid on a minimart; the plot engine here is much more personal. Crais's highly unorthodox private eye Elvis Cole is minding his girlfriend's son Ben at his house near LA when the boy is kidnapped from under his nose. The kidnapper taunts the unhappy Cole by phone with the words, 'I've got the boy. This is payback.' But Cole has something to work on: the words 'Five two', which was Cole's unit's designation in Vietnam. Elvis has put this hellish part of his life at the back of his consciousness for the last 20 years, but he decides that retribution is what the kidnappers are seeking, not money, and the solution to his current predicament lies firmly in the past. Crais has made his mark in an overcrowded field by characterising his dishevelled private eye with tremendous panache, and, by making the kidnapped boy who is the fulcrum of the plot the child of Cole's girlfriend (with the concomitant issues of trust and responsibility), Crais manages to make that old chestnut – 'This time it's personal' – seem as fresh as new paint.

The Wanted 2018
ROBERT CRAIS

In *The Wanted*, Tyson, a teenage burglar of upmarket homes, is being tracked by two brutal murderers, keen to retrieve a stolen laptop. Elvis Cole and Joe Pike are hired by the mother of the missing boy to find him, and soon both duos are converging on Tyson – with violent results. Not vintage Crais, perhaps, but he still expertly delivers his customary modern-day riff on the 1940s hardboiled idiom.

Calendar Girl 1994
STELLA DUFFY

Any proselytising is absolute death to a book's narrative drive, and the best writers are well aware that if points are to be made, it is essential that they simply crop up in the course of the story, rather than drawing attention to themselves. And Stella Duffy's feminist lesbian crime novel *Calendar Girl* is a good example of just how entertaining her work can be – for any reader, whatever their sexuality (although Duffy is dismayed by what she describes as heteronormative views). Saz Martin is having a hard time running a private eye business on an Enterprise Allowance scheme and is grateful for any clients. When a man named Clark hires her services, he tells her that he has lost £16,000 of redundancy money to a mysterious woman whom he knew only as 'September'. They met twice a month for dinner, but she remains an enigma to him. As Saz digs into a dangerous mystery, there are some graphic sex scenes in store for the reader. What makes the book so thoroughly enjoyable, though, is the other main protagonist, stand-up comedian Maggie, who Duffy deals with in alternate chapters. While it is sometimes a bit of a jolt to switch between two very different characters, Duffy handles the change of gear with gusto and conveys a genuine sense of menace without ladling on the violence. Duffy has proved capable of extending conventional crime scenarios in other ways, as shown by 1999's *Fresh Flesh*, in which Saz Martin is tracking down the natural parents of adopted babies. It goes without saying that if you're someone for whom unblushingly described lesbian sex scenes are a problem, you should steer clear. But Duffy's writing is a delight, and Saz is a strongly drawn heroine.

Steppin' on a Rainbow 2001
KINKY FRIEDMAN

There is no one quite like Kinky Friedman. He is the star of his own novels, and his musical private eye persona is a brilliant creation: witty, caustic and highly individual. Not since **Ellery Queen** cast himself (via his various ghost writers) as the hero of his own adventures has this conceit been brought off so imaginatively. Sitting disconsolately in his New York loft, Friedman finds himself musing on friendship and the fact that none of his friends are in town. But he's contacted by an old acquaintance, Hoover from Honolulu, who tells him that Village Irregular Mike McGovern has vanished while researching and writing a cookery book. When last seen, McGovern was heading for the beach. Kinky makes his way to Hawaii to begin a search for his missing friend. What follows is a hilarious – and suspenseful – series of wild goose chases that get Kinky very little closer to the heart of the mystery. But after identifying a corpse whose face is missing and trying to capture hoax kidnappers, he finds a life-size sculpted wooden head in the local museum that looks exactly like the missing Mike McGovern. This is thoroughly characteristic stuff from a unique writer. To say that it moves along with the speed of an express train doesn't tell the half of it: the plotting is as bizarre and diverting as ever. There are those who find Kinky a highly irritating figure, but if you are on the right wavelength to open yourself up to the quirky delights on offer here, you'll have a great time.

The Cuckoo's Calling — 2013
ROBERT GALBRAITH

When the secret was out – and we knew that it was Harry Potter's only begetter **JK Rowling** behind the masculine sobriquet 'Robert Galbraith' – we were all obliged to play catch-up with a book that created barely a ripple on its first appearance. Rowling's first adult novel, *The Casual Vacancy* (2012), incurred a decidedly mixed critical response, despite its prodigious sales, but the follow-up was an accomplished piece that thoroughly deserved its retrospective success, even were it not by a celebrity author. As the beleaguered military policeman-turned-private eye Cormoran Strike investigates the apparent suicide of a supermodel, we are granted a measured but subtly involving reworking of crime novel mechanisms as the detective moves across a variety of class divides, finding that the police have got things wrong. Strike himself is a distinctive addition to the overcrowded ranks of literary private eyes.

S is for Silence — 2005
SUE GRAFTON

The Trojan horse for women crime writers in the States, the late Grafton possessed a laser-sharp ability to read (and reproduce) human behaviour while not giving too much away about herself, a skill parlayed into her long-running female private eye series, which began in 1982 with *A is for Alibi* and ended, prematurely, with her last book, *Y is for Yesterday*, in 2017. While the adjective 'feisty' is routinely applied to **Patricia Cornwell**'s pathologist heroine Kay Scarpetta, Grafton's gumshoe Kinsey Millhone does not lend herself so readily to easy categorisation. While undoubtedly a survivor, and preternaturally gifted in getting under the skin of those she encounters, Kinsey has a chameleon-like quality that helps put her witnesses and suspects at ease – very often so that they will betray themselves. In this, she is something like an American distaff George Smiley, with an added taste for junk food and rather more changes of brassiere.

S is for Silence demonstrates why Grafton has such a dedicated following, with Kinsey Millhone as dogged (and perceptive) as ever, trying to crack a particularly intractable mystery. In July 1953, the promiscuous Violet (married to the abusive Foley) disappeared, driving off in her new Chevy, blowing a kiss to her daughter. Thirty-five years later, that daughter, the unhappy Daisy, has decided that finding out what happened to her mother is the only way she can put her own unresolved life in order. She hires Kinsey, who questions all those who knew Violet before her disappearance. Was she murdered by the brutal Foley? Or is the reason behind her vanishing a more complex affair? As Kinsey gets closer to the truth she finds the easy cooperation of the townspeople hardening into something more hostile, and the slashing of her car tyres is the first sign that things will turn very nasty. Grafton eschews the synthetic climaxes that other, lesser writers inject into their narrative to add spurious excitement, instead providing a steadier and more realistic unravelling of the central mystery. If there's a problem with that approach here, it's possibly the fact that Kinsey is told over and over again how sluttish the missing Violet was, and any description of the latter's husband is incomplete without the information that he used to beat her. But just as we're getting impatient, Grafton cannily moves things onto another level, and the revelations begin to come satisfyingly thick and fast. Like her great predecessor **Ross Macdonald**, Grafton foregrounds idiosyncratic characterisation at all times, and some of the observation of small-town American life here has the acuity of **Richard Ford**.

The Maltese Falcon   1930
DASHIELL HAMMETT

The definitive Sam Spade adventure is also the definitive private eye novel, forging the template that all future practitioners would adapt. Initially serialised in *Black Mask* magazine (and filmed on several occasions), the novel

Dashiell Hammett
(1894–1961)

Raymond Chandler may have burnished the crime novel to its brightest, but he was undoubtedly building on the foundations of the godfather of the genre, Dashiell Hammett. Hammett's first work was published pseudonymously in the 1920s, and he spent his last 30 alcohol-fuelled years without producing any novels. But for the brief time his flame burned, none burned brighter.

Hammett served in World War I, and his first contact with crime was with the real thing – he was employed for eight years as a detective for the famous Pinkerton agency in Baltimore. His varied experiences with the agency were later transmuted into the stories and novels featuring his overweight, middle-aged sleuth, the Continental Op, always unnamed. On leaving the agency, and dogged by lung complaints, he paid the bills by writing advertising copy, but he found his métier writing crime stories for such pulp magazines as *Black Mask*, rapidly expanding his pieces into longer, serialised novels. His first, *Red Harvest* (1929), was a bleak, astringent portrait of a corrupt city and defined his pared-down

features the ultimate literary McGuffin (the object that all the characters kill or die for) in the eponymous *objet d'art*. As so often in the genre, the plot and its machinations very much play second fiddle to the wonderfully sharp characterisations: of the dogged Sam himself, of course, but also of the urbane villain Casper Gutman and his homosexual henchman Joel Cairo. There is, too, the archetypal literary femme fatale in the beguiling and treacherous Brigid O'Shaughnessy. The novel begins with Sam tracking down the killers of his partner Miles Archer, and the blunted but resilient code of honour that is the private eye's stock-in-trade is given a definitive airing. And while Sam may lack the subtlety that Chandler was to bring to his heir apparent, Philip Marlowe, the economical, diamond-hard and witty dialogue is there, and the stripped-down prose echoes the contemporaneous writing of **Ernest Hemingway**. And there are those who would claim that Hammett's work (in this less respectable genre) is the equal of his more fêted colleague.

economical style. In the same year (1930) came *The Dain Curse* and then the Sam Spade outing *The Maltese Falcon*, which encapsulated all the great themes of the private eye novel. His favourite was *The Glass Key* (1931), about corruption and friendship, and he created an equally enduring staple of the private eye genre in *The Thin Man* (1934), in which the wisecracking husband-and-wife detective team Nick and Nora Charles embodied a lighter, more comic style without the bleakness of his earlier books.

All of Hammett's work retains its freshness and vigour, constantly reminding the reader what a loss the writer's final decades of non-productive alcoholism were. He did see service in World War II, however, and consistently spoke out for left-wing causes alongside the dramatist Lillian Hellman, with whom he had a long-term relationship but never married; both were blacklisted during the McCarthy witch-hunt.

THE MALTESE FALCON　　1941

Director: John Huston

From John Huston's impeccable screenplay (wisely utilising whole swathes of **Dashiell Hammett**'s dialogue) and direction (his debut), through Humphrey Bogart's matchless Sam Spade, to the most memorable duo of villains in crime movies (Sydney Greenstreet's saturnine, overweight Gutman and Peter Lorre's effeminate but dangerous henchman), all the elements in this definitive cinematic incarnation of the novel simply could not be improved upon.

Gravedigger 1982
JOSEPH HANSEN

Probably the most celebrated name in gay crime fiction, Joseph Hansen combines the flinty narrative skills of his many predecessors with a totally modern (and radical) gay sensibility. His protagonist, Dave Brandstetter, is probably the only gay character to make a mark comparable to the many straight heroes of the genre. Dave's humanity and professionalism are always to the fore, which makes his appearances very welcome indeed. In *Gravedigger*, a particularly enjoyable Hansen novel, Charles Westover is a lawyer who has been disbarred from his profession and files an insurance claim when his errant teenage daughter is murdered. Dave Brandstetter is assigned to the case and discovers that several young women have been killed by the guru of a sinister cult. But is the dead girl, Serenity, one of these victims? As Dave moves into more and more disturbing territory, he finds that even his own unshockable character is to be tested – not for the first time, as 1979's *Skinflick* dragged Brandstetter from an evangelical church to a sordid underworld of prostitution and drugs. *Gravedigger* is played out against brightly realised settings: the sultry Californian locales and the snowbound mountain camps are evoked with all the customary Hansen aplomb.

Prayers for Rain 1999
DENNIS LEHANE

With a background as a counsellor specialising in disturbed and abused children, Lehane writes with authority. His *Mystic River* (2001), filmed by Clint Eastwood, vaulted him into the star stream, but his Kenzie–Gennaro novels, beginning with *A Drink Before the War* (1994), established a firm basis for his growing reputation. In *Prayers for Rain*, the fifth in the cycle, Boston private investigator Patrick Kenzie meets an intriguing young woman, Karen Nichols, who six months later jumps from one of Boston's most cherished monuments. As Patrick finds himself becoming obsessed with the truth behind the tragic events that befell Karen, he is soon engaged in psychological warfare with a lethally intelligent sociopath who specialises in making his victims' lives hell. The byplay between Patrick, his ex-partner Angela Gennaro and his eccentric friend Bubba Rogowski is a particular pleasure, and even the shop-worn theme of the hyper-intelligent villain is handled with a freshness that keeps cliché at bay.

Fade to Grey 2019
JOHN LINCOLN

John Lincoln is the pseudonym for **John Williams**, the novelist, biographer and crime fiction reviewer, and *Fade to Grey* is a smart, highly contemporary private detective novel set in two vibrant and vividly depicted UK settings: Cardiff and Bristol. Gethin Grey is the man you call when there's nowhere else to turn; his Last Resort Legals team investigates miscarriages of justice. But Gethin is running out of options himself: his gambling is out of control, his marriage is falling apart and there's no money left to pay the wages. Izma M was sent down years ago for the brutal murder of a young woman. In jail, he has written a bestseller and become a cult hero, and now the charismatic fading film star Amelia Laverne wants to bankroll Gethin to prove his innocence. For Gethin – low on luck and cash – the job is heaven sent. But is Izma M really as blameless as his fans believe? This seemingly cold case is about to turn very hot indeed…

A Nasty Piece of Work 2013
ROBERT LITTELL

A Nasty Piece of Work is a relatively slim volume for Littell (weighing in at under 260 pages), but it is as finely honed a thriller as any reader might wish for. Ex-CIA agent Lemuel Gunn has left his profession behind him, swapping the bloodshed of Afghanistan for a cramped trailer in New Mexico and hopefully starting on a new career as a private investigator. But his first case involves a woman called Ornella Neppi, who is inexorably running her uncle's bail bond business into the ground. Ornella enlists Gunn's aid when a criminal called Emilio Gava jumps bail after an arrest for buying cocaine. But things – unsurprisingly – prove to be radically different from the initial impressions that Gunn has of the case. Those fearing that Littell has left his espionage comfort zone behind for the territory of the tough private eye novel can be reassured: Gunn is a winning protagonist, and *A Nasty Piece of Work* is every bit as richly characterised, quirky and mesmerising as his more usual fare.

Ross Macdonald
(1915–83)

The notion of a holy trinity of American masters of the private eye novel was somewhat slow in coming. While **Raymond Chandler** and **Dashiell Hammett** had long enjoyed exalted status, the reputation of **Kenneth Millar** (better known as Ross Macdonald) was rather slower in coming. But the wait was worthwhile, and – whisper it – there are even many fans of the genre who would consider Macdonald to be the finest writer the field has known. Millar/Macdonald was born in Los Gatos, California on 13 December 1915 but was brought up in Canada, returning to California in the 1950s. Writing under his own name and then as Ross Macdonald, such books as *The Dark Tunnel* (1944) established his reputation. As John Macdonald, he produced the first novel to feature his saturnine private eye Lew Archer: *The Moving Target* in 1949 (the book was subsequently republished under the Ross Macdonald name). Many novels of quite astonishing consistency followed, such as *The Wycherly Woman* (1961), *The Chill* (1964) and, one of his finest books, *The Blue Hammer* (1976).

Macdonald was principally concerned with the psychology of his characters, Lew Archer sometimes functioning almost as a therapist when addressing the variegated problems of his clients and those he encounters. Written with a rigour and richness of ambition that matches the finest literary fiction, Macdonald often eschewed the reflexive violence of the genre, although when violent actions demanded an appearance, they registered all the more strongly. Such writers as the Norwegian **Gunnar Staalesen** regard Macdonald as the *ne plus ultra* of the genre, and that is a view that is gaining more and more currency with the years.

One Fearful Yellow Eye 1966
JOHN D MACDONALD

American master John D MacDonald's Travis McGee novels (all with a colour in the title) made him a very rich man – and though he is far less consistent than the other proponent of the private eye genre with whom he shares a surname, Ross Macdonald, at his best he brings an energy and forcefulness to his material, married to keen social concern as voiced by his gumshoe hero, who lives on a Florida houseboat called *The Busted Flush*. *One Fearful Yellow Eye* is the perfect entry point for MacDonald. McGee is commissioned by the wife of an old friend to retrieve the missing money that a celebrated surgeon (mortally ill) was to leave to his long-suffering family. MacDonald's plotting here is tortuous, but in the best possible fashion, and the sense of the fragility of life and the social order is as acute as it is in the other McGee novel that many consider among MacDonald's best, *The Green Ripper* (1979).

The Galton Case 1959
ROSS MACDONALD

This 1959 novel was Macdonald's favourite among his own work and is the signature book for the writer many feel to be **Raymond Chandler**'s true heir apparent. The author's signature theme – the malign influence of childhood events over adult actions – is worked out with an exacting precision, and while Lew Archer fulfils all the customary behaviour patterns of the tough private eye, the novel itself is in the nature of a psychological investigation. Lawyer Gordon Sable commissions Archer to find Anthony Galton. He is the son of the elderly Maria Galton, who wants to see her long-missing child before she breathes her last – which will be soon. In the sumptuous Galton residence, Archer also encounters a doctor, August Howell, and his daughter Sheila, along with a companion, Cassie. The search for the prodigal son proves far more complex than Archer expects, but there are other things to distract his attention. The lawyer who hired him has a wife with mental problems, and a rude associate named Peter Culligan. Culligan is murdered by a man who then steals Archer's car, and it soon becomes clear to Lew that all of this is somehow connected to the missing Galton. While the accoutrements of the Chandlerian private eye novel are all firmly in place, Macdonald's prose is heavier and far less inclined to embellish the narrative with stinging one-

The Moving Target — 1949
ROSS MACDONALD

One of Macdonald's most popular novels, this is a quintessential outing for his private eye Lew Archer, with an ambitiously large dramatis personae, all impeccably characterised. Archer is hired to look into the possible kidnapping of millionaire Ralph Sampson, and at the same time a great many people are going to a great deal of trouble to get their hands on a hundred grand in small notes. Archer finds himself running up against Elaine Sampson, Ralph's disenchanted wife, ex-DA Albert Graves (not a man noted for philanthropy), and the violent chorus boy Dwight Troy. All of this is vintage Macdonald and one of the best post-Chandler private eye novels, with a palpable sense of evil.

HARPER/THE MOVING TARGET — 1966
Director: Jack Smight

Paul Newman as an oddly renamed Lew Harper in Jack Smight's updated adaptation of *The Moving Target* works on some levels: at the height of his career, an obvious choice, serious, handsome and enquiring, and bringing something of his **Tennessee Williams** stage experience to the role. He was also surrounded by a clincher cast (Lauren Bacall, Shelley Winters, Arthur Hill). But is he Lew? Not really. Nevertheless, the success of the film was enough to ensure a follow-up adaptation of *The Drowning Pool* (1975).

Sex Dolls — 2002
REGGIE NADELSON

Since 1995, Nadelson's crime series featuring Moscow-born New Yorker Artie Cohen has built up a considerable following, with such books as *Hot Poppies* (1997) and *Bloody London* (1999) full of the quirky, irreverent writing that is Nadelson's stock-in-trade. *Sex Dolls* struck out into new territory in its unflinching depiction of a snowbound Paris in thrall to a grim trade in sex slaves. Artie Cohen, disturbed by changes in his long-term girlfriend Lily, is summoned from London to Paris, where he finds that Lily has been savagely raped and beaten in an unused apartment. Her amnesia offers Artie few clues, and he finds that he must investigate a very seamy side of Paris, one little known to the tourists. Artie's interest in jazz and the darker side of life is not, he discovers, sufficient preparation for the world of abused hookers and human enslavement he finds. And as his search for Lily's attackers leads him into considerable danger, he is pitched into a truly international trade that takes no prisoners. New York-born Nadelson (she also lives in London) has created a strongly drawn, engaging protagonist in the womanising Artie, and his encounters with the various lowlifes of *Sex Dolls* makes for scabrous and involving reading. Nadelson is good, too, on the various locales of the novel: drawing on her journalistic background, from London to Paris, from Vienna to New York, all Nadelson's destinations are etched with colour and atmosphere.

Blacklist 2003

SARA PARETSKY

Despite this being a reappearance of Sara Paretsky's dogged heroine VI Warshawski after a layoff, *Blacklist* is quite as vibrant and astringent as the author's earlier work. VI remains the best single female private investigator in American crime fiction, and her survival (after numerous pummellings, both physical and emotional) is both plausible and – for readers – very welcome. Here, we're concerned with cover-ups and conspiracy: familiar Paretsky territory. A dead woman journalist turns up on the grounds of an upscale mansion (it's VI who discovers her body), and when the police take very little interest, she is convinced that the race of the victim is a determining factor. VI begins to dig into the background of the victim, and family secrets begin to crop up (much as in the great Lew Archer novels of **Ross Macdonald**, families can be threatening things in VI's world). The police, of course, are no help – and are even physically obstructive. Who is manipulating the police agenda? As often in Paretsky's books, the emotional involvement of VI in the case is both ill-advised and inevitable. In interviews, Paretsky has made it clear that this is one of her most personal books – that involvement is framed in every word here.

Stone Cold
2003
ROBERT B PARKER

Parker's tough private eye Spenser has long been recognised as one of the most accomplished facsimiles of Chandler's definitive gumshoe Marlowe, and it might have been seen as a foolhardy move to introduce another series character. But Parker clearly needed to recharge his batteries, and the introduction of Jesse Stone had a galvanising effect. Stone's chequered career in the LAPD has pushed him into the backwoods of Paradise, Massachusetts, where he holds down the job of chief of police and tries to keep his alcoholism in check. In *Stone Cold*, Jesse is on the trail of two random killers, but the number of victims – from all walks of life – begins to stack up at an alarming rate, and Jesse realises that he may be dealing with a serial killer (or killers). And Jesse has another problem – the pressure-cooker atmosphere of Paradise is putting a merciless spotlight on him, and his personal problems (his wife, his drinking) have to be sorted out before he tackles the greatest professional challenge of his life. The dialogue and the sense of locale here are as acute as vintage Parker – and vintage Spenser.

Hell to Pay
2002
GEORGE PELECANOS

Pelecanos's second book to feature black private investigator Derek Strange and his white colleague Terry Quinn (the first was *Right as Rain* (2001)) signalled that he may be digging into the messy emotional lives of its tough heroes. But Pelecanos also had bigger fish to fry: the hard-edged scenario on offer here is really a frame for a piece of scabrous sociological writing, in which urban deprivation darkens the future of generations of young black males. Pelecanos has written cogently before about the cycle of violence that cripples the potential of so many young men, and his anger has a keen personal edge (the author's adopted sons are African-American). Here, his two tarnished heroes become involved in the death of a youth, gunned down as an innocent bystander in a drug shooting, and Strange feels that he must take out the killers in bloody ghetto fashion. But he's forced to confront some unpalatable truths about himself. The writing at times has a genuinely epic quality, with an excoriating analysis of the dark underbelly of society echoing both **Fyodor Dostoyevsky** and **Nelson Algren**. The bizarre juxtaposition of privilege and decay that is the city of Washington DC has rarely been anatomised as acutely as here: drug lord Granville Oliver is given the gravitas and influence of one of Washington's uptown senators.

Angel on the Inside 2003

MIKE RIPLEY

Angel enthusiasts know what to expect from the reliable Ripley – crime writing shot through with inky humour – and *Angel on the Inside* delivers the usual sharp-edged antics. So why is Ripley's wry protagonist Angel trying to break *into* a prison? The trouble starts when the ex-husband of Angel's partner Amy is rearrested, having been released from prison only a month before. And some very seedy characters start taking a close interest in what the ex-husband was doing between his release from prison and subsequent rearrest for stalking Amy – but Amy's not talking. It's up to Angel to find out why she is being so reticent and why another mystery person is so fascinated by her ex's movements – and the only way to do that is to discover what was going on in prison prior to his release. So Angel has to figure out how to break in; he doesn't know yet how he'll do it, only that it's going to be just like breaking out – only in reverse… Grab some hard liquor and curl up with this.

Black Maps 2003

PETER SPIEGELMAN

A palpable sense of danger haunts the pages of *Black Maps*, and that pleasurable unsettling of the reader is a constant factor. Spiegelman's hero, private eye John March, is struggling to pull himself together after the misfortunes that have blighted both his life and his career. Manhattan is his beat, but when a Park Avenue client employs him, he finds himself with a case that has a million ramifications – most of them dangerous. Rick Pierro, March's client, is a self-made man who has transcended his low-

> ## Sleuths on screen
>
> For many today, Raymond Chandler's preference for the somewhat smart-arsed Dick Powell as Philip Marlowe ('You could imagine Powell playing chess,' he said) in *Murder, My Sweet* (an adaptation of *Farewell, My Lovely*, directed by **Edward Dmytryk** in 1944) may seem perverse. This is because for most it is the inimitable Humphrey Bogart's performances as both Marlowe and Sam Spade that appear definitive and threw a shadow it was difficult to best. The diminutive Alan Ladd proved irritating in Hammett's *The Glass Key* (**Stuart Heisler**, 1942), and **Robert Montgomery** rather too chirpy and earnest directing himself as Marlowe in *The Lady in the Lake* (1946). The only other viable 1940s candidate, Robert Mitchum, had such an air of moral ambiguity about him (both on screen and off) that he only got the chance to portray Marlowe as an old man (tremendous in **Dick Richards'** *Farewell, My Lovely* (1975) and barely retaining his dignity while all around lost theirs in **Michael Winner**'s ludicrous *The Big Sleep* in 1978). In fact, on screen, the knight errant PI became something of a figure of derision by the 1950s, when hard-bitten cops were in the ascendant. Affectionate nods were made

rent origins to become a star performer on Wall Street. But everything that Rick has acquired – including his desirable wife – is on the line when an unwelcome communication threatens to pull him into a massive financial scandal. John March tracks down a ferociously intelligent opponent who has left banks and people bleeding in his wake, and he discovers that the layers of corruption run very deep indeed. It's no longer a novelty for a thriller writer to have a financial background, but Spiegelman spent some 20 years in the banking, brokerage and software sectors, and there's no denying that he uses his knowledge more impressively than most.

Mr Clarinet   2006
NICK STONE

Let's face it, it's much easier to pick up a thriller by an author whose work we know well, rather than taking a chance on a debut novel by someone by Albert Finney in the British-based *Gumshoe* (**Stephen Frears**, 1971) and by Jack Nicholson in *Chinatown* (**Roman Polanski**, 1974, although the hapless Nicholson sports an absurd plaster across his nose for most of the movie), and in the hilarious tribute *Dead Men Don't Wear Plaid* (**Carl Reiner**, 1982, with an incompetent Steve Martin interposed into footage from a range of Hollywood noir classics); meanwhile an off-screen Bogart prompts Woody Allen on romantic gambits in *Play It Again, Sam* (**Herbert Ross**, 1972). Elliott Gould was an absurd postmodern anti-Marlowe in **Robert Altman**'s *The Long Goodbye* (1973); Altman's view of Marlowe as a loser and anachronism in modern-day LA has a very different resonance. There's the usual razor-sharp Altman characterisation of small parts, and a towering performance by noir veteran Sterling Hayden, but Gould's shambling, ineffectual detective – whose most significant relationship is with his cat – will not be to the taste of most Chandler admirers.

Interestingly, few of the modern private eyes have made it to the screen (although Kathleen Turner's feisty VI Warshawski made a great BBC radio series, after playing the character on film), and Robert Crais for one refuses to license his characters, preferring his reader's images of them to remain unadulterated.

we've never heard of. But sometimes playing safe is the wrong option – and readers would be doing themselves a disservice by ignoring Nick Stone. *Mr Clarinet* is a book that came weighted down with some heavy pre-publicity hype from his publishers, clearly hoping that Stone would be the Next Big Thing. Certainly, his biography is unusual: born in Cambridge to a Scottish father (in fact, the noted historian Norman Stone) and Haitian mother, Stone was sent to live in Haiti with his hard-drinking, gun-brandishing grandfather who used voodoo remedies. After Cambridge, he was back in Haiti when the country went down another bloody path. But all of this didn't guarantee that he could turn out a novel as interesting as his life had been. However, a few pages of *Mr Clarinet* are enough to prove that Nick Stone was indeed the find that his publishers were clearly hoping for, although that early promise has remained unfulfilled. For a start, his scene-setting is a revelation: a massive Haitian canvas against which the terrifying narrative plays out.

Miami private investigator Max Mingus will pocket $15 million if he can track down Charlie Carver, scion of an extremely rich family. Charlie has gone missing in Haiti, where many young people have disappeared. And it's here, of course, that Stone is able to make impressive capital from his years in this violent and exotic country. As Max digs ever deeper into the mystery surrounding Charlie, he discovers that voodoo is not just a come-on for the tourists, but an extremely sinister and forceful presence, behind which hovers the mysterious figure of Mr Clarinet, who the natives believe has been luring children away from their families. All of this is dispatched with tremendous brio by Stone, who never gives the slightest impression of being an apprentice novelist. Many elements are stirred into the heady brew: black magic, Baby Doc Duvalier, the cocaine trade and the incipient civil war in the country. Stone even persuasively draws parallels between the 1994 US invasion of Haiti and the Iraq situation in the 2000s. If he doesn't pull together every strand in this ambitious enterprise, few readers will have cause to complain.

Weirdo 2013
CATHI UNSWORTH

It was the London-based writer Iain Sinclair, no less, who provided the encomium for this rich and strange offering from one of Britain's most individual writers. And Sinclair is the perfect commentator, given that his highly idiosyncratic vision is one of the few that is a match for Unsworth's equally off-kilter perception. *Weirdo* is probably Unsworth's most fully achieved book, with the eponymous character described by the tabloids as the 'Wicked Witch of the East' who at the age of 15 was convicted of murdering one of her classmates. Two decades later, private eye Sean Ward (with an abruptly terminated Met police career in his past) begins to uncover new stratifications hidden within this multi-layered case from the past. There is, perhaps, a warning that should be given before picking up the novel: its density and atmosphere will make most other contemporary crime fiction seem etiolated fare. But Unsworth admirers need not hesitate.

CHAPTER 5

COPS
Police procedurals and mavericks

The private eye in crime fiction is always a maverick – it goes with the territory. But protagonists who earn their crust as police officers usually divide neatly into categories: organisation men (and women) who may be at daggers drawn with their superiors but who – largely speaking – buckle down and get the job done. There may be broken marriages, alienated children, battles with the bottle, but an innate professionalism always – finally – sustains them. But there's also the maverick cop – quite as much of a loose cannon as the private eye, even though he or she may be paid by the state. In novels featuring rogue policemen, their sacking is always a whisker away – or violent death, if they're corrupt cops (the Old Testament morality of even the most anti-establishment crime writers usually surfaces in a savage reckoning before the last page).

On the other hand, there are also the police procedurals, godfathered by **Ed McBain**, which set themselves the task of ensuring that the quotidian details of a cop's life are handled in an absorbing fashion, although this is an increasingly daunting task, as readers and viewers are smothered by an avalanche of cop novels and TV shows, endlessly rehashing the familiar tropes. But the very best writers of novels featuring coppers – like those below – are always aware that it's the character of their hero that keeps us reading quite as much as the impenetrable mysteries they're solving. And the dichotomy between deeply flawed individuals and their professional responsibilities is a sand and oyster scenario that has produced some shining pearls of crime writing. As with the private eye novel, the job of the literary copper – to strip bare the human soul – has often provided a fertile area for writing of penetrating psychological acuity, quite the equal of non-genre fiction.

The Doll's House 2015
MJ ARLIDGE

In *The Doll's House* (definite article, unlike **Henrik Ibsen**), by Matt Arlidge, a young woman wakes in a dark cellar, totally disoriented – she has no idea how she arrived there or who kidnapped her. The body of another young woman is found buried on a remote beach, but her family have been getting regular texts from her for years. Detective Inspector Helen Grace is soon on the track of a particularly unpleasant monster. With a manipulation of tension that is always fluid and cinematic, MJ Arlidge's novel grabs the reader by the throat – as does his single-minded, unconventional policewoman Helen Grace, with her unorthodox S&M sexual tastes. Later books, such as the taut *Liar Liar* (2015) and *Down to the Woods* (2018) have continued Arlidge's upwards trajectory.

Lifeless 2005
MARK BILLINGHAM

Billingham's breakthrough was inevitable: he made a considerable impression with the first two books in the Tom Thorne series, *Sleepyhead* (2001) and *Scaredy Cat* (2002), novels that instantly marked him out as one of the most impressive writers on the overcrowded British crime scene. Subsequently, *Lazybones* (2003) showed the author's willingness to tackle uncomfortable themes, dealing as it did with convicted rapists being savagely killed after their release from prison. And it has to be said that Billingham's novels take no prisoners in terms of extreme violence – he will never be a favourite read among those who want polite mayhem amidst the tea cosies, as *The Burning Girl* (2004), *The Killing Habit* (2018) and *Their Little Secret* (2019) amply proved. *Lifeless* is a novel that added more lustre to Billingham's achievements – not least for the element of social critique folded into this one. Detective Inspector Tom Thorne is aware of the downward trajectory of his career. Finding it difficult to cope with the recent death of his father, he is also smarting under bitter criticism of his professional life (he broke all the rules on his last case), and he finds that, against his wishes, he is forced to take gardening leave. But this enforced inactivity isn't to last. Homeless people on the streets of the capital have been savagely kicked to death, their corpses discovered with a £20 note pinned to their chests. Random killings of alcoholics and junkies? Or something more targeted? Thorne finds himself back at the sharp end as he takes dangerous journeys into the clandestine byways of the underclass, with their inflexible codes and strictures. *Lifeless* is not a comfortable read – Billingham never is, despite, or perhaps because of, his alternative career as a stand-up comedian – but it is easy to become addicted to the stronger fare that the author offers.

Sweetheart 2008

CHELSEA CAIN

Heartsick, Chelsea Cain's debut, had an unusual synthesis of familiar serial killer motifs and some intriguing innovations (notably the fact that her utterly ruthless murderer was a woman: the beautiful Gretchen Lowell). Cain is very much a member of the cadre of female crime writers who match their male counterparts in extreme, unsparing violence, and the subsequent *Sweetheart* was again in the sanguinary tradition of **Tess Gerritsen** and **Karin Slaughter**. Some weeks after the events of the first book, Cain's battered cop protagonist Archie Sheridan is at the site of the new murder scene at Forest Park. Simultaneously, Susan Ward is reporting on a political case involving statutory rape and making herself very unpopular with her paper – notably because the senator involved is an intimate of the newspaper's owners. But then a colleague of Susan's is killed in what appears to be a car accident, and the lethal Gretchen Lowell, the seductive serial killer of *Heartsick*, is raped by a guard at the prison where she is incarcerated. He subsequently kills himself, and while Gretchen is being transferred to another prison, she persuades an attendant to commit murder in order to help her escape.

Echo Burning 2001

LEE CHILD

Since the British writer Lee Child inaugurated his series of exuberant and edgy thrillers in 1997, he has maintained the standard of excellence that finds its apogee in *Echo Burning*. Ex-military policeman Jack Reacher – at a loose end, as so often – finds himself in Texas and hitches a ride with a beguiling young woman, a ride that will have serious consequences for him (Child often has Jack bump into his adventures in this fashion). Her name is Carmen, and she tells Jack that she has a daughter who is in danger – not least from her thuggish husband who is currently in jail but ready to murder her when he gets out. Clearly, what Jack shouldn't do is journey to Carmen's secluded Echo County ranch and get mixed up in the mess that is Carmen's life. So, of course, that's exactly what he does. Bent cops and lawyers add to the lethal mix. It's an exhilarating ride – for both Jack and the reader.

As ever, locales and characters are shot through with a pithy sense of the American landscape – nothing gives Child more pleasure than to be told by American readers that they were convinced that his novels were written by someone from their own country. He lives in New York, so it's easy for him to get things right, but it's a measure of how much things have moved on from the days when novels that appeared to be American but were actually the work of Brit writers (such as **James Hadley Chase**'s *No Orchids for Miss Blandish*) could be a little haphazard when it came to details of setting and society. Nowadays readers on both sides of the Atlantic require total verisimilitude – and that Lee Child delivers in every sentence.

The High Commissioner 1966

JON CLEARY

Jon Cleary has long enjoyed a reputation as one of the most accomplished of Australian crime novelists, although he worked in several genres, with a career that lasted for over half a century (and with over 50 novels under his belt) and a particular skill in using atmospherically realised international backdrops. Although the award-winning *Peter's Pence* (1974), concerning an IRA plot to steal treasure from the Vatican, is one of his most impressive novels, *The High Commissioner* is perhaps the best entry point for those new to Cleary. The Australian High Commissioner has been accused of murder, and rough-edged Sydney cop Scobie Malone is handed the assignment of travelling to London to bring him back for trial. But on arrival in the UK, Malone discovers that the High Commissioner is marked for murder, and saving his life becomes as much of a priority as getting him to Australia to face justice. The political dimension is intelligently handled, but the real skill of the novel lies in the creation of the tough, out-of-his-element cop, Malone.

NOBODY RUNS FOREVER 1968
Director: Ralph Thomas

While this adaptation of **Jon Cleary's** novel is undoubtedly a misfire, indifferently scripted and directed, it maintains a watchability through two canny pieces of casting: Rod Taylor as the bolshie Oz cop Malone and the urbane Christopher Plummer as the High Commissioner he has been instructed to bring back. The treatment of the action sequences is perfunctory, and the political dimensions are similarly underplayed, but the performances of these two veterans ensure interest throughout. Taylor in particular – using his own accent for once – is great value for money.

Cold Earth 2017

ANN CLEEVES

If Ann Cleeves' unkempt detective Vera Stanhope – the lead character in books including 2017's *The Seagull* – is not to your taste, you should sample her edgier sequence of books featuring Shetland Detective Inspector Jimmy Perez. Northern winters are unforgiving, and a landslide destroys a croft house. In the wreckage, Perez finds the body of a woman dressed in a red silk dress, but she was already dead before the landslide, and Jimmy becomes obsessed with discovering her identity – and why she died. There is a clue: a wooden box with photos and a handwritten letter bearing the line 'My dearest Alis'. Few British writers can boast Cleeves' consummate skill at evoking atmosphere, and the sense of weather and terrain is as crucial to the success of her Shetland novels as the characterisation of

Perez, whose Mediterranean ancestry ensures that he is always an outsider in this cloistered community. One of the most memorable entries in the series, and a demonstration of why Cleeves' books have proved TV-friendly.

Broken 2000
MARTINA COLE

The amazing success of all Martina Cole's crime novels must be a source of despair to those writers who have struggled for years. Right from the start, she has enjoyed unqualified approval for her distinctive and grittily written fiction. Even the workaday TV adaptations of *Dangerous Lady* and *The Jump* merely brought more kudos her way. In *Broken*, a child is abandoned in a deserted stretch of woodland and another on the top of a derelict building. Detective Inspector Kate Burrows makes the inevitable connections, and when one child dies, she finds herself up against a killer utterly without scruples. Her lover Patrick Kelly offers support in this troubling case, but he is under pressure himself. A body is found in his Soho club, and Patrick himself is on the line as a suspect. And Kate begins to doubt him… In prose that is always on the nail, Cole weaves her spell throughout this lengthy and ambitious narrative. Kate is an exuberantly characterised heroine, and the mocking Patrick enjoys equally felicitous handling from the author.

Damaged 2017
MARTINA COLE

Nothing cosily Golden Age in the caustic work of Martina Cole. In *Damaged*, Detective Chief Inspector Kate Burrows, although retired, is enlisted to help hunt down a serial killer. Kate's personal life with former gangster Patrick is thrown off balance when a young man appears (with his untrustworthy wife) claiming to be Patrick's son. Kate is faced with two problems – one of them having a notably higher body count. The unarguable success of Cole's sizeable tally of crime novels must be a source of envy to other practitioners. From the beginning, she has enjoyed massive sales for her gritty fiction, creating a new genre: the tough East End crime novel with a single-minded (if damaged) woman at the centre, usually sexually involved with dangerous (but often attractive) villains. Her copper protagonist Kate has the same DNA as her lawbreaking women, and it is Cole's ear for everyday speech (as much as her in-your-face, unvarnished storytelling) that grants her books such impact.

The Blue Nowhere 2001
JEFFERY DEAVER

Some authors are content to plough the same furrow for most of their working lives, while others need the recharging of batteries that a totally fresh approach brings. Jeffery Deaver is clearly in the latter camp, for despite the success of the Lincoln Rhyme books, such as *The Bone Collector* (1997), *The Blue Nowhere* moved off in a very surprising direction, with little of the Doyle-in-the-20th-century approach of its predecessors. He pulled off the coup of introducing two distinctive new heroes: Frank Bishop (a flawed but ruthlessly effective cop) and his reluctant associate, Wyatt Gillette, a talented young computer hacker released from prison to help Frank track down that most topical of modern criminals, the uber-hacker. The villain in this one is a kind of online Hannibal Lecter, a criminal genius (without the taste for fava beans) whose trawling off and on the net allows him to follow every move and detail of a victim's life, before moving in for the kill. Working against the considerable disadvantage of an online villain (he really had to work hard to make him truly sinister), Deaver created a high-tech thriller that suggested he need never go back to his Lincoln Rhyme books.

The Strings of Murder 2015
OSCAR DE MURIEL

Oscar de Muriel was born in Mexico City in the building that now houses Ripley's Believe it or Not museum but now lives in North Cheshire. For years he had been meaning to write a story about the Devil's Trill Sonata (de Muriel is a violin player), and it fit perfectly as his protagonists Inspector Ian Frey and Detective 'Nine-Nails' McGray's first case in a lively and colourful series. In Edinburgh in 1888, a virtuoso violinist is murdered in his home. Black magic symbols adorn the walls, and the dead man's maid swears she heard three musicians playing before the murder...

The Way Through the Woods 1992
COLIN DEXTER

Dexter is, of course, the poet laureate of Oxford crime, and his long-running series of Inspector Morse novels (shored up by the remarkably successful series of TV adaptations with John Thaw as the morose, crossword-solving, opera-loving copper) was something of a publishing phenomenon. These are gracefully written, atmospheric essays in classic crime, with the cultivated, beer-loving Morse one of the great literary curmudgeons (his sniping relationship with his sidekick Lewis is wonderfully entertaining). Dexter himself was notably wry about the sheer amount of Oxford mayhem that Morse encounters, reasoning that there would hardly be an Oxford don left alive if his novels were true to life. But that hardly matters, given the achievement of the individual books. Of these, *The Way Through the Woods* is one of the best. Morse is on holiday in Lyme Regis when he reads a letter in *The Times* about the disappearance of a Swedish girl who may have been murdered. Soon he's back in Oxford, where he encounters a multi-layered mystery involving both pornography and bird fancying. As so often, of course, a variety of plot strands are drawn together – and another characteristic of the Morse books is given an airing here, his sentimental attachment to a variety of intelligent women. The final icing on the cake is provided by literary allusions, another favourite device of Dexter, who knows his **AE Housman** quite as well as his **Arthur Conan Doyle**.

THE WAY THROUGH THE WOODS   1995

Director: John Madden

This is one of the better TV adaptations in the much-loved John Thaw Inspector Morse series – and further proof that the late actor supplanted any mental image readers may have possessed of the character. Running to 33 episodes aired from 1987 to 2000, many with an unprecedented two-hour primetime slot, what makes it particularly pleasurable is the series' preparedness to take the necessary time for the mystery to unspool at its own natural pace and Thaw's often glacial but considered performances were perfectly judged. The use of the Oxford locations – always a plus in this series – is as skilful as ever.

Streets of Darkness   2016

AA DHAND

AA Dhand's debut featuring charismatic detective Inspector Harry Virdee was released to critical acclaim in 2016, with TV rights being sold prior to publication. It is not hard to see why – this was the first crime series to feature an Asian lead who is far removed from being a tired cliché. Virdee is fiercely patriotic and proud of his British upbringing, so the fact that his family has disowned him for crossing a religious divide because he married his Muslim wife Saima takes us into a world where racism is seemingly alive within Asian communities. Quite simply, we have not been here before in crime fiction.

Dhand's second novel, *Girl Zero* (2017), firmly cemented him as a fearless writer looking into the world of Asian grooming gangs, while his third offering, *City of Sinners* (2018), once again uses the landscape of Bradford to transport us into a world that, on the one hand, feels familiar and, on the other, is uniquely terrifying. *City of Sinners* begins with a dead Asian girl hanging from the rafters of Bradford's Waterstones. Harry realises that a serial killer is setting the city up for a turbulent week of anarchy – and, most worryingly, this feels personal. Sporting pace, precision and eventful plotting, Dhand's work could not be timelier.

Medusa 2003

MICHAEL DIBDIN

Starting with an outrageous (but brilliantly ingenious) reworking of the Master Detective versus Jack the Ripper in *The Last Sherlock Holmes Story* (1978) – a book that truly put Doyle purists' noses out of joint – and a quirky outing for the poet Robert Browning as sleuth in *A Rich Full Death* (1986), Dibdin gave every sign that each new book would be quite unlike its predecessors – except in terms of adroit plotting. However, in 1988's *Ratking* he introduced his series detective, Italian Police Commissioner Aurelio Zen, an individual creation. But it's the informed, non-tourist renderings of Italian settings – Venice, Rome, Florence – that really give the books their insidiously gamey flavour. Government corruption seems to be endemic under Italian skies, and Zen's bruising encounters with more and more levels of bureaucratic chicanery make for riveting reading. Dibdin always had his finger on the political pulse – and Italian politicians moulding the law to their own ends seems more plausible than ever these days.

In *Medusa*, Zen's Roman superior Brugnoli unofficially assigns him to look into the grisly discovery of a corpse in a disused military tunnel in the Dolomites. But then the body is mysteriously removed from the morgue by the military police, the Carabinieri, and, as so often before, Zen finds government interference tying his hands; the Defence Ministry has dropped a veil over the case, describing the death as accidental. In trying to figure out the significance of a tattoo of the Medusa's head on the corpse, Zen stumbles across the mysterious 'Operazione Medusa'. We're into extreme right-wing conspiracies here, with a backstory of Red Brigade-style left-wing terrorism.

LA Confidential 1990
JAMES ELLROY

Is this the most impressive crime novel produced in the US in the last few decades? Many would argue so – and the claim would appear to be irrefutable if one considers it in the context of Ellroy's ambitious LA Quartet (*LA Confidential* was preceded by *The Black Dahlia* (1987) and *The Big Nowhere* (1988) and followed by *White Jazz* (1992)). Starting with a relatively simple premise (a killing at an all-night diner is under investigation by three LA cops, each of whom has a very different agenda), Ellroy utilises the discursive narrative to produce a massive panoply of Los Angeles in the 1950s, more assiduously detailed than the LA of that other great chronicler of the area, **Raymond Chandler**. Blending his fictional scenario with real events and characters, the picture-postcard vision of the city with its non-stop sunshine, glistening beaches and universal prosperity is swiftly undercut by Ellroy's penetrating vision of the darker side. His real subject, however, is the psyches of his three very different policemen and it is in this area that the true greatness of the novel lies – while the psychology of his protagonists is laid open with scalpel-sharp precision, the task is always accomplished in prose that is clean, unfussy and pared-down.

It is Christmas 1953. Bud White is young, brash and eager to make his mark in the LAPD, by whatever methods it takes. Sergeant Jack Vincennes has the glamorous sideline of being consultant on a popular TV cop show, and he revels in his celebrity, while Ed Exley tries to do his job without bending the rules (unlike his fellow officers). Associates of an LA kingpin are dying messily, and one of the suspects is a rich pornographer with a sideline in plastic surgery that transforms prostitutes into simulacras of movie stars. As the three cops dig deeper into a very complex mystery, they

LA CONFIDENTIAL 1997

Director: Curtis Hanson

Curtis Hanson's triumphant version of **James Ellroy**'s brilliantly written labyrinthine novel does it full justice, not least with its three star-making turns by Kevin Spacey, Russell Crowe and Guy Pearce, who between them perfectly encapsulate the glossy likeability, ruthlessness and boy-scout incorruptibility (in a deeply corrupt world) of their respective characters. The film, which seemed to herald a revival of the period-set crime movie, and which brought Ellroy to a much wider audience, has proved to have no offspring: **Brian De Palma**'s subsequent film of Ellroy's *The Black Dahlia* (2006), while stylish, proved stillborn.

Dark Tides 2014

CHRIS EWAN

The phrase 'If you've got a winning formula, why change it?' is clearly one that the writer Chris Ewan (or his publishers) didn't agree with. He made a mark with the titles in his witty and entertaining crime series the Good Thief's Guides, all of which enjoyed critical acclaim and respectable sales. So – one might legitimately ask – why rock the boat with an entirely different kind of book? The answer to that is simple – in their very different way, his later novels, set in the author's own Manx territory, proved to be just as accomplished as the earlier series. *Safe House* (2012) dealt with governmental corruption and international terrorism, and, impressive though it is, *Dark Tides* is even better, this time drawing on the Isle of Man Halloween convention of Hop-tu-naa.

Claire Cooper is just eight years old when her mother disappears without trace during Hop-tu-naa. The years do little to assuage her loss, until Claire, now a teenager, finds herself part of a group of five friends who celebrate Halloween with foolhardy dares. Claire is a participant, but she is more mature than her friends and her presence changes the nature of the group. Then one of the pranks takes a very grim turn and the group is torn apart. Six years pass, and one of Claire's friends dies in what appears to be an accident on the night of Hop-tu-naa. Claire has now become a police officer, and she is not convinced that the death was accidental – and what is the significance of the single footprint found near the body? After another Halloween death and another footprint, Claire begins to fear that somebody is seeking revenge – and the secret to the identity of the killer clearly lies in the past. If the above scenario – prank goes wrong, body count begins – sounds familiar from a hundred films, well, yes, it is. But such is Chris Ewan's skill that this is an accomplished piece of work. Ewan utilises the more sinister aspects of Manx folklore, forging from them a truly atmospheric thriller.

Die with Me 2008

ELENA FORBES

British writer Elena Forbes' *Die with Me* was a strong and assured debut. The hallmark of this one is psychological acuity, as persuasive here as from such experienced names as Gillian Flynn and Attica Locke. It's assumed that the young girl found dead in a London church has committed suicide – but Detective Inspector Mark Tartaglia isn't convinced. He finds that other suicides have presented the same features, but clashes with authority and colleagues interpose themselves between Tartaglia and the grim truth. Overfamiliar tropes aside, Forbes' novel delivers the goods.

Murder at the Nightwood Bar 1987

KATHERINE V FORREST

The Kate Delafield mysteries of Katherine V Forrest are always stylish, with crisply written dialogue that marks the author out as one of the most proficient in the mystery – let alone the lesbian mystery – genre. Here, Kate investigates the murder of a 19-year-old prostitute, an addict who has been living on the streets and whose body has been found outside a lesbian bar. There is zero cooperation from the girl's strict and repressive parents, nor even, surprisingly, from the women who might be thought to be her friends – the lesbian patrons of the Nightwood Bar. And things are further complicated by Kate's attraction towards one of these women, the alluring Andrea Ross. All this is handled with the quiet skill and authority that are Forrest's trademarks, and the sexual politics are never allowed to get in the way of some solid storytelling.

The Scholar of Extortion 2003

REG GADNEY

Readers still demand one key element in crime novels that may be quite as important as the protagonist: an atmospherically realised and detailed locale. We want to be taken to unfamiliar places, however dangerous. And the art of scene-setting is not a lost one: *The Scholar of Extortion* has a Hong Kong setting so pungent and distinctive that the reader will be checking their pockets for their passport. Gadney (who died in 2018) was one of the least parochial of English writers, sporting a gift for foreign settings. His hero here is Winston Lim, a stalwart of the Hong Kong police force whose palm has resisted greasing; he spends his time struggling against the bureaucracy and teeming chaos of his city. When Lim gets wind of a bloody act of terrorism that is to take place on the Hong Kong seas, he plunges into the city's foetid back streets to nail the instigator. This turns out to be Klaas-Pieter Terajima, the so-called 'Scholar of Extortion', a sadistic assassin hired by the ruthless Zhentung clan to facilitate their murky activities in southern China. While the trappings here are ostensibly modern and high-tech, this is basically an old-fashioned, rip-roaring tale of piracy in the Far East, with Winston Lim as doughty and winning a protagonist as one could wish for. The governmental corruption angle that surfaces seems a tad warmed-over, but there's little authors can do these days when this particular cliché beckons. Does it matter? If your nightmares are filled with terrorist bombs ticking in the luggage compartment of your plane, a smaller expenditure on this book will give you a distinctive holiday you won't forget. All from the safety of your armchair.

The Third Victim 2001

LISA GARDNER

Lisa Gardner has demonstrated in such books as *The Other Daughter* (1999) and *The Perfect Husband* (1998) that she's more than capable of delivering the genuine article: thrillers always couched in smart, well-turned prose. If *The Third Victim* isn't quite as involving as some of her earlier books, it's still a very impressive piece of work. A grim crime has torn apart the pleasant town of Bakersville and the residents are insistent that justice should be done. But although a boy has confessed, some of the evidence suggests that he may not actually be guilty. Officer Rainie Conner, assigned to her first homicide investigation, is caught up in the controversy. And it's hitting too close to home, bringing back memories of her past, and her worst nightmares. With the help of FBI profiler Pierce Quincy, Rainie comes closer to a deadly truth than she can imagine, because out there in the shadows, a man watches her and plots his next move. He knows her secrets and he has already brought death to Bakersville. But what he really wants is Rainie – and he won't give up until he has destroyed her. Gardner is a skilled writer, and this is first-rate stuff. We've encountered the policewoman struggling with her first case before, but the device is handled with freshness and imagination.

A Traitor to Memory

2001

ELIZABETH GEORGE

Don't underestimate the professional writer who knows exactly what he or she is doing – even if (superficially) the use of the crime genre is comfortingly familiar rather than innovative, as it is here. Concert violinist Gideon Davies is playing a piece by Beethoven when he realises that his ability has totally deserted him – nothing connected with music remains in his mind. But a woman's name is embedded in his consciousness – Sonia – and the sound of a woman crying. He becomes involved in an investigation into the death of a young woman, Eugenie, killed after being hit by a car. Seeking her murderer, aristocratic police detective Thomas Lynley investigates connections he has discovered between the violinist and a shadowy group of individuals who share a secret involving a 20-year-old crime. As ever, Elizabeth George (an American who chooses to set her mysteries in the UK rather than on her native shores) plays fair by all the rules of the classic English detective story, and it's a pleasure to see the machinery of the genre functioning with such smoothness.

A Ghost in the Machine — 2004

CAROLINE GRAHAM

For anyone familiar with the crime novels of Caroline Graham (perhaps inspired by the workaday TV adaptations in the *Midsomer Murders* series), one word will spring to mind: plotting. This is what Graham does – impeccably. In such books as *Death in Disguise* (1992) and *A Place of Safety* (1999), she has conjoined persuasive characterisation with narrative assurance of an impressive order. In *A Ghost in the Machine*, we're given a comfortable, in-each-other's-pockets community that is party to a dark secret. Kate and Mallory Lawson take possession of a relative's well-appointed house in the village of Forbes Abbot, and pleasurably anticipate the destressing that the move from metropolitan life will hopefully bring. But they're in for a disappointment: the village's internecine feuds seem to have a lethal edge. When violent death ensues, the doughty Detective Chief Inspector Barnaby finds himself with a very tangled web – quite as baffling as the many Midsomer murders that have kept him occupied. Lively, vigorous stuff.

Wrong Way Home — 2018

ISABELLE GREY

Isabelle Grey honed her skills working for television, and *Wrong Way Home* demonstrates her command of the thriller idiom. Detective Inspector Grace Fisher is working on a 25-year-old cold case in which a woman was raped and murdered near the site of a fire in Southend. DNA evidence opens up new avenues, but with a suggestion that the police force was less than diligent at the time of the original crime. As in earlier Grace Fisher outings, Grey furnishes a totally unpretentious thriller that keeps the reader pleasurably perplexed.

The Silent Room — 2015

MARI HANNAH

With her pithily drawn Northumbrian settings, Mari Hannah has produced a compellingly readable series featuring gay copper Detective Chief Inspector

Kate Daniels, which – while not as gritty as the books of her Scottish confrère **Val McDermid** – has maintained a satisfyingly dark and tense atmosphere matched by persuasive detail in the forensic and policing methods.

So where did the imperative for *The Silent Room* – with its different protagonists – come from? Publishers – always holding up a finger to see which way the wind is blowing – are well aware that introducing changes with established authors is often a good idea. So there's no sign of Kate Daniels here; we're in different territory, with a young Special Branch detective, Matthew Ryan, who finds himself under a cloud. His boss has been arrested on corruption charges, and the security van holding the disgraced officer is hijacked. Ryan is suspected of aiding and abetting the escapee. Locked out of the case, the young policeman knows that his career is on the line. However, the official investigation collapses, and Ryan discovers that the unexplained death of a Norwegian citizen may have serious repercussions, with a continent-spanning conspiracy that involves many individuals on both sides of the law.

Mari Hannah has always had two key specialities: a gift for genuinely ingenious plotting matched by a skill at choreographing suspense sequences that is the equal of more stellar names in the genre. Both characteristics are at full stretch in *The Silent Room*, with everyone involved (notably the warring police officers) leaping off the page. But a crime novel stands or falls on how vividly its central protagonist is conjured, and Hannah has come up with a real winner in Detective Sergeant Matt Ryan, a man cut adrift from all outside sources of aid and doubting his own judgement. His various crises of conscience (is his boss as innocent as Ryan believes?) are powerfully handled, and many readers will be perfectly happy for Kate Daniels to stay on extended leave – as long as Matt Ryan subs for her.

The Big Thaw   2000

DONALD HARSTAD

Having served as a sheriff in northeastern Iowa for 26 years, Harstad used his accumulated experience of the darker side of human experience to create the acclaimed *Eleven Days* (1998). And his second novel, *Known Dead*, was another thriller shot through with the intensity of its predecessor. This time, Nation County is suffering as the dead of winter exerts a paralysing grip. Deputy Sheriff Carl Houseman is dealing with the usual criminal fraternity of Iowa, while his partner and friend Hester Gorse has undertaken security duty on the floating casino *Colonel Beauregard*. Both will find themselves fighting for their lives when a ruthless group of men attempt a million-dollar siege of the economic assets of the state. Harstad's unerring tactics here involve a carefully orchestrated double jeopardy for his beleaguered protagonists: while Carl fights for control of the investigation, and finds himself at the extremes of his survival skills, Hester is trapped on the *Beauregard*, firmly in the eye of the storm. We've read the 'conflict between lawmen' scenario before, but rarely as adroitly handled as here – this is down to a combination of economical but rounded characterisation and a sense of verisimilitude that no doubt results from Harstad's long experience as a law officer. Hester, too, is a highly plausible creation – and her more direct experience of dangerous situations in the narrative means that she must carry much of the weight. That Harstad pulls this off as convincingly as Houseman's clashes with his fellow law enforcers is an index of his considerable skill.

The Treatment 2002

MO HAYDER

Success was something of a double-edged sword for the elusive writer Mo Hayder with her debut novel *Birdman* (2000): the book enjoyed astonishing success, but called down a fearsome wrath on the author for unflinchingly entering the blood-boltered territory of **Thomas Harris**'s Hannibal Lecter books. Part of the fuss was clearly to do with the fact that a woman writer had handled scenes of horror and violence so authoritatively, and *The Treatment* provoked a similar furore. Actually, it's a meticulously detailed shocker: less unorthodox than its predecessor, perhaps, but still a world away from the cosy reassurance of much crime fiction. In a shady south London residential street, a husband and wife are found tied up, the man near death. Both have been beaten and are suffering from acute dehydration. Detective Inspector Jack Caffery of the Met's major investigation squad is told to investigate the disappearance of the couple's son, and as he uncovers a series of dark parallels with his own life, he finds it more and more difficult to make the tough decisions necessary to crack a chilling case. As in *Birdman*, Caffery is drawn with particular skill, and Hayder is able (for the most part) to make us forget the very familiar cloth from which he's cut. The personal involvement of a copper in a grim case is a very familiar theme, but it's dispatched with panache here.

A Season for the Dead   2003
DAVID HEWSON

In a hushed Vatican reading room, a professor is shot dead after brandishing evidence of a grisly crime. Moments later, two bodies are found in a nearby church, each with a gruesome calling card from the killer. Thus begins David Hewson's electrifying novel, a bewitching blend of history and drama, set amidst a bizarre killing spree in modern Rome. As the August heat exerts its grip, the news of the two murders holds the Holy City in thrall. And as the media gathers and Vatican officials close ranks, a young detective is sent to tackle the case. Nic Costa is the son of an infamous Italian Communist, a connoisseur of Caravaggio, and a cop who barely looks his 27 years of age. Thrust into the midst of a slaughterfest that will rattle his city to its ancient bones, Nic meets a woman who will soon dominate both his consciousness and his investigation. A *soignée* professor of early Christianity, Sara Farnese was in the Vatican library on that fateful day, a witness to her colleague's strange outburst and death. But her role becomes even more puzzling as more bodies are found: each victim is killed in a gory tableau of a Christian martyrdom. And each victim had intimately known Sara, whose silence Costa cannot quite crack and whose sexual history becomes more lurid and unfathomable with every revelation. Soon, a nightmarish chase is implicating politicians and priests. A beguiling mystery, and an intriguing tour of the streets and alleyways of Rome.

Someone Else's Skin   2014
SARAH HILARY

There are writers who, while moving in familiar waters, demonstrate an innovative and quirky imagination, transforming narratives whose accoutrements are familiar. Sarah Hilary is most decidedly in that category, and even though her character Detective Inspector Marnie Rome may initially appear to owe something to other female coppers such as **Lynda La Plante**'s Jane Tennison, she turns out to be a singular individual – as is Hilary herself, with her crisp and direct style.

In *Someone Else's Skin*, DI Rome is dispatched to a woman's shelter with her partner Detective Sergeant Noah Jake. Lying stabbed on the floor is the husband of a woman from the shelter. Rome's investigation opens up the proverbial can of worms, and a slew of dark secrets are exposed before a final violent confrontation in a kitchen. As well as functioning as a well-honed police procedural, this is very much a novel of character – Marnie Rome in particular is notably well realised, and issues such as domestic abuse are responsibly incorporated into the fabric of the novel.

Two O'Clock Boy   2016

MARK HILL

Mark Hill has had previous careers as a journalist and as an award-winning producer for BBC Radio 2. None of this, of course, necessarily qualifies him to write the kind of storming debut that is now de rigueur if any fledgling crime writer wishes to make a mark, but that is exactly what he did in this ambitious novel. *Two O'Clock Boy* (republished as *His First Lie*) took the clichés of the modern police procedural and forged something new and impressive from them. His protagonist is morally ambiguous copper Detective Inspector Ray Drake; familiar, yes, but this is an interesting variation. Prior to the narrative of the book, a children's home, Longacre, was razed to the ground. In the present, a sinister figure, the 'Two O'Clock Boy' appears to be in the process of eliminating everyone who was brought up in the home. It is Drake's job to track down this murderous figure, but there are complications arising from the night of the fire that have massive significance for the troubled Drake. Those feeling that we do not need another London-set crime series may change their minds after tackling this authoritatively written novel. It's lengthy, but justifies its considerable wordcount at every turn.

The Death of Dalziel   2007

REGINALD HILL

Is he really dead? Has the Fat Man really sung his last? That's something Reginald Hill's admirers wondered in 2007 when this novel appeared. And there's no denying that many read this entry in the late Hill's exemplary series with an extra frisson of interest – had it really been 37 years since we first met the educated, sensitive copper Peter Pascoe and the coarse but lovable Andy Dalziel in *A Clubbable Woman*? And many mused: had Hill tired of Dalziel? The catastrophe that Reginald Hill lined up for his detective involves Middle Eastern terrorism being imported to these shores – and an explosion in a video shop on the security register that leaves Andy a bloody, comatose heap, while Pascoe (his life saved by the shield of his friend's considerable bulk) struggles to consciousness, his only thought being to get his partner to hospital. All of this happens in Chapter 1 – by Chapter 2, Andy is critically ill, incapable of movement – and this allows Hill to try one of the audacious experiments that he's partial to: we are taken into the chaotic impressions that crowd Andy's drugged consciousness. In the process, we learn more about him than we did in all the previous 21 books. With the customary wit suppressed (after a typically scabrous burst of it before the explosion to remind us of his take-no-prisoners attitude), we are shown a richer, more complex man than the bluff exterior has led us to expect.

This is one of the ways in which Hill kept the series fresh – with innovations that take the reader to surprising areas: *One Small Step* (1990), for instance,

PD James
(1920–2014)

The author of such books as *The Murder Room* (2003) and *Innocent Blood* (1980) had a busy lifestyle that kept her diary full: her commitments in the House of Lords, her foreign travel (transatlantic voyages to meet her legions of American admirers, for instance), her role as a wry late-night pundit for the BBC (she was, of course, a BBC governor). Oh yes – and that little matter of writing the most elegant and ingenious crime novels around, featuring her saturnine and cultivated copper, Commander Adam Dalgliesh. Her novel *The Lighthouse* (2005) showcased one of James's favourite themes: the murder in a cloistered community, this time an island retreat for the rich and influential. Dalgliesh and his colleagues are on hand to probe the dangerous internecine battles among the island guests. What distinguished James from her illustrious predecessors was her refusal to sanitise the murders in her books, dealt with the first murder on the moon in the year 2010. But another reason for the series' longevity (apart from the highly successful TV adaptations) is Hill's readiness to engage with important social issues – and that readiness is apparent here in the elements that set the violence in *The Death of Dalziel* in motion: religious fundamentalism in Britain's ethnic communities begins to foment the commission of lethal terrorism – and, in reaction to this, the host nation throws up its own men of violence, ready to greet what they see as a threat to Britain with an equally ruthless vigilantism. Peter Pascoe discounts the MI5 explanation of the explosion (an accident in which would-be bombers have blown themselves up) and looks into the mysterious activities of the Knights Templar, more deeply involved than the security services are prepared to admit. As usual, Hill is utterly unputdownable. But... does Andy Dalziel die? It will cost you the price of a paperback to find out...

---

which are often surprisingly brutal, and her need to ensure that they are crimes committed by individuals for real reasons, rather than simply to provide a body for the sake of the plot. It's almost as if James had taken to heart **Raymond Chandler**'s famous dismissal of the classic English murder mystery: 'Hammett gave murder back to the kind of people that commit it for reasons, not just to provide a corpse; and with the means at hand, not hand-wrought dueling pistols, curare and tropical fish.' She was also an author not afraid to take her time over exposition, and she eschewed any artificial ratcheting up of tension: if suspenseful situations arise, they are invariably generated by the plot rather than a feeling that several chapters have passed without something sanguinary happening.

Many crime readers have a pronounced affection for the book in which James's female private eye Cordelia Gray first appeared, *An Unsuitable Job for a Woman* (1972), but the best entry point for those new to the author remains *A Taste for Death* in 1986, which is also a good introduction to her beloved copper Adam Dalgliesh. The novel begins when a woman is decorating her church with flowers and stumbles across the bodies of a tramp and an important Tory politician, whose throats have been hacked open. Dalgliesh is charged with finding out whether or not the MP (subject of a smear campaign) killed himself after murdering the tramp.

The Murder Room 2003
PD JAMES

From her first book right up until her death, Phyllis James was firmly at the top of the tree in the British crime writing stakes. The secret of her success was a combination of elements: elegant writing, strong characterisation (notably her long-time protagonist Commander Adam Dalgliesh) and a refusal to write the same book over and over again, even though certain tropes often reappear. More than any other British writer, James elevated the detective story into the realms of literature, with the psychology of the characters treated in the most complex and authoritative fashion. Her plots, too, are full of intriguing detail and studded with brilliantly observed character studies. Who cares if Dalgliesh belongs more in the pages of a book than poking around a graffiti-scrawled council estate? A particular speciality is the isolated setting (a nod back to her predecessors, and none more isolated than in 2001's *Death in Holy Orders*). So where does *The Murder Room* stand in her particular pantheon? The doughty Dalgliesh finds himself obliged to take a trip to the Dupayne, a private museum on Hampstead Heath. One of the family trustees has been killed and the future of the museum is in the balance, as a new lease was on the point of being signed, while the trustees were at daggers drawn over whether or not the museum should remain open. In one of the galleries, the eponymous Murder Room, there is a recreation of Scotland Yard's famous Black Museum. But as Dalgliesh peels back the layers of deceit, his attraction to the beguiling Emma Lavenham begins to interfere with his job, and Dalgliesh finds himself having to make some stark choices. For years, James promised to give the lonely Dalgliesh a new relationship,

THE MURDER ROOM 2004
Director: Diarmuid Lawrence

If **Ian Rankin** was initially unlucky in the TV casting of Rebus (John Hannah was far too young and lightweight – the weightier, more mature Ken Stott was much better casting), **PD James** was luckier with the unlikely Roy Marsden as Dalgliesh for most of her TV adaptations. In this otherwise capable version, however, Martin Shaw (replacing Marsden) is clearly miscast as the poetry-reading copper. Other casting decisions in the piece also seem odd, and the sections involving Dalgliesh's love life don't really work. Leaving that aside, James's plotting remains substantially intact, and the director makes strong use of his locations.

and the fact that she delivered on her promise is particularly pleasurable, as the handling of the relationship is sympathetic and intelligent. But the real pleasure here lies in the black deeds in a classic cloistered setting, and there is no denying that James is unbeatable in this area.

Dead Like You 2014

PETER JAMES

Peter James's popular series featuring Brighton detective Roy Grace has sold prodigiously, even keeping crime heavyweights James Patterson and John Grisham from the number one slot in the UK bestseller lists. At the time of writing, the long-awaited television series is yet to be made – a series that would no doubt make Grace's stamping ground of Brighton as familiar as Inspector Morse's Oxford. After initially making his mark as a horror writer, James has refined his storytelling skills to acquire the full measure of the classic police procedural narrative. In *Dead Like You*, Brighton's Metropole Hotel is the scene of an unpleasant incident: a woman is violently raped when she enters a room. Some days later, another woman is similarly assaulted – and both have their shoes stolen by the offender. Assigned to the case, Detective Superintendent Grace becomes aware that these two incidents have disturbing echoes of a sequence of crimes that shook Brighton in 1997. The attacker (who had been described as the 'Shoe Man') claimed five victims, the last of which he had murdered before disappearing. Grace is faced with two unpleasant possibilities: that the original Shoe Man who cheated justice ten years ago has returned to wreak havoc again, or – equally disturbingly – that there is a copycat at work.

Head Shot 2002

QUINTIN JARDINE

Jardine's novels split into two series: the nine novels featuring reluctant actor/private detective Oz Blackstone, and the 30 or so following 'Britain's toughest cop', Edinburgh-based Deputy Chief Constable Bob Skinner, which has been one of the most consistent sequences in the crime field since he appeared in 1993's *Skinner's Rules*. For some time, the best entry was probably *Gallery Whispers* (1999; in which Skinner tackles a terrorist attempting to murder various heads of government), but *Head Shot* is one of the most interesting Skinner books – not least because the author cannily relocates his protagonist to a different country (the US), with all the extra problems such a move creates. And there's a personal element this time: Bob Skinner is obliged to identify the murdered bodies of his wife's parents, and exerts pressure on his colleagues to become part of the investigation. But this is New York State, and American policing methods are very different from those on his home Edinburgh beat. Skinner is not persuaded that the killings are part of a series of bungled burglaries (the prevailing theory), and ends up tackling the usual recalcitrant witnesses and false leads. Although not all his Stateside colleagues are unhelpful, his approach has to be less intuitive than usual – and considerably more direct. Meanwhile, things are not going well for Skinner's team back in Edinburgh, where a whole slew of problems cry out for the boss's attention. A quirky and individual work.

Breaking and Entering 2000
HRF KEATING

It is amazing to think that the much-missed Keating wrote his first Inspector Ghote novel, *The Perfect Murder*, in 1964, and was thereafter a stalwart of the Collins Crime Club stable. Here we are in the 21st century, and Keating is still delighting us with such expertly turned tales of Bombay-set mayhem as *Breaking and Entering*. The city is alive with the news of local bigwig Ajmani's savage murder, and the police force is unable to solve the mystery of how he could be stabbed in his heavily guarded mansion. Ghote has been given the less prestigious task of tracking down a cat burglar, who bears the nickname Yeshwant. With the dubious help of his old friend Axel Svensson, Ghote is on the point of revealing the cat burglar's true identity, and (needless to say) his investigation looks likely to throw light on the murder of Ajmani... What makes the Ghote series so beguiling is Keating's effortless conjuring up of the sultry Indian locales, along with the perfectly anatomised jealousies and infighting of the local police force. Ghote remains one of the most individual sleuths in crime fiction – he owes little to other classic models (except, perhaps, Holmes – but which literary sleuth doesn't?) – although Keating managed to ring the changes with his character, including a fish-out-of-water novel, *Go West Inspector Ghote* (1981, with the detective finding it difficult to function professionally outside India). *Breaking and Entering* has some of the smoothest and most ingenious plotting of the series, and there are no signs that Keating ever lost the freshness and inspiration that were characteristic of his very first Ghote book.

The Business of Dying — 2002
SIMON KERNICK

In 2002, this inaugural novel in a series of London-set thrillers displayed the hallmarks of a stylist – after a rather discursive opening, the plotting is as cogent as you'll find. Detective Sergeant Dennis Milne is a rogue copper with a speciality sideline in killing drug-dealing villains. But everything goes pear-shaped when (on the basis of some bad advice) Milne kills two straight customs officers and an accountant. At the same time, he is looking into the savage killing of an 18-year-old working girl, found with her throat ripped open by Regent's Canal, and his investigation draws him towards other police officers. Soon, it's a throw of the dice as to whether Milne will go down for his own dodgy dealings before he cracks a case that is steeped in blood and corruption. This is vigorous stuff that delivers all the grimly authentic storytelling that is the *sine qua non* of the best crime thrillers. But it's something more than that – there's a touch of **Graham Greene** in the redemption that's within the grasp of the hopelessly compromised Detective Sergeant Milne, a character with as many edges as you'll find in any first-rate novel, crime or otherwise. Another theme is the transitoriness of so much that we hold dear in life: ironically, even before the novel was published, the King's Cross gasholders that adorned the original jacket were swept away by the Eurostar extension, only to reappear in a new home… Nothing is permanent, as Kernick's rugged novel coolly argues.

Mr Mercedes — 2014
STEPHEN KING

When you are one of the world's most successful authors, it can be a risky business switching from the genre for which you are best known. Some years ago, the crime writer James Patterson felt the desire to get out of his system three saccharine romantic novels that barely caused a ripple. It is, however, a different matter for Stephen King, who has

Photo: Shane Leonard

long been the undisputed monarch of the horror thriller, but has a deep personal love for the crime genre. This is not his first venture into that field, but it is (so far) his best.

Mr Mercedes is a tense, ticking-clock thriller that sets a burned-out cop against a demented mass murderer who is planning an act of carnage to match the one with which he started his criminal career. The opening of the novel is a tour de force, the kind of curtain raiser that King admirers relish. In a Midwestern city, crowds of unemployed, desperate people wait in frigid temperatures for the slim chance that they will be hired at a job fair. We meet two people in the queue, a down-on-his-luck young man and a mother who has been forced to bring her baby, who is coughing in the cold. Their characters are described with such warmth that we are in no doubt that these will be the protagonists of the book. But then a Mercedes suddenly appears – which subsequently proves to have been stolen – and with shocking suddenness, the driver ploughs the car into the crowd, reverses and drives over his victims again. Eight people are killed and 15 wounded, among them the characters who we assumed we would be following throughout the book. The car is abandoned and the killer escapes, leaving no trace.

A year passes, and recently retired policeman Bill Hodges receives a deeply disturbing letter from a mysterious individual who lays claim to being the perpetrator of the act of random murder, and who tells Hodges that he is in the early stages of planning an even more gruesome attack. Hodges, still suffering guilt from being unable to crack the earlier case, finds himself drawn out of his unhappy retirement to engage in a battle of wits worthy of Holmes and Moriarty – or Hannibal Lecter and Clarice Starling.

Those who might be reluctant to follow Stephen King into an unfamiliar genre should not hesitate; all of the narrative skill that distinguishes his fantasy work is firmly in place here, including those shocking hints of what is to follow ('One of the young men... had been staring at Janice Cray – this was Keith Frias, whose left arm would shortly be torn from his body'), and the orchestration of mounting tension shows the author's usual command. And if the basic scenario is a familiar one, the characterisation is faultless. There is the depressive detective hero with an ever present gun on his table, toying with the idea of suicide; similarly memorable is the terrifying psychopathic killer (with perhaps a little of the DNA of motel proprietor Norman Bates), living with his alcoholic mother in a house filled with secrets. Admittedly, we are reminded that crime fiction is not King's default territory: a lengthy description of the horrors of daytime reality TV shows (which the suicidal Hodges glumly watches) outstays its welcome, and both hero and villain are familiar types. But King fans will be riveted from the first explosion of violence to the final, equally seismic, climax.

The Smiling Man   2018
JOSEPH KNOX

How do you manage to top – or at least match – that first effort which had reviewers scrabbling for encomiums? The British writer Joseph Knox was doubtless exercised by this syndrome – his debut *Sirens* (2017) swept all before it, but it had taken eight years to write. The follow-up arrived, *The Smiling Man*, but had Knox overcome the traditional jinx? We are once again in a Manchester that frequently seems like an anteroom to hell. In a massive disused hotel, The Palace, detectives Aidan Waits and Peter Sutcliffe encounter the eponymous smiling man. He is dead, with every identifying mark (including teeth and fingerprints) obliterated. But as Waits reconstructs the fragments of the dead man's life, there is a sinister nemesis scrutinising his own. A series of increasingly terrifying encounters are in store. Knox's first novel was pedal-to-the-floor stuff, and this one is even more powerful, with Waits, the less than admirable protagonist, reappearing after his first outing in *Sirens*. There are two narratives here – the second concerns a child living in mortal fear of his mother's lover – but neither offers much respite in terms of the escalating tension. One thing is sure: Knox is no one-hit wonder.

Sunset and Sawdust   2004
JOE R LANSDALE

Among writers in what is loosely called the crime and thriller genre, Joe Lansdale is an absolutely unique talent. In fact, his ironic, atmospheric novels barely fit in any recognised genre, although violent death can be counted on as a recurring factor. This is unsurprising, as he has also written westerns, science fiction, horror and even porn titles (pseudonymously). But the series featuring Texan sleuths Hap Collins and Leonard Pine, which launched in 1990 with *Savage Season* and includes such books as *Bad Chili* (1997) and

Captains Outrageous (2001), has carved out a Lansdalian universe unlike that of any other writer (apart, of course, from his host of imitators).

Sunset and Sawdust was something of a new departure when it appeared in 2004: Sunset is the widow of a constable who has been shot dead at a Texan sawmill camp, and her assumption of her husband's role is looked at askance by the uncooperative townsfolk. However, she undertakes to look into a double murder, leading to some bizarre encounters for the gun-toting Sunset. Over-the-top characters, delirious plotting, a well-drawn milieu and coruscating dialogue: all the customary Joe Lansdale tropes are in place.

Soft Target 2005

STEPHEN LEATHER

Let's face it: most thrillers are little more than a series of tenuously connected action set pieces with grudging, cursory moments of characterisation – the latter clearly of little interest to many big-name writers. But it's a formula that works: **Robert Ludlum** salted away a tidy fortune working in this fashion. However, it clearly didn't appeal to Stephen Leather, who largely avoids it. An ex-journalist who divides his time between the UK and Thailand, Leather has tried to ensure that his characters are human beings rather than Action Man dolls. He is also phenomenally productive, turning out an original thriller a year – if not more – since the early 1990s. *Hard Landing* (2004) introduced Dan 'Spider' Shepherd, an SAS trooper-turned-detective in an elite undercover squad. In *Soft Target*, Shepherd takes on a maverick police unit that has a sideline in ripping off drug dealers. Despite some damaging controversy concerning his unorthodox marketing tactics, Leather remains a reliable writer – even if he dropped off some writers' Christmas card lists.

Mystic River 2001

DENNIS LEHANE

Childhood friends Sean, Jimmy and Dave have their lives changed when a strange car turns up in their street. After one boy gets into the car and two not, a terrible event happens that terminates their friendship. Twenty-five years later, Sean is a homicide detective, while Jimmy has taken a criminal route. When Jimmy's daughter is found savagely killed, Sean is assigned to the case. And with his own personal relationships in deep trouble, he finds that he is obliged to go back to the life he thought he had left behind, coming to terms with his ex-friends and a confrontation with a human monster. As a character study and psychological thriller, *Mystic River* is unsurpassable.

MYSTIC RIVER — 2003
Director: Clint Eastwood

As an actor, Clint Eastwood has always been able to get the best out of his cast when directing; here, Sean Penn, Tim Robbins and Kevin Bacon give career-best performances as **Dennis Lehane**'s childhood friends dealing with their blighted adult lives. One of the many admirable qualities of the film (like so many of Eastwood's later films as a director) is its readiness to allow elements to fall into place at a judicious and natural pace, rather than pitching things at an audience with the attention spell of a gnat.

Dennis Lehane
(1965–)

When word of mouth among thriller enthusiasts is particularly good for a certain author, that's a reason to pay attention. But when similar acclaim comes from fellow writers, readers really need to mark their cards. Dennis Lehane became a must-read novelist on the strength of such gritty and forceful thrillers as *Darkness, Take My Hand* (1996) and *Gone, Baby, Gone* (1998) featuring private investigators Patrick Kenzie and Angela Gennaro. Praised for his taut, carefully orchestrated storylines and expressively drawn, vulnerable characters, Lehane is the kind of writer who has achieved his position by stealth rather than massive advertising campaigns. His 2001 magnum opus *Mystic River* (discussed in this section), confirmed his status as one of the most vigorous and skilful American talents in years.

Photo: (cc-by) David Shankbone

Uniform Justice

2003

DONNA LEON

How does she do it? Other crime writers falter – even the best – but not Donna Leon: virtually every outing for the urbane Commissario Guido Brunetti is as impressive as the last. And reading a Leon novel is almost as good as a trip to Venice, so evocative is the expat Leon when writing about her adoptive city – although her view of the dark side of Italy strays quite some way from the tourist point of view, with levels of corruption and double-dealing that perhaps Signor Berlusconi and his various successors would rather keep in the shadows.

Leon's cunningly wrought plots often take their own sweet time to establish an inexorable grip, and this is particularly true of this outing for Commissario Brunetti – but, boy, does it pay dividends. A mysterious death has Brunetti stumped. A cadet at a highly respected military academy has died. Is it suicide? Or is a murderer stalking the academy? Brunetti discovers that the boy's parents are separated, and that his father – who has had a chequered career in both medicine and politics – is a man with a lot to lose. What's more, the boy's sister has vanished. An implacable silence greets Brunetti – par for the course in his investigations – but he's soon uncovering institutional skulduggery and forbidden sexual behaviour. Leon winds things up in a surprising fashion – as always, she's too canny a writer to allow the reader to second-guess her when it comes to her denouements.

Dark Blood

2011

STUART MACBRIDE

Stuart MacBride has been corrupting the children of Britain; not content with writing his lacerating crime fiction for adults, he has polluted the youth of the nation with his young adult outing *Sawbones*, which had the Sunday papers fulminating against 'a novel full of expletives, sex and violence'. (One paper even calculated how many times the F-word and its variants had been utilised – 89 times, to be exact.) Needless to say, this tsunami of moral outrage did absolutely no harm to sales of the book. And it might be argued that the softly spoken Scottish writer has done young adult readers something of a service: when they move onto MacBride's adult titles, they will be perfectly primed for the incendiary mix of gruesome incident and idiomatic writing that is the hallmark of the author's crime fiction featuring tough copper Logan McRae. And what better place for that legion of fresh-faced new readers to start than with *Dark Blood*? As in such earlier outings as *Cold Granite* (2005) and *Broken Skin* (2007), we're served up some of the grittiest crime writing in the field. But while MacBride might seem to be setting out to make fellow Celts **Val McDermid** and **Ian Rankin** look as genteel as **Alexander McCall Smith**, there is much more to him than a readiness to turn the gruesome setting up to 11. The McRae books sport some of the pithiest snapshots of modern urban life this side of **Irvine Welsh**, and the plotting has a cohesion that puts most writers in the genre to shame.

Logan McRae is handed a particularly unwelcome job. He is to be involved in the relocation of a vicious rapist, Richard Knox. The latter has served his time and found God, putting his numerous sexual assaults behind him, and he is to be moved (at public expense) from his native Newcastle to McRae's beat of Aberdeen. The auguries are not good, particularly as Edinburgh hard man Malk the Knife is muscling into the property development boom and a gangland accountant has gone missing. This is quintessential MacBride: tartan noir etched in the darkest of hues and garnished with dialogue so sharp you may cut yourself. If you're the parent of a teenager, perhaps it would be best not to read any passages out loud. Or if you do, don't tell the Sunday newspapers.

Cruel Mercy 2017

DAVID MARK

The quality of mercy is not something that David Mark dispenses to either his characters or the reader. Those looking for cosily comforting crime fiction should steer clear of the author, whose police procedurals are deeply mordant. But fans of the grittiest crime fare love Mark's copper Aector McAvoy, who customarily moves in a darkly realised Hull (the author's own stamping ground) but is relocated here to upstate New York to resolve a bitter dispute within the travelling community. This new territory for

McAvoy pitches him against mafia hitmen (both Italian and Russian) and ecclesiastical corruption. Moving his protagonist out of Humberside was a risky move for David Mark, but he pulls it off with aplomb, energised by both the change of locale and the multi-layered levels of malfeasance on offer.

The Lewis Man

2012

PETER MAY

On the Isle of Lewis, villagers are stocking up on winter fuel in the usual fashion – cutting up peat – but they make a macabre discovery. Peat has the property of keeping bodies in a remarkable state of preservation over the centuries, such as the body found here – the Lewis Man of the title. But the assumption that this body may be millennia old is dispelled when a tattoo is discovered on the body – one referring to Elvis Presley. This wonderful touch is one of the many praiseworthy things about Peter May's novel, which showed that its equally accomplished predecessor, *The Blackhouse* (2009), was no flash in the pan. May has a prodigious inventiveness that springs off every page. Saturnine copper Fin Macleod has left the force and has made his way back to his ancestral home. As well as terminating his career, he has left his wife in Edinburgh and has doggedly set about the task of restoring the rural croft of his parents to a liveable state. Needless to say, Fin is soon involved in what appears to be a murder case – crime readers will struggle to think of a single novel in which a retired copper is successfully able to leave his old career behind him. The peat-preserved body undergoes DNA tests and is found (in an unlikely development) to share a family connection with the father of Fin's girlfriend when the detective was a boy. The old man, Tormod Macdonald, is suffering from progressive dementia – and has, in fact, claimed that he was an only child. But the body in the bog gives the lie to this statement, and Fin finds that the dark past has an awkward way of resurfacing – both for him and for the father of his ex-sweetheart.

This is terrific stuff, and a reminder that when a crime novelist of authority sets his sights high, the results can be as persuasive as the best writing in any genre. Particularly praiseworthy here is the parallel narrative of the old man Tormod's own story, conveyed to us with all the confusion of a drifting mind, but still as assertive as the main strand of the novel. Fin, as in the previous book, is distinctive in the field of fictional (ex-)coppers.

Ed McBain
(1926–2005)

One of the most influential of American crime writers, Ed McBain wrote children's books, science fiction and westerns before making an indelible mark on the crime genre. Under his other nom de plume, **Evan Hunter** (his real name was **Salvatore Lombino**), he utilised his background as a teacher to create *The Blackboard Jungle* in 1954, which was a massive hit (as was the film version in 1955, which spawned cinema riots with its Bill Haley soundtrack). However, McBain's greatest legacy lies with his 87th Precinct books. He wrote the first, *Cop Hater*, in 1956, and the series initiated the tightly functioning team of cops, all memorably – if economically – drawn. McBain also showed a readiness to tackle the grimmer aspects of police work; *Calypso* in 1980 had elements as grim as anything to be found in the work of later writers such as **Thomas Harris**. The 87th Precinct books appeared in quick succession (there were 13 from 1956 to 1960), but the standard was remarkably consistent and tough cop Steve Carella remains probably his strongest creation. McBain still found time to produce a slew of other books, principally as Evan Hunter. In the 1960s he moved into film writing with a brilliant screenplay for **Alfred Hitchcock's** *The Birds* in 1963. He also produced the Matthew Hope books (with over a dozen from 1977 to 1998), but these were less successful. McBain also created the forensic crime genre – and was notably nettled when other writers (such as **Patricia Cornwell**) picked up the ball and ran with his innovations.

The Empty Hours   1962

ED McBAIN

Ed McBain was one of the true immortals of the crime writing field, with his 87th Precinct series freighting in a whole host of highly influential innovations – not least the large ensemble cast, all developed to precisely the right degree, while never getting in the way of the exigencies of the plot. In *The Empty Hours*, one of his most distinctive books, we are given three razor-sharp episodes in the life of the 87th Precinct. The title tale has a young and well-to-do woman found strangled in a down-at-heel block of flats. Doughty cop Steve Carella has little to work with: just a handful of cancelled cheques. The second tale, 'J', centres on the bloody murder of a rabbi, with the letter J painted on the wall of the synagogue. And 'Storm' features (surprise!) another murder: Cotton Hawes, officially on holiday, mixes it with the local police when a girl is found dead in the snow. McBain confidently delivers the goods, as always.

Bloodline 2018

NIGEL McCRERY

Nigel McCrery is the creator of such popular – if unchallenging – TV crime series as *Silent Witness* (which borrowed the US notion of the feisty female pathologist) and *New Tricks*, with its new concept of a group of ageing coppers behaving like fractious schoolboys under the stern eye of their female boss. McCrery's novels, however, are considerably more astringent fare, frequently full-blooded in their delineation of the macabre. The author's predilection for televisual crosscutting is strongly in evidence in *Bloodline*, with his signature coppers Inspector Mark Lapslie and Detective Sergeant Emma Bradbury dispatched to investigate the disappearance of a young woman, Isabel Alarcon, in the secluded Spanish town that bears her name. Is Isabel's stepfather's history as an Essex gangster a factor? This sixth outing for Lapslie is sharply characterised and adroitly plotted; it may make readers hope that McCrery spends all his time on novels rather than screenwriting.

Broken Ground 2018

VAL McDERMID

McDermid's narrative skills since her unofficial coronation as the UK's queen of crime have not diminished, as proven by *Broken Ground*. Since ending her Northumbrian sojourn and resettling in Scotland, McDermid has swapped the north of England setting of her Tony Hill and Carol Jordan books for Edinburgh, despite the latter city being heavily populated with literary coppers these days, and we are once again in the eventful company of her alternative series character, Karen Pirie of Scotland's Historic Cases Unit. Alice Somerville, attempting to recover her inheritance (which turns out to be a pair of vintage motorcycles buried after World War II in a peat bog by her grandfather), comes across a bullet-ridden corpse and something else not dating from the war: a pair of Nike trainers. It's a classic Karen Pirie cold case setup. A fifth of the way into the book, McDermid switches the narrative to 1944 and incidents in the past that will have grim ramifications many decades later for the investigation. Pirie, bruised by office politics, is less interested in the 'down escalator that is Police Scotland promotion' than cracking her case. She is a satisfyingly wry and hard-edged protagonist, with the accumulating suspense maintained by McDermid's spare, dry tone of voice.

Bad Blood 2017
BRIAN McGILLOWAY

Let's forgive Brian McGilloway the overfamiliar title for this one. The Irish-born writer has long been adroit at bringing thorny issues to a general readership (in *Bleed a River Deep* (2009), featuring Garda Inspector Benedict Devlin, he tackled issues of organised crime and the treatment of illegal immigrants), and in *Bad Blood* he folds another provocative social concern into his rugged narrative. Detective Sergeant Lucy Black is investigating the death of a young man brutally killed with a rock, on his body an admission stamp for a gay club. Lucy finds a community divided between a gay rights group and a fundamentalist preacher who has called for the stoning of homosexual men. With far-right agitators at work on a local council estate, Lucy and her boss Tom Fleming discover that, immediately prior to the Brexit vote, the country is deeply divided in disparate ways. Caustic and committed, McGilloway proves that the mores of a society can be anatomised within its popular fiction.

The Fall 2012
CLAIRE McGOWAN

Claire McGowan became a familiar figure on the London crime fiction scene as director of the Crime Writers' Association, but it was clear from this assured debut novel that her real métier is delivering criminous diversions such as may be found in *The Fall*. There are elements of the police procedural here, with a well-drawn copper in Matthew Hegarty – though it has to be said that the latter is a familiar figure. The real achievement of the book, however, is its variegated cast of characters, particularly some expressively realised female protagonists who fairly leap off the page, displaying the author's keen ear for class and social nuance. No doubt McGowan felt that we needed a conventional copper to draw her narrative together, but it's the women here who count, such as the feckless mixed-race Keisha, in thrall to a pretty worthless male (in fact, the males in the book are a pretty sorry bunch). She is someone we find ourselves wanting to spend time with, however annoyingly she behaves.

Laidlaw 1977
WILLIAM McILVANNEY

The book that launched the tartan noir movement is undoubtedly the late William McIlvanney's *Laidlaw*, but the justified canonisation of this immensely influential writer has been a relatively new phenomenon. Even as recently as the first Bloody Scotland crime festival in 2012, despite the fact that his name could not be more honoured, not all of McIlvanney's books were available – a shameful situation that has now been remedied. Inspector Jack Laidlaw is investigating the rape and murder of the youthful Jennifer Lawson in Glasgow. Assisting him is newly transferred Detective Constable Harkness, who finds Laidlaw's methods eye-opening and unorthodox. Many of the traits that distinguish tartan noir – not least a memorable Celtic sleuth – are to be found in McIlvanney's work, and *Laidlaw* is the perfect place to start.

Arabesk 2000
BARBARA NADEL

Barbara Nadel has gone from strength to strength with her atmospheric and idiosyncratic Istanbul-set thrillers with the unorthodox Inspector Çetin İkmen as the protagonist. The first, *Belshazzar's Daughter* (1999), was immediately successful, while the third, *Arabesk*, evoked descriptions of the author as the Donna Leon of Istanbul, but Nadel needs no such comparisons: she is very much an individual talent in her own right. The scion of one of Turkey's most aristocratic families, Inspector Suleyman, is unfamiliar with the downmarket, noisy world of Arabesk singers, a world that hides depths of menace beneath its beguiling exterior. And when the peasant wife of one of its star performers is killed in a sumptuous Istanbul apartment, he is unable to cope with the case and his mentor, Inspector İkmen, is persuaded to become involved, despite being on sick leave. As in other books in the series, Nadel presents a gallery of richly created characters along with the assured scene-setting we expect from her. This remains one of the most original crime series currently in progress – at the time of writing, the most recent title is number 21, *A Knife to the Heart* – although Nadel, an Eastender, also has a second series set in World War II London.

Incorruptible 2018
BARBARA NADEL

Barbara Nadel's distinctive Istanbul-set series of Inspector İkmen thrillers dovetails brightly coloured settings with deliciously tortuous plots: İkmen is always struggling with intractable cases. In *Incorruptible*, the body of a young woman has been found crammed into a dustbin and festooned with cut flowers. İkmen discovers that she was hailed as 'the blessed woman', apparently cured of cancer by a miracle and subsequently declared a messenger of the Virgin Mary. This beatific Christian reputation has not endeared her to the Islamic community, and there were many who wanted her dead. But is there something in her family history that has brought about her murder other than religious intolerance? Nadel has never shied away from provocative issues, and the uncomfortable edge here makes this one of the most forceful entries in the series.

Turn a Blind Eye 2018
VICKY NEWHAM

At university, Vicky Newham acquired a fascination with psychopathology and serial killers, before teaching the subject for ten years. However, it was her experience of living and working in East London that prompted the characters and plot for her debut novel, *Turn a Blind Eye*. This is the first in a sequence set in the area, and features a female Bangladeshi detective, Inspector Maya Rahman – a strongly written character in a promising debut.

Jacquot and the Angel 2005
MARTIN O'BRIEN

Those lucky enough to have picked up O'Brien's first crime novel, *Jacquot and the Waterman* (2005), will have discovered an inventive detective story with colourful French locales creating the perfect backdrop, satisfying the English middle-class obsession with all things French. O'Brien, who lives in Gloucestershire, was, in fact, travel editor of *Vogue*, and it's hardly surprising that he utilised his globetrotting to produce his first crime novel featuring Daniel Jacquot of the Regional Crime Squad. In the third novel, *Jacquot and the Angel*, Jacquot is not happy with the work of his colleagues after a well-to-do German family living in Provence is savagely killed. It's a particularly grisly killing, involving a shotgun discharged over and over again at point-blank range. A gardener from the region is the chief suspect, but Jacquot isn't convinced. The answer to the mystery lies some 50 years in the past, when the Gestapo murdered a group of resistance fighters in World War II. As Jacquot struggles with intractable facts, an enigmatic young woman appears and claims to have crucial knowledge that might crack the case. And even Jacquot's own family plays a significant and tragic role. French country life has never been so fraught with sinister atmosphere, and the beauty of the settings is shot through with the heavy legacy of the past.

Written in Bones 2017

JAMES OSWALD

With *Written in Bones*, a résumé of the plot hardly conveys James Oswald's very individual tone of voice, but here goes: a corpse is discovered in the Meadows, a park in Edinburgh – a corpse that appears to have fallen from a massive height. Assigned to the case, Detective Inspector Tony McLean discovers ramifications stretching into Auld Reekie's troubled past. Unsettling atmosphere, strong sense of place and a canny twist at a key point that is sure to wrong-foot the reader: the success with which Oswald achieves his effects easily outstrips the formulaic work of bigger names than his.

The Murder Bag 2014

TONY PARSONS

Perhaps because of a reaction against what detractors called the laddish fiction of Tony Parsons (although he clearly had complex strategies in play in his examination of sex and relationships), the writer took a new direction, reinventing himself as a gritty crime writer. If you are shell-shocked from the army of novels featuring tough maverick cops – and are convinced that nothing new can invigorate the genre – perhaps you should pick up *The Murder Bag*. Yes, we've met detectives at loggerheads with their daughters (as here) before, from Wallander to Rebus. But there are two things that instantly lift this one out of the rut: parenting is a speciality of the author's work and it's treated with a nuance largely absent elsewhere in crime fiction. And Parsons, a quintessential London writer, evokes his city with pungency and elan. Bolshie Detective Constable Max Wolfe is investigating a homicide in which a banker's throat has been cut; a second victim is a homeless heroin addict. The connection: an upscale private school.

Four Blind Mice 2002

JAMES PATTERSON

Short chapters. Very short chapters. That's James Patterson's recipe for retaining his grip on a reader's attention, perhaps a tad overused. His other trademark is the use of nursery rhyme titles in his extensive Alex Cross series, which debuted with *Along Came a Spider* back in 1993. But his phenomenal sales – on both sides of the Atlantic – rout all criticism. The author knows precisely how to manipulate his readers, and his finely honed, utilitarian prose does get the job done – his Alex Cross novels have been besting the sales of his confrères in the crime writing field for many a moon. In *Four Blind Mice*, Cross is recovering from a savage duel with a murderous psychopath and finding consolation in a new relationship. But he agrees to tackle a fresh assignment: a man is accused of a double murder at an army base, and Alex soon comes to feel that this is a fix, with the real killer still at large. This is tense, pared-down stuff, authoritatively handled. But good detective series invariably have the deathwatch beetle chewing away at the central concept, which has led to authors from Conan Doyle to Colin Dexter trying to kill off their sleuths (Dexter succeeded, Conan Doyle didn't). Patterson's Alex Cross series was definitely showing signs of slipping into autopilot, but the first novel in a non-Cross series that focuses on four different women, *1st to Die* (2001), clearly had a galvanising effect on the author, with Lindsay Boxer, the only woman homicide inspector in San Francisco, making for a well-rounded and engaging heroine.

The Cruellest Month 2011
LOUISE PENNY

The Cruellest Month is a key entry in Penny's series featuring her doughty copper, Chief Inspector Armand Gamache of the Sûreté du Québec. Once again the Canadian locales are well drawn: in the pretty town of Three Pines, it's spring and spirits are high. But this is crime fiction, and – as all aficionados know – there is always a skull beneath the skin. Beneath the surface, destabilising secrets fester. A seance in a crumbling deserted house has had disastrous results, with one of the participants apparently frightened to death. Gamache is handling the case, but there are corollary distractions for his assignment: one of his team is about to throw a very large spanner into the works – one that may destroy Gamache (but which member of the team is it?). And there are things that even the detective himself is keeping hidden. In a limpid but subtly poetic style (the **TS Eliot** reference in the title is apropos), Louise Penny charts her narrative with the kind of quiet assurance that has so diverted readers in earlier books such as *Still Life* (2005) and *Dead Cold* (2007), and a particular pleasure is afforded here by the deeper personal involvement of Gamache in the story (as ever, he is satisfyingly multifaceted). The atmosphere of deferred revenge and incipient death is enjoyably unsettling.

The Listeners 2018
ANTHONY J QUINN

Carla Herron has swept through fast-track training at Edinburgh's police college and is immediately plunged into a disturbing case on the Scottish Borders. At the Deepwell psychiatric hospital, a patient has confessed to murdering one of the institution's psychotherapists. But there is no body, and the supposed murderer is under round-the-clock surveillance in a secure ward. Carla finds herself on two journeys: one geographical and one into the darkest reaches of human psychopathology. As in earlier books, Quinn sets up an intriguing Russian doll of a novel, with manipulation within manipulation.

The Falls 2001
IAN RANKIN

Ian Rankin's tough Scottish copper John Rebus is a key component of the UK crime scene, and the twelfth Inspector Rebus novel is one of

Ian Rankin
(1960–)

It must be something of a burden (albeit one to be fervently desired) to be the most successful male crime writer in the UK, but Ian Rankin (who was born in Scotland in 1960) carries his responsibilities lightly, and continues to produce a body of work that ensures his pre-eminence in the field for quite some time to come. If **Charles Dickens** is the ultimate chronicler of London, there are those who would maintain that Ian Rankin has performed a similar function for his beloved Edinburgh; his novels featuring the wry, damaged Detective Inspector John Rebus have produced a cumulative picture of the city – in all its splendour and squalor – that is quite as rich as anything to be found in more explicitly literary novels. While Rebus may be a familiar character to readers of crime fiction – messy private life, conflicts with his superiors, alcoholism – Rankin's skill as a novelist makes him quite as rich as, for instance, the protagonists of **John Updike**'s work, and serious issues are treated within his narratives, such as the duality to be found in the work of **Robert Louis Stevenson** (a key influence on Rankin). The first book to feature Rebus, *Knots and Crosses* (1987), demonstrated that his writing skills were already burnished to a fine degree, while such subsequent books as *Dead Souls* (1999) dealt with issues such as paedophilia in a harrowing (yet responsible) fashion. His most complex novel is possibly *The Hanging Garden* (1998), with the subjects of war criminals and sexual slavery as persuasively handled as one could wish.

---

the most substantial – and accomplished. Here, the complexity of the plotting affords subtle pleasures that perfectly complement the customary grittiness, and the scene-setting is as sure-footed as ever. In *The Falls*, the detective's private life is cannily sidelined in order to focus on a highly involving plot. A student disappears in Edinburgh, and Rebus is assigned to track her down, with added pressure coming from the fact that she is the daughter of a family of moneyed bankers. Is this an instance of a rich girl striking out on her own, away from family responsibilities? But a wooden figure in a coffin circuitously leads Rebus to an online role-playing game in which she was participating. And when one of Rebus's most valued team members, Detective Constable Siobhan Clarke, takes on the virtual quizmaster, is she to share the fate of the vanished girl? A considerable plus here is the welcome development of Siobhan Clarke as a powerfully realised character in Rankin's arsenal – we are quite as concerned with her dangerous situation as we are with Rebus's bushel of problems, and the tension is maintained whichever character is centre stage. The following year's *Resurrection Men* (2002) drove deeper into the groove, setting aside the aspects of Rebus we had become all too familiar with and bringing forward Siobhan Clarke – in an entertaining inside joke, Rebus is sent off to be 'retrained'. Rankin is clearly capable of running and running (as 2018's *In a House of Lies* proved), and of keeping several steps ahead of his readers.

The Babes in the Wood 2002
RUTH RENDELL

Rendell's books continued to grow in clarity and craftsmanship right up to the end of her life. *The Babes in the Wood* was one of her most stylish offerings featuring her long-term protagonist, Chief Inspector Reg Wexford. Rendell usually saved her most disturbing and nuanced writing for her non-Wexford books and her more psychologically driven plotlines for her alter ego **Barbara Vine**, but this novel imports all those elements into a narrative that begins in a typically macabre fashion and inexorably moves into the darker reaches of the human soul. The River Brede near Wexford's territory of Kingsmarkham has burst its banks after a torrential downpour. When his colleague Burden tells him about a woman who believes that her two teenage children, Giles and Sophie Dade, and their babysitter have drowned (even though all three could swim), Wexford launches an investigation that has him questioning some basic assumptions of human behaviour – even his own and that of his family. Wexford himself is delineated as economically as ever but remains a very persuasive literary copper, and Rendell's plotting skills ensure the usual seamless marriage between carefully structured storytelling and a restless probing of the psyche. As so often, Rendell writes unsparingly about the façades we all carefully maintain – and which can so easily slip.

Ruin Beach 2019

KATE RHODES

Kate Rhodes is riding high in the crime writing stakes with her beautifully plotted and elegantly written psychological thrillers, of which *Ruin Beach* is the most recent. The Scilly Isles' Deputy Chief of Police Ben Kitto is hankering for the buzz of working in the murder squad in London when the discovery of the body of a professional woman diver provides him with a challenge as rigorous as any he found in the capital – particularly when the islanders become deeply recalcitrant. All the elements that coalesced so perfectly in such earlier books as *Hell Bay* (2018) are firmly in place here.

Born Bad 2017

MARNIE RICHES

Marnie Riches is already ensconced as a leading light in the field of Mancunian noir, and *Born Bad* covers all aspects of her city, from its rundown backstreets and grime-covered civic buildings to its rich musical legacy. In 2018, Home Office figures identified Manchester as the most violent city in Britain, and the machinations of its crime bosses power the narrative here. *Born Bad* is perhaps more family drama than police procedural (with a desperate father attempting to save his endangered son), but whatever its genre, it's impressive.

Playing with Fire 2004

PETER ROBINSON

Peter Robinson has never quite achieved the upper echelons in terms of sales for his highly efficient crime novels – but those familiar with his work quickly latch onto the fact that he's one of the most reliable practitioners around. *Gallows View* in 1987 established him as a fresh and astringent voice in the field, and his hero, Inspector Alan Banks, has proved to be the perfect conduit for Robinson's canny narratives. However, the key to the appeal of a Peter Robinson book is not just the plotting, but a well-conveyed sense of place: the Yorkshire Dales are where the author locates his tales of murder and deception, and after a book like *Playing with Fire*, the reader feels very familiar with this atmospheric terrain. On a cold winter's day, fire destroys two narrowboats on the Eastvale canal. Inspector Banks and his colleague Detective Inspector Annie Cabbot are examining the charred corpses found in what's left of the boats. Who are the victims? There are several possibilities – and several possible killers, including the parent of a girl who perished in the flames, and an art dealer with some dark secrets. And then the arsonist strikes again… Perhaps not the equal of the assured *In a Dry Season* (1999), this is still a rounded piece of work by Robinson that weaves a binding spell.

Careless Love 2018

PETER ROBINSON

Describing a writer as 'a safe pair of hands' hardly raises the pulse in anticipation, and the fact that Peter Robinson had already written 24 entries in his Detective Chief Inspector Alan Banks series by the time this appeared may further suggest that the books have a certain rote quality – but nothing could be further from the truth; *Careless Love* is as reliable a read as the first Banks titles in the 1980s. The detective is investigating two deaths: a university student discovered in an abandoned car on the Yorkshire moors, and an elegantly dressed man found at the bottom of a moorland gully, partially devoured by animals. As Banks and reliable colleague Annie Cabbot struggle to find clues to both deaths, the presence of an old nemesis is slowly revealed – a figure who left an indelible mark on both coppers. Prolific Peter Robinson may be, but he always manages to ring the changes with some elan in each new book.

A Fear of Dark Water 2012

CRAIG RUSSELL

Arriving as it did festooned with encomiums from the likes of Mo Hayder, this is a highly individual detective novel. Russell's detective Jan Fabel operates in Germany, and a return to duty on the Hamburg murder squad leads to an encounter with a particularly terrifying killer. An environmental summit is due to begin in the city when the weather turns turbulent. As the floodwaters disappear, a body is found – decapitated. In his initial investigation, Fabel thinks that the body belongs to another victim of a serial murderer and rapist who tracks down his prey using social network websites. However, this explanation begins to seem inadequate when the detective's investigations uncover a clandestine cult with an environmental agenda.

Class Murder — 2017
LEIGH RUSSELL

Certain writers accrue a dedicated following without necessarily achieving the name recognition of some of their less talented colleagues. A prime example is the always reliable Leigh Russell, whose tenth Geraldine Steele mystery, *Class Murder*, is a signature outing. The novel reunites her doughty female copper with her former sergeant, Ian Peterson. Two people are murdered, their only connection in the past, and Steele is soon on the track of an enigmatic killer. Her quest is not helped by the fact that her reputation lies in tatters – and all the available witnesses are being killed. Russell's Geraldine Steele mysteries have sold over a million copies, and her secret is no doubt the sheer skill of her writing and her expertise in the police procedural field, which, while not notably innovative, is always expertly delivered.

The Birdwatcher — 2017
WILLIAM SHAW

It took very little time for crime fiction fans to realise that William Shaw was the real deal – a writer of immense command, who took the genre, shook it apart and came up with something fresh, hard and incisive. His series with Detective Sergeant Cathal Breen and WPC Helen Tozer bristles with a strong evocation of 1960s London and has taken on some provocative issues, such as the effects of colonialism and the new era of permissiveness. *The Birdwatcher*, however, is Shaw's first standalone novel (it features Alexandra Cupidi, who would subsequently become a recurring character) and is very different from previous books – though equally accomplished. The setting is the Kent coast, and his protagonist, Police Sergeant William South, has the best of reasons for not wanting to be part of a murder investigation in the area – he is, in fact, a killer himself. As a dark case grows ever darker (with people trafficking in the mix), we learn more and more about the troubled South as we are shown his childhood in Northern Ireland, the killing of his father (active in the paramilitaries) and his dramatic first involvement in a murder case. It is this rigorous analysis of personality – the impulses that can drive people to murder – that energises this powerful and astringent novel.

The Intrusions 2018
STAV SHEREZ

In this award-winning piece, Stav Sherez brings an incisive, galvanic force to the crime novel that must be the envy of his peers. The shade of **Émile Zola** no less (with that writer's notions of justice in an unforgiving society) hovers at Sherez's elbow in this outing for his coppers Carrigan and Miller, up against a case of abduction that begins in a Bayswater hostel but has tendrils that spread far wider. Geneva Miller, intransigent and vulnerable, is shaping up to be one of the most distinctive of female literary coppers in a desperately overcrowded field. The author is something of a polymath, and the echoes here of Zola, mentioned above, jostle with everyone from **Graham Greene** to **Fyodor Dostoyevsky**, but Sherez's learning is worn lightly – he is still a crime writer, and his immediate imperative is always narrative grip, here set against a jaw-dropping final development that will resonate in future books in the series.

Gorky Park 1981
MARTIN CRUZ SMITH (born Martin William Smith)

After the phenomenal success of Martin Cruz Smith's *Gorky Park* (with his brilliantly realised pre-perestroika Russian settings and wonderful Russian copper Arkady Renko), it was obvious that a major new talent had arrived on the crime scene, along with a detective who, at a stroke, joined the ranks of the most memorable in the field. But some disappointment was in store for new Smith readers: many of his 17 earlier books began to appear on the back of the success of *Gorky Park*, and readers were reminded that this former reporter had had a lengthy career as a novelist before this breakthrough book. And although the reissued books were perfectly capable pieces of work, they didn't begin to match the achievement of *Gorky Park*.

Gorky Park won the Crime Writers' Association Gold Dagger, and few previous novels had ever utilised a foreign locale with such attention to detail. Renko, Chief Homicide Investigator for the Moscow Prosecutor's Office, is handed a triple murder to investigate. Why have three corpses been mutilated and buried in the Moscow park of the title? As Renko tries to deal with intractable government departments and the whole vodka-swilling apparatus of the Soviet state, he finds that the solution may lie with some dangerous (and influential) foreigners. While Renko was a classic creation (and was used almost equally well in such successive books as *Polar Star* (1989) and *Red Square* (1992) – though the novelty was, of course, diminished), it is the Russian setting with its unremitting snow, May Day celebrations and indomitable – if repressed – citizenry that both made this novel one of the most popular crime thrillers ever written and led to a whole army of imitators.

GORKY PARK 1983

Director: Michael Apted

The excellent William Hurt as Renko; Lee Marvin as a duplicitous American businessman; a screenplay by no less than Dennis Potter. The auguries were all in place for a movie that would have done full justice to the novel. So what went wrong? Many things: Hurt's performance is so low key as to be almost invisible, director Michael Apted is not able to marshal the elements of the complex plot with sufficient rigour, and Dennis Potter gives every impression of being out of sympathy with the material. The film was shot in Helsinki, which makes a passable substitute for Moscow. Lee Marvin was, of course, characteristically charismatic.

Truth 2009

PETER TEMPLE

One of the ancillary pleasures of books is not shared by readers and publishers. Readers like nothing better than to proselytise to friends about a little-known author they have discovered – it's the satisfaction of knowing about a talented writer before he or she is taken up by the hoi polloi. Publishers, however, have no time for such concepts as 'deserves to be better known', 'caviar to the general', and so forth. They just want their authors out in the marketplace, well known, selling by the shedload. It must have been particularly irksome for the publishers who boasted the prodigally talented South Africa-born, Australia-resident Peter Temple in their list. They will have been aware that he is one of the most respected of literary crime novelists, with a back catalogue of considerable distinction. And they will also be aware that he never quite made the breakthrough that he so richly deserved – Temple enjoyed good reviews but modest sales (see how easy it is to play the 'underrated author you should know about' game?). Of course, the situation was very different in Australia, where Temple enjoyed the success that is his due.

In *Truth*, to all outward appearances Inspector Stephen Villani has made a success of his life. He is head of the homicide division in Melbourne, where his unbending dedication to duty has put him at the top. But Villani is a divided, damaged man whose attitude to his father is deeply ambiguous. The cracks in his private life begin to spread when a series of fires ravages Melbourne and a murder case becomes the catalyst for a meltdown, as his investigation is subsumed under a series of personal crises. Interestingly, the jacket comparisons for the book opted not for the customary **James Lee Burke** and **James Ellroy** but **JM Coetzee** and **Tom Wolfe**. And if these comparisons seemed a little vainglorious, Temple's writing (always terse and economical) demonstrated that the two non-crime novelists are apt models. Temple's conflicted, self-destructive protagonist is set down in a mordant evocation of a city in crisis; in fact, Villani's divided soul is presented, in understated fashion, as a metaphor for the society he lives in, with the capacity for organic regeneration as elusive for the city as it is for the man. Temple's award-winning *The Broken Shore* (2005) was good; this is better.

Then She Was Gone 2016

LUCA VESTE

When politicians make specious promises about facilitating a 'northern powerhouse', they are almost certainly not aware that one already exists – in terms of crime fiction, at least. Gritty northern writers who are injecting the genre with adrenalin include a talented Liverpudlian novelist, the counterintuitively named Luca Veste. Veste made an auspicious debut in 2013 with *Dead Gone*, and his caustic detectives, Inspector David Murphy and Sergeant Laura Rossi, reappear in *Then She Was Gone*, which re-energises the police procedural format. A politician disappears. And a year earlier Tim Johnson's baby daughter was kidnapped – or so he claimed – but the police saw him as a suspect. What's more – did the missing daughter actually exist? Murphy and Rossi find themselves opening a particularly nasty can of worms.

A major character in Veste's work is Liverpool itself, with every aspect of the city's evolving landscape, from its historic beauty to its self-deprecating humour. Veste's Italian and Scouse heritage has produced an intriguing hothouse flower, as shown in this assured series.

The Old Religion 2018

MARTYN WAITES

It was only a matter of time before the first post-Brexit crime novel appeared, and readers should be grateful that it's in the capable hands of Martyn Waites. Tom Killgannon is an undercover policeman forced by a career debacle into the witness protection programme and working as a barman in the isolated Cornish village of St Petroc. His unexciting life is rocked when teenage Lila, a runaway from a travellers' commune, steals his wallet, threatening the revelation of his identity and bloody retribution from the criminals from whom he has escaped. Meanwhile, the locals have realised that the stagnant local economy will not be booming despite parliamentary promises made to them. But village leader Morrigan counsels that there is a route to prosperity: a return to the 'old religion', with deeply sinister implications. Waites' taste for English gothic is in the mix here, and his customary evocation of atmosphere is firmly in place – as are some masterful plot revelations.

Bruno, Chief of Police 2009

MARTIN WALKER

Martin Walker has a solid journalistic background and is the author of several acclaimed works of non-fiction, including *The Cold War*, along with a historical novel, *The Caves of Périgord* – but none of this is necessarily a copper-bottomed guarantee of success in the crime fiction genre. Fortunately, *Bruno, Chief of Police* turns out to be a quietly assured piece of work, full of quirky touches and characterised with real exuberance. The eponymous Captain Benoît (Bruno) Courrèges is in charge of a modest force in the town of St Denis in the Périgord region of France – which allows Walker, of course, to utilise things he gleaned for his previous novel set in the region. But Bruno is not your typical hard-hitting copper: he never carries the gun he owns, and barely needs to arrest people. However, suddenly all is turmoil in the town as inspectors from Brussels swoop on the rural market, making many enemies. Bruno is worried by the fact that this phenomenon is invoking memories of the town's ignoble Vichy France past. Then an old man from a North African immigrant family is murdered...

Hollywood Station 2006

JOSEPH WAMBAUGH

It was truly a cause for celebration when one of the most influential and important crime novelists returned to the spotlight in the 21st century after a period of some neglect. The contemporary police novel owes a great deal to such Wambaugh classics as *The Choirboys* (1975) and *The Onion Field* (1973); in these novels, Wambaugh's years in the LAPD enabled him to evoke the immense pressures experienced by officers on duty, and the breakdowns of several of his characters have a power that is charged by this verisimilitude. His comeback novel, *Hollywood Station*, is proof that he hasn't lost his touch. His memorably drawn protagonists here are Hollywood cops Fausto Gamboa and Ron LeCroix, who have to deal with the kind of outrageous situations that one might expect of Tinseltown. But, unsurprisingly, things turn very dark indeed.

A Patient Fury 2017

SARAH WARD

After so many tired police procedurals, who can produce something quietly different in the genre? Sarah Ward, demonstrably, as *A Patient Fury* proves. Ward is a judge for a Nordic noir award, and – like **Ann Cleeves** – infuses a degree of Scandinavian chill into her resolutely English scenarios.

Here, a family is immolated (Ward has a gift for the macabre image – a burning body, strung from a ceiling, turns slowly to face those watching), and combative, diminutive Detective Constable Connie Childs finds that the key to the murders may lie with an as-yet-undiscovered fourth body.

The Devil's Dice 2018

ROZ WATKINS

The Devil's Dice was shortlisted for the Crime Writers' Association Debut Dagger and is the first in a planned series set in the Peak District and featuring Detective Inspector Meg Dalton. It was inspired by an incident in which Watkins' dog ran up to her with what looked like a human spine – in fact it turned out to belong to a large hare. The author was previously a patent attorney, so it was almost inevitable that a dead attorney would crop up in her writing – poisoned here, and found in a cave. His demise gives Meg Dalton a chance to prove to her sceptical colleagues that a slightly chubby vegetarian with a limp can make a great cop.

The Anarchist Detective 2013

JASON WEBSTER

A welcome antidote to the frigid climes of Scandinavian crime fiction may be found in Jason Webster's sultry (and elegantly written) Max Cámara series, of which this entry is particularly accomplished. In *The Anarchist Detective*, Webster's dyspeptic Spanish detective Cámara is in elective exile in Madrid, with a view to cultivating his cordon bleu skills – and enjoying some erotic indulgence with the seductive Alicia. But the day job exerts its hold again, and he is drawn back to his home town of Albacete, a place he has struggled to forget. Back on familiar territory, he is soon knee-deep in betrayal, lies and the grim residue of the Civil War, still poisoning lives.

Sideswipe 1987

CHARLES WILLEFORD

If you're lucky, you might be one of the people who can claim they knew all about Charles Willeford before he was really discovered – there are more and more people making that claim. Although well known to the cognoscenti, ex-boxer, painter, actor and journalist Willeford remains unknown to the great mass of crime readers – and that's undoubtedly their loss. Certainly namechecked by **Elmore Leonard**, **Carl Hiaasen** and **James Hall** as a key influence, it was only with **George Armitage**'s 1990 film of *Miami Blues* (1984) that he really came to public attention – but too late. Hardened cineastes might also recognise his credit as the author behind **Monte Hellman**'s controversial 1974 movie *Cockfighter*. Always one of the most individual of stylists – and one of the first crime writers, like James Hall, to run a university creative writing course – he combines a cockeyed view of the world with an inimitable prose style and wonderfully drawn characters, such as *Sideswipe*'s beleaguered Hoke Moseley (who also features in *Miami Blues*). Hoke is a cop who has struggled through a none-too-shining career and then decides to retire and attempt to run a down-at-heel hotel. This proves to be a mistake: he has got his girlfriend pregnant and his two teenage daughters are rapidly going off the rails. If all of this wasn't bad enough, a gang of wackos turns up at the hotel. All of this is handled with the kind of delirious energy that is Willeford's trademark, and his influence on later writers (and even filmmakers) will be evident to anyone who makes an acquaintance with his work. In some ways, it would be nice for Charles Willeford to remain a hidden pleasure for the chosen few – but that would be selfish, wouldn't it?

The Silent and the Damned 2004

ROBERT WILSON

It's a proud band, the knot of readers who extol the virtues of Robert Wilson, with such books as *A Darkening Stain* (1997) categorical proof that their man is something unique in the ranks of crime writers. His sagas of twisted loyalties and middle-level corruption in foreign settings are reminiscent of an earlier generation of writers – grimy urban noir is not for Wilson. He gleaned much praise for *A Small Death in Lisbon* (1999), and although *The Company of Strangers* (2001) was less well received, Wilson followers were pleased when *The Silent and the Damned* appeared, an outing for his conflicted detective Javier Falcón that pressed all the right buttons. Seville in summer: Falcon is investigating what appears to be a suicide pact in an upscale area. Needless to say, nothing is as it seems; Falcon dispenses with the obvious and begins to see the hand of a criminal strategist at work. Another double suicide follows – and one of the dead is a police colleague of Falcón's. Ukrainian prostitutes and people-smuggling Russian mafia are soon stirred into the brew – but then Falcón makes a significant discovery... While the trademark Wilson gift for locales is in evidence, he never forgets that the key to the best crime writing is sharp characterisation, and the large dramatis personae is drawn with skill. If some plot elements seem a tad warmed-over, Wilson still delivers a carefully structured but exuberant piece of work.

When Red Is Black   2004

QIU XIAOLONG

The author's debut, *Death of a Red Heroine* (2000), caused quite a splash when it first appeared, and *A Loyal Character Dancer* (2002) was a highly individual read, handling its culture-clash theme with real aplomb. For once, the 'cops from different backgrounds' concept was treated with real freshness. Here again we meet the resourceful Inspector Chen Cao, who has agreed to do a translation job for a Triad-connected businessman. When a murder is reported, Sergeant Yu is obliged to take care of business – but both men are soon knee-deep in a baffling mystery. This third Inspector Chen mystery set in contemporary China is quite the equal of its predecessors.

CHAPTER 6

PROFESSIONALS
Lawyers, doctors, forensic scientists and others

Barely a week passes without a well-paid lawyer deciding that they can become an even better paid writer of legal thrillers – for that dubious pleasure we can blame the unprecedented success of **John Grisham**, onlie begetter of this kind of lucrative career change. The law featured in fiction as a destructive element in the lives of the protagonists as far back as **Charles Dickens**' *Bleak House*, but the modern riff on the theme involves placing the lawyers centre stage, often functioning as detectives by default.

It was a source of some annoyance for the late **Ed McBain** that the two major innovations he brought to the crime novel were developed – and thoroughly colonised – by others: the police unit functioning as a tight-knit team, and the importance of forensics in detection. But McBain could hardly complain that his achievement in the field was undervalued – and there is no denying that two phenomenally successful American crime novelists in particular, **Patricia Cornwell** and **Kathy Reichs**, have parlayed forensic anthropologist heroines into total bestsellerdom. Another highly influential 'alternative profession' for a crime novel protagonist is the criminal profiler – and there, **Val McDermid**'s unassumingly brilliant Dr Tony Hill is almost as imitated as Cornwell's heroine Kay Scarpetta. On screen, the public's taste for the often gruesome technicalities of crime solving has been reflected in the continuing popularity of TV series such as *Silent Witness* (forensic pathology), *CSI* (crime scene investigation) and *Cracker* (criminal profiling).

And the future? There are other verdant areas of crime-related professionals for development: insurance investigators and bounty hunters, for instance.

The Corpse with the Sapphire Eyes — 2015

CATHY ACE

Born and raised in Swansea, Cathy Ace is the creator of Cait Morgan, a diminutive, plus-sized Welsh-Canadian professor and criminologist. Based in British Columbia, Cait has travelled widely over the course of the series, and in this one – book number five – Ace takes her heroine back to a rainy Wales. Cait is about to marry retired cop Bud Anderson, but the supposedly romantic Welsh castle feels anything but – possibly because there's a corpse on the stairs. What first appears to have been the untimely but accidental death of the wedding choirmaster turns out to be murder. And when strange events start occurring, Cait and her sister – together with Bud – need to solve the mystery before it ruins the wedding.

Whispers of the Dead — 2010

SIMON BECKETT

Forensic specialist David Hunter is recovering from the after-effects of a recent macabre assignment and has made an ameliorative journey to the research faculty where he learned his trade: the institution known as the Body Farm in Tennessee. Hunter has been asked by the man who honed his forensic skills to take a trip to a crime scene – a cabin in the woods, miles from anywhere, where the victim's body, though seriously decomposed, was clearly bound and tortured. Sometime later another body is discovered, and Hunter is once again treading familiar territory involving lethal mind games with an ingenious and relentless psychopath. Simon Beckett has the full measure of his material here; this is a key book.

Deep Down Dead   2017
STEPH BROADRIBB

Steph Broadribb's debut novel *Deep Down Dead*, while consummately readable, has no truck with restraint. If anything, Broadribb and her protagonist, tough Florida bounty hunter Lori Anderson, have more than a hint of **Lee Child** and Jack Reacher about them, with literally no punches pulled. The other parallel with Lee Child is, of course, the fact that this is an English writer making a sterling job of finding an American voice for both the narrative and the characters, and Broadribb proves to be just as adroit in this area as her better-known counterpart. *Deep Down Dead* involves the up-against-it Lori, desperate for money, taking on what proves to be a dangerous job. She has no choice, as medical bills for her ailing nine-year-old daughter (she is a single mother) are mounting up. Having browbeaten her boss into giving her this assignment, she makes a mistake – one that has the reader apprehensive from the start: she is obliged to take along her daughter when escorting her criminal charge. And soon she's encountering some very nasty people indeed. This was a promising debut, delivered with both energy and colour, with Lori an unusual protagonist, and follow-ups have appeared successfully since then.

The Gardens of the Dead   2006
WILLIAM BRODRICK

As in his first book, *The Sixth Lamentation* (1999), here Brodrick is primarily concerned with plotting. And his second concern after plotting is... more plotting. This isn't to say that the characters are not fully rounded; it's just that Brodrick is far more concerned with storytelling expertise. Elizabeth Glendinning is a QC who knows that her death is imminent. But she has a pressing agenda – she will bring a guilty man, now free, back into the law courts. The plan that will take effect after her death involves six individuals, all of whose lives were changed by a significant trial. Elizabeth's posthumous plan is that Graham Riley will be arraigned by this group, led by Father Anselm – barrister turned monk, and Elizabeth's former colleague. Anselm receives the key to a security box that will bring back memories of his previous life, when the case against Riley collapsed after a witness destroyed the prosecution case. This witness, George

Bradshaw, found his life ruined after these events, and wanders London as Blind George, his short-term memory in pieces after an assault. However, Elizabeth's carefully oiled planning begins to break down, and Anselm unwillingly takes on her mantle, investigating her life and that of her son, Nick. And there's an urgency to these investigations: lives are at stake…

Any fears that Brodrick's earlier book was a lucky accident were quickly allayed with *The Gardens of the Dead*. Certainly, the complexity of the narrative here is a little wearying at times. But as this labyrinthine tale unfolds, Brodrick is able to bring off a truly impressive sleight of hand.

Double Indemnity 1943

JAMES M CAIN

James M Cain's second most famous book is as febrile and hard-edged as *The Postman Always Rings Twice*. Insurance investigator Walter Huff falls for the middle-class femme fatale Phyllis Nirdlinger and (as in *Postman*) is persuaded to kill her husband for his insurance. This most cold-eyed of crime novels is one of the most impressive in the genre (hardboiled or otherwise), with nary a wasted word – the concision of Cain's prose is even more bracing today, when elephantiasis has taken hold of the crime novel. The basic scenario – the anti-hero led by his genitals into a murder for gain by a ruthless, predatory woman – was to become a crucial blueprint for the genre, never more coolly articulated than here. The famous **Billy Wilder** film consolidated the success of the book, but it would still be remembered today even without this helping hand – not least for Cain's very modern cynicism.

DOUBLE INDEMNITY 1944

Director: Billy Wilder

While many a noir masterpiece has undergone an ill-advised remake, no one has yet had the temerity to try to match Billy Wilder's ice-cold classic, in the cinema (there is an underpowered TV movie). The film is burnished with work on the screenplay by no less than **Raymond Chandler**, although **Lawrence Kasdan**'s *Body Heat* (1981) echoed Wilder. Barbara Stanwyck, Fred MacMurray (the definitive fall guy) and Edward G Robinson as MacMurray's colleague in insurance fraud investigation, who rumbles the plot, are a matchless cast for this reptilian tale of lust, greed and betrayal.

Patricia Cornwell
(1956–)

Patricia Cornwell is so unassailably ensconced in the bestseller charts that her name is routinely used to sell the legions of imitators who have followed in her path. Approbation arrived immediately for her first book, *Postmortem* (1990), and the astonishing success of this debut (and the multiple prizes it gleaned) acted as a spur for her successive books, in which the forensic anthropologist Kay Scarpetta – with a messy private life – encounters a series of increasingly grisly puzzles. It was no surprise when she received the Crime Writers' Association Dagger, about which she remarked that receiving an award from the home country of **Agatha Christie** was a tremendous honour – 'After all, in terms of plotting, we're all her heirs.' When Cornwell changed direction, temporarily abandoning Kay Scarpetta for the Judy Hammer books (Hammer being

The Defence
2016
STEVE CAVANAGH

Readers first met Steve Cavanagh's lively Eddie Flynn, a former conman turned trial attorney, in *The Defence*, a book guaranteed to push the requisite buttons for lovers of **John Grisham** and **Scott Turow**. Cavanagh's spirited debut novel takes us into the complex, shaded world of Flynn as he copes with a radical change of career – though perhaps the two roles aren't as different as one might think... Dialogue is a particular speciality for Cavanagh – always pointed and authentic.

Seizure
2003
ROBIN COOK

The name of the doctor/novelist Robin Cook has long been a byword for impeccably detailed, plausible thrillers, and even if his later writing is not always as powerful as such early books as *Coma* (1977) and *Outbreak* (1987), he is always totally professional, guaranteeing the reader a well-turned piece of work. That's very much the case with *Seizure*, where Cook's skills in the a more straightforward female cop), she took a measure of flak. Why wasn't she continuing to produce something that was a proven hit? But clearly Cornwell felt the need to keep the experience of writing fresh for herself, and the Hammer books have their virtues. However, most loyal Cornwell fans were glad to see Scarpetta return, reinvigorated. On the faintly risible subject of the painter Walter Sickert (who Cornwell identified as the most famous of serial killers in her controversial book *Portrait of a Killer: Jack the Ripper – Case Closed* (2002)), the author brooks no argument, and she spent a good deal of money adducing scientific opinions to support her case. However, her Scarpetta books represent her real legacy.

plotting arena are quietly brought into play. Biotechnology is the theme here, and an implacable opponent of all research in the field, ultra-conservative southern senator Ashley Butler, enjoys chairing a committee to put the brakes on cloning technology. Stem cell researcher Daniel Lowell is, of course, a key opponent, but both men have strange and conflicted personalities. When Butler contracts Parkinson's disease, he is forced to enlist the aid of his former enemy, but premature use of new technological advances has disastrous consequences for both of them. All of Cook's best thrillers utilise medical and scientific concepts like this (highly topical as America moves further to the right in such areas), and *Seizure* satisfyingly incorporates such ideas into a sprawling but taut narrative.

Blow Fly 2003

PATRICIA CORNWELL

After *Postmortem* (1990) launched her series of Kay Scarpetta novels – and created an army of imitation female pathologists – Patricia Cornwell seemed to lose her way. But this outing has all the energy and invention of the earlier work – although the levels of blood-boltered horror here make even the sanguinary excesses of the earlier books look restrained. Scarpetta's independence has made her *persona non grata* with her long-suffering bosses, and she's pursuing a freelance career in Florida. But the monstrous Chandonne, a serial murderer with lycanthropic tendencies she tackled in the past, is not quite out of her life. And if this doesn't make Kay's life complicated enough, her niece Lucy, no longer in the employ of the FBI, has Chandonne's bent lawyer in her sights, with intentions that are quite as murderous as those the serial killer had towards Kay. As so often before, Kay is forced to juggle her personal and professional responsibilities, with her emotional life a hostage to fortune – a settled love life is not on the cards for her. What follows is a richly unsettling melange of tortuous plotting (the synopsis here only hints at the complexity of *Blow Fly*'s multi-layered narrative) and the usual full-throated bloodletting, all hurtling along at a pace that rarely gives pause for breath. What a dark world the beleaguered Scarpetta plies her trade in! Being aware of the skull beneath the skin leaves her with few illusions about the imperfections of the human race.

A Dark Devotion 1997

CLARE FRANCIS

Although we have not seen much from her of late, the reach of Clare Francis as an author has been wide indeed: at least six of her bestselling thrillers (including *Red Crystal* (1985), *Wolf Winter* (1987) and *Deceit* (1993)) are among the finest in the field, and her non-fiction books describing her epic ocean voyages have become classics. Like many a crime writer, however, she is interested in blurring the boundaries between crime fiction and literature and, latterly, some may feel that she has been lost to the crime fraternity. But the enthusiast will still have books as impressive as *A Dark Devotion*, in which Norfolk's salt marshes are put to masterful use as a backdrop for an atmospheric tale of murder, legal skulduggery and sexual passion. Criminal lawyer Alexandra O'Neill is enjoying the rewards that her successful career is bringing her, but there is a fly in the ointment: her husband, a partner in a London legal firm, is becoming an alcoholic. The couple move among low-rent criminals, with petty crime on the daily menu. Then Alex is contacted by the man she was in love with as a child in Norfolk, Will Dearden. His wife has gone missing, and Alex is drawn into a complex web of intrigue that will irrevocably change her personal life.

Right Behind You 2017

LISA GARDNER

A modest cheer for the American Lisa Gardner, whose *Right Behind You* commendably eschews most of the clichés of the crime genre while keeping her ironclad storytelling skills firmly in place. Sharlah Nash once saw her brother kill in order to save her life. After she has spent time in foster care, retired FBI profiler Pierce Quincy is finally able to offer Sharlah, now 21, a safe new life – one she cannot refuse. But her unstable brother appears to be on a killing spree, and this time it looks like she is on his death list. Not Gardner's best work, but still pretty damn good.

Body Double 2004

TESS GERRITSEN

Tess Gerritsen's *Body Double* is a reminder that – **Mo Hayder** apart – many of the toughest female writers hail from America. She has upset some of her fellow crime writers with her readiness to hit her readers in the face, with absolutely no concessions to the squeamish, but – honestly – who would pick up a Tess Gerritsen novel expecting something suitable for readers of *The Lady*? In the first book in the series, *The Surgeon* (2001), a vicious killer returns from the dead to threaten the surgeon he held responsible for his demise, and Gerritsen's unrelenting style quickly grabbed readers' attention. Her heroines, detective Jane Rizzoli and medical examiner Maura Isles, are memorable figures, with a whole slew of unusual traits, and, what's more, they are two very different women – something Gerritsen emphasises. The early outings for Rizzoli and Isles consistently (and pleasurably) accelerated the reader's pulse rate, and that's something she pulled off again in 2004 with *Body Double*, even though this one has a deceptively slow-burning start.

Maura Isles is shown a woman stretched out on a slab – a woman who appears to share her appearance, age and blood group. And while a killer is wreaking havoc across the country, Maura has to journey to Maine to find out the truth about a mother she never knew. In Gerritsen novels, things are seldom what they seem – and that's very much the case here, as layers of reality are ruthlessly stripped aside. Once again, the author pulls no punches when it comes to confronting the most extreme and disturbing outer reaches of human behaviour, and, as they used to say, 'those of a nervous disposition' should take care. But Gerritsen fans are a hardy breed, and this scarifying novel delivers everything they go to her for.

The Broker

2005

JOHN GRISHAM

John Grisham has never let carefully textured writing get in the way of page-turning. The massive popularity of his novels – and of the mostly workaday movies that have been squeezed from them – is down to a killer combination of sheer storytelling and stripped-down, no-nonsense prose. Not to mention an authoritative way with the details of the milieus in which he sets his fast-moving tales (usually the American legal profession).

John Grisham
(1955–)

Not many authors can bask in the fact that their very name defines a genre – but John Grisham is in that select company. There's barely a legal thriller that doesn't hopefully invoke the author's moniker as a selling tool – but few of the army of Grisham wannabes have the sheer storytelling nous that the prototype possesses. As a trial lawyer, Grisham had the notion of using details of an existing case for a novel – a career trajectory emulated by all too many lawyers since, with results ranging from the excellent to the meretricious. For Grisham, the result was the accomplished *A Time to Kill* (1989), which remains a justified favourite of the author. And *The Firm* (1991), with its young lawyer protagonist who finds his hands are dirty with mob business, demonstrated that Grisham was no one-hit wonder. While subsequent books have not all maintained the impetus of the early books (and Grisham's once-trumpeted acquisition of a brand of born-again religious fervour did his work no favours), he is always professional, and has recently added a strain of sharp social comment to his books. His book sales remain prodigious.

Photo: Billy Hunt

But *The Broker* is proof that Grisham has also found other fish to fry. All the customary narrative muscles are exercised; ostensibly, the plot concerns slippery Washington power broker Joel Backman being sprung from a high-security cell by a departing president, principally so that the CIA can observe who murders him first: the Russians, the Israelis, the Saudis or the Chinese. But something more ambitious peeks out: this is Grisham's State of the Nation novel, masquerading as a chase thriller; some excoriating points are made about high-level corruption in the US – and, *inter alia*, the UK – in between heads falling under car wheels, and one doubts that *The Broker* will be on any White House bedside tables. It's a cold eye Grisham casts on his country, and its (fictitious?) president.

The Chosen Dead 2013

MR HALL

It is fortunate that most of us are not placed in the position of having to sacrifice our happiness in an ongoing battle with corruption. MR Hall's coroner heroine Jenny Cooper would clearly be sympathetic to Tolstoy's notion that his hero was truth – although the pursuit of truth has cost her dearly, and her fragile mental state has been stretched ever tighter over the course of five increasingly impressive books (there are a couple more after this outing). *The Chosen Dead* is slightly different from its predecessors in that Hall places his stress on a particularly intricate narrative rather than on the mental travails of his beleaguered, substance-abusing protagonist, who has a slightly easier time of it in this book than her creator has previously allowed her. Frankly, the obdurate Jenny has sorely tested our patience, and it's good that Hall makes her less exasperating than usual here – although people who are always right are invariably exasperating.

Without the support of her usual mainstay and colleague Alison (also going through a bad time), Jenny is in pursuit of the facts behind a case of meningitis that has taken the life of a friend's child. Steered by her pompous consultant ex-husband, David, she uncovers what appears to be a hospital conspiracy – while simultaneously looking into the unexplained death of an aid worker who has returned to the UK from Africa before falling from a high bridge. As Jenny peels back the layers of obfuscation, she comes up against the customary wall of indifference and hostility presented by various government bodies, telling her again and again that things are not as simple as she would like them to be. And even though the reader knows that it will take nearly 500 pages to accomplish it, Jenny will – as ever – be vindicated. In real life, most of us roll our eyes at the various conspiracy theories trotted out by the paranoid, but readers of crime fiction have to accept such things as de rigueur – and a belief in the slew of nasty cover-ups at the heart of the genre is as essential as a temporary belief in the existence of the Greek gods when watching *Medea* or *Oedipus Rex*. And those grandiose comparisons are not entirely inappropriate; Hall is undoubtedly one of the more ambitious crime writers, giving his books a texture that is both nuanced and persuasive.

The Rat on Fire 1981

GEORGE V HIGGINS

What to choose from the man whom **Ed McBain** described as 'the le Carré of classy sleaze'? All the books are great, and Higgins' background in the Boston legal scene gave him access to an enormous range of criminal briefs. But strangely, few of his books focus on legal practitioners – it was the clients (or defendants) who fascinated him. With *The Rat on Fire* he picked up on a standard insurance scam, when torching a tenement full of African Americans who default on their rent seems like a perfect way to make some easy money. But when the scheming landlord – a small-time lawyer – chooses a couple of incompetent lowlifes, Leo and Jimmy, to do the dirty deed, the plot unravels horrifically and, oddly, comically. Anyone with an ear for dialogue will enjoy Higgins' work, and the uneasy feeling that he actually likes the scummy crooks who populate his pages gives him a serrated edge as a chronicler of quite where, and how, the American Dream went off the rails.

Tell No Lies 2013

GREGG HURWITZ

With a multiplicity of elements to praise, it's difficult to know where to start first with Gregg Hurwitz's *Tell No Lies*, with its beleaguered probation counsellor Daniel Brasher knee-deep in a series of gruesome murders. The book exerts all the author's customary Ancient Mariner-like grip on the reader – and is sometimes reminiscent of another American master, **Harlan Coben** – but the author is always fully aware of the importance of character kept firmly at the centre of the helter-skelter plotting. Hurwitz brought new levels of sophistication to his much-acclaimed run on the *Batman* comic,

> # George V Higgins
> ## (1939–99)
>
> When devotees of crime fiction have a need to silence someone extolling the virtues of some overrated, bestselling writer, there's one name that will do it: one of the most underappreciated writers in the genre – the late, great George V Higgins. His specialities were twofold: characters as quirky and brilliantly characterised as anything in **Elmore Leonard** – and then there was the dialogue. Higgins' ear was unique, giving him the ability to reproduce the quotidian patterns of everyday speech, so that the exchanges between his lowlife protagonists were utterly cherishable. His first novel, *The Friends of Eddie Coyle* (1970), about a low-rent gunrunner at the end of his tether, is his masterpiece, but equally splendid work is to be found in *A Choice of Enemies* (1984), with its mordant take on political corruption, and *The Judgment of Deke Hunter* (1976), sporting a memorable cast of minor criminals. Higgins was an assistant to the US attorney in Boston, and the verisimilitude that his personal experience gave him was splendidly transmuted into his first-rate series of novels.

which demonstrates a welcome readiness not to be pigeonholed (although perhaps, that is not such a stretch – after all, the Dark Knight took over from Sherlock Holmes as the World's Greatest Detective).

Ties that Bind

2003

PHILLIP MARGOLIN

One of the reasons why readers go back to the legal thriller genre again and again is the delicious pleasure of plotting: nothing exhilarates more than some ingenious and surprising narrative, and that's something Phillip Margolin delivers with *Ties that Bind* – and in spades. Lawyer Amanda Jaffe is saddled with a case that makes her feel she's up against insuperable odds: her client is facing execution and has just killed his own lawyer. Jon Dupre is, self-evidently, a nasty piece of work: a wheeler and dealer in the dirty world of selling both drugs and women, and his fate is clearly sealed. But as Amanda digs beneath the surface of the case, she finds the proverbial can of worms. Dupre can claim friends in the most unlikely of places, not just at the criminal end of society. He is the custodian of some very dark secrets, and before he starts spilling them, there are people who will go to considerable lengths to maintain the status quo. Apart from the satisfyingly convoluted narrative, Margolin's skill here (also evident in such earlier books as *The Burning Man* (1996) and *The Associate* (2001)) lies in the creation of a strongly drawn, conflicted protagonist – and Amanda is certainly that. We've met her type before, but Margolin rings the changes with aplomb.

Val McDermid
(1955–)

There was a time when McDermid was just a solid, reliable crime novelist creating series such as the Lindsay Gordon mysteries and books foregrounding the gay journo Kate Brannigan. But then something happened: imperceptibly, McDermid joined the elite ranks of 'serious novelists who write crime fiction'. But had her work really changed? Did it justify the new gravitas she seemed to have acquired? Her early books were diverting, but better was to come. McDermid's series featuring profiler and clinical psychologist Dr Tony Hill was quite her strongest work yet, creating one of the richest pieces of characterisation of her career. And now she has the best of both worlds – a dedicated crime readership eager for every new offering, and the kind of serious attention her more literary peers might envy. In all modesty, it was this writer who christened her the 'queen of crime' in a national newspaper when the position fell vacant after the deaths of her older colleagues PD James and Ruth Rendell. It's a position she has comfortably held to this day.

Disturbing Ground 2014
PRISCILLA MASTERS

One of the pleasures of Priscilla Masters' well-turned thrillers is the way in which all the elements are satisfactorily integrated. We are shown the professional and emotional life of Dr Megan Banesto, who has come back to the small town in the Welsh valleys in which she grew up to act as the local GP. We are similarly presented with sharp character drawing in the figure of Megan's old flame, police chief Alun Williams, and the rekindled relationship between the two has genuine resonance. And smoothly meshing with these pieces of characterisation is a nicely honed plot in which the body of a paranoid schizophrenic patient of Megan's is found drowned in a pond. While the official findings point to suicide, Megan knows that the dead girl, Bianca Rhys, was terrified of water. Alun Williams flatters himself that Megan's theories are a device for the couple to get back together again and refuses to address the case with any rigour. But it slowly becomes apparent that this small Welsh town of Llancloudy conceals some nasty secrets, and perhaps Megan Banesto is the only one with the will to uncover them. The pace is quick, the local detail is interesting – even though we've been in this kind of cloistered village setting many times before – and the whole thing is very effective. Thriller fans will find this an efficient assault on their powers of deduction.

The Last Temptation 2002
VAL McDERMID

The Last Temptation takes Val McDermid's best-loved characters into truly disturbing territory. Tony Hill is up against a terrifying killer who has very specific targets in his sights: psychologists, no less. He has brutally murdered top names in the profession across Europe, and Hill has urgent reasons for cracking the modus operandi of his nemesis. But complications are added by the dangerous job that Hill's erstwhile partner, Detective Chief Inspector Carol Jordan, has undertaken: she is doing undercover work in Berlin, targeting a well-heeled criminal. Long-time thriller readers will not be surprised to discover that Hill and Jordan are soon pooling their resources to confront a force of evil that stretches back as far as the Nazi era, with both protagonists wrenched from their controlled environments and fighting for their lives. *The Torment of Others* (2004) was a resounding follow-up, and despite the question marks currently hanging over the value of criminal profiling, McDermid remains utterly convincing.

The Heirs of Owain Glyndŵr — 2016
PETER MURPHY

Peter Murphy has long had the measure of the law-based thriller and here utilises his legal expertise in a lively piece involving Welsh nationalist zealotry. It's 1 July 1969 and a nation awaits the investiture of the new Prince of Wales in Caernarfon Castle. But not everyone is celebrating. Lingering resentment over the treatment of the Welsh language and culture has led to several acts of terrorism – the planting of explosive devices in and around Caernarfon in advance of the ceremony. The devices are not well designed or made, and only one is successfully detonated: it was a long way from the castle, but nonetheless caused serious injury to a child. In the aftermath, a man is convicted of offences relating to explosives and sentenced to imprisonment. Peter Murphy has taken the real-life investiture and the history of the preceding years as the backdrop for the fourth novel in the series with his barrister protagonist Ben Schroeder – it is Murphy on top form.

Deep Water — 2016
CHRISTINE POULSON

Christine Poulson's earlier novel, *Invisible* (2014), combined effortless page-turning with subtle characterisation, and this book is a worthy successor. *Deep Water* may cheekily filch the title of a Patricia Highsmith novel, but it demonstrates once again the skill and psychological understanding of Poulson's writing.

Patent lawyer Daniel Marchmont is commissioned by the heavyweight biotech company Calliope and quickly finds himself in the eponymous 'deep water'. His predecessor at the company is dead, and a lab journal with crucial information has gone astray. Daniel has a personal interest – he and his wife Rachel are living in hope that biotechnology will find a way to cure the genetic disorder afflicting their daughter. Simultaneously, researcher Katie Flanagan suspects that dark dealings are in play in the company's laboratories, and – unsurprisingly – her life is soon on the line. There is an

Kathy Reichs
(1950–)

In an overcrowded field such as that of crime writing, it's difficult to establish a solid reputation. To achieve the acclaim that Kathy Reichs has – and in a relatively short time – is quite an achievement.

Reichs, like **Patricia Cornwell**, has used her medical background to create a series of tough and uncompromising thrillers. She was forensic anthropologist for the office of the Chief Medical Examiner of North Carolina and worked in a similar capacity in the province of Quebec. Her massive experience in the area of forensic science has been heavily drawn on, and at present she is one of only 100 people certified by the American Board of Forensic Anthropology. Like her leading character, Dr Temperance Brennan, Reichs found herself obliged not only to function but also to distinguish herself in the male-dominated world of law enforcement. *Déjà Dead* established her reputation in 1997, and Tempe Brennan made an immediate mark as a solid and reliable heroine. Brennan was, of course, similar to Patricia Cornwell's Dr Kay Scarpetta, but Reichs nevertheless rendered her a fully rounded character in her own right and managed to build new elements through successive books. The first novel had a relatively cool tone, but the follow-up, *Death du Jour* (1999), began to consolidate and refine elements present in its predecessor (such as character interaction) and the emotional temperature was higher. This new level of energy and invention clearly established Reichs as a more impressive writer than had been originally thought, decisively moving her out of the shadow of Cornwell. In Book 3, *Deadly Decisions* (2000), bikers are engaged in a war, and two of them appear to have blown themselves up. Brennan is largely unconcerned over what they do to each other, but a nine-year-old girl is killed in the crossfire. Not all Reichs novels maintain the same level of achievement, but *Break No Bones* (2006) was categorical proof that the author still knew how to intelligently ring the changes. There are undoubtedly too many female forensic experts in the field now, but Brennan remains one of the best.

echo here of such **Robin Cook** medical thrillers as *Coma* (with its notably Kate Flanagan-like heroine finding the company she works for is up to no good), but Poulson has a strong grasp of the exigencies of the medical novel of suspense. As well as maintaining the tension throughout the 250-odd pages here, her writing is both sharp and elegant.

Déjà Dead 1997
KATHY REICHS

As debut thrillers go, Kathy Reichs' *Déjà Dead* made more of a mark than most. Employing her background as a forensic anthropologist, Reichs ensures that the tradecraft of her heroine, Temperance Brennan, has complete verisimilitude. A woman's bones are found within the grounds of a monastery and Tempe, assigned to the case, suspects the work of a serial killer. The victim, she believes, is not the first woman to die at the hands of the murderer before being brutally eviscerated. Her point of view is not shared by the detective on the case, but Reichs' heroine is a woman who is always driven to prove herself, and she soon changes her colleague's mind. As the protagonists draw nearer to their quarry, the author is able to create a piquant picture of the province of Quebec as backdrop to the tension. Other details shore up the power of the narrative: the internal politics of a police division (with Tempe riding roughshod over some of the more fondly maintained protocols); the carefully maintained duality in the nature of the heroine, her professionalism sometimes at odds with her enthusiasm; and the steady accretion of flesh-creeping detail. This is not reading for the squeamish!

Faithless 2005
KARIN SLAUGHTER

The single-minded Karin Slaughter is a woman unafraid of dealing with unspeakable violence in her books. Her focus is not so much on the fashion in which the social contract is shattered, but on the reasons why – but that's not to say that she doesn't deal, unblinkingly, with the consequences of violence, and her name (appropriately enough) has become a byword for the toughest and most unrelenting of crime thrillers. She is much concerned with the factors that sanction the ruthless taking of life, but such things as the nature versus nurture debate are always embedded in narratives that are as well crafted as they are bloodcurdling. Her familiar protagonists – police chief Jeffrey Tolliver and coroner Sara Linton, who first appeared in *Blindsighted* (2001) – are two of the strongest characters in the genre, with a beautifully detailed relationship, and *Faithless* is as good an entry point for Slaughter as anything she has written. The duo discover a body in the woods, and it is revealed that the girl's death is the result of extreme terror. Aided by detective Lena Adams, the pair initiates an investigation in a nearby county, where a closed community offers little help in their search. All of this is handled with the assurance we expect from Slaughter, but perhaps the best thing here is the worm in the bud that Slaughter introduces into her investigating team: Lena's disturbingly erratic behaviour is as much a threat to the group as the implacable killer. Irresistible stuff.

Presumed Innocent 1987

SCOTT TUROW

It's not that easy to virtually hijack a genre, but the crown prince of the sharply written legal thriller may well be Scott Turow, since **John Grisham**'s born-again Christianity has crept into his work and vitiated it. And Turow's most famous novel is a virtual blueprint for the genre – one that subsequently became oversubscribed. Turow himself was an assistant US attorney in Chicago (1978–86), and the blizzard of legal detail crammed into the book ensures a strong sense of verisimilitude underneath the dirty dealings. *Presumed Innocent* is narrated by Rusty Sabich, a prosecuting attorney who is happily married. After an ex-work colleague of his is savagely raped, Rusty finds himself on a fatal collision course in both his professional and his private life. When his ex-lover Carolyn is killed, Rusty finds – to his horror – that he is accused of the murder. It isn't just the photographically detailed picture of the legal universe with its internecine squabbles and courtroom dramas that distinguishes *Presumed Innocent*: Turow is well aware that characterisation remains paramount, along with the kind of plotting that can constantly take the reader by surprise.

PRESUMED INNOCENT

1990

Director: Alan J Pakula

The presence of Harrison Ford, then at the peak of his career, ensured the massive box office success of this smooth and professional job, with an adaptation of a hot novel being the other key ingredient. Although it is undoubtedly true that director Alan J Pakula produced more personal work in less commercial projects, he turns in a professional job here. Good support from such reliable character actors as Brian Dennehy and Raul Julia, and the deliciously scheming Greta Scacchi, makes up for the fact that the complexity of the plotting has been somewhat smoothed out.

Reversible Errors

2002

SCOTT TUROW

Among the many legal thrillers that followed – including some by Scott Turow himself – few were able to capture the gusto of *Presumed Innocent* (1987), and it is a source of regret that so many other lawyers felt obliged to give up their legal careers and write indifferent copies of Turow's remarkable book. The background to the author's work is intelligence: he has talked about his faith in science and is dismissive of the idea that America is rushing headlong towards a kind of dumbed-down religious state. And although he is aware that the most distrusted group in the US is the legal profession, his books remind us that there are good eggs in with the bad. In *Reversible Errors* (2002), we find gritty and plausible legal detail, as we would expect from the author, and a cold-eyed, dispassionate examination of human behaviour. Tackling once again the collision of ordinary human existence and the exigencies of the legal apparatus, Turow brings to life not just the beleaguered attorney who is his protagonist, but also the hate-filled characters who populate this heady narrative. You may be tired of legal thrillers – but here's one to remind you why this genre became so damned popular.

CHAPTER 7

AMATEUR INVESTIGATORS

Journalists, other professionals and self-styled sleuths

Although many crime novels fit more or less comfortably into a clearly defined category – private eye, police procedural or whatever – the genre has many books that resist easy characterisation. As in much classic literary fiction, a crime in these novels is committed and the lives of the characters are irrevocably changed. Also like literary fiction, these non-category novels can explore with more penetrating analysis the murkier reaches of the human psyche, not being tied down to the exigencies of the professional or private cop working his way through a list of suspects. But the books in this section do occasionally have protagonists from other professions: journalists, art experts, jockeys, priests, modern Robin Hoods… and, of course, victims. Equally deserving of attention are **Dorothy L Sayers'** Lord Peter Wimsey and **Simon Brett's** Charles Paris – not to mention other non-police types such as Jane Marple, Gervase Fen, Albert Campion, Nigel Strangeways, **Jacqueline Winspear's** period investigator Maisie Dobbs, **MC Beaton's** Agatha Raisin, **Alan Bradley's** juvenile Flavia de Luce, **Elizabeth Peters'** Amelia Peabody, **Leye Adenle's** Amaka, **Jonathan Kellerman's** Alex Delaware and **Stieg Larsson's** Mikael Blomkvist.

Without Trace — 2016
SIMON BOOKER

I suppose that it should come as no surprise that Simon Booker's debut crime novel *Without Trace* is a notably assured piece of work. It was a first novel that spoke of years of experience rather than tyro good luck – which was in fact the case, as Booker had been honing his skills as a television writer for many years. Hence (one guesses) his command of both plotting and dialogue – the latter particularly idiomatic, which is not something that can be said for every crime novel, debut or otherwise. *Without Trace* inaugurated a series of psychological thrillers with the (female) investigative journalist Morgan Vine, whose career can hardly be said to be flourishing. She lives in a converted railway carriage on the beach at Dungeness (a nice touch, this, which marks the book out from the competition), and she has spent a great deal of time campaigning for the release of Danny Kilcannon, with whom she was in love when both were children. Danny has been arraigned for the murder of his stepdaughter, although Morgan is unconvinced by the evidence. But then Danny is released and Morgan's own daughter vanishes – which instantly throws her into confusion concerning everything she thought she knew about her ex-sweetheart. Is he innocent? Or is he a Machiavellian schemer who has pulled the wool over her eyes? The plot is based on real-life encounters in Simon Booker's life, but it isn't that fact which grants the book its verisimilitude – it's the writer's authoritative control of his medium.

Be My Enemy — 2004
CHRISTOPHER BROOKMYRE

Edgy, uncomfortable crime fiction with an acute awareness of modern society is the trademark of the talented Christopher Brookmyre – and, like the earlier *Quite Ugly One Morning* (1996) and *Boiling a Frog* (2000), *Be My Enemy* is characteristic stuff. There was a time when Brookmyre was filed under the generic heading of tartan noir, and certainly his books deliver the gritty diversions that such a label suggests. But Brookmyre was always keen to stretch the possibilities of the crime genre – and has been less focused on Scottishness than his crime writing confrère **Ian Rankin**. Brookmyre has always been more than ready to tread on the toes of the politically correct and to outrage those of a conservative bent, but his ideas are never pushed in our faces at the expense of the narrative. And the author is just as happy to offend those on the left as on the right – and it's this even-handedness that makes *Be My Enemy* so diverting. The book has many of the familiar Brookmyre fingerprints, such as cutting wit and danger – but it is also an attempt to do something new in its examination of the fascist leanings that even the best of us can harbour. Journalist Jack Parlabane, Brookmyre's regular protagonist, is obliged to participate in a corporate retreat at a secluded (and well-appointed) hotel. But some very dangerous things are to happen in conjunction with the team-building activities, and Jack is soon in trouble again. Using the isolated setting as a mixing pot for some of the most extreme views and attitudes in society acts as a metaphor for larger issues, as is often the case in Brookmyre's books.

The Innocence of Father Brown 1911

GK CHESTERTON

The affection in which the Father Brown books are held has slipped somewhat in recent years, possibly a result of a more secular age – and a toe-curlingly twee (though popular) BBC TV series with Mark Williams hasn't helped. But anyone prepared to sample the Chestertonian delights will not regret it. Chesterton was, of course, a remarkable figure in his day. After a stellar career in journalism, he became (like Graham Greene) a Roman Catholic in middle life, and from this grew his creation of the deceptively unassuming priest and detective Father Brown. This ecclesiastical descendant of Sherlock Holmes first appeared in *The Innocence of Father Brown*, and the standard of the stories rarely faltered thereafter. The Brown tales are a bright and idiosyncratic picture of their era, with as bizarre a selection of problems as the denizen of 221b Baker Street ever had to face. While the solutions to the mysteries are often a little strained, their ingenuity always wins the reader over. And possibly the real achievement for the modern reader is the way in which Chesterton avoids making the inevitably 'good' Father Brown insufferably pious – no easy task. This may be due to the tongue-in-cheek humour which is never far away in Chesterton's writing.

Time is an Ambush 1962
FRANCIS CLIFFORD

If there's any justice, the neglected Francis Clifford's time will come again. Clifford was one of the most accomplished of British novelists working within the parameters of the adventure/espionage field; his métier was creating situations of extreme danger for his protagonists and freighting in moral choices that push them to the limit. Clifford initially pursued a career in the rice industry in Burma before World War II. As a soldier, he undertook a gruelling odyssey of 1,000 miles through the occupied country, a trek he transmuted into the book *Desperate Journey* in 1979. He worked in the Special Operations Executive and – like many other writers – was to utilise this experience in his writing. Clifford was soon producing novels that showed an adroit mastery of plotting allied to a skill in the creation and manipulation of suspense worthy of **Alfred Hitchcock**. *Time is an Ambush* is vintage Clifford: a beautifully detailed, subtle yet tense piece in which a quintessential Englishman abroad, writer Stephen Tyler, becomes involved with the widow of a dead German in a small Spanish town. Originally published in 1962, *Time is an Ambush* reads as powerfully in the 21st century as the day it was written.

Dark Pines 2018
WILL DEAN

The notion of protagonists in crime fiction who succeed against the odds is hardly a new trope, but few writers have pulled off the trick with quite the aplomb that Will Dean has in this much-acclaimed debut novel. His heroine is Tuva Moodyson, a deaf reporter for a newspaper in the small Swedish town of Gavrik. In the elk-hunting season, two hunters are gruesomely killed, with their eyes removed, echoing an earlier murder case. Will Dean is English but has a thorough familiarity with the Swedish setting he has chosen, and the atmosphere of the small town – deeply eccentric and quirky – is brought off with great skill. Tuva, too, is a very memorable heroine, and the unalloyed praise that greeted this novel was thoroughly deserved.

The Woman in the Window 2017
AJ FINN

Alfred Hitchcock's *Rear Window* is a gift that keeps on giving for writers of crime fiction, from **Paula Hawkins**' variation on the theme, *The Girl on the Train* (2015), to AJ Finn's riff, **The Woman in the Window** (title courtesy of another director, **Fritz Lang**). (Finn is actually the controversial Dan Mallory, a US publisher who knows just what makes popular thrillers work – the controversy, however, is not relevant here.) As with Hawkins, we have a booze-addicted woman with a dysfunctional life, Dr Anna Fox. When not watching Hitchcock films (Finn is refreshingly open about the source of his inspiration), Anna uses the zoom lens of her camera to spy on the comfortable life of her neighbours, the Russells. But – as is de rigueur for this subgenre – Anna observes something horrific that she was not supposed to see. She is confronted with the inevitable question – will anyone believe her? The achievement here is that Finn does not to attempt to conceal the shopworn elements but confronts them head-on and rings some bracing changes.

Dead Cert 1962
DICK FRANCIS

The classic Dick Francis thriller *Dead Cert* has rarely been out of print for over half a century, but is it a relic of an era that has passed? Whatever one's feelings about horse racing – the late Francis's chosen territory – the book itself has not aged a day. Jockey Bill Davidson, riding on the favourite Admiral, has been murdered, and jockey Alan York takes on the mantle of detective to track down a group of savage criminals. His investigations get him nowhere, until he finds himself waylaid by a group of heavies. And then the answers to the problem suddenly start to come thick and fast until York loses his memory. The first-person narration here still leaps off the page, and it really doesn't matter whether or not the reader is interested in the world of racing: the background here is so idiomatic that it ensures the thriller mechanics move with total assurance. Many current thriller writers could pick this up and learn a trick or two – the very same qualities that made Francis such an immediate winner back in the 1960s hold true today: the machine-tooled plotting, the insider's knowledge of a closed world, and the elementary but sharply drawn characters. The author's son, the ebullient **Felix Francis**, has continued the franchise in a similar style with such books as *Pulse* (2017) and *Crisis* (2018).

DEAD CERT 1974
Director: Tony Richardson

Tony Richardson, director of such seminal British new wave films as *The Entertainer* and *A Taste of Honey*, might have seemed a curious choice for a straightforward thriller such as this, but by this stage of his career, Richardson had been choosing some very unsuitable projects. That proved to be the case with *Dead Cert*, but this tale of Grand National shenanigans has a strongly realised racing background, with all the horsey elements securely in place. A strong cast (including Judi Dench, before she became a national treasure) make the most of their characters.

Spend Game 1980
JONATHAN GASH

The character of Lovejoy, the ducking and diving antiques dealer (and sometime detective) is inextricably linked in most people's minds with the actor Ian McShane, who incarnated him in a long-running television series. But for the real Lovejoy, it's necessary to go back to the novels of Jonathan Gash (pseudonym of **John Grant**). The books are clever and always full of needle-sharp plotting. In *Spend Game*, an old friend of Lovejoy's who has also become an antiques dealer is killed, while Lovejoy watches. He is constrained from talking to the police because of complications involving a woman he is having an affair with – and this forces him to bring the murderer to justice himself and find out what was behind the killing. As ever, Lovejoy is a wonderful creation: comic, ingenious and only just this side of the law. And he remains the perfect guide for the reader through the fascinating world of antiques dealing and the many suspicious characters who swim in its deeper waters.

Winterland 2009
ALAN GLYNN

Although the credit crunch caused the odd hiccup in 2009, the city of Dublin maintained its frenzy of property development. Walking through such areas as **James Joyce**'s 'Nighttown' then, you would have seen something rather different from the locale celebrated by Joyce. The working girls may still have been there, but there were fewer of them and cranes now loomed above the narrow streets, preparing the way for the proliferating wine bars, coffee shops and upscale couture houses. But Dublin's basic identity seems to remain inviolable, however her face may change – and it is this struggle between the old and the new that has powered some of the most provocative fiction being written in Ireland in recent years. Interestingly enough, as Alan Glynn's *Winterland* comprehensively proves, it's the not entirely respectable genre of crime fiction that throws up some of the most incisive evocations of this protean city.

The central character, Gina Rafferty (who takes on some very powerful and dangerous people), may have wandered in from a **Martina Cole** novel, but the territory here couldn't be further from the East End of London, either geographically or in terms of the author's ambition: despite its popular pedigree, this is something of a state-of-the-nation novel. From the violent opening in a smoking section of a Dublin pub (where the dialogue has an authentic snap, maintained throughout the novel), Glynn keeps his narrative exuberant and fleet-footed. A young drug dealer, Noel Rafferty, is shot in a beer garden, and the police are happy to file it under gangland killings – one less thug to worry about. But on the same evening, Rafferty's uncle (who shares his relative's name) also loses his life in a suspicious car accident. Coincidence or conspiracy? Gina, Glynn's heroine, isn't buying the official explanation of either death and undertakes some amateur detective work. But she quickly realises that she is up against some influential opponents – movers and shakers in a world of crooked property deals and corrupt political influence. She discovers that her brother (the Rafferty who died in a car crash) was involved with the construction of a massive skyscraper, and with a property developer, Paddy Norton, whose ambition is to transform Dublin into something like downtown Chicago. The real crimes in Glynn's provocative and richly textured novel are not necessarily the killings, but the unfettered exercise of greed and political self-interest.

Dying to Tell 2001

ROBERT GODDARD

Robert Goddard's work remains the *sine qua non* of storytelling ability; it must amuse him to observe the vagaries of trends in crime fiction, particularly as his faithful readers largely ignore such things and continually return to his books. They're hardly cutting edge in terms of modern fiction, but who cares? *Dying to Tell* is a key entry in an illustrious line of Goddard winners. His less than energetic hero here is Lance Bradley, stewing in Somerset when he receives a request to trace Rupert Alder, an old friend who has cut his relatives adrift financially. Calling on the shipping firm Rupert worked for, it seems clear that he has been involved in a large-scale fraud. And other people are looking for Rupert too... Goddard fans will know what to expect – polished writing and reliable plotting.

Scrublands 2018

CHRIS HAMMER

Crime writing from Australia is clearly very fertile territory, as this strong debut proves. *Scrublands* had already enjoyed considerable success in its native country before UK publication and is a strikingly wrought piece of tension in an outback setting. In a tinder-dry town, a young priest is responsible for a mass shooting; when, a year later, journalist Martin Scarsden is sent to discover how the town has – or has not – recovered, he unearths a slew of well-hidden secrets. While rough around the edges in terms of its treatment of the emotional life of the characters, this is nevertheless an ambitious and accomplished piece of work.

Tokyo 2004

MO HAYDER

The sheer energy and invention of Mo Hayder's writing virtually obliterate any less than felicitous passages in her work, and the disapproval that greeted the violence of her early books (such as *Birdman* (2000) and *The Treatment* (2001)) was soon sidelined – perhaps because there are so many women around these days travelling in the same bloodstained territory,

Tess Gerritsen for one. But another reason why Hayder shows signs of having writing longevity is her reluctance to continue to tread paths she has trod before – as the ambitious *Tokyo* most satisfyingly proved. The central character here is a woman who is trawling Tokyo trying to find a missing piece of film revealing unpalatable truths about the Nanking Massacre in 1937. Grey Hutchins, Hayder's vulnerable heroine, tackles a job as a hostess in a nightclub and greatly increases the danger she is facing – and then finds a lead to the missing film, an academic who lived through the massacre. As the foregoing might attest, Hayder is painting on a large canvas here: it's audacious work, sometimes ill-focused, but always restlessly involving.

Angels of the Flood 2004

JOANNA HINES

A strong sense of place and an unusual take on the crime genre are two characteristics of the novels of Joanna Hines, although she has been absent from the crime scene for some years. *Angels of the Flood* is set in Florence, but it is a Florence few tourists have ever seen, and a Florence that no one will ever have the chance to see again. In November 1966 the city was devastated by a freak flood with catastrophic results for buildings, manuscripts and art, as well as for the Florentines themselves. The eponymous 'angels of the flood' were the young people who flocked to the city to help with the clean-up. Kate Holland, naive and full of enthusiasm, joins the volunteers. So too does Francesca Bertoni, an enigmatic Italian-American who is secretive about her reasons for hiding from her family. She is tracked down by Mario Bassano, the ambitious doctor who claims to be her fiancé, and tensions come to a head at a weekend party at the Villa Beatrice, which belongs to Francesca's uncle. The real strength of the novel is its picture of Florence during the disastrous floods and of an Italy that is very different from the present day. Hines knows her locales, and her writing is as good as a holiday under Mediterranean skies.

Dark Horse 2002

TAMI HOAG

Elena Estes is a woman who likes to live life on the edge, but her recklessness has cost her a job in the Miami PD and – more disastrously – the life of a colleague. She goes to ground in Florida, surrounds herself with horses, and attempts to regain her equilibrium. But her new-found peace isn't to last. Molly Seabright is convinced that something has happened to her stepsister, a groom at the stables that Elena uses, and soon the troubled ex-policewoman finds herself drawn into danger again, with the high rollers of the hyper-rich world around her quite as lethal as the scum of Miami. Hoag has carved out a career for herself as one of the most assured of American crime writers, and *Dark Horse* is a good entry point for new readers, with its troubled heroine, powerfully drawn locales and intricate plotting all well up to par, even though it's darker than most of her other work – after all, she began her writing career back in 1998 with romance novels. And whether or not you're interested in horses, the show season in southern Florida is an atmospheric backdrop to the skulduggery on offer.

Sleeping Cruelty 2000
LYNDA LA PLANTE

Although the TV incarnation of her *Prime Suspect* remains Lynda La Plante's calling card (due as much to Helen Mirren's memorable incarnation of Jane Tennison as any writing skills of the author), other La Plante books such as *The Legacy* (1987) demonstrate the range of her achievements. Her other television series, *Widows* (reimagined on the big screen by director **Steve McQueen** in 2018), utilises her trademark 'tough woman' motif, not a million miles from similar territory mined by **Martina Cole**. But (also like Cole), La Plante clearly wanted to show that she could create an equally strong male protagonist – and that's just what she does in *Sleeping Cruelty* with the ambiguous entrepreneur Sir William Benedict, a character the reader is invited to change their mind about – several times. Benedict has secured all the baubles that success can offer, including property in the Caribbean, and, as a mentor, has been financially supporting the younger, gay Andrew Maynard, a Tory MP. When Maynard takes his own life, a juggernaut is set in motion that looks set to destroy Benedict, but he isn't taking this lying down... All of this is writ large in trademark La Plante fashion, but the poster-coloured writing is absolutely apposite, with the dramatic effects pulled off spectacularly.

Rum Punch 1992
ELMORE LEONARD

Many crooks are amateurs too, and the great chronicler of the kinds of clowns that make life a misery for the rest of us was Elmore Leonard. *Rum Punch* is one of his Florida novels, featuring an array of classic Leonard types such as Max Cherry, a bail bondsman, and Ordell Robbie, an ambitious psycho who has the Mercedes and attitude and wants more, but is unlikely to achieve this with his posse of loser, weed-smoking ex-cons (junkie criminals rarely fare well in Leonard – see also *Fifty-Two Pickup* (1974)). Enter Jackie Burke, glamorous but ageing air hostess who is supplementing her income smuggling for Robbie. When she is caught red-handed by a couple of shady cops, Max Cherry raises her bail and falls in love with her at the same time. His problem is how to get her out of her dilemma, while not crossing the cops or Robbie. The usual sly plotting, narrative pace, matter-of-fact offhand violence and sharp street dialogue make for a Leonard classic, but the portraits of Robbie – dumber than he thinks he is – and his risible henchmen are what stick.

JACKIE BROWN 1997
Director: Quentin Tarantino

Hollywood *enfant terrible* Quentin Tarantino was born to direct **Elmore Leonard**'s novels. He has called the writer his 'mentor', and although Leonard has frequently been let down on the screen, this movie was a match made in heaven, restraining Tarantino's imaginative verve with a taut plot line – and surprisingly little upfront violence. With his usual quirky eye for casting, Tarantino used 1970s blaxploitation star Pam Grier as the subtly renamed sky smuggler and the suitably world-weary B-movie actor Robert Forster as Cherry. But his coup was casting Samuel L Jackson as a charmingly scary Robbie, Robert De Niro as his plug-dumb sidekick, Bridget Fonda as their doped-up nympho squeeze, and Michael Keaton as a corrupt cop. As always, there are great Tarantino set pieces, none better than the multi-viewpoint bag switch in a shopping mall, reminiscent of **Akira Kurosawa** or even **Jacques Rivette**.

The Executioners
JOHN D MACDONALD
1957

A novel of extremely dark menace that plays on many lawyers' or witnesses' fears about what might happen when a villain they send down finishes his sentence. Retired defence attorney Sam Bowden is seeking a new, quiet life with his young family in the picturesque resort of Cape Fear, North Carolina. Then Max Cady turns up, an illiterate rapist Bowden unsuccessfully defended in a case 14 years earlier. Blaming Bowden for a flawed defence, and clued up having spent his time profitably in the prison library, he is out for revenge. First the family dog is poisoned, then Bowden's daughter threatened, but Cady is careful to appear to be on the right side of the law. Then, in classic 'For God's sake don't do that!' mode, Bowden decides to retreat to their remote boathouse, providing Cady with the perfect setting to exact his planned vengeance by assaulting Bowden's wife. Will family man Bowden be up to vanquishing his nemesis?

CAPE FEAR
1962
Director: J Lee Thompson

Mauled by the UK censors upon its release, this stunning exercise in really nasty suspense benefited enormously from having Gregory Peck as the weak lawyer and a supremely threatening Robert Mitchum, reprising something of his *The Night of the Hunter* role, as Cady. Thompson wasn't a great director, but the balance works wonderfully between the bright daytime scenes of sunny small-town America and the night scenes as Cady's increasingly violent plan unravels.

CAPE FEAR
1991
Director: Martin Scorsese

Now Martin Scorsese *is* a great director, and his remake raised questions, the main one being 'Why?' With Nick Nolte as Bowden and Robert de Niro at his most disturbing as Cady, Scorsese ups the suspense quota considerably (especially when Cady stalks Bowden's daughter in her deserted school), not to mention upping the explicitly sexual drive of the original novel. Mitchum, Peck and Martin Balsam (who also featured in the 1962 movie) were given cameo roles.

Ruth Rendell
(1930–2015)

For many years, there were two women firmly at the top of the crime writing tree in the UK: **PD James** and Ruth Rendell, although a host of claimants for their dual crown jostled for attention. It is invidious to claim that either author had the greater talent, particularly as their similarities are matched by very different ambitions. Ruth Rendell's police procedural novels featuring her doughty Inspector Reg Wexford utilised the tropes of the classic English detective novel, with the characters of Wexford and his supportive wife subordinate to the truly ingenious plotting. But Rendell admirers usually claim that her best work lies in her non-series novels such as *A Judgement in Stone* (1977), where she addresses some of the darkest reaches of human behaviour and the lonely alienation of modern urban life; the characterisation of such books is much more complex and ambitious than in those featuring her long-serving copper.

When Rendell initiated a second writing career as Barbara Vine, sceptics who felt that she might overextend herself were quickly routed when it became clear that the Vine books were even more multifaceted and astringent. *Asta's Book* (1993) is a study in betrayal, personal identity and, of course, murder. Like all the Vine novels – as well as the best of the non-series Rendell titles – this is psychological crime writing of the most fastidious kind, always idiosyncratic in its treatment of character.

The Portrait
2005

IAIN PEARS

The literary crime novel is a rarefied form, always in danger of losing the primal compulsion of books in the wider crime arena by paying too much attention to carefully honed prose and prissily scorning the melodramatic effects of less ambitious fare. Some writers, however, are able to strike a judicious balance between the populist and the sophisticated – and Iain Pears is firmly in their number. He made his name with *An Instance of the Fingerpost* (1997), set in Restoration Oxford. *The Portrait* is another finely drawn exercise in malice, with Pears setting himself a difficult task: how to ensure that a restricted dramatis personae can maintain the reader's involvement. The setting is an isolated island, where the painter Henry MacAlpine has marooned himself, clinging to his seclusion. Then he is visited by a figure from his past, the influential – and often destructive – art critic William Nasmyth. Is Nasmyth there (as he claims) for a portrait sitting? Or for other clandestine reasons? What ensues is a sinister and lethal struggle of wills, delivered in Pears' understated but cutting style.

Adam and Eve and Pinch Me 2001

RUTH RENDELL

One of Ruth Rendell's most quirkily titled books is also one of her most individual, adapting a real-life event – the Paddington train disaster – in a fashion that is audacious but not meretricious. It seemed that Jock Lewis was one of the victims of the crash, and his girlfriend Minty has a double cross to bear – sadness at his death, and the fact that Jock was holding all her money, which has disappeared along with him in the accident. Rendell introduces another character, a woman called Zilla who has been notified by British Rail that she is a widow. But then Minty catches sight of someone – is it the supposedly dead Jock, alive and well and up to something sinister? Rendell is always at her best when dealing with the less comfortable fringes of psychopathology, and that's what she's up to here, balancing the disparate story strands with consummate skill.

Cold Desert Sky 2018

ROD REYNOLDS

Rod Reynolds is a relative newcomer, but his third novel, *Cold Desert Sky*, is as assured as its predecessors. Reynolds is a Brit who tackles the crime-blasted milieu of post-World War II America and presents as caustic and unflinching a picture as do such grizzled predecessors as James Ellroy, a clear influence. Disgraced journalist Charlie Yates, keeping his head down in 1946 Los Angeles, becomes involved with the disappearance of two young

Hollywood starlets. The trail leads back to the real-life crime boss 'Bugsy' Siegel, who wants Charlie dead. The plot – involving Charlie dodging both the FBI and the Mob – is much enhanced by an evocative vision of a nascent Las Vegas, the perfect backdrop to the menace of the narrative.

The Smile of a Ghost — 2005

PHIL RICKMAN

Phil Rickman's highly unusual protagonist Merrily Watkins, parish priest and single mother, is working in Ludlow with a new diocesan advisory panel – along with less than congenial colleagues – when a teenage boy falls from the castle ruins to his death. Two more deaths quickly follow, and Merrily must tread the mean medieval streets to uncover a lurking evil. Rickman's smoothly turned narratives always scrupulously avoid the tweeness that his heroine could so easily lend herself to; they remain tough-minded, atmospheric mysteries, with particularly sharp scene-setting.

The Predator — 2001

MICHAEL RIDPATH

Michael Ridpath made his mark in high finance but moved from the money markets to the book market, parlaying the expertise from his earlier profession into several novels that gleaned speedy acclaim. These distinctive and strongly written thrillers owe little to his writing peers, with *Free to Trade* (1995) being the most individual. *Final Venture* (2000) concentrated more firmly on a powerful linear narrative, and, while less immediately striking than his earlier work, was probably his best-written novel. Until, that is, the appearance of *The Predator*, which made a quantum leap from the author's previous books. The novel is in two parts: a brief first part and a more ambitious second section. The deal-making training in the world of investment banks counsels that participants should take no prisoners, as colleagues Lenka and Chris discover. But a pleasure trip by boat results in the death of a trainee – and the covering up of the death has disastrous consequences. Years pass, and Chris is horrified to see Lenka die before his eyes in a street assault in the Czech Republic – and it is down to him to nail the killer. As a legacy of his earlier career, Ridpath knows all about greed and its consequences, and he weaves a moral strand into his page-turning narrative.

Alan Williams
(1935–)

When the standards of current crime and thriller writing vary between the dispiriting and the excellent – sometimes in the work of the same author – it's salutary to read again the compact body of work produced by Alan Williams, the writer son of the playwright and actor **Emlyn Williams**. It's a highly pleasurable reminder of a time when crime writing of a rare order of excellence was the norm, and a novelist such as Williams could be on consistently blistering form, book after book.

Alan Williams is among the most impressive in what might be called the **Graham Greene/Eric Ambler** school of 'Englishman at bay in sultry climes'. Williams was educated at Stowe, Heidelberg and King's College, Cambridge. He was in Hungary during the uprising in 1956, and was forced to make his way out of East Germany by clandestine means. Like several of his writing confrères, Williams had some involvement with the espionage world, working for a Munich radio station with American intelligence links (which in turn was targeted by Soviet intelligence). After becoming

Snow Hill
MARK SANDERSON

2010

Over the centuries, much blood has been spilled in the antiseptic corridors of London's Smithfield market. Although the meat market itself is now surrounded by chi-chi bars and restaurants (with nary a bloodstained apron to be seen), there are signs that it is becoming a popular literary destination in the 21st century – but the blood flowing in modern Smithfield-set novels is human rather than animal. Frances Fyfield's *Cold to the Touch* married Smithfield and murder in sanguinary fashion, but Mark Sanderson's *Snow Hill* makes that book look like *Heidi* in terms of copious bloodletting. And if that isn't enough to ruffle a few feathers, there is some startlingly graphic transgressive sex. Struggling journo Johnny Steadman receives a tip-off about the death of a policeman at Snow Hill station, and thinks his luck is in. But Johnny finds himself blundering into a dark mélange of corruption a journalist, the author wrote in Britain for the *Western Mail* and *The Daily Express*, acting as foreign correspondent in the war zones of Vietnam and Algeria, where on several occasions he was suspected of being a spy.

Long Run South (1962) and *Barbouze* (1964) announced with a flourish that a major thriller writer had arrived. The former concerns a young Englishman, Rupert Quinn, who is sick of his job and seeking escape in Morocco at the time of the Algerian war. Quinn is offered a job as a courier on a coach tour into the interior, but finds himself unwittingly smuggling arms for the rebels, as well as becoming involved with the seductive Leila, liaison officer for the anti-government forces. This is no 007-style escapist piece: after the brutal torture of Leila, Quinn, despite his crippling fear, manages to survive more through luck than judgement.

Apart from his sheer storytelling ability, Alan Williams continually shored up his novels with a totally persuasive verisimilitude, utilising authentic historical detail to create narratives that generated considerable suspense. While not achieving the immense success of **Frederick Forsyth**, Williams demonstrated, in novel after novel, that he could produce books packed with as much persuasive detail as Forsyth's *The Day of the Jackal*.

and murder at the heart of the establishment. The London of the 1930s is conjured with skill, as are the less-than-enlightened attitudes of the day (notably towards homosexuality).

Derailed 2003

JAMES SIEGEL

James Siegel manages to match finely tuned plotting with a storytelling ability that takes the reader instantly by the throat. Admittedly, he starts with a sure-fire premise: the ordinary man torn from a boring, quotidian existence and plunged into a nightmare. This scenario has served many artists well (think **John Buchan**'s *The Thirty-Nine Steps* or **Alfred Hitchcock**'s *North by Northwest*), but this is one of the most assured treatments of the theme. Charles Schine is on his way to work, conscious that his life is moving along well-oiled tracks. But then he encounters the beautiful and enigmatic Lucinda Harris, and his association with her not only pulls apart the well-ordered fabric of his day-to-day routine, it threatens his very life. Charles has to learn – very quickly – some basic survival tactics, not to mention the niceties of dealing with some very dangerous people. And it's in the latter area that Siegel really shines: his villains, from petty thugs to more urbane and dangerous *éminences grises*, are drawn with a very varied and imaginative skill, with street language rendered quite as plausibly as the exchanges involving top-level corruption.

Pieces of Her 2018
KARIN SLAUGHTER

Karin Slaughter's standalones have maintained a uniformly bravura standard over the years. And in *Pieces of Her*, which shifts between two time periods – the present and the 1980s – she makes some cogent comparisons between changing attitudes. An example is this observation from decades ago: 'Men never have to be uncomfortable around women. Women have to be uncomfortable around men all the time' – an aperçu that has undergone a considerable shift in the #MeToo era. 911 operator Andrea Oliver, who has always been intimidated by her high-achieving parents, is celebrating her birthday with her speech therapist mother Laura in a shopping mall café when a shooter opens fire and is dispatched by the cool, implacable Laura. This devastating action changes Andrea's image of her mother, whose new celebrity allows her hidden past to erupt violently into the present. To call this high-intensity thriller writing is to understate the case, but Slaughter never forgets an oft neglected tenet of the genre – keep the individuality of your imperilled protagonists always to the fore.

Nine Lessons 2017
NICOLA UPSON

There is a notable strand of Englishness (as opposed to Britishness) in the work of the talented Nicola Upson – particularly so in this seventh entry in her distinctive historical series in which the crime writer **Josephine** Tey is dragooned into service as a detective. And in this outing, apart from the felicitous evocation of the Cambridge setting, Upson references our greatest writer of ghost stories, **MR James**. Two decades after that writer chilled his colleagues at King's College with his tales, Tey is spending Christmas in a town gripped by fear because of a serial rapist. Detective Chief Inspector Archie Penrose teams up as before with Tey to solve a series of vicious murders, with the supernatural stories of James proving crucial to the mystery. As well as furnishing a superior piece of crime writing, Upson is perceptive on the place of women in unenlightened 1930s England.

Cardiff Dead   2000
JOHN WILLIAMS

This, the second part of John Williams' celebrated Cardiff trilogy, is the most individual of the three books (the first was *Five Pubs, Two Bars and a Nightclub* (1999) and the third *The Prince of Wales* (2003)) – which is no mean praise, given the sharpness of the writing on offer in all of them. Set partly in 1999 and partly in the early 1980s, the book follows the stories of journeyman rock guitar player Mazz and sometime bass player turned single mother Tyra as they cautiously attempt to rekindle their love affair. There's also a (possible) murder and a surprising amount of discursiveness for a work of concentrated urban noir. John Williams' prose may be caviar to the general, but those open to the universe he so memorably creates will find rich rewards.

CHAPTER 8

DARK PSYCHOLOGY
External – and internal – pressure

Like another once-despised popular genre, science fiction, crime novels were routinely dismissed as a medium for superficial thrills – even though both genres have always been exploited by ambitious writers for many a pertinent commentary on the darker byways of psychopathology. Crime fiction in particular has long specialised in unsparing examinations of extreme states of mind and the psychology of crime. In the 19th century, **Fyodor Dostoyevsky**'s tale of murder and detection *Crime and Punishment* (the blueprint for many a later novel, with its dogged policeman wearing down a guilt-ridden killer) demonstrated that the genre could be infinitely more powerful and penetrating than more genteel fictional forms. The books discussed below all foreground the psychology of their characters *in extremis* – but never at the expense of the plot.

Give Me Your Hand   2018
MEGAN ABBOTT

Megan Abbott's nuanced and incisive books tend to focus on the complex psychology of her characters; the subject here is female friendship, but of the most toxic kind. In her teenage years, Kit Owens is inspired by her troubled friend Diane (who nurtures a dark secret) to drive herself hard to realise her full potential. The two women develop an almost symbiotic relationship, with both pursuing a shared goal: a science scholarship on disorders related to female sexuality. But there is a catastrophic sundering of the friendship, and Diane re-enters Kit's life as a bitter rival. What follows is traumatic and life-changing for everyone concerned. *Give Me Your Hand* provides a forensic examination of the female psyche, adding further lustre to Abbott's already stellar reputation.

The Forest of Souls
2005

CARLA BANKS

The father of Carla Banks (pseudonym of **Danuta Reah**) was an East European military officer who came to the UK as a refugee during World War II, a fact that undoubtedly influenced the plot here. Helen Kovacs has been researching the Nazi occupation of Eastern Europe, although she has chosen to keep her research from her close friend Faith Lange. But then Helen is killed, much to Faith's horror. At first, Faith believes that the police have found the murderer, but then she begins to suspect that the man in custody is not the man who killed her friend. At the same time, a journalist, Jake Denbigh, has also been led to believe that there is more to Helen's murder than meets the eye; he has discovered that several war criminals disguised themselves among a group of concentration camp victims who escaped from Minsk. And it would appear that Faith's much-loved grandfather Merek may be one of these men. But who is responsible for Helen's death? This is a commanding and persuasive piece of work, in which the heroine is taken to the furthest extremes of human behaviour and forced to confront the darkness of the psyche. (The novelist and journalist **Mike Phillips** similarly uses the medium to telling effect anatomising the customary banality of evil (and, in his non-fiction, the fashion in which that evil can flourish in a totalitarian state).)

The Wasp Factory 1984

IAIN BANKS

Who could have suspected from this remarkable and disturbing debut novel the many and varied directions that Iain Banks' subsequent literary career would take? Thrillers, political suspense, social commentary and, of course, as Iain M Banks, major works in the science fiction genre. *The Wasp Factory*, however, clearly marked out the dark territory that was to be his domain. Frank Cauldhame is, to put it mildly, a young man with troubles. He is a disturbed adolescent, living in an isolated Scottish household with two other invalid males: his disabled father and his psychopathic elder brother, Eric. Of all the members of this dysfunctional family, Frank is the most tragic case. And told in the first person, his autobiography is particularly chilling. His life began with a crime: the minor one of not having his birth registered. But more significant crimes lie in his future. Apart from his utter alienation from society and its norms, he particularly disapproves of the female sex, which he regards as weak and subservient. Much of this he blames on his mother, whom he regards as responsible for his literal castration. As a young boy, he was playing with the family dog when his mother was giving birth, and the dog bit off his genitals. As the above conveys, this is not comfortable reading, and as the narrative traces its shadowy trajectory, with more and more horrific details emerging about Frank's personality, squeamish readers will fall away. They will be doing themselves a disservice, however, for as well as the wholly original first-person narrative voice, there are some jaw-dropping revelations to be found in this study of the corruption of the sexual impulse.

A Noise Downstairs 2018

LINWOOD BARCLAY

What is Linwood Barclay territory? It's the sudden, destabilising event that changes the protagonist's life – and this is very much at the centre of *A Noise Downstairs*. Connecticut professor Paul Davis is battered unconscious with a shovel when he stumbles across a colleague, Kenneth Hoffman, attempting to dispose of the bodies of two women. Hoffman is imprisoned, but Davis, traumatised, is in therapy. Eight months later, he decides to exorcise the malign influence of his colleague by interviewing and writing about him. But then Paul is awakened one night by a sound – the clicking keys of a manual typewriter. The resulting typewritten notes, he decides, may be messages from the murdered women – but to those around him, his behaviour starts to seem delusional. There may be traces here of the supernatural novels of **Stephen King**, but the real cynosure of the book comes from Barclay's particular strengths: psychological thriller writing of authority embellished with his characteristic narrative twists.

The Suspect 2019

FIONA BARTON

The lineage of the psychological suspense novel is a long and fecund one, stretching back even beyond the masterly – if baleful – influence of **Patricia Highsmith**. And the current high standing of the genre is due to such writers as the skilful Fiona Barton, who manages to take overfamiliar scenarios and transmute them into something new and striking – as with *The Suspect*. Two teenage girls disappear on a gap year trip to Thailand and their families find themselves in a well-publicised nightmare. Ambitious journalist Kate Waters, always hungry to be first with a story, has a personal interest in the situation – she has not seen her own son in several years since he left home to go travelling. And things are to become even more personal – and fraught – for Kate. As in *The Widow* (2016), Barton has the full measure of the thriller narrative. A similarly fraught examination of the past is to be found in **Alex Marwood**'s unsettling *The Poison Garden* (2019).

Eye of the Beholder 1980

MARC BEHM

Often called the private eye novel to end all private eye novels, this is much more than a gumshoe narrative. *Eye of the Beholder* is unique in combining a fascinatingly baffling puzzle and a wonderfully realised love story with a highly subjective metaphorical descent into the underworld. In just 200-odd pages, Behm covers 40 years and a massive body count as his private eye, a disturbed and sociopathic figure, relentlessly tracks down a bisexual serial murderess whose speciality is disguise. As his protagonist – always referred to as 'The Eye' – follows the killer as she murders her way through a series of moneyed partners, we are taken on a nightmare odyssey through every state in the US to a grim and disturbing climax. One thing is certain: the reader is quite unlikely to encounter anything like this again. This is unquestionably a dazzling one-off. Or it would be if he hadn't written the similarly unnerving *Afraid to Death* (1990).

EYE OF THE BEHOLDER 1999
Director: Stephan Elliott

The cinematic qualities of Behm's novel are unsurprising – he had extensive experience writing screenplays, including **Stanley Donen**'s often underrated 1963 thriller *Charade* and, rather strangely, **Richard Lester**'s 1965 Beatles film *Help!* And, in fact, his novel began life as a screenplay for **Philip Yordan**. However, Elliott's misfiring adaptation hardly does it justice; it sidelines the psychological observation of the book and transforms the obsessiveness of the plot into a simple chase scenario. Ewan McGregor, displaying little charisma, is on the trail of Ashley Judd's ruthless assassin. The globetrotting is handled flatly, and it is interesting to speculate whether Elliott was ever aware that the novel he was adapting was far richer than anything shoehorned into his rather dull movie. However, it is worth tracking down *Mortelle Randonnée* (directed by **Claude Miller** in 1983), with the delicious Isabelle Adjani as the black widow.

The Craftsman 2018
SHARON BOLTON

Sharon Bolton (who also writes as SJ Bolton) has been living a double life. While marketed as crime fiction, her novels are full of minatory and gothic shadows, inspired by **Stephen King**. The gothic is given full rein in *The Craftsman*, in which Bolton is at her best. When police officer Florence Lovelady arrested coffin maker Larry Glassbrook in 1969 he confessed to a series of child murders. But 30 years on, following Glassbrook's death, Lovelady begins to suspect that the case is not dead and buried, and as she re-examines what really happened she is forced to acknowledge that deeply sinister influences are still at work. It's not a spoiler to reveal that witchcraft is a theme here – the book is set in Pendle, notorious for its 17th-century trials, and it examines society's attitude towards those who are seen as 'different'. This is well-crafted, blood-chilling entertainment; the supernatural element is ambiguous – as it often is with Bolton – particularly in the disturbing final chapter.

The Flower Girls 2019
ALICE CLARK-PLATTS

Former human rights lawyer Alice Clark-Platts worked at the UN International Criminal Tribunal for Rwanda and is the author of such incisive novels as *Bitter Fruits* (2015) and *The Taken* (2016). *The Flower Girls* channels elements from such real-life cases as the Jamie Bulger murder (as many others have done), but weaves something new and intriguing. A child goes missing, and a clue to the disappearance may lie in a disturbing crime from two decades previously: the eponymous 'flower girls', Laurel and Primrose, were involved in a similar case in which one was convicted of murder while the other was granted a new identity. The repercussions of this earlier judgement are to have fateful repercussions in the present. Clark-Platts maintains a visceral contact with her deeply conflicted characters in an impressive piece of work.

Tell No One 2001
HARLAN COBEN

David and Elizabeth Beck return to Lake Charmaine every year. This has been a part of their lives since they were children, but a grim event destroys their happy idyll. On their 13th visit, Elizabeth is kidnapped and murdered, and David is left for dead. For the next eight years, he attempts to come to terms with the horror of these events, while Elizabeth's killer waits on death row. Then an image appears of Elizabeth on his computer screen and the years are torn away. Is it a joke? Or is Elizabeth – somehow – alive? David finds the few remaining shreds of his life ripped apart as he is hunted down while he tries to track a ghost whose message to him is a warning to tell no one. Although we are in darker territory than usual here, the lean and mercurial narrative is delivered with customary panache by a genuine stylist of the thriller genre, and Coben fans will feel that the master is very much on form.

TELL NO ONE / NE LE DIS À PERSONNE 2006

Director: Guillaume Canet

Harlan Coben admirers were distinctly nonplussed when the adaptation of his bestselling thriller *Tell No One* arrived from a French source, but the resulting film was one of the finest thrillers of its day. Without imposing a Francophile identity on the American scenario, the film channelled all the elements that made the novel so successful: initially modulated tension followed by genuinely involving suspense. The film starred an understated François Cluzet as David (renamed Alex), the paediatrician whose wife was apparently murdered by a serial killer. The spare and finely honed narrative style was thoroughly apposite – and the royal seal of approval was conferred by having Coben himself in a cameo, not that he could have known the film would be so successful.

The Murmur of Stones 2006

THOMAS H COOK

The American writer Thomas H Cook slowly and surely became a must-read author. He bagged an Edgar award for his *The Chatham School Affair* (1996) and was shortlisted for the award a further six times (plus once for a short story), most recently with *Sandrine's Case* (2013). Family life as a source of psychopathological damage is the subject of *The Murmur of Stones*, a satisfyingly convoluted tale of which Peter Straub noted: 'With this book the crime novel had moved firmly into literature.' Cook's protagonist Diana has grown up caring for her schizophrenic father, and when her own son, Jason, is discovered to be similarly afflicted, Diana stoically accepts her responsibility. But her son will always be different – a fact that Mark, Diana's husband, cannot live with. When Diana leaves her son in the care of his father for a short time, she returns to discover her son has drowned, and she cannot accept the 'accidental' verdict of the subsequent inquiry. She begins to construct a case against her husband – and soon destabilising forces of madness and death are unleashed. The late **Ross Macdonald** wrote many unsettling novels in which the family was the sum of its various cupboarded skeletons, but Cook concentrates the notion to a more deeply unnerving degree.

Burial 2009

NEIL CROSS

Are novels supposed to make us feel elated? Or is it acceptable to feel guilty and soiled, identifying with a character who colludes in the murder of a woman after some sordid group sex? If you feel the second option is one you'd rather avoid, you'd better steer clear of Neil Cross's *Burial*. Such is the author's insidious skill that we are ineluctably involved in the messy private life of Nathan, a rather sad loser, whether we like it or not. We may feel queasy at the experience, but it is possible to argue (as Cross might do in defence of his deeply disturbing novel) that the reader might feel a certain scrubbed-with-a-brush scourging after reading *Burial* – not necessarily a pleasant sensation, but… energising. As in such previous books as *Holloway Falls* (2003), Cross marries literary values to the exigencies of a page-turning crime narrative – but that's literary with a small 'l'. No flourishes here: everything is pared to the bone. Nathan, stifled in a radio journalism job and in the last phases of a disintegrating relationship, attends a party given by his right-wing radio host boss and meets the slightly deranged Bob. After some ill-advised, cocaine-fuelled (and deeply squalid) three-way sex with Bob and a stoned young girl, Elise, in a car, Elise ends up dead. An accident? Bob was the last person in the car with her. The traumatised Nathan is persuaded to bury the body, and the death goes unsolved. Nathan endures agonies of guilt, until Bob reappears in his life and tells him that the woods in which they buried Elise are about to be dug up for a housing estate. Nathan is soon making one catastrophic decision after another, with an inevitably macabre outcome.

It's easier for an author to invite identification when a protagonist has certain attractive moral or physical qualities – we can all happily imagine we're 'featur'd like him, like him with friends possess'd', but it's a more complex achievement to put us inside the skin of a no-hoper like Nathan, which is just what Cross does. When Nathan initiates a relationship with the unknowing, damaged sister of the girl in whose death he is implicated, the reader is squirming – both at his colossal misjudgement, and in the fervent hope that he won't be found out. However, there are those who won't thank Neil Cross for taking us into such moral terra incognita. But even those feeling a little grubby won't be able to deny the author's sheer mastery of his unsettling task.

Sharp Objects 2006
GILLIAN FLYNN

Gillian Flynn is as much a contradiction as the vulnerable heroine of her debut novel. Flynn claims to be white trash from the hog capital of America – but she's actually a well-spoken, sharply dressed journalist (TV critic for US magazine *Entertainment Weekly*), both of whose parents are academics. *Sharp Objects* features journo Camille Preaker, who similarly calls herself 'white trash from old money', and Camille's plausibility is no doubt due to the dual traits of her creator – though one hopes that Flynn has a better relationship with her mother than the poisonous one between Camille and the neurotic, hypochondriac Adora. The book arrived in this country festooned with plaudits – but so do many other novels. But this one lived up to the hype – and, more than that, Flynn created something fresh (if that's the word) in this steamy synthesis of Southern Gothic, literary character study and Oprah Winfrey-style grossly behaving working-class Americans. We're hooked from Chapter 1, in which the journalist heroine, ill at ease with herself and her job on a bottom-of-the-barrel newspaper, is summoned by her editor, who makes it clear that she never quite lived up to the hopes he had for her. So when he suggests she return to her home town of Wind Gap, Missouri to write about the abduction and murder

SHARP OBJECTS 2018
Director: Jean-Marc Vallée

In an era of dumbed-down TV, it's refreshing to encounter something that demands so much from the viewer and, what's more, respects our intelligence. This edgy, elliptical version of **Gillian Flynn**'s novel comes closer to **Michelangelo Antonioni**'s oblique *L'Avventura* (1960) than a conventionally linear thriller – for instance, some crucial revelations are dispensed with almost subliminally during the end credit sequence of the very last episode. What's more, the acting is top-drawer, notably Patricia Clarkson's fearsome mother and Amy Adams in a career-best performance as the troubled reporter, some considerable distance from her film appearances as Lois Lane.

of two young girls, she feels obliged to go, despite her better judgement. Camille may be from one of the most moneyed families in the town, but the sprawling mansion that is her home is where she knows she will find her demanding mother – and only being in a different city has allowed her to attain some kind of mental equilibrium. And then there's her slutty half-sister, a desperately precocious 13-year-old who has an entourage of teenage girlfriends and some kind of hold over the town. Back with her estranged mother, Camille is once again caught up in a childhood tragedy that has left her scarred, and while identifying with the murdered girls, she begins to make the wrong decisions: she has sex with the investigator assigned to the case, and even beds the prime suspect, a troubled teenager. All of this is dispatched in fascinating fashion, more Southern Gothic à la daytime trash TV than **William Faulkner**. And there's a jaw-dropping twist that you may not see coming...

The Hunting Party — 2019
LUCY FOLEY

Word of mouth remains an important element in drawing the attention of readers to provocative and accomplished writers, and Lucy Foley has been a deserving recipient of praise. Her grasp of the demands of a compelling crime narrative are on the nail in *The Hunting Party*, and if her delineation of the psychology of her characters is writ large rather than with finesse, that hardly undercuts the sheer readability of the tale she tells. A camaraderie among a group of friends forged at Oxford has survived the years, and a New Year's celebration at a secluded Scottish hunting lodge is arranged. The initially pleasant gathering leads to more than the consumption of haute cuisine – only eight of the nine friends will return home from the party. There is a serial killer on the loose...

Land of the Living — 2003
NICCI FRENCH

Nicci French is in fact the husband-and-wife team of writer **Sean French** and journalist **Nicci Gerrard**. Quality has been a hallmark of French's books from the debut novel, *The Memory Game* (1997), and *Land of the Living* is part of a sequence of impressive psychological thrillers that combine detailed plotting with masterful characterisation, particularly of the off-kilter side of human behaviour. The basic situation in this book is immediately arresting. Waking up hooded and bound, Abbie Devereaux has no conception of how she arrived at this frightening state. She is being looked after by a man whom she never sees, but who does speak to her, and what he says compounds her terror: he promises that she will eventually be killed 'like the others'. Abbie finds that her very identity is at threat along with her life, and aspects of both her career and a failing relationship with a lover come under her mental spotlight. She has a dual problem: she must fight to retain both her sanity and her life in the face of an impossible situation. If the basic premise is reminiscent of **John Fowles'** 1963 debut *The Collector*, *Land of the Living* is far more than a reworking of the theme. The authors are fully aware that the best thrillers take us deep into the minds of their protagonists, a theme French extended into a memorable psychological battle of wits in *Secret Smile* (2004). The tension and suspense are ratcheted up with total assurance, and as the narrative moves towards its conclusion, readers will have to force themselves not to rush through the pages. Forget that terrible film of Nicci French's *Killing Me Softly* (directed by **Chen Kaige** (2002)): as a literary phenomenon, judge the work of this dual-identity author on the books.

Day of the Dead 2018

NICCI FRENCH

The duo who comprise Nicci French inaugurated their Frieda Klein series, featuring an intuitive consultant psychologist, with *Blue Monday* in 2011. At a meal to launch the series, the two ironically read out a letter in which I had said 'Thank God Nicci French writes standalones and have resisted introducing a series character!' But the success of the series was unarguable, although I continue to prefer their earlier books. They brought the sequence to a satisfying end in *Day of the Dead*, with Frieda Klein finding herself in a nightmare scenario when a criminology student writes a paper about her. Frieda has been in hiding from the serial killer Dean Reeve, who is slaughtering random individuals in a ruthless attempt to flush her out, and by halfway through the book the two are grimly hunting each other. If the Klein series has not possessed the rigour of French's superb standalone novels, it has offered many pleasures, not least the development of the protagonist, and it concludes with a suitable flourish.

The Trespasser 2016
TANA FRENCH

The recalcitrant Tana French's books appear at lengthy intervals, but she is one of the most penetrating and highly regarded of psychological crime novelists – and unquestionably a cult writer of considerable reputation. Beleaguered Detective Antoinette Conway's career is on the line, but an investigation into the violent consequences of a lover's quarrel offer her a kind of redemption. *The Trespasser* is Tana French on superlative form – but when is she ever anything less?

Seeking Sanctuary 2003
FRANCES FYFIELD

Writers such as Frances Fyfield (pseudonym of **Frances Hegarty**) have found their way into the upper echelons by dint of sharp psychological observation and stylish, elegant writing. The accumulated suspense of Fyfield's books in particular is hard to resist. Her novels featuring Crown prosecutor Helen West and police detective Geoffrey Bailey have built up a steady following since they first appeared in *A Question of Guilt* (1988) and draw on the author's own experience as a criminal lawyer. But *Seeking Sanctuary* is something else; Fyfield's customary delving into the more astringent aspects of the human mind is taken to a new level of intensity here. At the reading of the will of Theodore Calvert, it becomes apparent that this strangely worded document has been calculated to perpetrate revenge on the dead man's former wife, whose pietistic homilies destroyed the marriage. The beneficiaries of Calvert's will are his daughters Therese and Anna (his fastidiously religious wife Isabelle has died), but Therese has followed her mother's unceasing injunctions to piety by becoming a nun. When an enigmatic young man named Francis appears, he quickly makes himself invaluable at Therese's convent. But soon the lives of Anna and Therese are changed irrevocably by the handsome Francis, who is not everything he appears to be, and – Fyfield warns – violent emotions can be suppressed for only a limited time. The relationship between the three central characters is expertly drawn, and the rigorous constraints of religion add a further level of repression that mirrors the secrets at the heart of this idiosyncratic narrative. Books such as this – one of Fyfield's best – and *Staring at the Light* (1999) mine the same vein of psychological acuity and dark menace as **Patricia Highsmith**, the intense quality of the prose illuminating narratives that both celebrate traditional storytelling values and explode them. And if this sounds like your cup of tea, *Undercurrents* (2000), one of Fyfield's most disturbing books, is another title worth checking out.

The Shadow Tracer 2013

MG GARDINER

Here is the talented Meg Gardiner with an abbreviated moniker and one of her best books. Her heroine, Sarah, is living quietly with her five-year-old daughter Zoe, but then she hears that the school bus has crashed. When Sarah arrives at the hospital, although Zoe is uninjured, it is revealed that she is in fact Sarah's niece; her mother, Beth, died at the hands of a malign cult known as the Worthe family. What's more, the little girl possesses an even more dangerous secret. As ever with Gardiner, we are ineluctably drawn into the desperate plight of the heroine, and the orchestration of tension is superlative.

The Dry 2017

JANE HARPER

There are times – admittedly, not very often – when a crime fiction debut makes an almost physical impact on the genre, gleaning rave reviews, selling prodigious quantities and bagging key awards. All of this happened for Jane Harper's first book, *The Dry*, which accrued mountains of praise and a Crime Writers' Association Gold Dagger for its atmospherically realised Antipodean setting and the keenly realised psychology of her cop protagonist Aaron Falk. No crime entry in the year of the book's issue caused such a stir, and Harper's name became – at a stroke – iconic in the genre.

Force of Nature 2018

JANE HARPER

The second book is always a daunting prospect for a writer, so the follow-up to Jane Harper's remarkable debut (see above) inspired in readers a mix of anticipation and trepidation. *Force of Nature* is a very different kettle of fish from its predecessor, although once again we are in a life-threatening environment. Five women on a team-building exercise take a gruelling backpack hike across Australia's Giralang Ranges – but only four return. The missing woman, Alice Russell, is of keen interest to Federal Agent Aaron Falk as she is a whistle-blower in a case he is working on. Unsurprisingly, the powerful sense of place of the first book is once again evident, with a landscape wracked by appalling weather and natural dangers proving a testing ground for Harper's conflicted characters. In the subgenre of inexplicable disappearances in Australia (e.g. **Joan Lindsay**'s *Picnic at Hanging Rock* (1967)), this is a distinguished entry.

Strangers on a Train 1950
PATRICIA HIGHSMITH

What a debut novel! Looking back on the author's career as one of the most disturbing practitioners of the psychological crime novel, it's astonishing to see how she virtually arrived fully formed with this classic of the genre. Readers are now, of course, obliged to disentangle the original novel from **Alfred Hitchcock**'s celebrated adaptation, but the effort is worthwhile – particularly as censorship restrictions of the day forced the director to soften one key element in the narrative. Two men meet on a train. Guy Haines is the reader's surrogate: relatively normal, locked in a loveless marriage with the unpleasant Miriam. But Charles Bruno is a psychopath, and when he offers to swap murders with Guy (Bruno will dispose of Miriam if Guy will murder Bruno's inconvenient father), Guy doesn't take the proposal too seriously – until Miriam is killed. Soon, Bruno is asking Guy to complete his part of the bargain and commit murder himself. This, of course, is the point at which novel and film diverge. Hitchcock, in the cinema of the early 1950s, could not have his hero behaving in such a fashion, whereas Guy is forced by the unremitting assault of the mad Bruno to do just that. Nor could Hitchcock dwell on the homosexual undercurrent of the two protagonists' relationship. This is the first example in Highsmith's work of the dark moral equivocation that became her stock-in-trade – and the reader's changing attitude towards the apparently normal Guy is the kernel of the book. Bruno may have a mother who may be partly responsible for what he is, but how much can readers identify with Guy, either before or after he commits murder?

Patricia Highsmith
(1921–95)

Patricia Highsmith is an unlikely heir to **Henry James**, but, like her celebrated predecessor, Highsmith was an unromantic American writer of rarefied sensibility, living in Europe and treating her characters with a cool, Olympian detachment. Highsmith was born Mary Patricia Plangman in Fort Worth, Texas in 1921, and she inaugurated her career with the remarkable *Strangers on a Train* in 1950, instantly setting a benchmark she often had to struggle to maintain. Her books gleaned celebrated admirers such as **Graham Greene**, who particularly admired her perfectly formed short stories. In such books as *This Sweet Sickness* (1960) and *A Suspension of Mercy* (1965), Highsmith mapped out a terrain that was very much her own. Eschewing detectives as protagonists, she takes the reader inside the sensibilities of characters whose carefully constructed lives are often torn apart by the violent disruptions that – she hints – are not too far beneath the surface of most people's quotidian existence. Her admirers are most fond of the books featuring the totally amoral conman Tom Ripley (notably *The Talented Mr Ripley* (1955) and *Ripley Under Ground* (1970)) but, splendid though these are, the author's unquestioning sympathy for her murderous character is often dismaying. Highsmith bridled at the suggestion that Ripley was a psychopath, and her manner as an interviewee was often fearsome. Her body of work established a yardstick for edgy psychological crime writing that most of her successors can only aspire to – as well as inaugurating the current genre of domestic noir.

STRANGERS ON A TRAIN   1951

Director: Alfred Hitchcock

While the two disagreed, there is no doubt that **Raymond Chandler's** work on the screenplay of one of Hitchcock's supreme masterpieces ensured its classic status. There are, of course, caveats: Farley Granger is a rather bland Guy, and the censorship restrictions (see page 187) undercut the truly subversive nature of **Patricia Highsmith's** novel. But the command of cinema and narrative is Hitch at his best, and the presence of the superb Robert Walker as the immensely seductive gay psychopath Bruno ensures the creation of one of the cinema's great villains.

Confessions of a Romantic Pornographer   2004

MAXIM JAKUBOWSKI

As well as being one of the most respected editors in the crime genre, bringing back into print many neglected names, and proprietor of the much-missed London mecca of crime enthusiasts, Murder One in Charing Cross Road, Jakubowski is an idiosyncratic writer of fiction. His phantasmagorical novels synthesise a variety of elements into a heady brew indeed: hardboiled idioms, skewed psychology and the unabashedly erotic. It is the author's controversial treatment of the latter that has earned him the sobriquet 'King of the Erotic Thriller', but this understates the literary qualities of his work, with many clever postmodern concepts informing the always unsettling narratives. A good introduction is *Skin in Darkness* (2006), a blistering anthology collecting three of the author's most arresting tales in a melange of unbuttoned sexuality and noir sensibility. In *Confessions of a Romantic Pornographer*, the protagonist is Cornelia, a woman who has earned a living as a stripper but is also an adroit assassin. She is commissioned to track down the last, incomplete manuscript of the dead writer Conrad Korzeniowski (the literary reference to **Joseph Conrad** is not accidental).

Half Broken Things
2003

MORAG JOSS

Morag Joss bagged the Crime Writers' Association Silver Dagger for this novel, a book that built on the achievement of such earlier successes as *Funeral Music* (1998) and *Fearful Symmetry* (2000). *Half Broken Things* is concerned with the lies we tell ourselves to conceal unpalatable truths. The protagonist, Jean, is a house-sitter, living a pointless life as her mature years approach. But in Walden Manor, her current house-sitting assignment, she has access to sealed cabinets and cupboards – which also gives her, she finds, access to proprietorship of the house. As she settles into her new role, she acquires a couple of unsuccessful individuals like herself, and a semblance of happiness seems possible in this damaged group. But the past erupts into the present, wreaking destruction. Joss readers will have an inkling of the dark treats in store here: the elegance of her prose probes the loamy ground of the darkest human behaviour.

Flesh and Blood
2001

JONATHAN KELLERMAN

Jonathan Kellerman's Alex Delaware thrillers have amassed a devoted following, and the reasons for this are readily apparent. In such books as his debut *When the Bough Breaks* (1985) and *Over the Edge* (1987), Kellerman used his background as a paediatric psychologist to create a profession for his hero of total verisimilitude. Kellerman also writes textbooks on clinical psychology; in fact, the Kellerman clan – including wife Faye and son Jesse – almost seems to have cornered the market in psychiatrically based tomes, building up a catalogue of disturbing case studies of the disturbed. In the first books, Alex, though officially retired, took on cases referred to him by Milo Sturgis of the LAPD, and a recurrent theme was that of damaged children suffering from emotional or physical abandonment by their parents – and that is, to some degree, the theme of *Flesh and Blood*. When Alex Delaware first sees Lauren, she is a teenager with all the usual problems – moody, uncommunicative, resentful of her parents. But years later, at a bachelor party, Alex finds himself watching two strippers go through a graphic display – and one of them is the unhappy Lauren. Then she disappears and we're off into familiar Delaware territory, delivered with all the aplomb we expect from the reliable Kellerman. In earlier books, Alex was occasionally portrayed as being a little too prescient, but Kellerman has given his hero a satisfyingly conflicted emotional life, and his personal involvement here gives *Flesh and Blood* a strong underpinning of drama that counterpoints the central mystery and sharpens it at every point. Only Kellerman's earlier, non-Delaware, *Billy Straight* (1998) displayed the same degree of penetrating psychological insight and unvarnished view of human nature – and here the plotting is even more assured.

The Burning Air 2013

ERIN KELLY

Erin Kelly has written several novels of psychological suspense, of which this one is perhaps the most disturbing – and also the one that lays out most clearly the corrosive areas in which she moves. Her first two books, *The Sick Rose* (2011) and *The Poison Tree* (2010), borrowed titles from William Blake, but *The Burning Air* takes on most tellingly Blake's line about a destructive and dark secret love.

It is a family tradition for the MacBrides to visit Devon each bonfire night, but there is a pall over the latest gathering. The matriarch of the family, Lydia, is dead. Her husband, the customarily sober Rowan (a retired headmaster) is drinking himself into a stupor. The family is in meltdown, with the eldest daughter Sophie watching her marriage crumble, while grandson Jake (who is mixed race) has the police breathing down his neck. But there is one ray of optimism: Felix, Sophie's brother, has brought along his beautiful new girlfriend Kerry, who charms the unhappy family. She appears to be a natural babysitter, and Sophie leaves her daughter in her care. But both Kerry and the baby disappear. Has she abducted the baby? Or have both of them been taken? The distraught Sophie turns on her brother, claiming that the missing girl could – for all they know – be some kind of psychopathic monster. And the truth, when it arrives, is shocking.

When even the best writers of standalone novels of suspense are obliged to observe commercial imperatives and adopt continuing characters (for instance, **Nicci French**), one can only hope that the talented Kelly is not persuaded by her publisher to write about a series protagonist, be they damaged male detective or alcoholic female forensics specialist. Not that there isn't plenty of damage at the heart of this book – Blake's 'invisible worm' has been doing his worst in the MacBride family – but the balancing of the very different characters has an intensity similar to that of chamber music, with each player proving as crucial as the last the author has presented for our attention. If Erin Kelly has not quite attained the rarefied psychological astuteness of a **Barbara Vine** (and if the final revelation is a touch underwhelming), she has proved herself to be among the most accomplished and pin-sharp of writers at work in the crime genre, with family dysfunction a speciality. And William Blake can continue to be a source of appropriate future titles: 'Cruelty has a human heart'? 'Hire a villain'?

She Lies in Wait 2019

GYTHA LODGE

She Lies in Wait is a striking debut, even though the basic premise is a familiar one. In 1983, six school friends spend a night in a forest. They have a single rule: that anything can happen. But it isn't just erotic abandon that envelops the group – one of their number, Aurora, is not to return from the evening. Three decades pass, and the legacy of those fateful events hangs heavily on all of those present. And then Aurora is found. What follows is, needless to say, traumatic for all concerned. Lodge takes plot devices we may have seen before, but manages to invest them with a new and unsettling charge.

Bad Things 2011

MICHAEL MARSHALL

Michael Marshall (who also writes as Michael Marshall Smith) has firmly established himself as a very unusual practitioner of the modern thriller, following an innings as a superlative writer of fantasy. A four-year-old boy, Scott Henderson, walks out onto a jetty in Black Ridge, Washington State and is not seen again. His father, John, is devastated but struggles on – until he receives an email from a stranger who says he knows what happened to the boy. John decides to return to Black Ridge but, instead of a satisfactory solution, chaos is unleashed, and John is likely to lose what little is left to him.

Candyland 2001

ED McBAIN AND EVAN HUNTER

As Ed McBain, he created the groundbreaking 87th Precinct series, whose innovations were much plundered by TV series such as *Hill Street Blues* and crime writers including **Patricia Cornwell**. As Evan Hunter, he wrote such indelible 1950s novels as *The Blackboard Jungle* (1954) and the screenplay for **Alfred Hitchcock**'s *The Birds* (1963, adapting a **Daphne du Maurier** piece), but with *Candyland* the names of both personae appear on a novel for the first time (is this a publishing first?) to produce an authoritative piece of work – and both are pseudonyms, with the writer's real name being **Salvatore Albert Lombino**. Architect Benjamin Thorpe has an obsession: unknown to his family, he wanders the New York streets in the wee small hours looking for dangerous female companionship, and he has a confrontation in a seedy brothel that will change his life. A teenage prostitute known as Heidi has crossed paths with him, but ends up strangled and viciously mutilated in an alleyway. Thorpe is the obvious suspect… but is he too obvious? McBain had stated that he felt many readers had forgotten who Evan Hunter was and so he decided to give this writing persona another spin, but the portmanteau writing credit was actually something of a marketing ploy. This is a crime novel of some considerable psychological power – and, in fact, it doesn't read like either of the 'two' authors' previous books.

The Guilty Party 2019

MEL McGRATH

The scenario of Mel McGrath's *The Guilty Party* may sound familiar, but the writer can always be relied upon to come up with unusual variations. The novel follows four university friends who witness a sexual assault on a stranger and agree not to intervene. A couple of months later, at a weekend away, their inaction comes to haunt them. Was the victim really a stranger? And why was her body discovered in the Thames? Will the secrets they are keeping from each other ultimately destroy them? This is a novel about the power and limitations of friendship in the face of a devastating crime.

Vanish in an Instant 1952

MARGARET MILLAR

When speaking of crime writers from earlier eras, a mention should always be made of the excellent – and neglected – Margaret Millar, whose *Beast in View* (1955) and *Vanish in an Instant* are reminders that she should be best remembered for her own considerable accomplishments rather than as the wife of novelist **Ross Macdonald**. In *Vanish in an Instant*, a young girl from an upscale background is found in a snowstorm at night, drunk and covered with someone else's blood. Is she a murderess? Millar's simultaneous command of psychology and plotting is a thing of wonder.

Trust No One 2018

ANTHONY MOSAWI

A young girl is locked in a sensory deprivation tank, forced to listen to a repeated message: 'My name is Sara Eden.' It is the only thing she knows about herself. Anthony Mosawi's harrowing *Trust No One* may lazily use a hackneyed title (there are at least seven books currently in print so designated), but there is nothing second-hand about the film industry-trained writer's debut novel. Years pass, and Sara – now an adult – has begun to piece together things about her enigmatic past. She knows that she was subjected to her ordeal by sinister, clandestine figures who are now trying to track her down. As we – along with Sara – learn about secret government manoeuvres involving the use of her particular abilities, we are barely given pause for breath in a hurtling narrative that is squarely aimed at the blockbuster market. The furious action wisely allows the reader no time to consider the implausibility of the scenario – even though Mosawi's book is based on a real-life figure: Helen Duncan, a Scottish medium who came to the attention of Winston Churchill during World War II.

I Was Dora Suarez 1990

DEREK RAYMOND

Of all the highly impressive Factory novels by Derek Raymond, cult writer and famous Soho drinking club habitué (including *He Died with his Eyes Open* (1984) and *The Devil's Home on Leave* (1985)), *I Was Dora Suarez* is one of the most original. The Factory books were narrated by the unnamed Sergeant and set in the Metropolitan Police's 'Department of Unexplained Deaths', codenamed A14. In his autobiography, the author (the Raymond moniker was a pseudonym of **Robert Cook**) chose this book as the pinnacle of his career and pointed out the unpleasant effect the writing of this frequently painful book had on his psyche. The raw materials of the novel are unsettling indeed: necrophilia, extreme and graphic violence, and various other odd forms of sexual behaviour (including a felching club) coexist in these bitter pages, but the final effect is cathartic – a genuine purging of evil through a confrontation with its furthest reaches. The murderer in *Dora Suarez* is a psychotic who decapitates his luckless victims before arranging them in bizarre tableaux to facilitate his black rituals of mutilation. Astonishingly, Raymond is able to take us inside the mind of a monster and, if not sympathise, perhaps understand.

Bellevue Square — 2018
MICHAEL REDHILL

Bellevue Square is a doppelgänger novel haunted by ghosts – not so much **Edgar Allan Poe** (who created the most memorable malign double in 'William Wilson'), but **Guy de Maupassant**, Redhill's literary hero (this book is the first in a projected trilogy called 'Modern Ghosts', after the Maupassant story). The same unsentimental view of human nature as the French novelist's – and the sense that chaos is just a worrying step away – informs *Bellevue Square*. The novel is narrated by Jean Mason, who runs a bookshop in Toronto, and at first we warm to her witty, self-deprecating voice, even though we may be wary of the novel's first sentence: 'My doppelgänger problems began one afternoon in early April.' Jean learns from a client that she has been spotted in a different place with a slightly altered appearance, and cracks swiftly begin to appear, both in the structure of the narrative and in Jean's increasingly fractured psyche. By the time she is accused of murdering a woman friend, she is already scanning the faces of those around her in search of her terrifying human shadow. Is she losing her mind? Certainly, those around her seem to be – the surface of reality becomes increasingly viscous as the book moves towards its phantasmagorical climax.

Lost — 2014
MICHAEL ROBOTHAM

It could hardly be said that Michael Robotham's earlier career as a writer prepared him for the field of the tough and clever thriller; the author earned his crust as one of the best ghost writers in the business. Were you amused by the cuttingly funny Scouse first-person voice in Ricky Tomlinson's autobiography? In fact, that was a highly professional piece of ventriloquism on the part of the talented Robotham. Did you really think that was Geri Halliwell's breathy confessions coming to you directly from the side of her pool in her memoirs? No, once again, it was the invisible Mr

R, sitting in the next deckchair to the bikini-clad Ginger Spice, copying down every pearl of wisdom so that he could write the book in what would appear to be her tone of voice. (One of these personalities was happy to acknowledge Robotham's ghost-writer role: guess which one...)

But although the author was much in demand for his ghosting skills, his preference was for the more personal style of thriller writing that he first essayed in the highly adroit thriller *The Suspect* (2004). That book had more individual style and imagination than anything in his previous clandestine efforts, and it's good news for readers that *Lost* is every bit as diverting as its predecessor. The central theme here is amnesia: Detective Inspector Vincent Ruiz is a sufferer, and the dangerous fashion in which he cracks the mystery of his past makes for an extremely involving 400 pages. The author has done his homework on transient global amnesia, in which a key event is erased from the memory. Ruiz has been shot and dumped, apparently dead, in the Thames. He can remember being assigned to a kidnapping case that went disastrously wrong: the kidnapper may have been jailed, but the child died and the body was never found. When Ruiz wants to reopen the case, he meets a wall of opposition – and his colleagues accuse him of faking amnesia. But he comes to believe that the child is not dead after all, and that her father is a sinister Russian mafioso. The answer may be found by Ruiz teaming up with a psychologist who can help him relive that fateful night...

Ghost of a Flea
2001

JAMES SALLIS

The reader is forever being cast adrift in this disorientating novel by one of the American grand masters of the genre (who was kind enough to write a foreword for my book *American Noir*). Questions of memory and the past are handled with the allusiveness of **Marcel Proust**, although it has to be said that Sallis is a considerably more plot-focused writer. The central character is black writer-cum-detective Lew Griffin, who first appeared in *The Long-Legged Fly* (1992) – the books in the series all feature insects in the title. As the novel starts, Lew has given up the craft of novel writing and is living an off-the-grid existence in New Orleans as a part-time journalist. A friend in the police force has been shot during a holdup, and at the same time his relationship with the intriguing Deborah has collapsed. Only engagement with criminal activity and the darker side of the human psyche can kickstart Lew's life and propel him from his torpor. While Sallis never forgets the imperatives of the crime narrative, this is a far more deeply philosophical book than most people will be used to encountering in the genre – and some will find it forbidding. Literary references abound, and those seeking a straightforward, uncomplicated narrative should look elsewhere. But for fans of more ambitious writing, Sallis is a key author. In fact, this jazz-loving polymath has also written a critical work on pulp writers, *Difficult Lives* (1993), and a biography of pioneering black crime writer **Chester Himes** (2000).

Sleep
2019

CL TAYLOR

Readers are in something of a state of siege when it comes to psychological crime novels at present, but certain books – with perfect justification – jostle their way to the top of the pile, principally via insidiously involving narratives and sharp characterisation. For some time, CL Taylor has been shifting huge quantities of her various entries in the genre, and *Sleep* is a solid example of her craft. Her protagonist, Anna, is suffering from serious insomnia accompanied by night terrors – a legacy of a dark incident in her past. Seeking escape from her tormented life, she takes a job in a hotel on the secluded Scottish island of Rum, but her thoughts of escape are short-lived. A variety of guests arrive at the hotel and – in a knowing nod to **Agatha Christie** – all of them are harbouring secrets. One of them, needless to say, is a killer – and it isn't long before the luckless Anna finds that her card has been marked. CL Taylor studied psychology at the University of Northumbria, and that is perhaps why the mental processes of her characters ring true despite the conscious artificiality of the situation. Such writers as **Karin Slaughter** have commended Taylor's skills at producing claustrophobic tension, and it should be noted that such praise is appropriate here – Taylor is a dab hand at shredding the nerves of the receptive reader.

Disordered Minds
2003

MINETTE WALTERS

With nary a false step, Minette Walters burnished her reputation as one of the most powerful yet nuanced practitioners of the psychological thriller. In fact, Walters' winning streak had continued for an unfeasibly long time, with each book slightly more ambitious than its predecessor. She

Minette Walters
(1949–)

What happened to Minette Walters? As a crime writer, she began at the top and stayed there for many years, sustained by her creativity in the genre. Her first book, *The Ice House* (1992), won the John Creasey Best First Crime Novel award, with subsequent books such as *The Sculptress* (1993) and *The Scold's Bridle* (1994) similarly gleaning prizes. This critical acclaim was matched by an enthusiastic following among readers, possibly because Walters disregarded advice given to her when setting out: she had been told to avoid 'one-offs'. Walters was assured that **Ruth Rendell** could only do it because she was so well known, and she still had to use the **'Barbara Vine'** alter ego to get away with it. But even early in her career, Walters was very reluctant to write a series. When *The Sculptress* won the American Edgar award and *The Scold's Bridle* won the Crime Writers' Association Gold Dagger, she felt that her 'right to be different' was confirmed. Walters' sales were prodigious – which suggested that many readers responded to the deeper psychological profile she could give to characters only appearing in one novel, along with a sense of closure.

built up a total picture of modern Britain that cut across all social strata, while still using the apparatus of the crime novel, but *Disordered Minds* reached into darker areas of the human psyche than usual. Howard Stamp is an educationally subnormal man who died in prison by his own hand in the 1970s, after apparently murdering his grandmother. But, years after his death, anthropologist Jonathan Hughes looks into the case again, not persuaded of Stamp's guilt. He meets a man convinced of the dead man's innocence, but as the move towards the truth begins, the real murderer is keen to retain the status quo – violently. All of this couldn't be further from the cosy Home Counties mystery that gently comforts the reader; Walters is in the business of disturbing us, but not merely out of a desire to shock. As ever, she depicts fully rounded, conflicted characters with whom it's impossible not to identify, and there are truths spoken here about society. Walters' readiness to tackle larger themes than her more parochial English peers remains her most salient attribute.

The Shape of Snakes (2000) was a provocative example of the author's interest in incorporating social issues into her novels: the plot is set in motion by the death of a black woman living on the edge of society. By having a woman from a different social background taking an interest in the death (which no one else believes to have been a murder), Walters was able to tackle issues of commitment and white, middle-class guilt, while avoiding making her protagonist a noble doer of good deeds.

There was much speculation as to why Minette Walters appeared to abdicate from a natural position – the heir apparent of **PD James** and **Ruth Rendell** (a position finally filled by **Val McDermid**). The reason was that Walters had undertaken a radical new writing departure into the field of the historical novel. *The Last Hours* (2017) was relatively well received, but admirers of her earlier work still wistfully wish that she will once again take up the crime writing baton.

In a Dark, Dark Wood

2015

RUTH WARE

Many people (to their regret) have incautiously said yes to a friend's invitation to a stag or hen night. They can be pretty grisly occasions, but thankfully few of them have the grim consequences of the gathering in Ruth Ware's *In a Dark, Dark Wood*. Ware's central character Leonora (who narrates the novel) finds that there is a price to be paid for deviating from her generally antisocial behaviour when she accepts such an invitation. The event, held in a Frank Lloyd Wright-style house in an isolated forest, brings up betrayals and guilt from the past and proves to be a recipe for catastrophe. While functioning as an exemplary crime novel, there is much keenly observed social comedy here – not a million miles away from the acerbic work of **William Trevor** – and spiky characters are a particularly strong suit for Ware. Crime readers may have more than enough on their plates at the moment, but there is no ignoring this provocative writer.

Hello Bunny Alice 2003
LAURA WILSON

Laura Wilson has never been happy staying within the parameters of the conventional crime novel; in *My Best Friend* (2001), she brilliantly deploys a device in which the novel is narrated by three strongly delineated protagonists. However, her succeeding book, *Hello Bunny Alice*, returns to the single narrative voice. Alice has displayed her wares as a bunny girl, and has been engaged to the celebrated comedian Lenny Maxted. The novel opens with her receiving an anonymous clipping concerning a corpse discovered in an English lake. Slowly – and tantalisingly – Alice discovers that her involvement in this mystery will change her life. The other cleverly realised plot strand involves Maxted's former comedy partner, Jack Flowers. After Maxted commits suicide, Flowers is cut adrift and unable to make it on his own. The way in which Wilson ties together the various storylines is masterly, although some patience may be required – Wilson is not interested in providing a popcorn read. But the demands made on the reader are more than repaid. Her more recent books, such as 2017's *The Other Woman* (with its sardonic tone), have demonstrated her desire to avoid repeating herself.

Rear Window 1942
CORNELL WOOLRICH

Woolrich, one of the great workhorses of the pulp era, turning out an immense body of work for minimal rewards, is a writer whose name conjures up psychosis, threatening cityscapes and plots of tortured complexity, and there are few of his many books that are not worth attention. Having said that, it is easier to appreciate his work as a totality, rather than through an assessment of individual books. *Rear Window*, however, is a good entry point and exemplifies many of the pulp writers' interest in psychology and aberrant behaviour. Photographer Hal Jeffries is virtually imprisoned in his apartment after he breaks his leg, and he begins to clandestinely observe his neighbours from his window. Slowly, he becomes convinced that one of his neighbours has murdered his wife, and his attempts to prove this turn out to be very dangerous indeed. While **Alfred Hitchcock** made much more of the voyeuristic elements of the scenario, Woolrich's novel can also be read as a metaphor for the way in which fiction writers construct scenarios from observing the traits and sometimes intriguing activities of people around them. Woolrich is no stranger to the quirkier elements of human behaviour, and it's that as much as the adroit plotting that makes this short story (originally titled 'It Had To Be Murder') work so well.

REAR WINDOW 1954

Director: Alfred Hitchcock

Undoubtedly one of Hitchcock's greatest films, *Rear Window* investigates the very process of watching in a voyeuristic fashion – much as the film's audience is doing. The celebrated 'transference of guilt' theme has its richest exploration here, with James Stewart exemplary as the troubled, housebound hero. But more apparent than in the book is the nagging suspicion that the supposed crime is purely a figment of the frustrated voyeur's imagination, adding a further psychological twist. Interestingly, the studio settings actually enhance the claustrophobic feel of the movie, and only **Michael Powell**'s notorious *Peeping Tom* (1960) approximates Hitchcock's examination of the dark pleasures of voyeurism.

CHAPTER 9

PSYCHOPATHS AND SERIAL KILLERS

As discussed in Chapter 6, bestselling American crime writer **Patricia Cornwell** was clearly bemused when her attempts to prove that the great English painter Walter Sickert was, in fact, Jack the Ripper were met with massive scepticism and scorn in the UK. After all, Cornwell had spent jaw-dropping amounts on research (buying – and forensically examining – Sickert paintings, hiring experts, etc.), and it can hardly have been a ploy to sell her book on this nigh-obsessive quest (after all, Cornwell needs no help with her sales figures). So – she wondered – why the UK hostility? Actually, the answer is straightforward: Jack the Ripper is not only claimed as the first serial killer in history, but he was (presumably) British and a national icon, however bloodstained and psychopathic. But the US need hardly worry; after all, the massively successful serial killer novel was virtually created by an American – and one of prodigious skill at that. But **Thomas Harris** is by no means the only proponent of this most modern of literary forms – nor, indeed, the inventor of the genre. For every cynical Hannibal Lecter imitation there are a dozen writers forging innovations, such as the highly successful **Mark Billingham**, **Lauren Beukes** (with *The Shining Girls* (2013)) and **Tess Gerritsen**, not to mention non-crime writers such as **Cormac McCarthy** with his lacerating *No Country for Old Men* (2005). It's a field that is now becoming overcrowded... time for a cull, maybe?

Hour Game
2004
DAVID BALDACCI

After the floodgates were opened for the serial killer genre by **Thomas Harris** and his cannibalistic aesthete Hannibal Lecter, this book may have you groaning 'Not another serial killer thriller!' But if this is your response to *Hour Game*, you're not reckoning on the fact that this one is written by David Baldacci, a man who would rather give up writing than repeat himself – or, for that matter, copy other writers. Yes, a lot of the territory here has been traversed before, but this isn't Thomas Harris-lite – *Hour Game* bristles with a bushel of innovations that obliterate any sense of overfamiliarity, even if the grisly opening chapters come perilously close to things we've often read about before. Ex-secret service duo Michelle Maxwell and Sean King, having inaugurated a partnership that best combines their individual skills in *Split Second* (2003), look into the disappearance of some highly confidential papers owned by the well-placed Battle family. The decomposed body of a young woman is found, arranged in a bizarre position, and two teenagers are bloodily slaughtered while having sex in a car. It seems that a serial killer is at work – and King and Maxwell soon learn that the Battle family (needless to say) is involved up to their necks. So what's new here? Baldacci has come up with something we haven't encountered before: a murderer who mimics the methods of a series of famous serial killers, such as the highly intelligent psychopath Ted Bundy and several other real-life monsters. And it goes without saying that the horrific narrative is dispatched with maximum effectiveness by the author.

The Beautiful Dead
2017
BELINDA BAUER

Her publishers might have cheekily borrowed the winged insect cover motif from **Thomas Harris**'s *The Silence of the Lambs* (1988), but if any writer can give the American master of the macabre a run for his money, it's the formidably talented Brit Belinda Bauer. From her first book, the award-winning *Blacklands* (2010), onwards, she has demonstrated two notable characteristics: a plucky willingness to take the crime novel into completely unexpected new territory, and a sure-fire grasp of exactly what it takes to unsettle the reader. In *The Beautiful Dead*, Eve Singer's career as a TV crime reporter is flagging and she realises that there is a dividend for her in the fact that a serial killer is plying his bloody trade in London. But the murderer, who sees himself as an artist, is soon counting on Eve to showcase his gruesome 'performances'. Bauer admirers will find she's on typically scabrous form here.

The Killing Habit 2018

MARK BILLINGHAM

Those who consider Mark Billingham to be one of the most reliable practitioners of the modern British crime novel point to some added value: he has been building up through his books an all-embracing picture of modern British society. *The Killing Habit* utilises real-life crime – the 'Croydon Cat Killer', allegedly responsible for the death of hundreds of animals and still at large. Tom Thorne, satisfyingly un-PC as ever, is not pleased to be handling the case of a similar pet killer. Working once again with Nicola Tanner – one of the few people who knows how to deal with him – Thorne begins to suspect that, rather than building from animal to human murder (the standard trajectory of the psychopath), the killings may represent a reversal of this scenario. A host of unsolved cases may lead the duo to a malignant opponent. As ever with Billingham, a rich cast of characters and tense situations are marshalled with panache, leading to a final terrifying encounter.

The Crucifix Killer 2013

CHRIS CARTER

The Crucifix Killer has been caught and convicted. The monster who claimed seven victims – subjecting them to torture before ending their lives – had a grisly trademark: he carved a double crucifix emblem into the necks of his prey. But he has been executed, and his bloody endeavours are at an end. Detective Robert Hunter should know this – he's the man who took the killer down, at some emotional cost to himself, and he has struggled to put the disturbing game of cat and mouse with a devious psychopath behind him. But the nightmare isn't over, it seems – a horrifying series of new murders has begun, as bizarre and operatically sadistic as those committed by the Crucifix Killer. And the crucifix mutilation of the victims is back. What makes this even more devastating for Hunter is a niggling fear he has long nurtured: that he brought the wrong man to justice. Can Hunter (the name Chris Carter has chosen for his protagonist is no accident) salve his own conscience by tracking down the real murderer? And will he be able to keep his own personal demons in check? (Failing to nail this lethal criminal is only the most egregious of several professional mistakes that have marred his career.)

If ever there was a writer with the requisite credentials to pull readers down the darkest corridors of criminal psychology, it's Chris Carter. His background in studying criminal behaviour and pathology at Michigan University – not to mention his stint as a member of the State District Attorney's Criminal Psychology Unit (where he interviewed and studied a variety of serial killers) – has ensured that his writing has a chilling, and totally plausible, authenticity. But sporting the background knowledge for a novel such as *The Crucifix Killer* is only half the battle; is Carter a skilled enough wordsmith to keep us transfixed for the length of a novel – and to overcome a formulaic plot? That Carter's book is such a relentless page-turner firmly demonstrates two things: the author has all the right novelistic smarts to put us firmly on the side of his tormented detective; and there is plenty of life in the serial killer narrative.

Good Samaritans 2018

WILL CARVER

While it attempts to blend a variety of different genres, including domestic noir, Will Carver's tense novel perhaps functions most successfully in the serial killer arena. His protagonist Hadley is looking for comfort from the Samaritans, but the call back she receives is from a troubled individual called Seth who deals with his insomnia by dialling people at random. What follows is a truly disturbing series of events involving a strong cast of characters – including a murderer who uses bleach on his victims to remove forensic evidence. The shifting tone of the book, which initially appears to be inconsistent, proves to be very cannily organised, and Carver draws together all the various strands with great skill.

Bad Men
2003

JOHN CONNOLLY

Irish-born Connolly's treatment of human degradation and retribution has quickly established him as one of the most provocative writers in the UK; utterly unafraid to alienate his readers, his books plunge us into a dark world where nothing is safe, nothing is secure. *Bad Men* synthesises two of the writer's favourite themes: the devastating effects of crime as performed by men of zero morality and a dark vision of the supernatural. Sanctuary was once the name of what is now known as Dutch Island, near the coast of Maine. In the novel's prologue, massive bloodletting in the 17th century establishes it as a very black place indeed, but now the area has been tamed. The one lawman, the outsized Joe Dupree, finds his role hardly a challenge to his abilities, but he senses that the ghosts of the past are merely dormant. Things soon change after the arrival of a man called Moloch, an immensely cruel criminal who is sprung from jail by his team of killers. While he has been doing time, his wife and son have settled on the island, and things become very hard for them after the breakout. And Dupree and his rookie female colleague soon have to deal with both the living and the dead.

As always with Connolly, this is pulse-racing stuff. His series of books featuring the detective Charlie 'Bird' Parker (which kicked off in 1999 with *Every Dead Thing*) are essential reading for his admirers, but this headlong dive into macabre crime is the perfect test for readers uncertain as to whether or not they can stay the course of a Connolly novel.

American Psycho
1991

BRET EASTON ELLIS

Occasioning an outraged furore on its first appearance, this biting black comedy was certainly never conceived as a 'crime' novel in the genre sense, but rather as a satire on the Wall Street 'preppy' generation for which brand names were all-important, and anything, but anything, could be acquired. Patrick Bateman is the archetype: he has everything – good job, fat salary, Brooks Brothers clothes, charm and intelligence. It seems he is also a psychopath, treating his 'hardbody' one-night stands with increasing disdain, until he discovers the simple delights of killing them after, or preferably during, sex. And, as the novel progresses (with wonderful discursive passages on brand names, clothes, the quality of one's business card, etc.), the more dangerous the situation, the more exciting Bateman finds it. What makes the book truly disturbing – and controversial – is the first-person narration, which not only absolves the author from any moralising judgements, but, indeed, reverses this position, Bateman as narrator treating the escalating body count (and increasingly horrific means of achieving it) as matter-of-factly as a shopping spree on Fifth Avenue.

AMERICAN PSYCHO — 2000

Director: Mary Harron

Interestingly directed by a woman, this (superficially) most misogynist of texts naturally proved unfilmable – even by modern cinematic standards. Chain-saw eviscerations during group sex were challenging enough, but the real problem lay in the internal monologue, which only the novel could really provide. The movie played to the audience who read the book as a slasher-fest and who would normally never consider reading a 'literary' novel. Casting innocent-faced Christian Bale against type (at the time) as Bateman was daring, but the ironic satire that lies behind the novel was dulled, although the elements that remained granted the film a cult status.

A Quiet Belief in Angels — 2007

RJ ELLORY

Roger Ellory had been a midlist writer who watched in amazement as his career went through the roof with this book. Of course, such dizzying success carries a price: reader expectations for successive books were high, and the massive authority of *A Quiet Belief in Angels* (not to mention its ambitious panoply of American society – Ellory is a Brit who sets his books in the US) made it a difficult act to follow – not helped by fallings-out with his fellow writers. In *A Quiet Belief in Angels*, Joseph Vaughan has grown up in the 1950s, his teenage years affected by a series of mutilations and killings of young girls in his cloistered rural village. His attempts to safeguard his community and classmates as part of a group called 'The Guardians' fail. Years pass and the killer appears to be dead, but, inevitably, the past returns in grim fashion. Ellory has been productive since this novel, but without recapturing its impact.

Silent Terror/Killer on the Road — 1986
JAMES ELLROY

If Thomas Harris hadn't pipped him at the post, this little-known early Ellroy masterwork would be regarded as *the* seminal modern serial killer text.

Thomas Harris
(1940–)

History can repeat itself. While Thomas Harris's novels *Red Dragon* (1981) and *The Silence of the Lambs* (1988) represented a double whammy that permanently reconfigured the crime fiction genre – and, as a subsequent by-product, the entire field of horror fiction – the successful films of the books led to a shift in popular crime/horror cinema. *The Silence of the Lambs* in particular inaugurated a sea change in thriller cinema – and its effects are still being felt to this day, not least in the freighting in of extra layers of texture and resonance into narrative structure. Many writers – whether in the crime or the horror field – envy Thomas Harris his unparalleled storytelling abilities (something I celebrated in a book on the novelist). But Harris has gone beyond being merely a top-flight writer: he is now a brand, and his sanguinary serial killer novels are the defining works of the

Photo: Robin Hill

Probably inspired by the high-profile activities of real-life serial murderers Ted Bundy and David Berkowitz ('Son of Sam'), the novel intelligently penetrates the mind of an apparently motiveless mass murderer on the move. Known as the 'Sexecutioner', Martin Michael Plunkett takes deep personal pride in his job. And we know this because of Ellroy's chilling use of a first-person narrative. As often with this author, we almost find ourselves in sympathy with his protagonist as he wreaks his awful revenge on the demons that torment him and the uncompassionate universe he sees around him. Until, that is, he teams up with a like-minded serial killer, in a twist that seemed unlikely at the time, but which increasingly seems not far from the mark.

---

genre. His name is routinely invoked for every new writer who attempts to cover the same territory – mostly in vain, as there is only one Thomas Harris, and each novel (along with the inevitable film adaptations) featuring the super-intelligent aesthete and monster Hannibal Lecter is an event.

The Silence of the Lambs (1988) was ground-breaking, but the first outing for Thomas Harris's music- and art-loving psychopath, *Red Dragon*, is as comprehensively gripping as its successor. As well as the brilliantly delineated villain, there is a strong hero in ex-FBI profiler Will Graham, assigned to such cases as Lecter's because of his ability to intuitively place himself in the mind of monsters. As Harris had demonstrated in previous thrillers (such as *Black Sunday* (1975), with its increasingly relevant terrorist atrocity theme), his grasp of narrative structure is unswerving, and the careful, precision-timed parcelling out of plot information is one of the author's trademarks. But while others have attempted to imitate such tropes, none possess Harris's consummate mastery of characterisation – everybody in the novel is limned with painterly skill, whether in a few well-chosen lines or (like the monstrous Lecter) at satisfying length. Readers quickly realised that they could forget the imitators who swiftly followed: Thomas Harris was the *locus classicus*. (After a lengthy hiatus, Harris published an underwhelming non-Lecter novel in 2019, *Cari Mora*.)

The Silence of the Lambs   1988

THOMAS HARRIS

Red Dragon (1981) was the first book to introduce the cultivated serial killer, and its plot – including a unique symbiotic relationship between detective and prey – was very swiftly being imitated. *The Silence of the Lambs*, however, took the phenomenon to a whole new level. Clarice Starling is a trainee FBI agent, working hard to discipline mind and body. She is sent by her boss, Section Chief Jack Crawford, to interview the serial killer Dr Hannibal Lecter, who is kept under the very tightest security, to see if he is prepared to help in the case of a killer using a bizarre modus operandi. The inexperienced Clarice is no match for the Machiavellian Lecter, and he begins to play highly sophisticated mind games with her – while the other monster – the one still at large, known as 'Buffalo Bill' – continues to ply his bloody trade, chopping up women and skinning them. It's not hard to see why this book achieved such acclaim: it is, quite simply, a tour de force. And while Lecter may not be like any serial killer who ever walked the earth (most are dull, stupid men with predictably abused or damaged childhoods, from a less privileged social class than Lecter and unlikely to lecture on Italian Renaissance art), he remains the most iconic uber-criminal in modern fiction.

THE SILENCE OF THE LAMBS   1991

Director: Jonathan Demme

Given the phenomenal success of his novel, **Thomas Harris** could certainly have survived a maladroit cinema adaptation when the inevitable movie was made. In fact, Harris was lucky: Jonathan Demme got everything right, orchestrating the tension with the skill of a latter-day **Alfred Hitchcock**. The real success of the movie, however, lies in the casting: Jodie Foster, impeccably incarnating the out-of-her-depth Clarice against Anthony Hopkins, masterly as the urbane Lecter – even sidestepping the Hollywood cliché of casting all well-spoken intelligent villains as Englishmen by developing an indiscernible but distinct American accent. Above all the film (like the novel) is intelligent, a sharp contrast to most dumbed-down slasher Hollywood fare.

Dexter in the Dark 2007
JEFF LINDSAY

If you are a fan of one of the most outrageously entertaining shows on TV, you clearly have a taste for the darkest of humour; *Dexter* is not for those of a conventional mindset, or, for that matter, the squeamish. Dexter Morgan is an alienated serial killer – a psychopath who is barely in touch with everyday human emotion and who relates to those around him with an outsider's eye. The twist, however – author Jeff Lindsay's masterstroke – is that Dexter is also a Miami cop, an expert on the bloodiest of murder scenes, and the killers he clandestinely eliminates are monsters, far worse (he thinks) than he is.

The third of Jeff Lindsay's novels is *Dexter in the Dark*. After the macabre delights of *Darkly Dreaming Dexter* (2004) and *Dearly Devoted Dexter* (2005), that's surely a cause for celebration, isn't it? Well, yes... up to a point. At a grisly crime scene (with two Miami college students immolated and decapitated in ritualistic fashion), Dexter Morgan has a queasy realisation that he is up against a force more ruthless than the Dark Passenger, his own motivating inner voice. And then something happens that begins to change the shape of the narrative: Dexter's Dark Passenger falls silent. Something else is to change Dexter's life: he is about to marry his fiancée (who has two young children), but more to provide cover for his homicidal activities than to turn him into a normal human being. The gruesome killings continue – and Lindsay gives the grim force behind the murders a name – 'It' (this is only the first of several reminders of **Stephen King**'s supernatural horrors). All of this is as entertainingly idiosyncratic as usual, but the tone of the book is very different from its predecessors – not least for the puzzling absence for most of the novel of the Dark Passenger, so effectively used in the earlier outings. Some readers may query Lindsay's decision to make Dexter's guiding force a supernatural being rather than just a metaphor for the more plausible psychosis resulting from the hideous death of his mother. But there are still quirky pleasures galore here, such as Dexter's panicky dealings with his two newly acquired children, who take a very unhealthy interest in his bloody hobbies. Is he to have a couple of youthful apprentices?

The remarkable Mr Ripley

What, you may ask, is a box for the character Tom Ripley doing in this chapter rather than alongside the entry for his creator, **Patricia Highsmith**? The answer is simple: he is a serial killer – at least in terms of the prodigious body count that he racked up over several books. But can a calculating fictitious killer be cool? Well, some 20 years before Hannibal the Cannibal was projected onto our collective consciousness as a cultural icon, Patricia Highsmith wrote a remarkable book, *The Talented Mr Ripley* (1955), which follows Ivy League preppy Tom Ripley living an unfocused expat life in Europe. To our grim fascination, Ripley exploits his enormous capacity for guile, deceit – and murder.

Following his first appearance, Ripley is comfortably ensconced in France, has a beautiful partner and is busily collecting paintings but occasionally needs extra funds. Who would stoop so low as to convince a vulnerable man that he has a terminal disease in order to get him to

A Cold Mind 1983

DAVID LINDSEY

It is an unrecognised fact that Lindsey was among the first crime writers to focus on serial killing and the motivations behind such behaviour, not least its frequent links with sexuality. This novel was the first in a short series featuring Houston cop Stuart Haydon, who has a way with multiple murderers, and it was rapidly followed by *Heat from Another Sun* (1984). Quite why Lindsey didn't capture the public's attention in the way that Harris was to do is a mystery, and it would be several years before *Mercy* (1990) really established his reputation. Nevertheless, he is a powerful writer, whose ability to create a tense narrative that balances the problem confronting the cop with the many problems motivating the murderer remains remarkable.

carry out a crime for you, to ensure his family's future (*Ripley's Game* (1974))? Who would connive to encourage an innocent child to be a killer (*The Boy Who Followed Ripley* (1980))? As Ripley regularly reappeared in Highsmith's work – in contrast to her impeccable standalone novels – it became clear that she was not prepared to make moral judgements concerning her amoral protagonist, even as the body count continued to rise. What's more, it was apparent that the author had a certain tacit admiration for Ripley's Gordian knot approach to problem solving.

Of course, this is the fascination of Ripley, a fascination played out in a handful of films (all accomplished) based on Highsmith's character, films that display an interesting array of portrayals of this most ambiguous of anti-heroes: Alain Delon in *Plein Soleil* (**René Clément**'s 1960 version of *The Talented Mr Ripley*), Dennis Hopper in **Wim Wenders'** *Der Amerikanische Freund* (*The American Friend* (1977), based on *Ripley's Game*), and Matt Damon in **Anthony Minghella**'s glossy and assured *The Talented Mr Ripley* (1999).

Deviant Ways 2000
CHRIS MOONEY

While Mooney's persuasive and edgy thriller may recycle familiar elements from the overcrowded serial killer genre, it largely does so with imagination and invention. After all, there are now so many dogged cops with fragile private lives stalking (and being stalked by) grimly ingenious psychotics, it's impossible to avoid certain ideas popping up again and again. The real question remains: can an author make the material seem fresh? Largely speaking, Mooney pulls off the trick with real panache, and his troubled ex-FBI profiler hero Jack Casey is a very plausible protagonist, even if his struggle with a life shattered by an earlier encounter with a psychopath is one we know well from many another thriller. His nemesis is the Sandman, a terrifyingly prescient madman who is slaughtering not just one individual at a time but whole families and whole neighbourhoods. His method is explosives (shades of the Oklahoma bombings), and he knows quite as much about Jack Casey as he does about his well-researched victims – and particularly how to really twist the knife in his opponent. Mooney kicks off with a joltingly orchestrated prelude, and the simmering threat of appalling violence keeps the reader transfixed throughout. Unless you've a serious case of serial killer fatigue, this may be one for the shopping list.

The Rottweiler 2003

RUTH RENDELL

Ruth Rendell turned out a body of work notable for both teasing ingenuity and seamless literary style. She is the British writer who is closest to her American predecessor **Patricia Highsmith** in dealing with the darker corners of human psychology, and that's very much the case here. London is at the mercy of a vicious serial killer, dubbed the Rottweiler after bite marks are found on the neck of his first victim. When a second murder takes place near an antique shop, the narrative focuses on the owner of the store, Inez Ferry, and her neighbours, a rich gallery of character portraits. Inez herself is wasting her life, forlornly watching videos of her dead actor husband, while the Asian woman who works for her, Zeinab, enjoys an active sex life, having liaisons with two separate men while living with a third. Then there is the solitary Jeremy, while Will, a boy with learning difficulties, lives in an unhealthy relationship with his aunt. But this is not standard whodunnit territory, with a hidden killer and stubborn detective; as before in Rendell, the mystery is almost casually thrown away with the killer's identity dispensed relatively early. What concerns her is the insidious progress of evil in the human soul; **PD James** may have been the writer with the more religious sensibility, but Rendell has the bleaker vision, with the murderous possibilities of human behaviour given full rein in her dark world. A blackmailer, too, is stirred into this heady brew, and this character is a mirror image of both the killer's evil and the less savoury aspects of the other protagonists. With the minutely observed portraits of Inez and her neighbours counterpointed by the horror of a seemingly psychopathic killer, we're in safe hands with Rendell.

The Killer Inside Me   1952

JIM THOMPSON

Stanley Kubrick was one of the famous admirers of this remarkable novel, and its terrifying picture of a psychopathic consciousness conveyed in the first person has not dated. It is still a truly disturbing read. Lou Ford is the deputy sheriff of his modest Texas town and is well thought of by the small populace. The general view of him is that he is efficient but unexciting – but Lou has a very dark secret, which he describes as his 'sickness'. His adopted brother was blamed for an act of violence that Lou committed when he was younger, but this twisted part of his psyche is on the point of emerging again, and the consequences can't be shrugged off onto others this time. In some ways, Thompson's technique here echoes

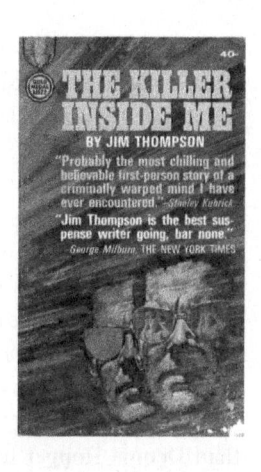

THE KILLER INSIDE ME   1976

Director: Burt Kennedy

While Burt Kennedy was an efficient director of no-nonsense westerns, he was signally out of his depth in this misguided adaptation of **Jim Thompson**'s classic, which is a shame, as the actor playing the tormented Lou was the excellent Stacy Keach, a man more than able to deal with troubled inner states when the right director could channel such things. On this occasion, Burt Kennedy wasn't that director, and Thompson's novel is traduced.

THE KILLER INSIDE ME   2010

Director: Michael Winterbottom

I attended a showing in Nottingham of Michael Winterbottom's unsparing film of Jim Thompson's novel in the company of the director, and he was unfazed by the walkouts over the film's unsparing violence (notably a gruelling scene in which a woman is systematically and dispassionately beaten to death), but those hardy souls who stayed the course were rewarded with an uncompromising film that did justice to the nihilistic vision of Thompson's original novel, with Casey Affleck grimly memorable as the psychopathic anti-hero.

that of the existentialist novelists **Albert Camus** and **Jean-Paul Sartre**, with the cruel, affectless prose conveying intense inner turmoil through indirect impressions. Once read, *The Killer Inside Me* is not easily forgotten.

Dead Calm 1963
CHARLES WILLIAMS

Williams, like **Charles Willeford**, is an unsung hero of the US post-pulp mystery thriller and can often be found sidling alongside him on the bookstore shelves. His career started with Jim Thompson-style small town 'erotic' thrillers such as *Hill Girl* (1951) and *The Diamond Bikini* (1956), and his *Hell Hath No Fury* (1953; filmed impressively as *The Hot Spot* by no less than **Dennis Hopper** in 1990) bears comparison with his mentor. *Dead Calm* is one of several sailing thrillers that Williams produced. Newlyweds John and Rae Ingram are cruising in the Pacific, an idyllic dream come true until, becalmed in the doldrums, they drift across a sinking hulk. They rescue the lone passenger, but not before the experienced navigator John senses something is clearly wrong. The young survivor claims that his wife and another couple on the vessel died of lead poisoning. In a dramatic reversal of roles, John Ingram is left on the sinking death vessel, while the clearly psychopathic survivor makes off with his wife on the honeymooner's yacht. A tense slow-motion chase ensues, with Rae doing her best to outwit her unwelcome sailing companion, while John uses all his maritime skills to come to her rescue. Genuinely spine-chilling and enormously suspenseful.

DEAD CALM 1989
Director: Phillip Noyce

Australian 'new wave' director Noyce introduced a family tragedy as the reason for the Ingrams' cruise, giving a certain edge to the relationship between John (Sam Neill) and his young wife (introducing... Nicole Kidman). The photography and pace is superb, as is Billy Zane as the unhinged killer, and Noyce wrings every drop of suspense he can out of a small cast and beautifully placid ocean setting.

CHAPTER 10

IN THE BELLY OF THE BEAST
Criminal protagonists

While – theoretically – most readers of crime fiction don't actually commit the bloody murders or ambitious thefts they enjoy reading about, there's no denying the frisson produced when we put ourselves inside the consciousnesses of these ruthless protagonists. In the cinema, **Alfred Hitchcock** seduced us into feeling how exhilarating it was to identify with a criminal – and feel suspense over whether or not they'll be caught – and we fell for this strategy every time, however impeccably law-abiding our instincts. And this moral equivalence has long been the principal stock-in-trade of the best crime writers. Some authors moved exclusively in this dark universe – **Patricia Highsmith**, for instance, with her murderous dramatis personae. And admirers of **Ruth Rendell** often feel that her best work lies in her books *sans* the doughty Inspector Wexford, where the central characters perform terrible, destructive deeds. In the crimefighter-led novel, we feel the compass of universal order will rest at the correct point by the final page; it's a more disorienting experience to be dropped into the psyche of a murderer or a thief – individuals who (more often than not) have a tragic destiny. There is, however, a fragile sense of morality at work here, however off-kilter: if we're ever tempted by the world of crime, writers such as **Elmore Leonard** (with his luckless protagonists) and **Bill Beverly** will quickly disabuse us of the notion that this is a glamorous life.

Here's a batch of top-notch writers who, despite our ordered, non-transgressive lives, put us into the heads of individuals who live life at the very edge...

The Killing of the Saints 1991
ALEX ABELLA

With a US population built on the 'melting-pot' foundations of different races, religions and cultures, a novel such as Alex Abella's *The Killing of the Saints* is instructive. Two crack-head losers plan a jewel-shop robbery, which goes horribly wrong, resulting in mass, unmotivated slaughter. What makes this book so disconcerting is not the drug use but the influence of santeria religious ideas on the killers, where effectively all responsibility for their actions can be placed on a deity and the cult that exists behind it. Conceived by the Cuban-born author as an examination of one of the many subcultures that constitute modern America, on its publication this powerfully written book nevertheless had a prescient feel in a post-9/11 world.

Brothers in Blood 2018
AMER ANWAR

Brothers in Blood is a tough crime thriller set in West London's Asian community. Zaq Khan, an ex-con, is working a dead-end job at a builders' yard. All he wants to do is keep his head down and put the past behind him. But when Zaq is forced to search for his boss's runaway daughter, he finds himself caught up in a deadly web of deception, murder and revenge. With time running out and pressure mounting, Zaq has to find the missing girl before it's too late and, if he does, keep her – and himself – alive long enough to deal with the people who want them both dead. Anwar grew up in West London and is both a winner of the Crime Writers' Association Debut Dagger and a recipient of an Eric Ambler award from the Society of Authors' Foundation.

Dodgers 2016
BILL BEVERLY

A key modern crime novel in which a teenage drug dealer in Los Angeles is dispatched by his boss to murder a judge. This brilliantly written study of violently corrupted young lives is both biting social document and crime narrative. Beverly (who has the manner of a quiet American academic – which he is) was widely considered the crime find of the year in which the remarkable *Dodgers* appeared, and he bagged the Crime Writers' Association Gold Dagger along with a slew of other prizes. Since the appearance of the book, Beverly's reputation has grown prodigiously; it's rare that a debut novel has had quite the impact of this one.

The House of Wolfe 2015
JAMES CARLOS BLAKE

There are so many disparate elements crammed into Blake's remarkable novel that it is at times in danger of bursting at the seams. But just when the reader might think that the author has over-egged the pudding in this catalogue of kidnappings, torture, gunplay and death, he unerringly steers the helter-skelter narrative back on course. And there is a highly distinctive voice at work; admittedly, **Elmore Leonard** and **Cormac McCarthy** seem to be in the DNA here, but Blake is his own man. The rain is pouring down in Mexico City when the members of a wedding party are kidnapped at the mansion of the groom's family. Low-rent gangster El Galán has ambitions to join a major cartel, and sees the kidnapping as a PR stunt as much as a money-maker. But one of the captives belongs to a family of outlaws, so things are about to become chaotic and bloody. *The House of Wolfe* is cogent and exhilarating.

No Beast So Fierce 1973
EDDIE BUNKER

Eddie Bunker was the real thing. 'Mr Blue' in **Quentin Tarantino**'s signature 1992 film *Reservoir Dogs*, Bunker was a battered ex-con who knew all too well the inside of a penitentiary. His writing had both the raw energy and dark poetry of writers with a more heavyweight though still shady literary reputation, such as **Jean Genet**, **William Burroughs** and **Charles Bukowski**. In the small cadre of American prison writers, Bunker was *numero uno*:

he had lived the life, and this bleak and gripping novel about an ex-con's fraught attempt to deal with the depressing prospect of going straight after a lengthy spell inside is both mercilessly unsentimental and utterly gripping. As Bunker's anti-hero begins the slow and inevitable slide back towards crime, the reader's guts are twisted as painfully as they are when reading the novels of other great lowlife chroniclers such as **Nelson Algren** (with whose *Never Come Morning* (1942) this book shows some similarities). Intriguingly, Bunker makes the prospect of a straight, crime-free existence for his born-under-a-bad-sign protagonist more terrifying than the exhilarating return to lawbreaking, however disastrous the prospects of the latter may be. Bunker spent some 30 years of his life in and out of prison, and his writing – with its echoes of a broken home and alcoholic father – is never reassuring. But it is always razor-sharp and coolly observed.

STRAIGHT TIME 1978

Director: Ulu Grosbard

For a commercial Hollywood movie, Ulu Grosbard's adaptation of **Eddie Bunker**'s novel is truly audacious in its complete refusal to elicit sympathy for its ill-fated ex-con protagonist as he moves through a bleak and unyielding universe; but perhaps this was one of the reasons why the film was a commercial failure. Dustin Hoffman underlines this decision with an uningratiating performance that is both understated and powerful, even if the final effect of the film is dispiriting (and slightly dull).

Maura's Game 2002

MARTINA COLE

Martina Cole immediately established herself as a bestselling voice in crime fiction when her debut thriller *Dangerous Lady* appeared in 1992. That book introduced us to her tough and canny protagonist Maura Ryan, queen of the underworld, who returns in *Maura's Game*, now bent on going straight as she has salted enough away from her crime days to be comfortable. Needless to say, all her good intentions go up in smoke when she finds that she can't leave her old life behind – her old associates won't let her. In prose that is always blunt and incisive, Cole weaves her spell throughout this scabrous narrative. Maura is an exuberantly characterised heroine, and the supporting cast enjoys equally gritty handling from the author.

The Final Country 2001
JAMES CRUMLEY

Among modern practitioners of the American hardboiled crime genre, few would deny that the late James Crumley is in the upper echelons. His hard-edged, racy prose, his dangerous, quirkily drawn characters and – most of all – his exuberant narrative skills pretty comprehensively see off the competition, although he is surprisingly little known outside the US. But such supremacy brings a price: reader expectations for each new novel meant that Crumley had to raise the stakes in each successive outing. The first chapter of *The Final Country*, featuring a dangerous head-to-head with a shotgun in a redneck bar, instantly makes it clear that we are in for vintage Crumley, every bit as grimly diverting as such earlier winners as *Bordersnakes* (1996) and *The Mexican Tree Duck* (1993). Enos, Crumley's tough anti-hero, is out of jail and on the trail of the partners in crime who set him up. But a drug dealer pulls a gun on Enos and ends up dead, so the police are set to add murder to Enos's charge sheet. The one person who can save him from a death sentence is Crumley's long-term protagonist, low-rent, 50-something private investigator Milo Milodragovitch – but Milo is struggling (as so often before) with corrupt politicians, heavy-duty crime bosses and two women keen to get him into bed, despite his bad back. Crumley once called himself 'the bastard son of **Raymond Chandler**', but *The Final Country* is a reminder that he was an individual talent: the plotting here is outrageously inventive, while a very dangerous Montana is created with skill. Milo is one of the most strongly realised characters in Crumley's fiction, and, as always, the heady cocktail of drugs, violence and dark humour makes for an irresistible read.

The Day of the Jackal 1971
FREDERICK FORSYTH

The problem for an author who creates a ground-breaking, highly distinctive book early in their career is the singular one of following it up, and it has to be said that nothing Frederick Forsyth has written since *The Day of the Jackal* has matched this remarkable thriller. But that's not to say that Forsyth's subsequent career is not studded with some remarkable successes. *Jackal* is, of course, a book with one of the most unusual premises in all crime/thriller fiction – a notion that would be described in Hollywood parlance as 'high concept'. An anonymous Englishman is hired in the early 1960s by the Operations Chief of the paramilitary OAS to assassinate the French President, General Charles de Gaulle, and thereby alter the political landscape irrevocably. With this premise, Forsyth set himself an intriguing task: the reader knows that de Gaulle was not assassinated, so how can suspense be maintained throughout the novel when we know that the mission is doomed to failure? As in **Geoffrey Household**'s *Rogue Male* (1939), this is, of course, the audacity of the novel: Forsyth makes the tradecraft of an assassin's work utterly fascinating. With every stage of the planning and execution assiduously detailed, we suspend our knowledge of the inevitable outcome – or, more precisely, begin to wonder how such a professional killer will fail to change the course of history. The methodical detail of the book has been copied many times since – not least by Forsyth himself – but never with such success, although books such as 1972's *The Odessa File*, still exert a powerful grip. Another, less acknowledged triumph of the book is the way in which we are involved in the activities of a protagonist whose humanity is ruthlessly suppressed.

THE DAY OF THE JACKAL — 1973

Director: Fred Zinnemann

The considerable success of Zinnemann's film consolidated that of the novel, with the honours evenly divided between the director's cool and efficient approach to his material, a clever and fastidious script by Kenneth Ross, and the charismatic performance by Edward Fox as the super-efficient assassin. The most surprising thing about the success of the film is that it did not turn Fox into an international star, although he has subsequently enjoyed a strong career as a character actor. The novel was filmed again in 1997 as *The Jackal*, with Bruce Willis as the eponymous killer. While Willis turns in a creditable performance, almost everything that made the earlier movie memorable is jettisoned by director **Michael Caton-Jones**.

Brighton Rock — 1938

GRAHAM GREENE

Even in the 21st century, this remains one of the most blistering and galvanic pictures of urban crime in all British literature. When not addressing the problems of guilt (Catholic or otherwise), Greene remains fascinated by the extremes of human behaviour, and his teenage gangster Pinkie, cutting a violent swathe through the seaside underworld of Brighton, is one of the great monsters of fiction, inarticulately wrestling with the religious faith that is merely a source of negativity and retribution as he jockeys for position against what prove to be insuperable odds. The details of gang war in Brighton are brilliantly delineated, with Pinkie's violent killing of a man in the early chapters marking him out as a young man not to be trifled with. But set against the terrifying Pinkie is the figure of Ida Arnold, blowsy but sympathetic, and determined to bring about revenge for the death of a man she knew but briefly. Ida could easily have been a sentimental figure, but Greene is, of course, much too good a writer for that and creates a fully rounded, confused but positive character who acts as the perfect counterweight to the teenage hoodlum. The celebrity of the novel is fully justified, and the moral qualms of all the characters – even the most irredeemable – are marshalled with immense skill. Many non-religious readers are put off by the Catholicism in Greene's books, but there is never a sense of evangelism: for Greene, belief merely alters the quality of misery for those who possess it. Graham Greene was pleased with the fact that he was not considered a good advertisement for the Catholic Church, and he lost his faith towards the end of his life.

BRIGHTON ROCK 1948
Director: John Boulting

Even today, the razor-wielding violence of John Boulting's seminal British gangster film has a considerable impact. It's intriguing, therefore, to muse on the fact that we are familiar with a censored version of the film, softened after the moral guardians of the day threw up their hands in horror. But while Boulting does sterling work, working from **Graham Greene**'s own script of his novel, it's Richard Attenborough's truly unpleasant – but fascinating – Pinkie that remains in the mind, a British gangster to set beside the memorable portrayals of James Cagney and co. No accident, then, that Attenborough went on to play other memorable monsters in **Bryan Forbes'** *Seance on a Wet Afternoon* (1964) and **Richard Fleischer's** *10 Rillington Place* (1971). An updated remake directed by **Rowan Joffe** in 2010 with Sam Riley as Pinkie was less successful.

The Last King of Brighton   2011
PETER GUTTRIDGE

It seems a million years ago that Peter Guttridge was one of the sharpest and wittiest writers of comic crime that the UK has produced. He's still an excellent writer, but his territory has shifted – not that his sequence of Brighton-set crime novels (of which *The Last King of Brighton* is the second) dispenses with humour, but the tone is decidedly darker, as the world presented to the reader is a much more dangerous one than any of the author's lighter novels featuring beleaguered detective Nick Madrid. As in the acclaimed first volume in the new sequence, *City of Dreadful Night* (2010), we are in a benighted Brighton that is every bit as menacing as that conjured by **Graham Greene**. Criminal kingpin Dennis Hathaway maintains a successful criminal empire by a combination of ruthlessness and greasing of police palms. His son, John, has no idea how his father makes his money and pursues the customary teenage enterprises of the 1960s: playing in a group and seeking sexually available girls. But as he reaches 17, John is made aware of the corruption on which his father's legacy has been built. In the present day, John is now in charge of his father's empire and has learned just how the world works. But then a man is found brutally murdered on the South Downs, having been tortured to death – and this act of monstrous violence will have a considerable effect on John's life. Guttridge combines pithy and evocative scene-setting with dialogue that has the ring of authenticity, and this book is every bit as visceral as its predecessor in his Brighton sequence.

Night and the City   1938
GERALD KERSH

Unquestionably the key book by the dizzyingly prolific British pulp-meister Gerald Kersh, *Night and the City* is a heady, rich delight. Critical attention came late – but when it did, there was a definite sense of a wrong being righted: despite the very mixed nature of his achievements, at his best Kersh was a considerable writer. Harry Fabian lives life at the very edge, ducking and diving through a grittily realised London, playing both ends against the middle as he tries to make his mark as the leading wrestling promoter in the city. Harry needs money – just a hundred pounds, but scams and blackmail aren't paying off for him. Can he squeeze the dosh out of a corrupt nightclub owner and his predatory wife? As Harry's enemies close in and his options narrow, he begins to assume a genuinely tragic status. If you only ever read one novel by Gerald Kersh – guess which one it should be?

NIGHT AND THE CITY — 1950
Director: Jules Dassin

Night and the City has inspired two films, the classic 1950 film noir starring Richard Widmark and Gene Tierney, filmed in London by blacklisted American director Jules Dassin, and **Irwin Winkler**'s 1992 workaday remake set in New York and starring Robert De Niro and Jessica Lange. Dassin's phantasmagoric film still completely eclipses the indifferent remake, with Richard Widmark's nervy, career-defining performance unassailable.

Swag 1976
ELMORE LEONARD

The best entry point for Leonard remains his mid-period work (1970s–1980s), and such books as *Fifty-Two Pickup* (1974) will demonstrate to any reader why Leonard is thought of so highly. In *Swag*, a highly entertaining outing by Leonard, two bottom-feeding crooks, Frank and Stick, are taking a crash course in armed robbery and trying to gain the necessary experience while knocking over liquor marts and other small joints. They have coined the 'Ten Golden Rules for Armed Robbery', but when they start to bend these rules themselves, trouble is in store. As lean and efficient as the ever reliable Leonard can deliver: just reading this book is in itself a crash course in how to write the very best modern crime fiction. Leonard is particularly good on the banality of crime and its practitioners: no criminal masterminds here, just none-too-efficient low-level types trying to behave in a vaguely coherent fashion.

The Drop 2011
HOWARD LINSKEY

Many of the best crime fiction novelists – from **Elmore Leonard** to **Donald Westlake** (when writing as **Richard Stark**) – are well aware that

Elmore Leonard
(1925–2013)

Elmore Leonard's influence on modern crime fiction is incalculable. In fact, that sentence can be expanded to say that his impact on modern popular culture has moved his name out of the ghetto of crime writing into wider areas. **Quentin Tarantino** is a fan, and even before he filmed an Elmore Leonard novel, the filmmaker's best work (such as *Pulp Fiction* (1994)) demonstrated the influence of the Master. But while Leonard's quirkily plotted, ironic tales of criminal lowlifes suffering various reverses of fortune have most of what one might expect in contemporary crime writing, there is one aspect of his books in which he reigns supreme: dialogue. None of his rivals, however prestigious, have Leonard's gift for rich, idiomatic and often very funny dialogue, and the way his characters speak has been much imitated. Interestingly, his early career as a writer of sharp westerns has now been re-evaluated, even by those of us who knew it only through the excellent Paul Newman movie *Hombre* (1967; directed by **Martin Ritt**) – which has elements of Leonard's later stripped-down crime work. But, ah, those crime novels! *Fifty-Two Pickup* (1974), *Unknown Man No. 89* (1977), the complex *LaBrava* (1983)... pick up any one of them and you'll see why 'Dutch' Leonard enjoys godlike status among crime aficionados.

---

the withholding of moral judgements on their violent characters is a risky endeavour. It's undoubtedly true that stripped-down prose about totally amoral characters performing lethal actions can have an exhilarating effect, but those readers who are not criminals themselves (the majority, one would have thought) might be likely to feel alienated from such protagonists. But when the trick can be pulled off, the result can be writing that leaps off the page in its lacerating forcefulness. This is very much the case with Howard Linskey's *The Drop*, a classic British gangster novel that evokes and matches some of the best writing in the genre, notably the iconic *Jack's Return Home/Get Carter* (1970) by **Ted Lewis**, in its use of an unromanticised northeast England setting. In fact, it's a measure of Linskey's audacity to go up against Lewis in using a milieu that was so thoroughly colonised by the earlier novel, but such is Linskey's authority that we admire both his chutzpah and his ability to stand comparison with any of his predecessors.

White-collar criminal David Blake works for the gangster Bobby Mahoney, relishing his comfortable lifestyle. But then a lot of money – the eponymous 'drop' – goes astray, and Blake finds himself in the frame, with extremely dangerous results a possibility. All of this is handled with great panache, and it's clear that Linskey is a writer worthy of attention. **Simon Kernick** – no slouch himself in this area – said of the book: '*The Drop* is a brutal, hard-hitting debut which opens up Newcastle's dark, violent underbelly like a freshly sharpened stiletto.'

Sunburn 2018

LAURA LIPPMAN

Laura Lippman's diamond-hard prose and quirky characterisation epitomise the best in American crime writing, but *Sunburn* represented something new for her: a touch of **Anne Tyler** (there are echoes of Tyler's astringent portraits of American families) and also of the hardboiled writer **James M Cain** – this is a modern take on his blue-collar narratives.

Polly walks out on her husband and daughter to lead a new life as a waitress. She is pursued by her husband and a shadowy figure who hires a laconic detective to track her down. Soon, Polly and the detective, Adam, are all over each other. We're a third of the way into *Sunburn* before Lippman begins to tell us what's really going on, but by then we are mesmerised by her combustible cocktail of the erotic and the malign. (For full disclosure, I should point out that the novel features a sleazy lawyer called 'Barry Forshaw'…)

The Sudden Arrival of Violence   2015

MALCOLM MACKAY

Few novelists in the last decade have enjoyed such comprehensive acclaim among the critical fraternity as the young Scottish crime writer Malcolm Mackay. His books (the first of which was *The Necessary Death of Lewis Winter* (2013)) suggested a Scottish equivalent of the hardboiled **James M Cain** (author of *Double Indemnity* (1943)): a writer who didn't waste a word but who had a certain poetic sensibility, as evinced by the titles of the other two books in his trilogy, *How a Gunman Says Goodbye* (2013) and this acerbic final volume, *The Sudden Arrival of Violence*. That debut, *The Necessary Death of Lewis Winter*, burst upon the scene with incendiary impact, uneasily placing the reader in the mind of a hitman. While using the familiar trappings of the crime novel, the book was still utterly original. What makes all three novels in the trilogy particularly impressive is the terrifyingly laid-back, authentic toughness – surprising, coming from a quiet, unassuming author from Stornoway (where Mackay still lives).

Mackay has conjured an astringent vision of the Scottish underworld, brilliantly sustained throughout these three books. Crucially, he has not forgotten the importance of pithy characterisation, particularly where his relentless protagonists are concerned. In this third book in the sequence, the author draws a variety of strands together, but not in a too schematic fashion. Calum MacLean is working for two criminal bosses and is always watching with the closest intensity, alert for the weaknesses that will give him an advantage. But as he begins to arrange his retirement, a gang war breaks out between one of his bosses and a bitter rival, and inevitably the gunman is drawn into the bloodiest of showdowns.

I don't know about my fellow reviewers, but to me there wasn't the slightest doubt that Mackay – whose youth belies a crime novelist of worldly authority – would pull off this concluding volume with the kind of understated panache that distinguished its predecessors… and so it proved. Perhaps the book's most signal achievement is keeping us captivated by the reptilian protagonist – but then cinema viewers in the 1930s would have had precisely this attitude towards James Cagney in such films as *The Public Enemy* (1931). Cannily, this young novelist realises that when it comes to our fascination with ruthless anti-heroes, it's definitely a case of *plus ça change*.

Running Hot 2004
DREDA SAY MITCHELL

A variety of accolades, from 'edgy' to 'original', have been lavished on Mitchell's highly individual brand of urban noir, with its distinctive black orientation. Her early books utilised the London underworld as a setting, with the police largely offstage in her work. She made her debut on the crime writing scene in 2004 with her first novel, *Running Hot*, the inaugural book in a trilogy about three working-class characters who live on a fictitious housing estate in East London. The book gleaned a slew of enthusiastic reviews, reached a wide readership and was awarded the Crime Writers' Association's John Creasey Memorial Dagger, a seal of approval that quickly established Mitchell as a writer who deserved attention. The protagonist of this book, Elijah 'Schoolboy' Campbell, a small-time drug dealer, makes a decision he knows will be hard to achieve: he wants to escape from the underworld of petty criminality that has been his milieu and make something of his life outside the world of his dangerous cohorts. The novel – using the accoutrements of the chase thriller – perfectly illustrated Mitchell's ability to adopt the crime genre as a springboard for exploring key contemporary social issues, something that motivated her both as a novelist and as a social commentator. 'Schoolboy' Campbell is a victim of the disadvantaged background he is struggling to escape from, and in many respects he represents the lives of some of the young men Mitchell grew up with in the East End of London, and with whom she has spent much time talking about their restricted lives.

The Crust on its Uppers 1962
DEREK RAYMOND

A quite extraordinary book – as extraordinary as its author (see page 231). It is one of the few novels that has a glossary of terms at the start, and most readers would be lost without it. Written entirely in an odd argot of Cockney rhyming slang and London underworld *spiel* from the post-World War II period, this book is a form of confession, and reveals as much about the author's shady life as it does about England over half a century ago. It describes a world – indeed a universe – in which chancing and criminal activity are the norm, and one by no means exclusively inhabited by social underdogs. Everyone, from the ex-Eton author sideways, is on the make, whether it's rigging horse races, recycling stolen vehicles or simply blagging and poncing (literally) on the backstreets of Soho. The late Raymond, frequently out of print but never forgotten, can unfortunately be blamed for the hypnotically jokey style of London gangster films such as *Lock, Stock and Two Smoking Barrels* (1998; directed by **Guy Ritchie**) and *Sexy Beast* (2001; directed by **Jonathan Glazer**), but Raymond was a considerable cut above this sort of stuff. A masterpiece of unexplored social history.

Clubland 2002

KEVIN SAMPSON

Why do we read thrillers? Part of the fascination of the genre is that we know we will be taken into a different and dangerous world, where the rules that govern our existence count for little. With Kevin Sampson's *Clubland*, that world is a particularly unsettling one, and at no point can the reader feel comfortable – but then we don't read thrillers to be comfortable, do we? Sampson's protagonist Ged Brennan combines his expertise in violence with a strongly moral streak. He has absolutely no intention of becoming involved in seedy clubs, drugs and topless bars. But then he receives an offer to assume control of the clubland empire of an executed gangster. He gives the opportunity to his cousin Moby (a man obsessively addicted to sex), but – unsurprisingly – this proves to be a disastrous move.

Desperation Road 2017

MICHAEL FARRIS SMITH

Mississippi-born Michael Farris Smith can point to an impressive back catalogue, with at least two signature novels, the blistering *Desperation Road* and *The Fighter* (2018), both of which set uncompromisingly described incident against an unsentimental humanity. *Desperation Road* can be compared to Daniel Woodrell's *Winter's Bone* (2006) and is set in a tough Mississippi town where drugs, whisky, guns and the desire for revenge create a dangerous cocktail. After 11 years in Parchman penitentiary in the Mississippi Delta, Smith's protagonist Russell Gaines feels that he has paid his debt, but he returns home to find that his troubles are by no means over. On the day of Gaines' release, an exhausted woman and her young

Derek Raymond
(1931–94)

America may be famed for its hard-drinking crime writers (notably **Raymond Chandler** and **Dashiell Hammett**), but the UK can boast a man who could match these red-eyed titans drink for drink – and, what's more, who was responsible for one of the most impressive bodies of crime fiction ever produced in Britain (before he pushed his body beyond its limits). Robert William Arthur Cook adopted the nom de plume Derek Raymond after about 1970, as there was already a Robin Cook writing crime in the States. He came from a privileged background and spent a great deal of his life under French skies before making the watering holes of Soho his personal fiefdom.

Raymond's first book, *The Crust on its Uppers* (1962), was written as Robin Cook and explored the darker recesses of human behaviour; it had a considerable impact, particularly in France – at one time, Raymond was more respected abroad than in his own country. The later *He Died with his Eyes Open* (1984) began a series focusing on the Factory, a London police unit handling assignments for the Department of Unexplained Deaths, and is a favourite of crime readers. Raymond's bleak, unrelenting body of work has now emerged from its period of neglect to assume its rightful position in the pantheon.

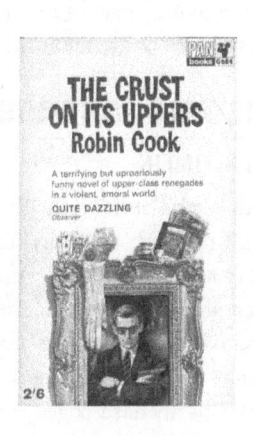

daughter spend their last cash on a motel room for the night, but the night ends with the woman running through the darkness with a pistol and a policeman lying dead in the road. As the destinies of Gaines, the woman and her child converge, the novel's resolution for all three characters is as rigorous as anything in crime fiction.

Tough Luck 2003

JASON STARR

As his adroit psychological thriller *Hard Feelings* (2002) comprehensively demonstrated, the American writer Jason Starr has a uniquely penetrating style, and this book has all the impressive marshalling of character, plot and action that marks his best work. Mickey Prada works in a neighbourhood seafood market in Brooklyn and has delayed college for a year to help his father, who is ill. But Mickey has made some unfortunate friends, and his bookie is after him. So when his best friend asks him to come in on a sure-fire scheme, Mickey agrees. But nothing is ever foolproof, and Mickey ends up in a hidden part of Brooklyn where catastrophe awaits. A sharp, edgy and stylishly written noir thriller.

Answers from the Grave 2004

MARK TIMLIN

In his Nick Sharman thrillers, London writer Mark Timlin performed a sleight of hand: while giving every impression of depicting gritty urban reality and the life of a cynical London private eye, the plots functioned on an almost hyper-real level, with plausibility less important than sheer narrative drive. *Answers from the Grave* shows the rebarbative Timlin taking his writing to a new level, with its notions of dreaming built into a customarily hard-edged story. Mark Farrow's father was a criminal who moved to the other side of the law and died at the hands of the brutal Jimmy Hunter in a 1960s bank robbery that went wrong. Mark has been patiently waiting for Jimmy to serve his lengthy prison sentence to exact an appropriate revenge. At the same time, Sean Pearse, the criminal's alienated son, has become a cop. When this incendiary cast of characters gets together, it's inevitable that there will be fireworks. Timlin's long-term protagonist Sharman makes a cameo appearance, but this is a more ambitious crime novel than most of the author's other works.

Savages 2010

DON WINSLOW

If you haven't heard of Don Winslow, don't worry – it's not a cause for shame. But if you *have* heard of him – and you have now – you've joined a coterie of people who know the name of a very special talent. This laconic New York-born writer is regarded by the *au courant* as one of the best in the field; his sprawling, visceral drug crime novel *The Power of the Dog* (2005) rivalled the Grand Master of that genre, **Robert Stone**. Opinion has been more divided over recent books set in California's surfer territory, in which Winslow has tried (and sometimes succeeded) to suggest that this laid-back community is in possession of more than a single brain cell. But did admirers' pleas for a return to the massive reach of *The Power of the Dog* result in *Savages*? In the latter novel, violent drug-dealing conflict is back, but now shot through with the mordant humour of his surfing novels – and the result is quite splendid.

Despite Ben's apparent environmental concerns, he's more than ready to handle big-time marijuana deals with his ex-mercenary friend Chon in Laguna Beach. Chon is the muscle, securing their territory against incursions, and they share a girlfriend, an Orange County beauty called Ophelia. Needless to say, everything turns sour. A video arrives, with shots of severed heads suggesting that there will be bloody consequences when the Baja cartel moves in. Ophelia is snatched, and Ben and Chon are instructed to hand over the business. It's obvious they don't stand a chance going up against such a ruthless nemesis. But guess whether or not they decide to try?

Winslow is not concerned with keeping his readers in a comfortable place, and the challenges begin with making us complicit with his less-than-admirable dope-dealing anti-heroes. The badinage of the beleaguered protagonists – one a laid-back save-the-planet type, the other a tough ex-SEAL (between them, a ragbag of SoCal attitudes) – is wonderfully funny, but there's also a slew of acidic socio-political commentaries on American society, and some nifty wordplay; Winslow has few equals in the latter area.

CHAPTER 11

ORGANISED CRIME
Wise guys and godfathers

If, as the Prussian theorist Carl von Clausewitz claimed, warfare is a 'cultural activity', well, so is crime. And if, as he suggested, warfare is 'diplomacy conducted by other means' then organised crime is free-market capitalism by other means. J Edgar Hoover's Federal Bureau of Investigation refused to acknowledge that organised crime existed in the US, until a cascade of cases from the 1960s onwards – often the result of squealers such as Joe Valachi and Henry Hill, or deep-cover cops including 'Donnie Brasco' – made it all too clear that criminal activity on an industrial scale was endemic in America and had infiltrated not just the police force but possibly the corridors of political power too. After all, JFK's father (and America's World War II ambassador in London) Joe Kennedy had made a fortune running illicit liquor across the Great Lakes during the Prohibition years. Organisations such as the Sicilian Black Hand, Jewish gangsters, Chinese Triads, Japanese Yakuza and Irish republican support groups had existed in localised ethnic enclaves, richly documented in journalist **Herbert Asbury**'s excellent series of books on 19th-century US crime, most notably *The Gangs of New York* (1928), filmed rather disappointingly by **Martin Scorsese** in 2002. But it was the Volstead Act, instituting alcohol prohibition in 1919, which not only immediately turned many American citizens who liked a highball in the evening into criminals by default, but provided the impetus for the growth of industrialised crime. And when the Act was repealed 1933, like any other corporation, the big guys – notably the immigrant southern Italian mafia families – needed to find new products and new markets. Prostitution, extortion and, above all, gambling and narcotics became their turf. But the turf was becoming overpopulated. While, in truth, British organised criminals were pretty amateur (the activities of the Kray twins and the Richardson gang have been glamorised out of all proportion), traditional and historical high rollers including the Chinese Triads and Tongs and the Japanese Yakuza saw international opportunities opening up. And then, following perestroika, a new and menacing breed of organised criminals emanating from Russia and Central Asia began to rewrite the rulebook – if there ever was one.

The Long Firm 1999

JAKE ARNOTT

As a picture of the London underworld in the 1960s, Arnott's brutal and impressive novel is social history with impeccable thick-ear credentials. As in **Akira Kurosawa**'s classic *Rashomon* (1950), different characters give us different perspectives on one thing – in this case, Harry Starks, a brutal gangster. But as the reader learns more about Harry, we realise that there is more to him than simply the bone-crunching violence. Arnott describes Harry through the prism of East End proletarian gangland subculture, as seen through the eyes of a sociologist involved with him. The gangster himself combines charm with his ruthlessness, and his intelligence wins over the reluctant, appalled reader. The characters with whom Harry interacts – seductive blondes, Marxist writers – are drawn with the same colour, and the surprising analyses of cultural behaviour (not least from the mouth of Harry himself) are as entertaining as the more visceral elements.

THE LONG FIRM 2004

Director: Bille Eltringham

This TV adaptation of **Jake Arnott**'s blistering novel created a considerable stir, not least for its canny casting of Mark Strong in the role of the charismatic anti-hero. While the screenplay inevitably simplified the more intriguing aspects of the novel (often reducing it to a straightforward tale of lowlife brutality), the impressive sheen of the production often did full service to Arnott's prose. Powerful casting of other parts, too, backed up Mark Strong's memorable central turn.

Little Caesar 1929

WR BURNETT

Perhaps best remembered these days as the source for Edward G Robinson's career-forging performance as the ruthless gangster making his fatal way to the top of the heap as a Capone-style mobster (while repressing a secretly gay nature), Burnett's novel reads as caustically as when it was written, its flinty prose as bluntly effective as ever. *Little Caesar* was Burnett's first novel and is often described as the first gangster novel. Cesare 'Rico' Bandello is a small-time hood who claws his way to an all-too-brief period as King of the Mobs before a fatal flaw in his character destroys him, conforming to the trajectory described in **Robert Warshow**'s famous essay 'The Gangster as Tragic Hero' (1948). The novel is played out mostly in dialogue, but it's perhaps difficult for the modern reader not to see – and hear – Robinson's strutting protagonist, particularly as Burnett keeps the reader at some distance from Rico and our post-Robinson perceptions are wont to creep in. For those unfamiliar with the **Mervyn LeRoy** 1931 film, though, the lack of any stylistic flourishes – once criticised as a failing – can now seem like a rather modern virtue.

Bordersnakes 1996

JAMES CRUMLEY

Crumley's world, like that of **Cormac McCarthy** and **Sam Peckinpah**, is the arid zone of the American southwest, where moral borders are as invisible as the now all but dried up Rio Grande. It is a world of deserts, tumbleweeds and local crime barons, on either side of the river, sweating pesos and dollars out of illegal immigrants, migrant workers and drug-running mules aiming for the rich pastures of 'El Norte', LA and its environs. Although wryly humorous, Crumley paints a picture of an updated, but still lawless, Wild West, where anything goes and nothing is predictable. To not carry a Savage pump-action shotgun in your car, let alone a handgun in your waistband, would be a sign of severe vulnerability, and as Crumley's protagonists play a dangerous criss-cross game of chance, he paints a portrait of a frontier of America where organised criminal activity is more normal than white picket-fence 'normality'. And as with the landscapes painted by Cormac McCarthy, this cruel region is dominated by law-breakers rather than law-enforcers.

And Then You Die 2002

MICHAEL DIBDIN

Despite Michael Dibdin's efforts, Reichenbach Falls-style, to do away with his series protagonist, we all knew Aurelio Zen wasn't dead – it would take more than an exploding car to finish off that tenacious Italian copper. In *And Then You Die*, the star detective of Rome's elite Criminalpol is back, recovered from the bomb attack in *Blood Rain* (1999) and lying low under a false name at a beach resort on the Tuscan coast. Using the fact that many think he's dead, Zen is waiting to testify in an imminent anti-mafia trial. His brief is straightforward: enjoy the Italian sun and seafood, and do nothing else. But a mild flirtation with the attractive woman under the next beach umbrella doesn't stop Zen from becoming restless, particularly as people are dropping dead around him. And how long before the Mafia realises that it didn't finish the job it started on that secluded Sicilian road? It's a cliché to remark that an author and his work need no introduction, but it's the phrase that is most apposite here. Dibdin had no peers in this kind of elegantly written, brilliantly plotted crime writing, and the Italian locales are conjured as strongly as ever.

American Tabloid

1995

JAMES ELLROY

American Tabloid is an authentic American masterpiece. While the Updikes, Mailers, Fords and DeLillos mud-wrestled for the trophy of 'The Great American Novel', wild man Ellroy crept up, pulled the carpet from under them, and stole the prize. *Tabloid* takes the defining era of post-World War II America, JFK's Camelot, head-on, no holds barred. Using the technique he honed in his LA Quartet (see *LA Confidential*), mixing real-life characters such as the president, his brother Bobby, FBI supremo J Edgar Hoover, Teamsters boss Jimmy Hoffa, and mobsters including Santo Trafficante with fictional (but entirely credible) shadowy fixers, he creates a heady cocktail of political and criminal intrigue in which all moral margins are shaken, stirred and then served over ice. The novel concentrates on both the Bay of Pigs fiasco and the Kennedy assassination, although Ellroy interestingly stops minutes short of the day in Dallas that everyone remembers. The next novel in the cycle, *The Cold Six Thousand* (2001), begins in November 1963 minutes after the assassination, with Wayne Tedrow Jr, a young Vegas cop, arriving in Dallas as the American dream explodes in Deeley Plaza. As usual with Ellroy, fact and fiction rub shoulders, with appearances by key figures of the era, and the Ellroy style is as perfectly honed as ever – though many find the prose in *The Cold Six Thousand* (short sentences, minimal punctuation) mannered and irritating.

Get Shorty

1990

ELMORE LEONARD

Once he abandoned writing very good westerns to the benefit of crime enthusiasts in the late 1960s, Leonard's novels fell mainly into two geographical locales: Miami and his home town of Detroit. This highly enjoyable novel takes us further afield, to Hollywood, and it reflects something of Leonard's jaded view of the place, where he was courted as a scriptwriter. Chili Palmer is a loan shark and debt collector for Miami gangsters, who follows a defaulting client to Hollywood, where he makes a surprising decision to move from his enforcing work and get into the movie business. This is absolutely wonderful stuff, with such strongly drawn characters as Chili's defaulting customer Leo, who has faked his own death in an air crash and has absconded with the $300,000 his wife received from the airline. And then there's the thick-headed mafia cruiser Ray 'Bones' Barboni, who has no love for Chili since the latter shot him in the head. Sublime.

GET SHORTY 1995

Director: Barry Sonnenfeld

Casting is the key to the success of this sharp and witty adaptation of **Elmore Leonard's** unsparing picture of Hollywood and organised crime. John Travolta's turn as Chili Palmer has the superficial appearance of some of his lazier work, but is actually spot on in conveying the ambiguities of a quintessential Leonard character. And with Gene Hackman as a sleazy producer, not to mention Danny DeVito and *The Sopranos*' James Gandolfini in the cast, the excellent Sonnenfeld has great material to work with. Talk about biting the hand that feeds you, though.

Jack's Return Home/Get Carter 1970

TED LEWIS

There's no doubt that **Mike Hodges'** film of Ted Lewis's gritty novel was the primary factor in granting the novel cult status; Lewis had initially done himself no favours with one of the most clunky titles in crime fiction. But as our image of the vengeful Jack Carter is forever stamped with Michael Caine's indelible performance, how does the original novel read in the 21st century, viewed in its own right? While, in all honesty, Hodges undoubtedly added layers to the original, there's still much to commend, notably the brilliantly drawn northern locales. As gangster Jack Carter takes leave from his Kray-like employers to return to his home town to arrange the burial of his estranged brother, he quickly realises that the circumstances of the death are suspicious. Soon, Carter is cutting a brutal swathe through the local hoods (gambling, prostitution, blue movies, corporate corruption), trying to find out why his brother died. Lewis's speciality is the pithy evocation of place, and few novels – even those of such northern literary specialists as **John Braine** – place the reader so securely in this territory. The grim industrial vistas, the down-at-heel private clubs and porn cinemas – all are as luminously painted as the amoral cast of characters.

GET CARTER 1971

Director: Mike Hodges

There's no getting away from it – this is a film that really does fully justify its cult reputation. Quite simply, Mike Hodges' version of **Ted Lewis**'s remarkable novel about organised crime in the provinces (Hodges relocated the action to Newcastle) is the best British gangster movie ever made, and a career best for just about everyone associated with it. **Guy Ritchie** and other more recent genre specialists can only wistfully dream that they could create something as hard-edged and brilliant as this – but then Hodges himself was never able to top this film, despite the critical success of later work, such as *Croupier* (1997). As the brutal, affectless Jack, Michael Caine has never been better, and playwright/actor John Osborne as the local crime baron is utterly convincing.

The Godfather 1969

MARIO PUZO

The novel that put the Mafia on the map has exerted an inestimable influence, and the ripples from Mario Puzo's massive blockbuster (not to mention its various film adaptations) continue to spread to this day. Deploying the hyper-detailed format later perfected by **Frederick Forsyth** in *The Day of the Jackal* (1971), Puzo relates in exhaustive detail the day-to-day dealings of an influential Italian family in America – who just happen to be ruthless mafiosi. Other writers had dealt before with the acrimonious meetings between heads of families and the often bloody business that followed, but Puzo was the first to render these as nigh-operatic set pieces. In fact, all the criminal business is essentially a backdrop for what is a violent version of a classic Shakespearian theme: the education and corruption of a young man. Michael Corleone, back from a stint in the army, is slowly and steadily prepared for accession to the throne vacated by his father, the patrician Don Corleone, who dispenses wisdom and summary justice in the manner of a Renaissance pope. Puzo's prose is a tad penny plain and the characterisation is lacking in any deep psychological insights – also true of other books by the author, such as *The Sicilian* (1984) and *The Last*

Don (1996) – but there is no denying that *The Godfather* touched a nerve, not just with the reading public but also with a number of the New York 'families' who felt that this was a *roman-à-clef* cut too close to the bone. This is one of the most important novels in the crime genre, though it is also a rare example of a novel topped by its film adaptation (see below).

THE GODFATHER 1972

Director: Francis Ford Coppola

Generally speaking, it goes without saying that Hollywood adaptations of celebrated books usually simplify and dilute the essence of the originals, but Coppola's famous adaptation of **Mario Puzo**'s novel is an exception: with its top-drawer cast (Marlon Brando, Al Pacino, Robert Duvall, James Caan) and cool measured pace punctuated by moments of bloody violence, it is a richer and more intricate experience than Puzo's original, with a career-restoring performance by Brando, effortlessly charismatic – and sinister – as Don Corleone. Coppola went on to make a follow-up that was even better – *The Godfather Part II* (1974) – examining both Michael's developing career and his father's early life (a unique prequel and sequel formula), and completed the trilogy with *The Godfather Part III* (1990), where his star Al Pacino had aged sufficiently to play the role of the Don facing eternity. And there's that haunting Nino Rota score...

The Hunter/Point Blank 1962

RICHARD STARK

While **Donald Westlake**'s achievement as a crime writer is legendary, many readers have a sneaking regard for the cold, spare Parker novels he wrote under the pseudonym of Richard Stark. Rarely was a nom de plume so well chosen: the Parker books, with their ruthless, largely unemotional mob hitman as a central character, are truly existential enterprises – everything is stripped away that does not facilitate the fast-moving plot. In *The Hunter* (now better known by the title given to its celebrated film adaptation, *Point Blank* (see page 242)), Parker is shot and left for dead on the instructions of his associates following a successful heist. Later, bent on revenge, he cuts a bloody swathe through 'the Outfit'. And, as Parker gets ever closer to the money he feels is his, he also tracks down the source of his betrayal: his own wife, who has had an affair with a treacherous associate. All of this is delivered in uncluttered, affectless prose that allows readers to make up their own mind about the characters. A certain sleight of hand is evident on Westlake/Stark's part: every so often an innocent bystander will have the misfortune to get in Parker's path, as the author tries to remind us that it's not just gangster scum who get hurt by people like his anti-hero. But readers will forgive this piece of sophistry, so fast moving and involving are the always compact Parker novels.

POINT BLANK 1967

Director: John Boorman

John Boorman claimed never to have read **Richard Stark**'s original novel, while Stark/Westlake claimed never to have seen the film. Whether or not we buy either of these highly dubious statements, this is the perfect match of novel and film, with British director Boorman marrying the disorienting time shifts of the art-house movie ('**Michelangelo Antonioni** with a bullet') to the thick-ear exigencies of Stark's no-nonsense plot. And casting the ultimate icon of dangerous cool, Lee Marvin, as the hunter (unnecessarily renamed Walker) is the icing on the cake.

The Getaway 1959

JIM THOMPSON

A late entry in Thompson's extraordinary oeuvre, this remains an outstanding read. The novel opens with Doc McCoy being sprung from prison as a result of his girlfriend sleeping with an influential local politician and crime boss. Little does she know that the real reason is that Doc is needed for a heist. Doc, ever professional, pulls off the score, but with backup not of his choosing. The robbery results in bloody mayhem, and Doc, proceeds of the job in hand, wants to settle old scores. In doing so, he makes enemies of the local Mob and is forced to flee with his girl. Using insider contacts, he is introduced to a bizarre Mexican resort for past-their-sell-by-date villains on the run. As usual with Thompson, there is a very unpleasant and off-the-wall twist at the end of the tale, but, until then, the story of Doc and his girl, the heist and their getaway over the border is pulp crime writing at its best.

THE GETAWAY

1972

Director: Sam Peckinpah

The self-destructive director Sam Peckinpah shared more with **Jim Thompson** than did **Stanley Kubrick**, the writer's most noted cinematic collaborator/patron. A dyed-in-the-wool westerner, a loner, an alcoholic gambler regarded as a pariah within his industry, and yet capable of moments of sustained genius, Peckinpah's film of *The Getaway* remains high in his canon, focusing on the characters of Doc (Steve McQueen) and his girlfriend (Ali MacGraw) and the mechanics of the heist and its bloody aftermath. The set piece – a high-calibre shoot-out at a dingy southwest motel – is cinematically outstanding, and Peckinpah's abbreviated ending (Doc and his girl escape in a garbage truck and are then ferried across the Rio Grande by another Peckinpah stalwart, Slim Pickens), although disliked by Thompson, is a great example of the director's less surreal and more refined sense of irony. A pointless remake (1994) by **Roger Donaldson** with Alec Baldwin and Kim Basinger merely glamorised the 'crucified heroes' of the Thompson/Peckinpah source material, and the action sequences only served to emphasise Peckinpah's mastery in this area.

CHAPTER 12

CRIME AND SOCIETY
Class, ethnicity and politics

The best crime writing has always addressed key issues affecting society – often with more forcefulness than more self-consciously 'literary' fiction. **Raymond Chandler**'s Philip Marlowe moved between the various strata of LA society – from the dispossessed underclass to the luxurious homes of the rich – and a detailed canvas of an American class structure emerged. Forensic examinations of US society continue with such remarkable writers as **James Ellroy** and **James Lee Burke**, with a broader political dimension than was ever tackled by **Dashiell Hammett** and Chandler. The massively talented **Robert Stone** has used the apparatus of the thriller to paint a picture of post-Vietnam America that continues to be relevant in the light of more recent US overseas interventions; and **George Pelecanos** and **Walter Mosley** tackle issues of race quite as forcefully as writers who wrote exclusively about such concerns (such as **James Baldwin**) ever did.

In the UK, the class system, of course, remains a pertinent factor in crime fiction – and when the doyenne of British crime writers, **PD James**, suggested that the well-educated middle classes were confronted with moral choices more often than those living in circumstances where crime was a fact of life, a furore erupted in the crime writing fraternity and beyond. The bitter division that appeared, however, was not always along predictable class lines: many of the 'Young Turks' who took issue with James were notably middle class (and not, for that matter, particularly young).

Writers such as **Minette Walters** and **Henning Mankell**, along with, more recently, **Eva Dolan**, **Stav Sherez**, **Pierre Lemaitre** and **Anya Lipska**, continue to anatomise such societal divisions with great acuity, while the multifaceted **Ruth Rendell** managed to turn over stones to examine what was lurking beneath the veneer of modern England. Another factor having an impact on society is science, and many writers – such as **Michael Crichton** in the US and **Michael Marshall** in the UK – have brilliantly synthesised the imperatives of crime and thriller fiction with the major changes technological developments have wrought on all our lives.

Acid Casuals 1995
NICHOLAS BLINCOE

Nicholas Blincoe may have abandoned the crime genre in the 2000s, but for some time he was a writer who cannily negotiated the parameters of flashy, fashionable writing and genuine literary brio. In *Acid Casuals*, the reader is taken into a variety of bizarre underworlds within the city of Manchester; the beat that Blincoe has made his own is the sometimes dangerous world of the Manchester club scene, with its plentiful drugs and some pretty nasty criminals running things behind the scenes. The protagonist is a young man, Paul, who lived on the edge of this world and now has another identity as a transsexual, Estela. She is back from Brazil to settle a score by putting an end to her old boss, a deeply unpleasant club owner. This is by no means standard gangster fare – that's not Blincoe's territory; the outrageous trappings, along with the sharply observed Mancunian locales, are the things that give real pleasure here. Blincoe has also written more serious, politically engaged books, but most readers will find this a more diverting entry point.

Gagged and Bound 2005
NATASHA COOPER

Another writer who has withdrawn from the crime genre of late, Natasha (or NJ) Cooper's strengths are her characterisation and the way she sets her London-based novels in well-realised, credible backgrounds. She also boldly explores ideas of responsibility – parental, professional and emotional; she gives the impression that she writes to ease her own nightmares. Her first series character, initially appearing in 1998's *Creeping Ivy*, is Trish Maguire, a 30-something barrister whose career began in family law but who now works mainly with commercial cases. Her involvement with the crimes of each novel comes out of her rage at any kind of injustice and her inability to refuse help to those who need it. Whether the people she interacts with

Ethnic crime writing

Crime fiction as a lens through which society can appear in harsh relief is exemplified by those writers who have focused on particular ethnic communities. But defining the limits of such work can be tricky. Are **Harry Kemelman**'s books (such as *Friday the Rabbi Slept Late* (1964)), in which Rabbi Small solves crimes by Talmudic reasoning to be considered 'ethnic'? But there are a number of crime writers who have not just looked at remote parts of the world, but who have dug deep into the peoples and cultures to be found there.

Arthur Upfield's novels reflect the characters among whom he lived and worked in rural Australia. Of English origin, Upfield had a passion for the country and its landscape, which is almost like a character in several of his books, such as *Death of a Lake* (1954). His detective, Napoleon Bonaparte, is half Aborigine and half white. Although in some ways the books are dated (they appeared from the 1930s to the early 1960s) and may seem un-PC to critical eyes today, there can be no doubt that Upfield was making a point about the terrible wasted potential of so many native Australians; 'Bony' dares not fail, because then it will be said that Aborigines always fail. Similarly, Upfield points up the cruelty and social imprudence of forcing Aborigines to leave their lives behind and face probable degradation on the fringes of white society, for example in *Murder Must Wait* (1953). Upfield's novels were very popular in both England and the US, but not in Australia, no doubt in part because an aboriginal hero was unacceptable, but also because, for Australian readers, the background was too familiar; the books lacked the nostalgic exoticism of English country house mysteries.

Canada and America can offer a number of examples of domestic ethnic detective stories, some written by people with an excellent knowledge are successful professionals or denizens of inner-city estates, such as Mikey and his loan-shark grandmother in *Out of the Dark* (2002) or retired soldier Daniel Crossman from *Keep Me Alive* (2004), they are absolutely credible. In *Gagged and Bound*, Cooper tackles various ways of silencing people who know too much: the legal, by means of a libel case; the emotional, by rubbishing a would-be whistle-blower; and the physical, in a horrific 'bag-and-gag' killing.

---

of the people they use in their books. The popular series of novels by **Tony Hillerman** featuring the Navajo tribal policemen Joe Leaphorn and Jim Chee provides a large amount of background information on the Navajo and Hopi Native Americans, and, by using the men's different personalities, the author can explore their attitudes to the majority culture and their interaction with it. Much less known are the two novels by the Canadian sports journalist **Scott Young** – *Murder in a Cold Climate* (1988) and *The Shaman's Knife* (1993) – both set in the Arctic Circle and featuring an Inuit detective, as does the Arctic series of English writer **MJ McGrath**. Her *White Heat* (2011) may have borrowed its title from an old James Cagney film, but in every other respect it is a totally original piece of work, demonstrating – for a first novel – an authoritative grasp of the thriller idiom. McGrath's lead character is female Inuit hunter/sleuth Edie Kiglatuk, who knows every inch of the Alaskan forests; she is a heroine with whom it is extremely easy to identify, however alien her lifestyle will be to most readers. But the author's real skill lies in her astonishing evocation of the frigid landscape, along with the sharply conjured details of Inuit life. Also worthy of attention are the Kate Shugak novels of Alaskan author **Dana Stabenow,** notably *A Cold Day for Murder* (1992). Kate is an Aleut ex-investigator who lives on a 160-acre homestead in a generic national park in Alaska, with no neighbours for miles around and a half-wolf, half-husky dog for company.

The novelist **Daniel Woodrell** is by no means exclusively a crime writer but his 'Ozark noir' books, notably *Winter's Bone* (2006; successfully filmed in 2010 by **Debra Granik**) describes a modern American backwoods society in which crime is a way of survival, with the old trope of bootlegging replaced by illicit crystal meth outhouse factories – and guns (and the ruthless use of them) as commonplace in this milieu as inbreeding.

Darling 2018

RACHEL EDWARDS

Political concerns are at the heart of *Darling* by Rachel Edwards, which focuses on the Brexit referendum result and its effect on levels of racism in the UK. Shortly after the 'leave' vote, the eponymous narrator is abused in the street because of the colour of her skin. She is defended by another single parent, a white widower called Thomas. The couple develop a relationship and marry, but Thomas's teenage daughter Lola has no affection for her new black stepmother, and the conflict between the two is to have disastrous consequences: a prologue tells us that one of the characters is to die. But which one? The writing here is unvarnished but persuasive, and Edwards' societal concerns are threaded through her novel without cut-and-dried judgements. Some readers may balk at the way in which Edwards makes virtually every character irritating – no easy sympathy is invited for Darling herself, with her faux-ingratiating tone of voice, while Lola has all the off-putting characteristics of a resentful teenager. There is clandestine evil at the heart of the book, treated with ambiguity rather than straightforward condemnation.

9tail Fox 2005

JON COURTENAY GRIMWOOD

Combining alternative North African history with a crime sensibility, Jon Courtenay Grimwood (now writing as Jack Grimwood) came to critical notice with his three 'Arabesk' mysteries (2001–03), finely detailed crime novels set in the city of El Iskandriyah (Alexandria) and featuring Ashraf Bey, ex-US prisoner and half-Berber detective. These were followed by *Stamping Butterflies* (2004), a novel hung around the attempted murder of the US president and an investigation into a killing in 1970s Marrakesh. As always with Grimwood, magic realist elements combined with sly humour and straight police detection to produce a novel that can be read on many levels. *9tail Fox* begins with the murder of the main character, Sergeant Bobby Zha, and then, instead of working backwards to explain the killing, the plot moves forward to allow the victim to investigate his own death. Having failed as a father, husband and SFPD officer, Zha finds himself at his own funeral, unable to recognise the glowing description of the officer being honoured. A flashback to the siege in Stalingrad during World War

II ties Bobby Zha's murder to medical research carried out on the orders of Stalin and lets the reader begin to tie this research to the current situation in Russia. Set in San Francisco's Chinatown and drawing on Chinese myth, genetic manipulation and the rise of the Russian oligarchs, *9tail Fox* displays Grimwood's habitual obsession with finely detailed location, narrative twists and sudden outbreaks of violence. As in all his novels, the hero's need for redemption is linked to wider questions about identity and what constitutes justice.

Ash and Bone

2005

JOHN HARVEY

There were many who felt that John Harvey was robbed when his novel *Flesh and Blood* (2004) failed to bag the prestigious Crime Writers' Association Gold Dagger award (the American **Sara Paretsky** pipped him to the post). Ms Paretsky used her acceptance speech to rail (by proxy) against the iniquities of her government, but Harvey casts quite as cold an eye on the UK as his American colleague does on the US, although his understated social criticism sports a British patina that is more quietly effective than Paretsky's in-your-face rant. Harvey's world-weary detective Frank Elder has problems with his ex-wife and daughter that seem to be beyond his ability to resolve. But – wait a minute – is Elder the principal character here? While he handles the police procedural business, he doesn't appear until Chapter 4, while the sympathetic female copper Maddy Birch launches the book, eyeing herself in the mirror and snapping her ponytail tight before fastening the Velcro on her protective vest and setting out on an armed raid to bring down a north London Mr Big. Things go bloodily wrong: the gangster is shot by another policeman who appears to plant a weapon near the dead man. Frank Elder, unable to cope with his daughter's hostility, welcomes the opportunity to get back into harness, investigating the murder of a female colleague with whom he had a one-off sexual encounter. The picture of Britain painted by Harvey is a dark and minatory place: everywhere from London's Crouch End (where the disused railway line is the site of a murder) to a Lincolnshire where crumbling houses have been the site of sadistic sexual murders. And Harvey's UK seems to be at the mercy of an army of barely socialised council-estate kids, their small-scale crime mirroring the more serious mayhem committed by their elders.

Cotton Comes to Harlem   1965

CHESTER HIMES

The best-known book by one of the most celebrated of black crime writers, this idiosyncratic and engaging thriller features Himes' classic characters, 'Coffin Ed' Johnson and 'Grave Digger' Jones, New York City cops with good reputations (despite their unorthodox methods) assigned to Harlem. Using their carefully maintained network of informers, the duo is looking into the murky background of the 'Back to Africa' movement, inaugurated by ex-con Deke O'Malley. Deke has skimmed nearly $90,000 from trusting families wanting to buy berths to the Motherland on ocean liners – berths, of course, that don't exist. The money is stolen by white thugs who hide it in a bale of cotton that ends up with an exotic dancer at the Cotton Club. And all the time, the body count is rising. The knowing Himes has great fun at the expense of racism (the stress on cotton, classic by-product of slavery, is no accident), and the rich gallery of eccentrics encountered by the two dogged black coppers is matched in interest by the duo themselves. Dialogue, as ever with Himes, positively leaps off the page and demands to be spoken aloud, whatever your ethnic background. Missouri-born Himes was certainly not

COTTON COMES TO HARLEM   1970

Director: Ossie Davis

Directed by the talented black actor Ossie Davis, the strength of this sometimes hit-and-miss adaptation of **Chester Himes'** most celebrated novel lies largely in the judicious casting, with Godfrey Cambridge and Raymond St Jacques essaying larger than life – and highly entertaining – versions of Himes' bickering protagonists. The quirky talent on offer raises this above the more standard blaxploitation movies of the period.

afraid of confronting issues: his first novel, *If He Hollers Let Him Go* (1945), is an edgy book dealing with a crew of black workers in a Los Angeles shipyard in the 1940s. As an examination of the social strictures placed on black Americans in this era, this is cold-eyed and intense fare, but the author's anger is always kept in proportion to the narrative he is creating: Himes always wrote a solid novel above all else, never a piece of agitprop. Admired in France, Himes migrated there (like contemporary black novelist **James Baldwin** and numerous jazz musicians), finding the European temperament more congenial than a racially segregated US in the 1950s.

The Good Sister 2018

MORGAN JONES

Chris Morgan Jones dropped his first name for *The Good Sister*, in which Sofia, a young British Muslim woman who is alienated from her father and the life in London she sees as corrupt and irreligious, comes to a fateful decision: she will make the fraught journey to Raqqa in Syria. Brimming with zeal, she sees the new caliphate as the greatest goal of her faith. She accepts that marrying a battle-hardened ISIS fighter is part of her religious duty, as is enduring the hostility of the other jihadi brides from various countries, all confined to a foetid, claustrophobic house that they are not allowed to leave. It's an audacious project for a male English writer, but Sofia's visceral chronicle of self-radicalisation is delivered in an utterly persuasive voice. This could have been a literary novel along the lines of **Kamila Shamsie**'s award-winning *Home Fire*, but a tense second strand is added – the journey of Sofia's desperate father Abraham, whom she regards as westernised and lost to the faith, who travels to Syria in an attempt to save her. His terrifying encounters with people traffickers and violent jihadis pulse with rigour and tension. But the real achievement of Morgan Jones' novel lies in the portrait of a naive young woman realising that the pure religious caliphate to which she has committed her life is a place of betrayal, misogyny and lethal danger.

The Language of Secrets 2017

AUSMA ZEHANAT KHAN

Detective Esa Khattak, a second-generation Pakistani Canadian, made an auspicious debut in Ausma Zehanat Khan's highly accomplished novel *The Unquiet Dead* (2017), and is proving to be one of the most intriguing characters in contemporary crime fiction. He is a devout Muslim constantly being obliged to deal with the violent distortions of his faith espoused by some of his coreligionists. In *The Language of Secrets*, Khattak encounters distrust and hostility from both his fellow detectives and his Muslim co-workers. When he is tasked with looking into the death of an undercover officer who had infiltrated a murderous jihadist cell, he finds his loyalties are even more painfully divided. As well as being a superlative crime novel, this is a sophisticated examination of western society's attitudes to the collision of fundamentalist Islam and terrorism. The writer was inspired by a real-life event: a 2006 attempt to blow up the Canadian parliament.

The Constant Gardener 2001

JOHN LE CARRÉ

The Spy Who Came in from the Cold was the book with which John le Carré set the world of espionage thrillers on its ear back in 1963. That novel is still the coruscating, unflinching picture of Cold War betrayal that obliterated all le Carré's rivals and marked out the author as the pre-eminent writer in the field – a position he's held (with some hiccups) ever since. Of course, it was the imposing Karla trilogy featuring George Smiley (beginning with *Tinker Tailor Soldier Spy* in 1974) that enriched and deepened le Carré's achievement. While some readers lamented the loss of the tautness of the earlier books, the massive panoply of the Smiley saga allowed le Carré to transcend the thriller category and produce profound works of literature, using the duplicity of his troubled protagonists to offer insights into the human condition.

After the end of the Cold War, le Carré (like his talented contemporary **Len Deighton**) seemed adrift for a while, until he found a way to address the new issues threatening our world. *The Constant Gardener* took on the unfettered power of the great pharmaceutical concerns and delivered the author's most resounding success in years. Justin Quayle is in the Diplomatic Corps, with a position in the British High Commission in Nairobi. His wife, as socially engaged as he is complaisant, changes his life as he tries to accommodate to her anti-establishment views (an embarrassment to him in his job). But she is murdered, and Justin finds himself on a nigh-obsessive quest to find the reason for her death. Justin is in the line of British expats in dangerous countries most memorably created by **Graham Greene** and **Eric Ambler**, but le Carré's concerns and targets are very much his own.

This ex-civil servant's anti-establishment fury makes leftist rebels seem mere dilettantes – and that is the engine for this brilliantly sustained novel.

Death Can't Take a Joke 2014
ANYA LIPSKA

Where the Devil Can't Go (2011) marked out the socially conscious Anya Lipska as a bravura crime writer, and this distinctive novel consolidates her reputation. An edgy, visceral vision of modern London at the mercy of ambitious Eastern European criminals, *Death Can't Take a Joke* boasts complex protagonists, well-realised locales and a keen social awareness. It's to be hoped that commercial success begins to match her currently underrated achievements.

Pleasantville 2015
ATTICA LOCKE

To say that Attica Locke's debut, *Black Water Rising* (2009) – ambitious, socially committed and beautifully written – created a stir is almost to understate the case, and one wonders if it weighed heavily on her shoulders that she would be obliged to deliver something equally impressive as a follow-up. But she did just that with *The Cutting Season* (2012) and the third book, *Pleasantville*. Here, the setting is Houston, 1996, where a mayoral election is in the offing and a key swing area is the African-American neighbourhood of Pleasantville. The nomination of Houston's mayor seems to be assured: Axel Hathorne has the perfect pedigree – ex-chief of police and the son of the district's founding father Sam Hathorne. But a late entrant in the mayoral competition is defence attorney Sandy Wolcott, who has achieved fame after a much-publicised murder trial. And then things begin to get considerably worse for Axel: a girl canvassing for him disappears, and when her body is discovered, Axel's nephew is charged with the murder. Sam Hathorne is keen for Jay Porter (whom we first encountered in *Black Water Rising*)

to defend his grandson – even though a disenchanted Jay is reluctant to do it. But his attempts to stay out of the courtroom are doomed to failure, and a truly destabilising court case is about to change the lives of everyone involved and expose the venality of some powerful people.

As in Locke's earlier work, awkward political issues bristle at the edges of the narrative: for instance, the black families who have achieved some success find themselves at odds with the resentful Latino families fighting in vain for the same advantages. Jay, increasingly out of his depth in an explosive situation, remains a satisfyingly conflicted character, and the sultry, edgy atmosphere of the town is reminiscent of the novels of one of the American masters of crime fiction, **James Lee Burke** (this appears to be no accident: Locke names the family of the murdered girl Robicheaux after Burke's durable sleuth). But Locke is moving in different territory, notably that of the riveting courtroom drama – and at that particular discipline she is already the equal of such writers as **John Grisham**.

You Don't Know Me 2017

IMRAN MAHMOOD

Imran Mahmood – a barrister specialising in crime – grew up in Liverpool before moving to London (as did I, though neither of us has the authentic Scouse accent). His massively acclaimed debut novel, *You Don't Know Me*, was praised by **Lee Child**: 'A daring concept executed to perfection, a hypnotic and authentic voice, and questions for us to answer as readers and people.' A young black man is accused of murder, with powerful evidence incriminating him. But at his trial he relates a remarkable story, which comprises the bulk of the book – an audacious move on Mahmood's part. Few debut novels make such an indelible mark as this.

White Devils 2004

PAUL McAULEY

We live in a dangerous world. What is it that's going to finally do for us all? Once it might have been rat-borne plagues, but we've learned to be wary of many more things in the centuries since the Black Death: sexually transmitted diseases, undercooked burgers, bird flu... And, of course, genetic engineering. McAuley's chilling *White Devils* plays cannily on our fears of unrestricted experimentation in such areas (it's not giving too much away to say that the 'devils' of the title are the grotesque product of GE experiments), but this is only one of the many elements the author mixes into a particularly heady brew. It's an all-too-plausible biotech thriller, certainly, but McAuley's consummate skills also extend into the areas of characterisation and sociological observation. Nicholas Hyde is doing volunteer work with a humanitarian charity in a strife-torn African country when he is caught up in a scene of carnage in the dense Congo forests. Nick's team is suddenly under attack – but from what? The things that lay siege to Nick and his crew are bizarre ape-like creatures, pale in colour and possessing enormous strength. Only Nick and a government observer escape the bloody slaughter with their lives – and Nick finds that the truth about the encounter does not chime with the government-approved view of events. The team was, apparently, attacked by 'rebel troops in body paint'. But who is behind the government cover-up? All of this is handled with panache and the science aspects are described with total assurance – as one would expect, since the author has a background in scientific research. McAuley has built a reputation as a purveyor of meta-fictions that defy category, and since 2001's *Whole Wide World* really established his reputation, his books have transmuted futuristic tropes into bizarre artefacts that illuminate the darker areas of psychology; his best books, however, look at alternative societies that refract the more arcane aspects of our own.

The Cold Cold Ground 2012

ADRIAN McKINTY

Comparisons have been drawn to David Peace's blistering 'Red Riding Quartet', specifically suggesting that the talented Adrian McKinty is doing for Northern Ireland what David Peace did for Yorkshire. And these comparisons are not far-fetched: the effortless grasp of genre that Adrian McKinty has demonstrated in such books as the powerful *Dead I Well May Be* (2003) is matched by a prodigious literary reach that is every inch the equal of its ambition. Detective Sergeant Sean Duffy, promoted and posted to Carrickfergus CID, finds himself with a challenge involving two very different cases: what appears to be the county's first serial killer and a young woman's suicide (which may well be murder). Things are complicated by the involvement of one of the victims in the IRA. This is powerful writing that takes on social issues along with its storytelling impetus.

Exile

DENISE MINA

2001

Denise Mina won the John Creasey Best First Crime Novel prize for her remarkable *Garnethill* (1998), but high reader expectations can be a heavy cross to bear, and more than one writer has come to grief attempting to recreate earlier triumphs. *Exile*, however, proved that Mina was in for the long haul. The Glasgow setting of this piece is rendered with a gritty authority that anchors the narrative in a strongly realised universe. Mina's central character is Maureen O'Donnell, who is used to encountering damaged women at the Glasgow Women's Shelter where she works, but one particularly badly treated woman, Ann, affects her. To Maureen's horror, she later learns that a body dumped in the Thames is the luckless Ann. Her corpse has been treated appallingly, and she is wrapped in bedding. Maureen has reasons of her own for leaving Glasgow, and a trip to London results in her looking into the death of her charge. But any feelings that she has seen the worst of life in terms of drugs and abuse in Glasgow are soon set side when she discovers the dark underbelly of London and tries to track down Ann's killer. The social issues addressed by the book are as cogently handled as the satisfying plotting.

The Red Road

DENISE MINA

2013

The Red Road again reminds us that Denise Mina, along with being one of the finest practitioners of the criminous art, is also a social commentator of perception and humanity. The story begins in 1997, with 14-year-old Rose Wilson being pimped by her 'boyfriend' and compromising her already ignoble life by committing two desperate crimes. Rose is arrested, and defence lawyer Julius McMillan decides to take her case. Although she ends up in prison, she is visited by her sympathetic counsel, and after her rehabilitation she joins the McMillan household and even acts as an assistant in Julius's law practice whenever darker corners need to be probed. Unsurprisingly, all of this is handled with the assurance that we routinely expect from Mina, who is second to none in the creation of damaged female protagonists – and Rose is one of her most fully rounded and convincing creations. But then the novel moves to the present, where a deeply unpleasant arms dealer, Michael Brown, is involved with a murder in the eponymous Red Road flats, and Detective Inspector Alex Morrow is a witness in the case.

These disparate elements (and a host of others – Mina is always spendthrift in her plotting) are brought together with authority, intricately drawing us into a narrative that engages with a variety of issues, all equally provocative. Concealed beneath the surface is an agenda that has been a consistent element of Mina's work over the years: a passionate concern for the vulnerable and damaged in society – and a rage at injustice. Our sympathy is both invited and tested in the most rigorous of fashions (it is to Mina's credit that she is never sentimental towards her victims), but if the unpleasant characters here are writ larger than usual, their unspeakableness serves the function of galvanising our responses to a complex, crowded novel.

Walkin' the Dog   1999

WALTER MOSLEY

Walter Mosley has long been one of the most respected names in the black crime writing fraternity, his Easy Rawlins series, which launched in 1990 with *Devil in a Blue Dress*, being a firm favourite of fans – who include Bill Clinton – although such non-crime novels as *Blue Light* (1998) demonstrate the same mastery of atmosphere and idiom as the Rawlins books, and *The Man in my Basement* (2004) was a powerful study of prejudice and the nature of identity. In *Walkin' the Dog*, Socrates Fortlow (who first appeared in 1997's *Always Outnumbered, Always Outgunned*) is struggling to come to terms with life after prison. He's living in a dingy two-room shack in Watts, maintaining a relationship – against the odds – and even holding down a job. But, as so often in this kind of narrative, the past won't leave him alone, and Socrates has to risk everything he's achieved to bring down some savage enemies. Ghetto life has rarely been delivered with such a dark-edged panache, and Socrates is a character with whom readers cannot help but identify – for all his (plentiful) misjudgements.

The Dispossessed — 2004
MARGARET MURPHY

Margaret Murphy writes with a textual immediacy, creating complex plots peopled by sensitively drawn, flawed and believable characters. Her trademark is compassion for the victim, and she never lets you forget that there are devastating consequences to violent crime, but judicious splashes of humour lighten the darker aspects of the narrative in all her work. *The Dispossessed* is the first book in a Liverpool-based series, featuring police detectives Jeff Rickman and Lee Foster. Rickman is investigating an Afghan refugee's sordid death, but he faces a community that can't – or won't – talk to him. Then, as the body count starts to rise, Rickman is framed for a crime he didn't commit. Is he on the trail of a serial killer? Or something even more sinister? In this challenging novel, Murphy presents a clear-eyed exploration of the dual themes of voicelessness and the exploitation of the disenfranchised, within the context of an underworld of migration scams, racism and prostitution in Liverpool.

The Twelve — 2010
STUART NEVILLE

Stuart Neville is a Northern Irish crime writer whose first novel took the genre by storm. But he is becoming well known for something other than his literary skills: he enjoys the imprimatur of no less an American crime writing legend (and larger-than-life personality) than James Ellroy – and apart from being able to use encomiums on his jackets from the great man (the surprisingly epithet-free 'This guy can write!'), he has even survived two Ellroy interviews, one in Neville's native Belfast. Apart from a sure grasp of the mechanics of suspense, Neville's real coup here is his portrayal of a markedly multifaceted and conflicted protagonist – prey to ghosts from Ireland's troubled and violent past – about whom readers are frequently obliged to change their mind (how often do we encounter that approach in modern crime fiction?). When the book appeared, comparisons were made to a host of other writers, but Neville was – and is – a very individual novelist.

Red Riding Quartet

1999–2002

DAVID PEACE

Is it possible to create a new genre in crime fiction? Amazingly, the answer seems to be yes: at the turn of the 21st century, David Peace produced what can only be called Yorkshire noir. His caustic quartet comprised *Nineteen Seventy Four* (1999), *Nineteen Seventy Seven* (2000), *Nineteen Eighty* (2001) and *Nineteen Eighty Three* (2002). All four are breathtaking and violent Yorkshire-set thrillers that tackle police corruption set against real-life events.

In *Nineteen Seventy Seven* we are in the year of punk and the Queen's Silver Jubilee. And the Yorkshire Ripper is plying his bloody trade. This is the dark world into which beleaguered copper Bob Fraser and over-the-hill journalist Jack Whitehead are drawn together in their sympathy for the prostitutes of Chapeltown. And as Peace's narrative treads inexorably towards the bonfires of Jubilee night and more grisly deaths, the two men come to the grim conclusion that there may be more than one killer at large. This is tricky work that Peace has undertaken: weaving a real-life tragedy into a work of fiction. But such is his way with idiosyncratic characterisation and remorseless plotting that the result is a totally convincing novel that is also, thankfully, highly responsible. As crime fiction chases its tail and vainly attempts to create innovation in an overcrowded genre, Peace seems able to effortlessly render everything anew in his lacerating and unsparing novels. His journo hero Whitehead is a particularly sharp creation, and comparable at times to the anti-heroes of **Graham Greene**.

Drama City

2005

GEORGE PELECANOS

Lorenzo Brown has left his criminal background behind and is struggling to scratch a humble living as a dog warden. And his parole officer, Rachel Lopez, is finding that Lorenzo, despite his good intentions, is her biggest problem. As the dangerous challenges facing George Pelecanos's beleaguered characters proliferate, the world in which they move is realised with the kind of casual skill that we expect from this outstanding novelist – he is a key modern American writer, not least for his edgy work with David Simon on such US TV series as *The Wire* and *The Deuce*. Here, the blue-collar ambience has a grittiness and plausibility that bespeaks the author's sympathy for those making their way far from middle-class comforts – and once again Pelecanos freights a subtle social commentary into his narrative in a fashion that always foregrounds the narrative imperatives.

The Harbour Master 2016
DANIEL PEMBREY

Amsterdam detective Henk van der Pol is approaching retirement when a woman's body is found in the harbour. It's not his case, but he becomes involved in the search for a ruthless killer – and in an investigation that has tendrils stretching into the corridors of government, people trafficking and the police. This is familiar territory, but Pembrey is a debut novelist of rare skill, marshalling his material with rigour and intelligence. Novelist **Nicolas Freeling** made Amsterdam his turf, but only a handful of subsequent writers have tackled the city. Pembrey is masterful at evoking its atmosphere, but the real achievement is to be found in his portrait of the ageing copper following a tangled, picaresque trail through Holland and Scandinavia. *The Harbour Master* suggests that Pembrey has a lengthy career ahead of him.

A Masculine Ending 1987
JOAN SMITH

This is the first of Joan Smith's detective novels featuring her academic-cum-detective, Loretta Lawson. She arrives in Paris after a fraught journey to stay at an apartment on the Left Bank she has borrowed from a friend. To her dismay, Lawson finds a stranger asleep there; creeping into another bedroom, she spends an uncomfortable night and leaves early the next morning to give a paper at a symposium organised by a feminist literary journal. Returning to the flat that night, she finds the stranger gone – and a tangle of bloody sheets on the bed. Her reluctance to go to the authorities runs deep; like many people on the left, she has been distrustful of the state since the British miners' strike of 1984–85. Returning to England without contacting the French police, she decides to investigate herself, with the assistance of her journalist ex-husband. Her inquiries lead her to Oxford

University, and a mystery involving a missing don, his estranged wife and one of his most talented students. *A Masculine Ending* cannily plays with the conventions of the traditional British crime novel, presenting Lawson as an intelligent woman who is an outsider on account of her politics and her feminism. It offers a perspective deliberately at odds with that of Golden Age writers such as **Agatha Christie**, especially in its scepticism about the idea of resolution. This is most evident in its ending, which enraged some readers but is in keeping with the ambivalence evident throughout the novel. The fourth Lawson book, *What Men Say* (1993) takes its title from Catullus's poem about Theseus and Ariadne, signalling its concern with loyalty and the darker side of relationships between men and women, Smith's constant theme, although she avoids facile misandry.

A MASCULINE ENDING — 1992

Director: Antonia Bird

Intelligent direction from Antonia Bird and a strong cast of some of the most interesting British performers (Janet McTeer, Imelda Staunton, Bill Nighy) – all of this guarantees a creditable stab at **Joan Smith's** intriguing novel, but one that irons out the complexities. As so often, there is no substitute for the richer texture of a book over its adaptation, however sympathetic.

Wolves Eat Dogs — 2004

MARTIN CRUZ SMITH

You've heard it before: 'It's Martin Cruz Smith's best book since *Gorky Park*!' But surely each outing since that first Arkady Renko novel of 1981 has been impressive? Well, up to a point; all have been imaginative, making full capital out of the novelty of having a Russian detective in well-realised Russian settings (even when the novelty was no more). Only the sequel, *Polar Star* (1989), really had the same power as that first book, with its cloistered shipboard setting and sharp characterisation, but *Wolves Eat Dogs* also reminds us just how good the Renko books are – and there are several new elements added to this one. First of all, this is not the antediluvian Russia that Renko moved in when *Gorky Park* appeared; this is the Russia of Vladimir Putin (Putin himself is described as always looking like he's 'sucking on a sore tooth'), a country half in the modern age of mobile phones, home cinema and sushi bars, and half mired in the time-worn government double-dealing that has beset the country since **Fyodor Dostoyevsky**'s day. Complex relationships with western big business are now part of the scene and form an element of the plot here: the death of a businessman after plunging from a high window can't be categorised as murder, Renko is told, as suicide is less likely to frighten away foreign businesses from a country still nervously perceived as being in thrall to organised crime. Apart from the virtuoso realisation of his locales, Smith has deepened the characterisation of his hero here: Renko is facing the scrap heap, dealing wryly with daily humiliation and shoring up the emptiness of his life by acting as friend and visitor to a silent, sociopathic boy (who he takes at weekends to an amusement centre at Gorky Park). As Renko tries to ferret out the truth behind the suspicious death, he encounters the usual stonewalling and often violent interference, and the solution has ramifications that reach to the most privileged echelons of Russian society.

Dog Soldiers 1974
ROBERT STONE

Other writers may have earned higher advances, but the late Robert Stone was considered by many to be one of the finest American novelists of his day, with a body of work (most of which utilises the thriller format) far more accomplished than that of many better-known names. My conversations with him revealed a writer of the widest ambition. *Dog Soldiers*, a typical Stone novel, is so much more than a tale of drug dealing that goes wrong: as one of the premier US writers of the Vietnam era (and beyond), Stone may have exploited the tropes and conventions of crime fiction, but he always had much bigger fish to fry. The story is set in Saigon during the final months of the war in Vietnam. The journalist John Converse has decided that he can guarantee his future fortune with one large-scale drug deal. But back in the United States, divided loyalties and double-dealing ensure that things quickly go wrong. The 3kg of heroin that Converse has smuggled from war-scarred Southeast Asia to the streets of San Francisco plunges him and his colleagues into a nightmare trip through the deserts of California. Hot on their heels are both the drug-dealing thugs on whose patch they've encroached and some very nasty bent cops. While Stone is unquestionably a literary novelist, with a lambent prose that brilliantly delineates his characters and a cool sensibility that informs his narratives with a real sociological edge, he is able to handle the violence and menace of his plots with the assurance of **Ernest Hemingway**. While the tough accoutrements of *Dog Soldiers* allow the book to function on a straightforward thriller level, its formidable achievements lift it several notches above most American novels written in the 1970s.

Stone continued, if sporadically, to hit the right nails. *Outerbridge Reach* (1992) tackled ambition, celebrity and self-defeat in a boat race circumnavigating the globe, while *Damascus Gate* (1998) is an outstanding analysis of the clash of interests centred on the Israel–Palestine conflict. The stripped-down *Bay of Souls* (2003), with a naive academic unexpectedly embroiled in Third World corruption, threatening local drug dealers and duplicitous expats, allowed him once again to explore notions of redemption and crises of conscience. Here, as elsewhere, the author shared with another of his heroes, **Joseph Conrad**, a startling skill at creating a melange of the poetic and the horrific: the sudden surfacing of the bloated corpse of a drowned pilot, looking like some fabulous sea monster with an attendant host of beautiful but flesh-consuming fish, genuinely chills the blood. But *Dog Soldiers* should remain your entry point to this fascinating writer's work.

WHO'LL STOP THE RAIN   1978

Director: Karel Reisz

What a glorious period for truly individual cinema the 1970s were! Karel Reisz may have drifted since his early success with films such as *Saturday Night and Sunday Morning* (1960) and *Night Must Fall* (1964), but he was very firmly back on form with this adaptation of **Robert Stone**'s blistering *Dog Soldiers*. As a picture of the post-Vietnam *zeitgeist*, it's full of insight – and as an edgy thriller, it's equally engaging. Strong performances from Nick Nolte and Tuesday Weld.

Acid Row   2001

MINETTE WALTERS

'Acid Row' is the ironic name given to their home by the luckless inhabitants of a sink estate. Disenfranchised, dangerous youths roam the streets, and into this no man's land of one-parent families comes Sophie Morrison, a young doctor visiting a patient. But she is unaware that she is entering the home of a paedophile known to the police. The first pages of *Acid Row* clearly mark the book out as a further step in the author's move into the kind of crime novel in which social significance is every bit as important as the page-turning imperatives of a thriller. Once again, Walters is just as interested in the psychology of the characters and the problems of modern life as in the dictates of the classic crime story. The use of the young Sophie as the protagonist is a brilliant stroke. When reports circulate that a disturbed child called Amy has disappeared, Sophie finds herself caught between dangerous vigilantes and a man she dislikes intensely. As in 2002's outstanding *Fox Evil*, Walters keeps the cutting-edge aspects of her plots to the fore, cleverly wrong-footing the reader at every turn: although we think we have decided how we feel about the endangered paedophile and the vigilantes, she never allows these aspects to overwhelm the nagging, disturbing power of her narrative. At heart, *Acid Row* is still a mystery. Is Amy, the supposed victim, really missing?

The Prince of Wales 2003

JOHN WILLIAMS

Cardiff. Local paper features editor Pete Duke, 40, has split up from his wife and is looking to have some fun. He meets Kim, 28, who works for the BBC. Bobby, 36, is a lesbian pimp who sees her world coming to an end as the demolition of the Custom House nears. Pete and Kim go to the last night of the Custom House, where they meet Bobby and her prostitute girlfriend Maria and shoplifter/failed pimp Mikey, and all of them get drunk and go for a joyride. A complex web of intrigues and messy relationship shifts ensues in Williams' scabrous picture of society in the Welsh capital city as the millennium approaches. In earlier books (such as *Cardiff Dead* (2000)), Williams staked out his claim to be the definitive, cold-eyed chronicler of his home town, and he has been refining his unforgiving canvas ever since. The black-economy Cardiff trilogy, of which *The Prince of Wales* is the culmination, displays writing of both ambition and idiosyncratic skill; the bid by Cardiff to forge an identity as the city's appearance and economy undergo turbulent changes is matched by the rich smorgasbord of relationships and characters in this novel.

CHAPTER 13

ESPIONAGE
Spooks and betrayals

It looked for a while as if the literary espionage genre was on the ropes. The field that had produced some of the most sophisticated and profound writing (as well as some of the most suspenseful) in what is loosely called the crime/thriller genre was dealt a body blow by the end of the Cold War, and two of the most acclaimed contemporary practitioners, **John le Carré** and **Len Deighton**, showed signs of being cast adrift by international events. But, to different degrees, both writers adjusted to this new landscape with its new threats and found fresh challenges for their protagonists. Le Carré turned his attention both to the nefarious modern-day activities of multinational corporations in *The Constant Gardener* (2001) and to sniffy criticism of Anglo–US unilateralism in *Absolute Friends* (2003). It's still a dangerous world, after all, and more recent writers have found great mileage in such areas as fundamentalist terrorism and ruthless big business exploitation of the Third World. Meanwhile, **Henry Porter** and **Robert Wilson** have woven different fabrics out of the legacy of Nazi and Soviet ambitions, often spanning parallel historical and contemporary plotlines – all the more prescient as neo-Nazism gets a second wind and Russia takes its old, familiar clothes out of the wardrobe – while **Charles Cumming**, **Mick Herron**, **Dan Fesperman** and other writers are keeping the genre fresh in the 21st century. Of course, the spy thriller enjoyed a magnificent birth with such works as **Joseph Conrad**'s 1907 masterpiece *The Secret Agent*, whose vision of fanatical terrorists is still relevant over a century later. Inaugurating the action-driven narrative, **Sapper**'s Bulldog Drummond stories (despite their now-questionable ideology) had great exuberance and foreshadowed the quick-witted espionage hero – burnished to perfection in **John Buchan**'s Richard Hannay in such classics as *The Thirty-Nine Steps*, the prototype for the modern thriller. Clubland hero Hannay's direct descendant was, of course, **Ian Fleming**'s James Bond, who interpolated more exhilarating sex, violence and gracious living into the bone-crunching action. The political complexities of espionage had previously been explored by **Somerset Maugham** in his Ashenden stories, but the right-wing assumptions of such classic spy fiction were to be challenged by **Eric Ambler**.

Journey into Fear 1940

ERIC AMBLER

As noted above, some of Ambler's finest books are finding their way back into print, embellished with the glowing imprimatur of many modern practitioners who are still in his debt. In this novel, the engineer Graham, an Englishman undertaking a terrifying flight across wartime Europe, is the archetypal Ambler hero: an ordinary man attempting to survive against an extraordinary backdrop of danger and corruption. There's no denying that certain elements of the narratives have dated a trifle, but the modern spy story begins in Ambler's consummately well-written thrillers.

JOURNEY INTO FEAR 1942

Director: Norman Foster

Eric Ambler was particularly lucky in this adaptation of one of his best novels, but the force of the film is not down to the credited director, Norman Foster. This was, in fact, **Orson Welles'** third film as a director (uncredited): as well as providing a memorable portrayal of the creepy Colonel Haki, Welles handled most of the direction, as well as working on the screenplay with principal star Joseph Cotten. While the storytelling is, at times, a touch muddled, the atmospheric *mise-en-scène* contains many pre-echoes of Welles' later noir masterpiece *Touch of Evil* (1958).

Eric Ambler
(1909–98)

At the time of the publication of his last book, Eric Ambler's publisher Ion Trewin lamented to me that the venerable writer had to be 'sold' to younger booksellers almost as a new name: the writer who forged the style adopted by the espionage novels of **John le Carré** and **Graham Greene** was almost a forgotten man – at least to a later generation of readers. The situation is better these days, with sporadic reissue programmes making such masterworks as *Journey into Fear* (1940) available again – and it's to be hoped that new readers will be drawn to this most gifted of writers. Ambler was born in 1909 and sampled a variety of careers (comedian, playwright, advertising copywriter) before publishing his seminal thriller *The Mask of Dimitrios* (1937), featuring the journalist Latimer – the first of Ambler's ordinary men caught up in dangerous situations in threatening, sultry foreign climates. While Ambler enjoyed a very successful second career as a screenwriter, he continued to produce skilfully crafted novels such as *The Light of Day* (1964), several of which were filmed.

Ambler's greatest innovation was probably the shift of political balance in the genre: the right-wing certainties of **William Le Queux**, **John Buchan** and **Sapper** were replaced by a marked left-wing bias; establishment figures were no longer to be trusted, and there was little moral difference between the espionage services of different countries. Ambler was able to accommodate the modern world in such books as *The Levanter* (1972), although the flame of his talent burned less brightly in later years.

Ian Fleming and his legacy: stirred but never shaken

The phenomenal durability of Ian Fleming's secret agent 007 continues to amaze. Few fictional heroes concocted in the early 1950s remain in the public consciousness – or indeed in print – but the James Bond franchise, whether on the page, at the cinema, in graphic novels or in computer games, or simply in the popular imagination, seems impervious to the years or to the vagaries of fashion.

When the *Sunday Times* journalist Ian Fleming (1908–64) settled down to pen his first novel, which appeared as *Casino Royale* in 1953, he came up with a remarkable formula: a secret agent whose 'licence to kill' on behalf of Her Majesty's government meant that he could be unleashed both as a counterespionage operative in the Cold War novels such as *From Russia with Love* (1957) and in the fight against organised crime (in *Live and Let Die* (1954) and *Diamonds are Forever* (1956), for example).

Bond was also charged with taking on a range of megalomaniac super-criminals, often members of the sinister SPECTRE organisation,

Running Blind   1970

DESMOND BAGLEY

Is this the first Nordic noir novel? The opening lines of Bagley's most impressive thriller immediately arrest the attention: 'To be encumbered with a corpse is to be in a difficult position, especially when the corpse is without benefit of a death certificate.' The reader is then launched into what is essentially a breathless chase through a stunningly realised Iceland, as well drawn as any locale in crime and mystery fiction. Bagley had a long and distinguished career in the field, but most of his books (even such impressive pieces as *The Spoilers* (1969) and *High Citadel* (1965)) have fallen from favour these days. If there is any justice, his work should regain its former lustre, and *Running Blind* is his most ingenious and pacey novel. Alan Stewart is told by his employers that he is to be just a messenger boy, including the eponymous villains of *Dr No* (1958) and *Goldfinger* (1959), *Thunderball*'s Emilio Largo (1961), and Bond's arch-enemy, Ernst Stavro Blofeld (*You Only Live Twice* (1964)).

In truth, Fleming's novels themselves – while exemplary pieces of popular writing – are now period pieces (for instance, Bond is privileged to sample – unlike Fleming's readers of the 1950s – a truly exotic foodstuff that turns out to be a kebab). But Fleming's command of narrative and colourful detail remains exemplary even to this day.

The continuing reinvention of Bond on the screen and the page has provided 007 with quite remarkable longevity; he has been portrayed by a variety of very different actors from Sean Connery to Daniel Craig and has been tackled in print by **Kingsley Amis, John Gardner, Sebastian Faulks, Anthony Horowitz** and others. Nevertheless, it is Fleming, with his Eton and the Guards pedigree, background as a dirty tricks planner for naval intelligence during World War II and subsequent work as a journalist, who retains ownership of the concept decades after his death. Bond's snobbery, ruthlessness, sadism and rampant libido continue to represent a refreshing beacon of political incorrectness in an increasingly buttoned-down, sex-averse world.

---

a carrier of unimportant materials. But before long, he finds himself on a deserted road in Iceland with a corpse at his feet. Is the parcel he is carrying more important than he has been led to believe? And who are the people who are following him, seeking his death? Stewart's increasingly desperate flight for life – together with a girlfriend – through inhospitable territory is brilliantly detailed. All of this is conveyed in breathless but literate prose, and Bagley's knowledgeable authorial voice ensures an irresistible read.

Night Heron 2015

ADAM BROOKES

There is an honourable tradition of foreign correspondents turning to the thriller genre – perhaps the most famous being **Frederick Forsyth**. Those ranks were swelled with another impressive addition: Adam Brookes, formerly the BBC's China correspondent, with assignments in Iraq, Afghanistan, North Korea and other countries under his belt. Of course, such experience, even when combined with solid journalistic talent, does not guarantee thriller success, but Brookes arrived as a fully formed talent with a complete mastery of the genre. The plot involves a Chinese spy and a British journalist, with a whole nation hunting them, and we are gripped by the sinewy narrative from the very first page. A desperate prisoner whose name is Peanut escapes from a brutal labour camp at night, braving the frigid desert of northwest China. Twenty years earlier, he worked for British Intelligence, but now he must use his skills to vanish into the crowded streets of Beijing – and those streets are covered with surveillance cameras. Increasingly fearful of being returned to the labour camp, he contacts his ex-paymasters at MI6 via ambitious journalist Philip Mangan. In return for safe passage out of China, he has a bushel of state secrets that he is prepared to trade. Mangan, sensing the scoop of his career, agrees to take part in this highly dangerous adventure, but what neither he nor the escapee realise is just how significant the secrets for sale really are; the fate of governments is involved, not just the fate of two men on the run.

Like earlier masters of the thriller from a reporting background, Brookes knows exactly how to convey the essence of the situation in the most economic and effective way possible – and local colour is always conveyed with maximum impact; the reader always knows exactly where they are as the tension begins to mount. But more importantly, Brookes turns out to be a writer with a keen grasp of character, and his increasingly out-of-his-depth journalist is a nicely rounded protagonist – not always a given in this kind of novel, where plot reigns supreme. The author's experience of China adds great authority, and his laser-sharp portrayal of a compromised media and oppressive, omnipresent security ensures tremendous authenticity. You may not want to visit Beijing after reading *Night Heron*, but you will certainly want to read more thrillers by Adam Brookes.

Red Rabbit 2002

TOM CLANCY

Certainly, his sales and royalty advances indicate that readers voted with their wallets and put Tom Clancy at the top of the bestselling charts, a lack of finesse clearly being no disincentive. Clancy's credibility-stretching novels featuring ace CIA operative (and later politician) Jack Ryan were initially promoted as anti-James Bond thrillers, but this was something of a smokescreen. Ryan may be more of a family man than **Ian Fleming**'s creation and less given to serial promiscuity, and 007 never achieved – or wanted to achieve – high office, but both protagonists are usually the key players in high-octane action in which a combination of their wits and brawn often bring the world back from the brink of catastrophe.

Clancy can be counted on to deliver his expected trademarks: this one is full of well-researched detail and is studded with the adroitly staged action set pieces we have come to expect. *Red Rabbit* sketches in details of Ryan's early life, with him working on the bottom rung in the CIA's analysis department. He is given the unenviable mission of debriefing a key Soviet defector but discovers a dark secret: there is a plot afoot to murder Pope John Paul II.

The Quest for Anna Klein 2012

THOMAS H COOK

Why is it that as readers we are almost always intrigued by a novel that takes the form of a quest? Is it because there is usually a satisfying resolution in literature, unlike in real life? One of the most original quests in some considerable time is launched in this beguiling novel by Thomas H Cook. *The Quest for Anna Klein*, as good as anything Cook has written, begins with Thomas Danforth, a man whose life appears to have been carefully laid out for him: successful importing company in New York in the 1930s, financial success, secure future. But then a friend from the government comes to him with a highly unusual request. Danforth is to facilitate the training of an enigmatic young woman at his large estate in Connecticut. The woman, the seductive Anna Klein, is to throw Danforth's carefully ordered existence into chaos. The war in Europe is about to burst forth in all its fury, and Danforth is forced to choose between his dull, regimented existence and a dangerous and exciting new life – a new life, what's more, that may even change history. The linguist Anna Klein's training involves weaponry and bomb making, with a view – initially, at least – to assisting refugees from the Spanish Civil War residing in France when the inevitable German invasion takes place. But when it becomes clear that the refugees cannot deliver what is expected of them, the plan for Anna and her colleagues changes to something more concrete: the assassination of Adolf Hitler.

There are several things that make Cook's novel so winning, not least the fact that all of this is described retrospectively after the Al Qaeda destruction of the World Trade Center, with an older Danforth telling the story to secret service man Paul Crane. Cutting between the two time periods – Anna Klein's story in 1939 and the terrorist atrocities of 2001 – the quest that Danforth and Crane are involved in is to discover the truth behind Anna Klein's story. This is complicated by the fact that Danforth fell in love with her – obsessively – before her disappearance. And the uncovering of the truth here is as shocking as anything in Cook's inventive, steadily paced novel.

A Spy by Nature 2001

CHARLES CUMMING

Within the space of just a handful of books, Charles Cumming established an enviable reputation as one of the most adroit practitioners of the modern spy novel – a worthy successor to titans such as **John le Carré** and **Len Deighton**. And with *A Spy by Nature* – and the follow-up, *The Hidden Man* (2003) – Cumming triumphantly proved that the literary spy novel is still a genre that has much to offer in the field of betrayals and dissemblings. This is a disquieting study of Alec (the name is clearly a nod to le Carré's ill-fated Alec Leamas in *The Spy Who Came in from the Cold* (1963)), a young MI6 operative who finds himself caught between two masters. *The Hidden Man* deals with difficult relations between fathers and sons (a recurrent theme, of course, in le Carré), and sports a canvas stretching from London to Moscow and Afghanistan. Plotting in both books is exemplary – and if you haven't investigated Charles Cumming yet, now's the time.

The Man Between 2018

CHARLES CUMMING

Charles Cumming's *The Man Between* continued the author's steady run of winners. This standalone thriller has naive novelist Kit Carradine drawn into the duplicitous world of espionage. Carradine, seduced by what he sees as the glamour of British Intelligence, is more than ready to take on the task of travelling to Morocco to track down Lara Bartok, an enigmatic fugitive who may be linked to global terrorism. She is a key figure in Resurrection, a Baader-Meinhof-like group that kidnaps and murders right-wing politicians and journalists (an early victim here is a female journalist who bears a resemblance to a controversial UK pundit). Inevitably, Carradine is attracted to the seductive Lara and is forced into a fateful decision.

The Ipcress File 1962

LEN DEIGHTON

It's hard to realise today what an impact Len Deighton's remarkable spy novel had on its first appearance in the 1960s. Like **John le Carré**, Deighton was reacting against the glossy, unrealistic depiction of espionage in the novels of **Ian Fleming** (a certain puritanism was a factor at the time). But certainly *The Ipcress File*, with its insolent working-class hero and low-key treatment of all the quotidian details of a spy's life (endless futile requisitions for petty cash, a decidedly unglamorous secret service HQ), was astonishingly fresh, while the first-person narrative was a Londoner's refraction of **Raymond Chandler**'s wisecracking Philip Marlowe two decades on. Another radical touch was the refusal to neatly tie up the narrative with a cathartic death of the villain – the shadowy opponent of Deighton's unnamed protagonist goes unpunished for political reasons. A series of novels in the same vein followed, none quite as impressive as this debut but all highly accomplished.

THE IPCRESS FILE 1965

Director: Sidney J Furie

Although Furie's reliance on eccentric camera angles may look a touch mannered today, it's worth remembering that this was remarked on at the time of the film's initial release. In fact, camera angles and all, this is a career best for Furie – a perfect reworking of **Len Deighton**'s quirky anti-Bond novel, with the inspired casting of Michael Caine as the low-rent yet epicurean spy. The dingy sets are by Ken Adam – hard to believe, given the elaborate work he was simultaneously doing on the Bond films for producer Harry Saltzman (whose project this was) – and 007 score composer John Barry was also on board. But almost the single most cherishable element in a film crammed with subtle pleasures is the late character actor Nigel Green as Caine's supercilious, pernickety boss – another career best.

The Amateur Spy
DAN FESPERMAN

2009

In an isolated house on a Greek island, Freeman Lockhart and his Balkan wife Mira (whom he met while doing dangerous work in Sarajevo) are asleep when Lockhart awakes with a flashlight shining in his face and a hand pressed against his sternum. There are three men in the room – he scrambles for a gun under the bed, but a foot stamps on his hand while a fist slams into the bridge of his nose. 'Time to get up,' one of the assailants says quietly. This powerful scene occurs some 20 or so pages into Dan Fesperman's novel, and reminds us that the author has few equals when it comes to generating tension. We're quickly on the side of the compromised Lockhart, forced by his three sinister visitors to spy on an old friend, Omar, while working for him in Jordan. Against his will, Lockhart agrees to give clandestine reports on Omar to a secret organisation investigating the latter's finances.

But just as we think we have an idea where this novel is going, Fesperman introduces two more major characters into his ambitious narrative. Aliyah Rahim and her doctor husband Abbas are commuting in Connecticut when they realise they're in the middle of a pending crash between an out-of-control Ford SUV and a Metrobus. Abbas manages to swerve out of the path of the other vehicles as they collide, but while he is attempting to help the bloody and helpless victims, a hostile cop shouts 'Who's the Arab guy?' Aliyah angrily defends her husband, but the incident painfully shows the couple the suspicion with which Arab Americans are viewed in a post-9/11 US. Abbas is sent into an emotional tailspin by the death of the couple's daughter, and he is convinced that US resentment of his race is responsible. Soon, his wife Aliyah suspects that he is plotting a violent and massive act of vengeance. Against her will, she, like Lockhart, agrees to spy on someone close to her.

The way in which Fesperman handles these simultaneous plot lines is quite as authoritative as one would expect from the author of such books as *The Prisoner of Guantánamo* (2006). It goes without saying, of course, that Fesperman is a master of the orchestration of tension – but he is equally good at characterising his vulnerable, conflicted protagonists. And in this queasy universe, reluctant betrayal jostles with constant physical danger.

Safe Houses 2018
DAN FESPERMAN

There are two leading strands to the thriller genre: the globetrotting blockbuster in which paper-thin characters crack a ridiculously complicated code, and the intelligent, character-based novel with psychology foregrounded. American writer Dan Fesperman is firmly in the latter camp but can also raise the reader's pulse. In *Safe Houses*, CIA employee Helen Abell has been murdered in Maryland along with her husband. Helen's daughter Anna, rejecting the notion that her mentally ill brother was responsible, commissions investigator Henry Mattick to find out the truth. She is shocked to discover that her mother was a spy in Europe, and Fesperman's ambitious time-split narrative – moving between Maryland in 2014 and West Berlin in 1979 – allows the author to explore the very different attitudes of the two periods, not least the endemic sexism of Helen's era of espionage. The duplicity of the secret world becomes a metaphor for wider human betrayal.

Blood of Victory 2002
ALAN FURST

Furst's impeccably written *Kingdom of Shadows* (2000) invoked comparisons with **Graham Greene**, **John le Carré** and **Robert Harris**; his brilliant recreation of the 1930s and Europe at the time of World War II has the kind of richness and authenticity that only the best writers can boast, and the sense of danger and foreboding that informs this earlier tale of intrigue and betrayal brings a rare rush of excitement. *Kingdom of Shadows* dealt with the growing tide of fascism in Europe and injected new vigour into the espionage tale, and *Blood of Victory* has the same assured scene-setting and felicitous grasp of character as its predecessor. The setting is once again wartime Europe, and Furst's protagonist is Serebin, a journalist from Odessa with aspirations to fine writing. He is making his way to Istanbul to arrange the release from jail of an ex-lover, backed by a powerful spy network located in the Parisian community of Russian émigrés, but then he is recruited by the British…

Furst is an American author who considers himself European, and his lineage as a writer stretches right back to **Joseph Conrad**. He is not afraid to challenge the reader, and his radical reinvention of the espionage novel is the happy result of the authority and fastidiousness of his writing. As in *Kingdom of Shadows*, Furst is careful to ensure that not all loose ends are tied up: that, and the multi-layered characterisation of Serebin, gives the novel the kind of weight more typical of literary novels than of the thriller genre.

The Foreign Correspondent 2007
ALAN FURST

Wartime Europe is the territory to which Furst returns in *The Foreign Correspondent* (Furst's cheeky appropriation of a famous **Alfred Hitchcock** title is misleading – this is a far darker piece than Hitch's *jeu d'esprit*). In fact, the book is set in the feverish period just before World War II, and the eponymous foreign correspondent is Carlo Weisz of Reuters, covering the final campaign of the Spanish Civil War. But a double death at a Paris hotel (a favourite spot for clandestine sexual liaisons) propels him into a new job. The victims are the editor of émigré newspaper *Liberazione* and his lover – and both have been murdered by OVRA, the secret police of Mussolini's fascist regime. Carlo, seduced by the laudable ideology and the romance of the idea, unwisely agrees to take over editorship of the paper – and puts himself into a dangerous position. But it's equally dangerous to rekindle an old affair in Berlin with the intriguing Christa, now married to a rich older man. As Carlo becomes the target of the murderous OVRA agents, the French *Sûreté* and even British Intelligence, political imperatives assume second place to the task of simply staying alive. Once again, *The Foreign Correspondent* is a reminder that the espionage novel (if that's what we're going to call this) can still be a vehicle for fine writing, and Furst's audacious reinvention of the genre is a constant delight.

The Ministry of Fear 1943
GRAHAM GREENE

The scarred and darkened London of the Blitz has never been so memorably portrayed in fiction as in this consummate piece of thriller writing by Greene, who chose to bracket the book as one of his *soi-disant* 'entertainments'. As so often, the distinction between his entertainments and more serious work doesn't preclude an examination of moral issues quite as profound and harrowing as anything in, say, *A Burnt-Out Case* (1960). The atmosphere of the novel is almost surrealistic in its accumulation of sinister detail. The protagonist is Arthur Rowe, suffering agonies of guilt after having brought about the death of his ailing wife. Ignoring the realities of the war, he guesses the weight of a cake at a charity fête, and subsequently finds himself pitched into a world in which he is hunted, on the run from murderous, shadowy figures, with his only chance of survival lying in cracking the truth behind his predicament. While the mechanics of the storytelling are kicked along by standard thriller imperatives, they have rarely been brought off with the brio that Greene demonstrates here, and the picture of a bomb-damaged London will stay in the mind of any reader of the novel.

MINISTRY OF FEAR 1944

Director: Fritz Lang

Given that **Graham Greene** himself was once a film critic, it's perhaps not an accident that he was so lucky in his choice of directors. His association with the gifted British director **Carol Reed** produced some of the novelist's best work (notably *The Fallen Idol* (1948) and *The Third Man* (1949)) but here his novel was sympathetically filmed by the great German Expressionist director Fritz Lang, doing wonderful work in the crime genre after his move to America (his later gangster thriller *The Big Heat* (1953) was to anticipate *The Godfather*). The film is lucky, too, in having the ever dependable Ray Milland as the hapless hero/victim.

Moskva 2016

JACK GRIMWOOD

Sometimes it's a good idea to change horses midstream. Jon Courtenay Grimwood has had a distinguished career as a writer of imaginative science fiction, but here he is resurfacing with the more blunt moniker 'Jack Grimwood' as a writer of thrillers, with the jacket of *Moskva* hopefully describing it as '*Fatherland* meets *Gorky Park*'. But has the gear change worked?

1985, Red Square. The naked body of a young man is found near the Kremlin, frozen solid. When the teenage daughter of the British ambassador disappears, doughty Army Intelligence Officer Tom Fox is tasked with finding her, but he discovers that the ruthless Soviet establishment doesn't take kindly to having its secrets exposed. There is much to admire here: the operatic sweep of this mesmerising novel; the orchestration of tension; and the strongly realised sense of time and place – all of these factors mark Grimwood's *Moskva* out as innovative in the arena of international thrillers.

Nightfall Berlin
2018

JACK GRIMWOOD

The rejuvenation of the espionage thriller continues apace with *Nightfall Berlin* by Jack Grimwood, his follow-up to the well-reviewed *Moskva* and the second book to feature British Intelligence officer Major Tom Fox. In 1986, with the Cold War showing signs of thawing, Fox is sent to East Berlin to engineer the repatriation of a defector. The mission is compromised, and Tom, accused of murder, soon has pitiless Stasi agents on his trail. Grimwood's previous career as a science fiction writer is echoed in the off-kilter, vaguely phantasmagoric atmosphere.

Spook Street
2017

MICK HERRON

It's not often a reviewer can say 'You've never read anything quite like this', but it's a safe encomium to use in the case of the prize-winning Mick Herron. The author's idiosyncratic writing is something unique in his genre, which, one might venture, is the spycraft of **John le Carré** refracted through the blackly comic vision of **Joseph Heller**'s *Catch-22*. Herron's trips to the outer reaches of British espionage already have a cult following, not least because his humour is wedded to a genuine sense of tension. We are back at Slough House, where superannuated agents are salted away. The confrontational leader of the team, Jackson Lamb (as unprepossessing as ever), is looking into what might be the murder of one of his associates – and mass killings by a suicide bomber in the Mall in London may have a connection. Herron's cutting dialogue, as ever, is priceless.

Bad Company 2003
JACK HIGGINS

A typical Jack Higgins novel? Let's look at *Bad Company*. Higgins trundles out a title that's seen much service before, but it's no doubt harder and harder to come up with thriller titles that haven't been used previously. In any case, this unvarnished outing for the tough intelligence man Sean Dillon is quite as fast-moving and uncomplicated as any of its predecessors, even though it's a long time since the glory days of 1975's *The Eagle Has Landed*, Higgins' celebrated World War II thriller. This time, dark secrets from World War II are resurfacing to cast a shadow over the present. Hitler's diary was placed in the custody of a youthful aide, the German nobleman Max von Berger. After the Führer died ignominiously in the bunker, the canny von Berger parlayed his inheritance into a great deal of temporal power, not least in terms of consolidating an association with the sinister Rashid clan, implacable opponents of British Intelligence – and specifically of Sean Dillon and his colleague Major Ferguson. The diary contains an incendiary secret – details of a clandestine meeting between representatives of Roosevelt and Hitler – and the present-day ramifications may bring down the current US president. Higgins fans will recognise this as standard-issue Sean Dillon territory – all the customary tangled plotting, bursts of action, and a studied avoidance of nuance are here.

The Spy Who Came in from the Cold 1963
JOHN LE CARRÉ

The greatest favour an admirer of thrillers could do for themselves is to read John le Carré, and start with *The Spy Who Came in from the Cold*. Even if you've read it – more than once – you'll be reminded anew how impeccably written is this finest of all modern espionage novels. The story of the ill-fated British spy Alec Leamas achieves a genuine tragic dimension, and there is not another novel in the genre that has plotting as exemplary as this, with every sleight of hand played on both the characters and the reader supremely satisfying. Finally, though, it's the not-a-wasted-word economy of the book that astonishes. Later novels by the author, however accomplished, are nearly always of epic proportions. This is a reminder that le Carré could – and perhaps should – be much more concise.

John le Carré
(1931–)

More than any other British writer (including even his great influence, **Graham Greene**), John le Carré (pseudonym of **David John Moore Cornwell**) has made the novel of espionage and adventure a respectable literary form – one that can be a repository for insights into human nature, politics and the moral bankruptcy of the developed world. It might be argued that another influence le Carré is happy to acknowledge, the novelist **Joseph Conrad**, performed this same feat, but Conrad had long been entrenched in the 'classic' category before le Carré began his genre-stretching activities. As with Graham Greene, le Carré could draw on his own period in the security services when he added a literary career to his civil service one – but his early novels, such as the splendid *Call for the Dead* (1961) and *A Murder of Quality* (1962), were essentially detective novels. The unassuming secret service man George Smiley made his first appearance here, however, before moving centre stage in the later, far more expansive novels. *The Spy Who Came in from the Cold* (1963) is the writer's first unalloyed masterpiece, and one of the great espionage novels, but more ambitious work was to follow in such multifaceted books as *The Little Drummer Girl* (1983). This novel's use of the Arab–Israeli conflict demonstrated that le Carré would negotiate the end of the Cold War to move on to other threats. If his hatred of current British and American politics has resulted in the kind of polemics in his novels that he would once have shunned, le Carré remains one of Britain's greatest writers.

THE SPY WHO CAME IN FROM THE COLD — 1965

Director: Martin Ritt

It's interesting to speculate how much of his massive popularity **John le Carré** owes to this perfectly honed adaptation of his classic novel. Of course, he would have enjoyed immense success, but that final plateau of celebrity may be down to Martin Ritt's movie. All the key elements of the source novel are incorporated in the top-notch Paul Dehn screenplay, while those elisions that were necessary are seamlessly done – it's hard to imagine a more satisfying adaptation. The icing on the cake is, of course, Richard Burton as Leamas. Too often the actor made unfortunate choices in his film roles – a fact he was all too aware of – but, thankfully, he seized this opportunity with both hands.

The Company — 2002

ROBERT LITTELL

If you find slim novels insufficiently demanding, and have a taste for *War and Peace*-sized thrillers, Robert Littell's remarkable *The Company* is for you. Littell gleaned comparisons as jaw-dropping as **Don DeLillo**, **Norman Mailer**, **Homer** and **Charles Dickens**; when it appeared, the general consensus was that *The Company* is the definitive CIA novel. The narrative details the search for a mole in the CIA against a massive panoply of key events in world history. New Haven, 1950: the CIA recruits from the country's most promising students at Yale – but is the KGB recruiting too? Budapest, 1956: what was the CIA's role in the Hungarian revolt against communist rule? Cuba, 1961: what was behind the debacle of the Bay of Pigs and its catastrophic aftermath? Afghanistan, 1983: the CIA is torn between bankrolling Afghan rebels and giving weapons to Islamic fundamentalists. What did the CIA know about Bin Laden and his ambitions? Moscow, 1991: during the fall of the Soviet empire, the CIA supports the forces of Boris Yeltsin, while the KGB aims to overthrow Gorbachev. Washington, 1995: the intrigues escalate. Spooks hand secrets to the Russians, but no longer for ideological reasons: filthy lucre is the motivator now. With a vast cast of characters, *The Company* skilfully integrates fictional espionage with an ambitious, panoramic canvas of the latter half of the last century, offering an unbeatable picture of the endless ramifications the secret world has on all our lives.

Littell was always going to find this novel a hard act to follow. If *Legends* (2005) is more compact than its predecessor, it's still a weighty tome. In it, Littell once again demonstrates his mastery of literary espionage, but this time shifts his attention to the dangerous life of a lone CIA operative who finds himself in a wilderness of mirrors. The singular achievement of this notable follow-up novel is the way in which the author allows it to function on two levels: firstly as a powerfully atmospheric, labyrinthine espionage narrative, and simultaneously as a penetrating study of divided personality. The latter aspect is never handled in a po-faced fashion, but always remains at the service of storytelling impetus.

The Bourne Identity 1980

ROBERT LUDLUM

Starting with the straightforward *The Scarlatti Inheritance* in 1971, Robert Ludlum was top of the thriller tree for so many years that it was quite a surprise when he appeared to vanish from view. But he made a lukewarm comeback – albeit aided by a co-author – and fans of his blockbuster thrillers eagerly embraced these new books. The real Ludlum? That's in *The Bourne Identity*, with all the author's familiar tropes in place. Jason Bourne is a man without a past, pulled from the sea full of bullets. He also has a surgically implanted microfilm and a reconfigured face. The trick is to find out who he is – and soon Bourne is fleeing from his erstwhile colleagues in the security services. Using his instinctive tradecraft (and a woman with whom he once had a relationship), he decides to test the premise that attack is the best form of defence. And taking the fight to the enemy is also a way of finding

THE BOURNE IDENTITY 2002

Director: Doug Liman

Memories of an indifferent earlier Richard Chamberlain television movie were erased by this lean and efficient adaptation of **Robert Ludlum**'s novel, with Matt Damon as the beleaguered Bourne. The film proved to be the progenitor of a successful new franchise – and even influenced an older series, with Daniel Craig's Bond debut, *Casino Royale*, following in 2006. Some have argued that Liman's movie (and its successors, *The Bourne Supremacy* (2004) and *The Bourne Ultimatum* (2007), both directed by **Paul Greengrass**) actually improved on Ludlum's sometimes by-the-numbers novels.

the missing pieces of his own identity. *The Bourne Identity* delivers all the requisite action and never neglects the essentials of economical scene-setting. If the characterisation is rough-hewn, that's par for the course with Ludlum, and admirers don't turn to him for subtleties of psychological insight.

Palace of Treason — 2016

JASON MATTHEWS

Jason Matthews has a CIA background, which guarantees a strong whiff of authenticity in his espionage novels. His debut, *Red Sparrow* (2013), was much acclaimed, and in this follow-up we are again in the seductive company of Dominika Egorova of the Russian Intelligence Service, who loathes what she sees as her own gangster state. While *Palace of Treason* may not quite live up to the promise of its predecessor, it's still a solid piece of work. Egorova is working as a CIA mole in the Kremlin when she comes to the attention of Vladimir Putin himself. But her passionate sexual affair with her handler Nate Nash breaks every rule in the CIA book, even as she tries to get a compromised agent out of Russia. Matthews admits little nuance in his view of the CIA and its foreign opponents (the former is good; the latter are bad), but he knows exactly what he's doing in maintaining a comprehensive grip on the reader.

Old Boys — 2004

CHARLES McCARRY

Elegant, pared-down prose. A measured, richly characterised picture of a secret world. A continent-spanning narrative. A middle-aged hero and a largely mature cast of characters. Betrayal and sudden death. These could be the constituent elements of a classic Cold War novel from **John le Carré**, but they are also typical of the *éminence grise* of the American espionage novel, Charles McCarry – a writer whose considerable reputation had been built up since the 1970s in a widely spaced series of diamond-hard, ruthlessly logical novels, positively burnished with high-end CIA tradecraft. McCarry appeared to write *finis* to the career of his protagonist Paul Christopher in 1983's *The Last Supper*, and he was just as recalcitrant when asked about the CIA stalwart's return as he was when quizzed on his years at the Agency; unlike certain British ex-spooks, McCarry remained close-mouthed about his earlier clandestine activities. But Paul Christopher was back in *Old Boys*

– even if he appears to be dead shortly after the first chapter. His ex-CIA colleague and cousin Horace Hubbard (with whom Christopher, now in his 70s, has just had a valedictory meal) inveigles other ageing Agency men into finding out if Christopher is really dead – as Hubbard suspects that he is not. Was it worth the protracted wait between books? The answer is an unqualified yes. McCarry was not an apologist for his country's less defensible actions, and the moral equivocation of his book, combined with fascinatingly handled spy tradecraft, confirms his place in the pantheon.

Dark Winter 2003

ANDY McNAB

Let's face it – we once thought that Andy McNab was all set to become a one-book wonder, parlaying his experiences with the SAS into a single, and highly readable, book, *Bravo Two Zero* (1993). But with such popular books as *Crisis Four* (1999), which was marginally more sophisticated than his first outing (not difficult) but with all the brute force fans want from him, he established a solid following. *Firewall* (2000) is a streamlined thriller in which Nick Stone (ex-SAS, now working for British Intelligence on 'deniable operations') is handed the freelance job of snatching a mafia warlord and taking him to St Petersburg – lucrative but highly dangerous work. More unusual, though, is *Dark Winter*, where the narrative has some fresh moves, with the bolshie protagonist sharply drawn and the action loaded with the energy that we expect from McNab. This one has Nick dispatched to Southeast Asia, and reluctantly putting up with a female partner on the trip; there, he is to tackle a scientist in the pay of Osama Bin Laden. But before the end of the book, Nick is turning up a host of terrorist plots in both Britain and America.

Pieces of Modesty 2010

PETER O'DONNELL

The Modesty Blaise comic strip was unarguably the most intelligent, best-written and sophisticated comic strip created for adults – but let's not forget how good creator Peter O'Donnell's subsequent novels were. For some time, one of the hardest-to-find Modesty Blaise books was this six-story collection, with the resourceful woman of action and her loyal sidekick, Willie Garvin, travelling and fighting their way around the world, from South America to Berlin, Finland to London, using everything that comes to hand, from a circus cannon to human kite flying, to survive against the odds. Peter O'Donnell, who is a favourite of many key practitioners, started as a professional writer in 1937, creating – together with the respected illustrator Jim Holdaway – the character of Modesty Blaise for a strip cartoon in 1963. The series was eventually syndicated in over 42 countries and O'Donnell produced 13 Modesty books.

Empire State
2003

HENRY PORTER

Henry Porter's *Empire State* consolidates the impression made by his earlier *A Spy's Life* (2001): here is an espionage writer with panache and assurance, turning out work that is ingenious and exuberant. Heathrow is the setting for a major assassination: the Special Counsel on Security to the United States is killed, and it is discovered that his family has been similarly murdered elsewhere in Britain. Porter's protagonist Robert Harland is obliged to tackle the most complex mystery of his career, but a clue resides in another seemingly random event: an osteopath in New York (Harland is one of his patients) is sent postcards of the Empire State Building, dispatched from Iran and Turkey, and the man who sent them is murdered in Macedonia. Harland has to draw these strands together before another major atrocity occurs. While the narrative here is quite as discursive and mystifying as one might wish for, it's the always felicitous characterisation that raises Porter above the level of many less ambitious peers. Henry Porter might well be among those writing the key espionage thrillers for the 21st century.

Firefly
2018

HENRY PORTER

After a hiatus of nearly a decade, the excellent thriller writer Henry Porter returned with *Firefly*, in which a 13-year-old boy has escaped from the refugee camps in Greece and is on a dangerous odyssey to Germany and freedom. But he has knowledge that has put him in the firing line of an ISIS terrorist cell; they are determined that he must die before he can reveal details of operations in Europe. Former MI6 operative Paul Samson is tasked with tracking down the boy (codenamed 'Firefly'), using his expertise in Arabic to win over his terrified charge and save him from his ruthless pursuers. *Firefly* sees the welcome return of a writer and journalist who has often decried the surveillance society, which he sees as an unacceptable intrusion into our personal freedom. And it's perhaps that very concern that drives this galvanic novel: it's not the all-seeing eyes of the security services that will prevent a large-scale atrocity, but the actions of one good man, Samson. With its portrait of the flood of refugees moving west from Macedonia, Serbia and Turkey, the book could not have been more timely, and Porter's sympathy for the dispossessed is as cogent here as his skill at sustaining narrative tension.

The Accidental Agent 2016
ANDREW ROSENHEIM

Andrew Rosenheim's *Fear Itself* (2011), the first book featuring Special Agent Jimmy Nessheim, was set in the turbulent political world of late 1930s America, with President Franklin D Roosevelt in an assassin's gunsight. As well as being a superlative thriller, that book presented a sophisticated and rounded picture of a society and an era, a trick pulled off again in the equally accomplished *The Accidental Agent*. The development of a superweapon will win World War II, but while the Allies work on the atom bomb, the Germans are bent on acquiring a nuclear weapon. Nessheim goes undercover at a secret nuclear programme at the University of Chicago, joining the team of physicist Enrico Fermi – which has been infiltrated. But is Nessheim the right man for the job? Ex-lover (and ex-communist) Stacey Madison has re-entered his life. Conspiracy and betrayal are set to derail the American war effort. There is much to praise in this complex and ambitious narrative, not least the adroitly handled ticking clock scenario.

Land of Fire 2002
CHRIS RYAN

Chris Ryan writes the kind of books that virtually dictate the pace at which they are read. Many a reader will have settled down for a chapter or two with such books as *Tenth Man Down* (1999) and *Stand By, Stand By* (1996) and found themselves unable to put the book aside. There is a fine balance between assiduously observed professional detail (often military) and the plausibility of the highly dangerous tasks Ryan sets for his protagonists. We're told just as much as we need to know, and it never gets in the way of the action. *Land of Fire* follows senior NCO Mark Black coming to terms with his past. During the Falklands conflict, he captured a young woman who was an Argentinian spy. And as a new military junta makes bellicose noises about invading the Falklands again, Black is forced to confront the girl once again – and possibly even trust his life to her. While all the usual suspense is on offer, Ryan has added some depth to his characters here, demonstrating that, at this point in his career, he had tired of simply dashing off straightforward thrillers.

A Treachery of Spies — 2018
MANDA SCOTT

Manda Scott's formidable Boudica quartet – not to mention her literary excursions to Ancient Rome – hardly prepared the reader for the abrupt change of gear in her Inès Picaut novels such as *A Treachery of Spies*. The novel begins in the present day with a murder whose tendrils stretch back to World War II. An elderly woman is savagely killed in Orléans, France, her throat cut and her tongue removed – a death in the manner of those who betrayed the Resistance. Dogged inspector of police Inès Picaut must investigate the actions of the Maquis in the 1940s, fighting a bloody hidden battle against the German occupiers. The dead woman, it transpires, was trained in Britain and parachuted into France. Scott adroitly balances the present-day murder investigation with the bravery and betrayal of the French Resistance. Moral questions are cogently addressed here – such as what happens when the virus of fascism infects the body politic – and Scott's writing is as commanding as in her novels set in ancient times.

Traitor's Kiss — 2003
GERALD SEYMOUR

Many publishers make grandiose claims for their pet authors, but Gerald Seymour's publishers can put their hands on their collective heart and unequivocally claim that they have the best thriller writer currently working in the UK. Seymour remains, quite simply, the most intelligent and accomplished practitioner of the genre in Britain today, and even his misfires (of which there aren't many) are more interesting than most of the competition. When so many novelists in the field are happy with hand-me-down characterisation and familiar storylines, Seymour always manages to create fresh and original protagonists, and weaves for them plots that are unlike anything he (or his rivals) have come up with before. In *Traitor's Kiss*, a high-ranking Russian naval officer, Viktor Archenko, is a source of much arcane information for the special services. Alarm bells begin to ring in MI6 when the usual lines of communication with Archenko are abruptly severed. London man Gabriel Locke, like his colleagues, knows that this precious contact was living life on the edge, but he remains an enigma. How to proceed? Locke decides that the best course of action is to get Archenko out – and while the Cold War may be over, this is a strategy that is fraught with immense danger. Locke is a classic spy hero and is one of Seymour's most forceful and unusual protagonists.

A Deniable Death 2011

GERALD SEYMOUR

Nothing can be more bitter, said **Lytton Strachey**, than to be doomed to a life of literature. Strachey was wrong – it is far worse to find oneself encountering a slew of bad thrillers. Which is why picking up a novel by Gerald Seymour is like taking a deep breath of fresh air after spending a month in a cellar. Why is it that this veteran writer has so comfortably maintained his reputation as the best in the business for so many years? His sales are steady but perhaps don't match those of other, far less talented writers – many of whom are well aware that they are minnows to his whale. *A Deniable Death* once again proves that age cannot wither his skills. Having tackled everything from the search for war criminals in the former Yugoslavia to suicide bombers in the UK, his subject here is the Middle East, presented with a convincing veracity.

MI6 have in their sights a bomb maker in Iraq, a man who has exported so much death and destruction to the neighbouring countries that his assassination is a matter of urgency. But tracking him down will be far from easy – terrorists have long been able to go to ground in the savage untamed territory around southern Iraq, an area that does not lend itself to surveillance. In fact, covert rural observation posts (or CROPs) are crucial to MI6, and the men who use them are tested to the limits in mosquito-ridden swamps while watching a dangerous enemy. One individual, Gibbons, is charged with selecting two men for this punishing infiltration mission. From a hide in the marshes, they will gather information on the bomb specialist before they escape to the border. This deniable mission – it can have no official sanction – carries the threat of murderous tribesmen and wild animals. And to make things even worse, the two men that Gibbons chooses have an intense dislike of each other.

As always with Seymour, it is impossible to know what to praise first. The customary grip of accelerating tension; the sense of a minatory foreign landscape acutely rendered (Seymour's days as a reporter covering conflicts in Vietnam, Borneo and Northern Ireland have sharpened his unerring eye for that precise piece of detail that conjures up the locale: never have the badlands of Iraq been evoked with such oppressive rigour). And for fans of the thriller, there are also the welcome echoes of past masters – writers who no doubt inspired Seymour in his tyro efforts. Here, it's **Geoffrey Household**'s *Rogue Male* (1939) that comes to mind, with men struggling to survive in a subterranean 'hide' where the slightest wrong move will be fatal. But perhaps what distinguishes Seymour most from his contemporaries is the level of sophisticated moral choice on offer. How many other writers would have fleshed out the bomb maker? Seymour allows us into the consciousness of this man and his life – notably his marriage to a mortally ill woman. And when readers get to the final nail-biting climax involving an agonising wait for airborne rescue, they may be wondering why they should bother with any other thriller writer.

All the Old Knives 2015

OLEN STEINHAUER

Sitting in the top-floor restaurant of London's Centre Point – before the area became a semi-permanent building site – the American writer Olen Steinhauer told journalists dining with him (including me) that he would rather trade in his keyboard than write the same novel twice – and, true to form, *All the Old Knives* is subtly unlike his earlier books. Yes, it is an espionage piece, sporting much of the psychologically acute, conflicted characterisation of the 1960s school, but it is also has the constraints of being set in a California restaurant for a long and crucial period, and this elective restriction has paid dividends.

Two ex-lovers arrange to meet for dinner. Six years previously, Henry Pelham and Celia Favreau began a sexual relationship while working as agents at a CIA station in Indiana. But everything changed when terrorists took over a plane at the airport, and a rescue attempt ended catastrophically with everyone aboard killed. The investigation threw up a series of text messages coming from an Austrian CIA agent on board the plane – had the agent been compromised? Years may have passed, but Henry and Celia have paid a heavy price for the debacle: the end of their relationship and – in Celia's case – the termination of her career. He arranges to see his ex-inamorata one more time. As the past is exhumed during a painful tryst over the pan-seared red snapper, Steinhauer provides a wine-fuelled long, dark night of the soul, in which the betrayals of the lovers' profession are laid bare.

Crime and thriller writers often set themselves particular challenges to refuel their creative juices, such as the detective solving a case from a hospital bed (a scenario adopted by authors from **Josephine Tey** to **Håkan Nesser**), and the restricted setting that Steinhauer has used here grants the narrative a concentration rare in the genre. The pace is moderato, but it exerts a grip as the two protagonists pick over the bones of their shattered relationship and the professional fiasco in which they were involved. Henry discovers that, as is often the case in a relationship, one partner loves more than the other, and as the exhumation of incidents from the past reaches a devastating conclusion, Steinhauer eschews easy excitement for the slow accretion of detail in the amoral, slippery world of the spooks. *All the Old Knives* is closer to the rigorous and masterly **Charles McCarry** than to **Robert Ludlum** and his heirs. Stephen King said of Steinhauer's earlier *The Nearest Exit* (2010): 'The best spy novel I've ever read that wasn't written by **John le Carré**.' This one isn't quite in that league, but it's a creditable effort.

The Whitehall Mandarin 2014

EDWARD WILSON

Edward Wilson is something of a hothouse flower in the greenhouse of current espionage novelists, closer to the quirkiness and wit of **Len Deighton** than the more sombre **John le Carré** furrow ploughed by **Charles Cumming**. *The Whitehall Mandarin* is a distinctly unorthodox Cold War novel, its clandestine cast spending as much time scratching their sexual itches as they do on espionage tradecraft. William Catesby (Wilson's recurring sort of hero) is an MI6 operative keeping a close watch on Cauldwell, an American cultural attaché in London; there is a suspicion that Cauldwell is supplying the Russians with sexually compromising photographs of British officials (not a difficult job in London in the early 1960s). As in earlier Wilson novels, Catesby is a spook who never takes the easy option, and the elaborate minuets he dances around the equally elaborate terpsichorean games of his opponents provides great satisfaction for the reader, as we attempt to second-guess both Catesby and his crafty creator – being soundly outfoxed at every turn. There are some richly characterised players here, such as the eponymous female Whitehall mandarin, a woman with a ruinous secret, and her rebellious proto-hippy daughter. Catesby, too, is sharply drawn, and notably unlike other secret service types in the spy novel redux. The only orthodoxy here is the standard tarring of East and West with evenly spread moral disapprobation – but Wilson is now firmly ensconced in the new firmament of espionage writing.

The Girl in Berlin 2012
ELIZABETH WILSON

One of the most accomplished espionage novelists is Elizabeth Wilson, whose *War Damage* (2009) and *The Twilight Hour* (2006) combined glittering, dark-hued prose with penetrating psychological insight. Wilson's success is continued with *The Girl in Berlin*, a sinewy thriller that takes us back to the summer of 1951 and the national obsession with the defection of Burgess and Maclean. Colin Harris is a member of the Communist Party and has spent several years in Germany before turning up in Britain to visit his old friends Dinah and Alan Wentworth. He has startling news: he has decided to return to Britain, and is bringing with him a young woman he has fallen in love with in East Berlin. Needless to say, the eponymous girl in Berlin is not all that she appears to be, and Colin and his friends are soon in very deep waters. As is Special Branch man Jack McGovern, struggling to retain a moral code in his compromised profession. Jack encounters secret service maven Miles Kingdom, who is convinced that there is a mole at MI5 and is keen to enlist McGovern's aid. Betrayal is in the air – multiple betrayals, in fact, in which the protagonists are forced to examine their core beliefs; **EM Forster**'s famous dictum about betraying country before friends has a crucial application here.

Wilson is an academic with a speciality in popular culture, so it comes as no surprise that her storytelling ethos is so ironclad. The picture of an earlier era of austerity Britain – and, *inter alia*, Berlin – has a confident sweep and truthfulness that establishes *The Girl in Berlin* as something rather special in contemporary writing in the espionage genre. If the characters are not as rigorously delineated as in **John le Carré** (or, for that matter, **Graham Greene**, whose shadow also falls here), that is perhaps an unfair caveat – after all, how many contemporary writers could match that duo? But as a fascinatingly detailed examination of vulnerable, all-too-human characters and ruthless political creeds, Elizabeth Wilson's novel demands – and rewards – keen attention.

The Company of Strangers 2001
ROBERT WILSON

Robert Wilson's tales of danger and betrayal in foreign settings echo those of **Graham Greene**, but with an added, individual strain that is entirely Wilson's own. When he won the Crime Writers' Association Gold Dagger for *A Small Death in Lisbon* (2000), he quickly acquired the literary gravitas that goes with this kind of celebrity. And following up this novel with *The Company of Strangers*, he built on this success. This tale of divided loyalties and a bitter war fought behind polite façades is an ambitious and sprawling novel, set in the stupefying heat of Lisbon in 1944. We are shown a city that echoes Bogart's Casablanca, where spies and informers make every conversation a minefield. The Germans have developed rocket technology and are on the brink of an atomic breakthrough. The Allies are keen to stop the German secret weapon, and their operative is Andrea Aspinall, a young mathematician struggling to come to terms with the sophisticated world in which she finds herself, living in the house of a rich Irishman who may well be a German sympathiser. Andrea meets Karl Voss, a military attaché to the German legation, who is embittered and compromised by his part in the death of a Reichsminister and traumatised by the death of his beloved brother in Stalingrad. This ill-assorted couple attempts to forge a relationship in a world of treachery and death. After a terrifying climax, the novel moves to the paranoid world of Cold War Germany, and Andrea finds that she must make grim choices in a snowbound East Berlin. At nearly 500 pages, this is truly a book of ambitious reach. But those who allow themselves to fall under the author's spell will find this to be among his most rewarding novels.

CHAPTER 14

DOMESTIC NOIR
Lies and murder in the family

At the time of writing, it's easy to discern what is the genre du jour: domestic noir. It may be a contemporary genre, but its principal antecedent in narrative terms – a woman marries a man who may be a murderer – is **Daphne du Maurier**'s *Rebecca* (1938). When the writer **Julia Crouch** coined the term for work including her own books, such as *Her Husband's Lover* (2016), and **SJ Watson**'s *Before I Go to Sleep* (2011), she was identifying what had become a clearly delineated field in the second decade of the 21st century. As Crouch put it: 'Domestic noir concerns itself largely (but not exclusively) with the female experience, is based around relationships and takes as its base a broadly feminist view that the domestic sphere is a challenging and sometimes dangerous prospect for its inhabitants.' Lately, the genre has taken a distinctly predictable turn, with the male sex invariably the repository of all that is dangerous and duplicitous. But perspicacious crime writers are no fools – they are well aware that their trade is cyclical. Readers will eagerly consume a new variation, but will tire of it if it is overused. And the evidence is that British crime writers are always keen to move on and to innovate – when they are obliged to.

Her Husband's Lover 2016

JULIA CROUCH

As mentioned on page 293, Julia Crouch christened the 'domestic noir' genre, so it's hardly surprising that she is one of the most adroit practitioners of the genre – in which marriage is a minefield and sexual betrayal is the order of the day. Louisa survives a car crash, but her husband Sam and children are killed. The eponymous 'husband's lover' is Sophie. Louisa is convinced that her late husband was prepared to exact terrible revenge if she ever left him, but Sophie defends his reputation – not, however, without self-interest. Sam is dead, but she feels that his house and his money really belong to her. The reader is constantly – and satisfyingly – wrong-footed when deciding which of the two women they should place their sympathy with. Some may find the book's considerable length daunting, but Crouch largely justifies the nearly 500 pages, proving that the domestic noir genre is safe in her hands.

After You Die 2016

EVA DOLAN

An unfair accusation often levelled at British crime fiction is the suggestion that the American and Scandinavian varieties are more often 'about something', with provocative issues energising the narrative. But there are UK writers who make serious points amidst the skulduggery – such as Eva Dolan, whose novels *Long Way Home* (2014) and *Tell No Tales* (2015) featured keen social engagement. That element is present again in *After You Die*, which tackles the emotive topic of disability-related hate crime. The subject is a case clearly based on real life, in which a woman complained to the police about the harassment she and her severely disabled daughter had suffered. Dawn Prentice is dead, viciously stabbed while her daughter starved upstairs. Detective Sergeant Mel Ferreira, her career derailed after being injured on duty, is troubled; she had met the dead woman – was she negligent in not taking her accusations more seriously? The authority and command of Eva Dolan's writing grow from book to book.

Photo: Mark Vessey

Apple Tree Yard
2013
LOUISE DOUGHTY

Louise Doughty is the author of some very different (and challenging) novels tackling a wide variety of subjects, including *Apple Tree Yard*, which was nominated for many prizes, translated into over 20 languages and adapted with great success for television. Yvonne Carmichael has achieved considerable success in the field of genetics, and has a strong relationship with her husband and their two adult children. But an encounter with a stranger at the Houses of Parliament leads to a passionate, clandestine series of sexual trysts, to Yvonne risking everything of value in her life, and finally to betrayal and murder. Doughty's other novels include *Black Water* (2016) and *Whatever You Love* (2010), which was shortlisted for the Costa Novel award and longlisted for the Orange Prize for Fiction. She has won awards for radio drama and short stories, along with publishing one work of non-fiction, *A Novel in a Year* (2007), based on her newspaper column.

APPLE TREE YARD
2017
Director: Jessica Hobbs

Written by **Amanda Coe** and **Louise Doughty** herself, and starring a well-cast Emily Watson and Ben Chaplin as the lovers, much of the discussion about this solid TV version of Doughty's novel focused on the fact that it dealt unapologetically with a middle-aged woman's sexual instincts – still novel enough even in 2017 to be a cause célèbre in a way that it wasn't for the book. Ironically, some of the virtue-signalling feminist criticism was directed at Yvonne Carmichael's ill-advised behaviour, as if suggesting that professional women in fiction should always be presented as admirable, aspirational role models.

A Place to Lie
2018
REBECCA GRIFFITHS

The domestic noir genre may have become overloaded, but *A Place to Lie* by Rebecca Griffiths adroitly delivers a tense narrative with stylish writing that keeps her a cut above many of her rivals. In 1990, Caroline and Joanna are staying with their Great Aunt Dora near the Forest of Dean, but the bucolic idyll is brought to an abrupt end with a death in a dark wood. Years pass, and a violent assault sends Joanna back to her aunt's crumbling cottage for a final confrontation with the various people who may have blighted her life. While there is nothing radically new in the plotting, Griffiths has a comprehensive grip on the reader's attention.

Our Kind of Cruelty   2018
ARAMINTA HALL

Sexual role-playing games – in Araminta Hall's impressive novel – have dangerous undercurrents. Privileged London couple Mike and Verity have a clandestine erotic strategy called 'the crave', in which Verity allows herself to be semi-seduced in a bar in order that Mike can appear at a crucial moment and rescue her, a charade that both find highly erotic. But when Verity opts to marry another man, Mike decides that this is the game taken to another level, and what follows has disastrous consequences for both. Hall's considerable achievement here is to keep the narrative persuasively within Mike's consciousness – and we learn that he is deeply damaged by an abusive childhood. The accumulating tension of the novel leads to a high-profile trial in which both protagonists are in the dock. While the orchestration of suspense is masterly, Hall's real agenda becomes apparent in a feminist subtext: the way in which active female sexuality is judged more harshly in modern society than male desire (although nowadays the latter is receiving criticism too).

The Girl on the Train   2015
PAULA HAWKINS

How do you capture lightning in a bottle? It's a trick that publishers are customarily desperate to pull off, and when it happens – as, for instance, with the massive success of **Gillian Flynn**'s *Gone Girl* (2012) – it engenders great excitement and considerable envy in the book world, with editors casting around ever more desperately for the next breakout book. That book wasn't long in coming. When Paula Hawkins' *The Girl on the Train* first appeared, response from the critical fraternity was muted but favourable, with admiration expressed for the solid storytelling (along with wry observations on the central theme being cheekily borrowed from **Alfred Hitchcock**'s *Rear Window*). The premise of the plot – the half-observed murder with a witness who is not believed – is, of course, one of the most familiar in the history of the cinema, and one that has been paid homage to (or, if you prefer, ripped off) innumerable times in such books as *The Woman in the Window* (the 2018 novel by AJ Finn rather than the vintage Fritz Lang film from 1944) as well as Hawkins' *The Girl on the Train*. But then the unexpected happened, and – in a demonstration of the fact that critics know nothing – the book became a prodigious, all-conquering bestseller, with the inevitable film adaptation adding more lustre to Hawkins' reputation and bank balance.

The author, however, was no debut writer – she had previously written about how women could manage their own finances (something that she presumably found very useful). She seemed bemused by her fame as a novelist – and when it was time for a follow-up to *The Girl on the Train*, Hawkins had to face the fact that this was a hurdle at which many a novelist has fallen, producing a successor to a mega-hit. What to do? Write a second novel that replicates the structure and narrative of the first book, or strike out in a completely new direction? In the event, Hawkins opted for the latter, perhaps secure in the knowledge that *Into the Water* (2017) would be comfortably presold. Certainly, this is a very different book from its predecessor. We are once again given damaged female characters, but there is no single protagonist to compare with the vulnerable alcoholic heroine of the first book. *Into the Water* adopts the risky strategy of multiple viewpoints – so many, in fact, that even the attentive reader may struggle to keep up with which particular character we are reading about at any given time. Many readers have found their patience tested by the fragmentary nature of the narrative, often with the same events revisited by different characters (not to mention shifts from the past to the present). But in an era of dumbed-down popular culture, the intricate plotting perhaps suggests that Hawkins respects our intelligence and assumes that we will make that extra effort to keep mental tabs on the large cast of characters.

THE GIRL ON THE TRAIN 2016

Director: Tate Taylor

The inevitable film of **Paula Hawkins'** mega-selling novel relocated the British milieu to the US, but with an impressive Emily Blunt retaining her English accent and nationality. While a latter-day **Alfred Hitchcock** was probably needed here, director Tate Taylor does respectable service to his source material.

In the Dark 2018

CARA HUNTER

Echoes of criminal investigations such as Austria's Fritzl case from 2008 are to be found in Cara Hunter's *In the Dark* – a novel that boasts a strong premise: a silent woman and a child are discovered locked in a basement room of an Oxford home, both starving and near to death. The ageing resident of the house is possibly suffering from dementia and claims to have no knowledge of either of them, and nor do any other locals. Detective Inspector Adam Fawley (who appeared to advantage in Hunter's *Close to Home* (2017)) finds that the old man's house is opposite that of a woman who went missing two years previously. A nanny implicates the missing woman's husband in that disappearance – though she is not necessarily to be trusted. This is a complex mystery in which apparent innocence conceals egregious guilt. Admirers of the dark undercurrents of Jacobean tragedies will find knowing echoes of that genre here, but Hunter also incorporates a variety of modern twists.

Bitter 2018

FRANCESCA JAKOBI

Francesca Jakobi's provocative *Bitter* is a reminder that the crime fiction genre is nothing if not gender-neutral when it comes to stalkers. Gilda Meyer was dispatched from a well-heeled German Jewish background to an English boarding school when the Nazis came to power; now, in 1969, she is a middle-aged woman on the brink of bringing chaos into her own life and that of her newly married son, Reuben. She resents her attractive new daughter-in-law for stealing her son's love – something that Reuben never showed her. The results are as hilarious as they are unsettling as Jakobi exploits the stereotype of the needy Jewish mother and we are drawn against our better judgement to side with the out-of-control Gilda.

What We Did 2018

CHRISTOBEL KENT

Christobel Kent is best known for her intuitive Italian sleuth Sandro Cellini but has also moved into the territory of the psychological thriller. *What We Did* is set in a sedate English university city where the heroine, Bridget, works hard at her business, secure in the love of her husband and son. But she has a troubled past: her music teacher abused her as a student, and he now arrives menacingly back in her life. When Bridget is driven to the edge, the consequences for everyone – including herself – are devastating. Kent's writing has always possessed literary elegance, and that is fully in evidence here. Her earlier work maintained a balance between tense frissons and the allure of sultry foreign climes, but her subject here is the limit to which human beings can be led by the behaviour of others. Few will miss the baking sun of Italy, given the suspense Kent engenders these days in her own rainy stamping ground.

Cross her Heart — 2018

SARAH PINBOROUGH

Another malign male terrorises the heroine of *Cross her Heart* by Sarah Pinborough. Lisa's life has been blighted by her violent alcoholic father John, but she has managed to escape with her daughter Ava. Her friend Marilyn also has secrets – notably that her marriage is by no means as happy as it appears on the surface. Then Ava saves the life of a child and the media coverage alerts John to their whereabouts. In extremis, Lisa and Marilyn resort to drastic measures. Pinborough's approach to the psychological suspense novel has sometimes utilised supernatural elements (eschewed here) and invariably possesses a surreal, dreamlike quality. If the steely grip of the earlier *Behind her Eyes* (2017) is more fitfully evident here, the juggling of multiple viewpoints shows great elan, and the author's storytelling is as sure-footed as ever.

All the Beautiful Lies — 2018

PETER SWANSON

The US author Peter Swanson has drawn on **Alfred Hitchcock** in earlier books to good effect. In *All the Beautiful Lies*, he looks instead to **Daphne du Maurier**'s *My Cousin Rachel* (1951), with its seductive female who may have murdered the hapless hero's close relative. Harry Ackerson is told by his alluring stepmother Alice that his father has died in a fall. Visiting her, Harry, a feckless young man whose life has been drifting aimlessly, comes under Alice's spell, even as he begins to believe that she may have committed murder. The reader is soon gripped and wondering which will come first: Harry's seduction or his death? Swanson's magpie borrowings are always finessed into something fresh and piquant.

Anatomy of a Scandal 2018

SARAH VAUGHAN

Kate is a barrister, prosecuting a public figure accused of the rape of his mistress, who is also his aide. James Whitehouse's wife, Sophie, is keen to shield her family from what she sees as the lies that threaten to destroy him. Kate, however, is determined to expose a man she sees as corrupt. While Kate is very much the key character in Sarah Vaughan's impressive *Anatomy of a Scandal*, the three main protagonists are all expressively drawn. The novel makes some provocative points ('Juries are keen to convict the predatory rapist,' Kate observes, 'the archetypal bogeyman down a dark alley, yet when it comes to relationship rape, they'd really rather not know'), and no doubt in the febrile #MeToo climate – in which men in positions of power can be brought down by accusations of sexual abuse before such claims are substantiated – there will be a slew of books in which this subject is central. Few, however, are likely to have the rigour and intelligence of Vaughan's novel.

The Wrong Girl 2015

LAURA WILSON

Are crime readers suffering from detective fatigue? Or is the turn away from dyspeptic, sociopathic sleuths towards ordinary individuals whose lives are based on a lie more to do with the current domestic noir trend? Take *The Wrong Girl*, in which Laura Wilson's copper Inspector Ted Stratton is nowhere to be found: the focus here is a woman, Janice, returning to Norfolk to be reunited with the daughter she painfully gave up for adoption years before, and discovering the grim truth behind several carefully contrived façades. In fact, it's not such a switch for Wilson, whose earlier books concentrated more on the darker recesses of the human psyche than the exigencies of the detective novel. *The Wrong Girl*, in which certain characters are not what they seem to be, is perfectly in tune with the tenor of what readers are currently consuming. Hopefully, those readers will not be put off by the impenetrable plot synopsis on the book jacket.

CHAPTER 15

COSY CRIME
Dialling down the sex and violence

When I was editing the magazine *Crime Time* in its print version (I now do that particular job online at www.crimetime.co.uk), I received two reader letters in fairly close succession. The first said something to the effect that: 'I note that *Crime Time*'s ethos leans towards the "cosy crime" idiom.' A second letter said: 'You clearly have a preference for tough, hardboiled crime over the unthreatening variety!' The two contradictory responses suggested that I was doing something right in maintaining a balance. I suspect that there's less of a balance to this study, as the cosy crime section that follows is relatively brief compared with some of the others. However, such writers as the doyenne of the field, **Agatha Christie**, are covered elsewhere. But there are a few choice examples here that avoid the seamier and more violent side of crime fiction to channel something which is more comforting and purely entertaining. And there is absolutely nothing wrong with the latter – as any writer on crime fiction will tell you, the genre is a very broad church and cherishes all its denominations.

A Mysterious Affair of Style

GILBERT ADAIR

2007

In an age in which fiction teems with scalpel-wielding psychopaths and alcoholic coppers, is there still room for crime novels of a more genteel demeanour? Written by novelists who set their faces against cutting-edge grittiness and embrace the gentler, never-never land virtues of an earlier era? The late Gilbert Adair clearly thought so, and this second novel featuring his middle-aged female sleuth Evadne Mount attempts once again to pull off a double whammy: a reinvention/recreation of the Golden Age crime novel à la **Agatha Christie** and simultaneously a ruthless parody of the fripperies and absurdities of that era. Does Adair repeat the trick of his earlier *The Act of Roger Murgatroyd* (2006)? The answer to that is not as clear-cut as it might initially seem. Adair has an impressive panoply of cultural references, displayed proudly and entertainingly in his books – the first line in *A Mysterious Affair of Style* is the exclamation 'Great Scott Moncrieff!!!' (although the reference to Proust's translator doesn't actually have any relevance beyond showing us that we are in for a clever parody). Adair clearly yearned for a variety of crime fiction in which the spilling of entrails is done tastefully offstage, and pleasure is simply to be found in the solving of an ingenious puzzle – the very artificiality, in fact, that **Raymond Chandler** so ruthlessly anatomised in an essay, using the darker reality of American crime fiction as a stick with which to beat the thin-blooded British variety of the day. But Adair was having none of Chandler's caveats and threw himself enthusiastically into the well-heeled 1940s milieu that clearly got his creative juices flowing.

It's a decade since the murder case that Evadne Mount tackled in *The Act of Roger Murgatroyd*, and she accidentally runs into her lugubrious ex-colleague, retired Chief Inspector Trubshawe. The duo are soon on the track of a clever killer who has murdered an actress on a film set (the director clearly modelled on **Alfred Hitchcock**), even as the cameras were rolling. As in classic Christie, we are presented with five suspects who might have slipped the dead woman the poisonous draught. The characterisations here are as outrageously over the top as ever, and the skill with which Adair reinvigorates the tropes of the Golden Age affords some light-hearted fun. But there is a problem with this one that is less evident in its predecessor: Adair so unerringly points up the silliness and contrivance of this kind of vintage narrative that the book finally functions only on the level of a rather cold-eyed detonation of the genre. It's almost as if Chandler – with all his loathing of this era – had written a merciless Christie pastiche in order to drive a final nail into the old girl's coffin.

Agatha Raisin and the Quiche of Death 1992
MC BEATON

In this first book in a long-running series, MC Beaton's much-loved character Agatha Raisin abandons her PR company, despite the fact that it is doing well, leaves London and heads for what she hopes will be a pleasurable early retirement in a tranquil village in the Cotswolds. She enters a local baking contest and is convinced that her quiche will see off all opposition – but then the judge who has disqualified her shop-bought entry suddenly dies. Needless to say, it transpires that Agatha's quiche has been poisoned. With its spikey, less-than-likeable central character and wit, Beaton's recipe for success is clearly laid out in this enjoyable offering.

A Bird in the Hand 1986
ANN CLEEVES

Pre-Vera and pre-Shetland, Ann Cleeves' first protagonist was the elderly naturalist George Palmer-Jones, a character reminiscent of those penned by the writers of the Golden Age of British crime fiction. In *A Bird in the Hand*, the first entry in a sequence of birdwatcher novels that Cleeves produced between 1986 and 1996, a young man is discovered murdered in a marsh on the Norfolk coast. He was one of the best-known birders in the country and something of a celebrity in the village of Rushy. Palmer-Jones looks into the murder and discovers a multiplicity of possible motives, even as he simultaneously looks into rumours of rare bird sightings. Rather in the fashion that the crime writer **Dick Francis** took the reader into the world of horse racing in his books, Cleeves immerses us in the esoteric field of birdwatching. And while the considerable accomplishment of her later books is still in embryo here, there is clear evidence that Cleeves was already a writer of skill.

The Mitford Murders 2017

JESSICA FELLOWES

There are several ready-made markets for this novel by the niece of the writer **Julian Fellowes**: the *Downton Abbey* audience (who will note the surname shared with that show's creator), readers of Golden Age crime, and those with an appetite for the privileged world of the Mitford sisters. In 1919, Louisa Cannon jumps at the idea of working with the upper-crust Mitfords in Oxfordshire, finding the youthful Nancy already an accomplished storyteller. But the death of a nurse, Florence Nightingale Shore (a real-life murder victim and the goddaughter of her celebrated namesake), has Louisa and Nancy on the track of a killer in an **Agatha Christie**-esque narrative that offers a solution to an unsolved crime from the past. Fellowes' plan is to focus on a different Mitford sister with each book; the spiky Nancy is credibly characterised here, and *Bright Young Dead*, which followed in 2018, features Pamela. On the strength of these entries, commercial success is assured – though the Hitler-admiring Unity will be a challenge.

The Monogram Murders 2014

SOPHIE HANNAH

The trustees of the **Ian Fleming** estate adopted a risky strategy with new outings for 007, accepting different approaches from such writers as **Sebastian Faulks** and **Jeffery Deaver**, but they were flexible enough to accommodate both modernised and retro adventures. But as **Agatha Christie** herself was well aware, the Hercule Poirot formula is far more rigid, and straying too far from the parameters would upset devotees. Which is why the choice of writer for this much-trumpeted 2014 reboot seemed at first to be counterintuitive. Sophie Hannah is a key practitioner of modern psychological crime, with a discursive approach to plotting; how would she adapt to the narrative-led, psychology-lite demands of Poirot? In fact, she dialled back on her own concerns to forge a simulacrum of the Christie style, with Poirot obliged to deal with three bodies discovered in different rooms of the same London hotel. Hannah is no more able to make Poirot a real human being than his creator was, but it's a noble effort. Subsequent entries include *Closed Casket* (2016) and *The Mystery of Three Quarters* (2018).

Magpie Murders 2016

ANTHONY HOROWITZ

Of late, the versatile Anthony Horowitz has been protean indeed. Having taken largely successful tilts at **Ian Fleming** and **Sir Arthur Conan Doyle** pastiches, with *Magpie Murders* he attempted something different – his take on a typical **Agatha Christie**-style whodunnit – and in its ingenuity and exuberance, it is perhaps his most pleasurable channelling of another author yet. Editor Susan Ryeland is not enthused by the thought of working on a manuscript with the writer Alan Conway, as her shepherding of the novelist and his detective Atticus Pünd has not been a happy experience. She discovers, however, that this new outing by Conway in the 'cosy' crime genre has some hidden secrets. Buried within the murder plot (with its surplus of red herrings) is another tale – one that carries a charge of genuine betrayal, ambition and murder. The narrative notion here (which it would be criminal to expand upon) could have lent itself to a tricksy, writerly *jeu d'esprit*, but Horowitz ensures that it functions on a variety of levels.

Murder at the Grand Raj Palace

2018

VASEEM KHAN

For those weary of the eviscerations of much modern crime fiction, Khan's witty and colourful books in the Baby Ganesh sequence offer a pleasing, but not overly cosy, alternative. This fourth novel featuring Mumbai detective Ashwin Chopra finds him charged with investigating the death of a wealthy American stabbed in his room at the upscale Grand Raj Palace hotel. The authorities – and the luxurious hotel itself – would be happiest with a verdict of suicide, but Chopra isn't persuaded. And his sidekick, baby elephant Ganesha, is here less help than hindrance. While each entry in this cycle has sported a familial resemblance, Khan has demonstrated a capacity to ring the changes, not least in his richly textured picture of modern Mumbai. Those who feel that the element of whimsy in Khan's tales renders them too comfortable are doing themselves a disservice; there is an element of the caustic along with the charm that makes this a most beguiling series.

The No. 1 Ladies' Detective Agency

1998

ALEXANDER McCALL SMITH

Talk to readers about the phenomenally successful Alexander McCall Smith, and you'll find there are no half measures. People either see this Scottish writer's Botswana-set crime series as a breath of fresh air in an increasingly clichéd genre, or find their gentleness and whimsy totally resistible. Mostly, though, the naysayers are outnumbered; McCall Smith's books featuring the lovable Precious Ramotswe have gleaned a massive following, mainly through something that most publishers would dearly like to buy (but can't) – word of mouth. The books in the series may initially have had something of a cult following, but this quickly burgeoned into massive sales. The secret of this success is not hard to fathom: firstly, the universe of the books is not a million miles from **Agatha Christie** (they're ingenious, non-violent mystery narratives; the author has made clear his objections to the sex and violence of most contemporary crime writing). But, added to this, the beautifully realised Botswana settings were quite unlike anything crime readers had encountered before, while Mma Ramotswe and her eccentric associates were a unique cast, singularly unlike the burnt-out alcoholic coppers that seemed to be populating every other crime novel – although it might be argued that Precious is a very original riff on Miss Marple. There is no plot as such: more a succession of small puzzles that the amiable Precious takes on – and if everything is a touch decorous, the wit and invention continually sparkle.

Friends, Lovers, Chocolate 2005
ALEXANDER McCALL SMITH

McCall Smith was not content to rest on his laurels with his *No. 1 Ladies' Detective Agency* series (see page 306); in *The Sunday Philosophy Club* (2004), he inaugurated a new crime series with amateur sleuth Isabel Dalhousie, located in Inspector Rebus's Edinburgh – although Isabel could not be further from **Ian Rankin**'s detective. Isabel is a philosopher who uses her calling to crack 'unsolvable' mysteries, and she also hosts the Sunday Philosophy Club at her house. The plotting has all the quirky inventiveness of the Botswana-set books, but, of course, this series can't call on such exotic backgrounds – although McCall Smith invokes the highways and byways of Edinburgh with as much detail as he can muster. Isabel, too, is a very different character from Precious Ramotswe, her philosophical discourses being much more sophisticated than the homespun charm of the Botswana sleuth.

Here, McCall Smith presents his second heroine with some moral challenges more complex than those she faces in her professional life. She finds herself reluctantly reviewing her feelings for a younger man, Jamie, who was to marry her niece, Cat. Her attempts to maintain a philosophical distance crumble in the face of a more physical response to the attractive young man. But her troubles have only just begun: Cat is on holiday in Italy and has asked Isabel to run her delicatessen. One of the customers, a recent recipient of a heart transplant, is disturbed by memories that he feels are not his own. Needless to say, Isabel investigates, and once again finds herself in far more dangerous territory than her philosophy classroom. While some will be keen for McCall Smith to get back to African climes, this is rather seductive stuff. In the course of the book, there are all kinds of charming asides on everything from the messiness of relationships to the difficulties of resisting temptation (in everything from chocolate to handsome Italians).

Dandy Gilver and the Proper Treatment of Bloodstains 2009

CATRIONA McPHERSON

In the bar of the House of Commons, you'll find MPs from both sides of the house happily quaffing together, with none of the animosity one might expect. But such a collegiate atmosphere isn't present at crime fiction conventions when two types of writer rub shoulders: the writers of tough urban crime tend to gravitate together, while those who specialise in less sanguinary Home Counties mysteries – the 'cosies' – tend to keep to their own company. Of course, there are exceptions: Val McDermid may plumb the most gruesome reaches of human psychopathology, but she's a passionate **Agatha Christie** devotee. What would McDermid make of Catriona McPherson's *Dandy Gilver and the Proper Treatment of Bloodstains*, a novel that appears to be firmly in the cosy camp – but is it? The comparison evoked on the jacket is to **Dan Brown** and **Barbara Pym**, but McPherson is more intelligent than the former and more political than the latter. The Dandy Gilver series (which began with *After the Armistice Ball* (2005)) demonstrates the author's faultless assimilation of this idiom: a genteel note is sounded throughout, with the middle-class Dandy, an amateur female sleuth in the 1920s, solving knotty mysteries. But McPherson is actually more postmodern than this might suggest; there's a subtle detonation of the cosy genre, soothing the reader while clandestinely taking on more serious concerns. This book is possibly the most radical in that sense, dealing with the politicisation of the serving classes and national strikes under cover of a murder-the-wife plot owing not a little to **Patrick Hamilton**'s *Gas Light* (1938).

The nervous Mrs Balfour has a new maid who is not all that she seems. She is, in fact, a disguised Dandy Gilver, hired by the young wife to protect her from the murderous designs of her husband. But can Dandy – in between writing letters back to her husband, complaining about the strikes sweeping the country – foil this bit of domestic malfeasance? The tactics here include an acute sense of period, sharp observation of the mores of the day (both above and below stairs), a nicely judged infusion of humour and a winning – if unlikely – heroine. All this is 'cosy' enough, but Dandy's acid disapproval of the social upheavals of the day is not necessarily shared by her creator, and it's this meshing of gears that adds a piquancy to the untroubled surface of the novel.

Sidney Chambers and the Problem of Evil 2014

JAMES RUNCIE

If you're from an ecclesiastical bloodline, is there a temptation to rebel against family traditions? After all, **Ingmar Bergman**, son of a fiercely devout pastor, made films about the futility of faith in the modern world, while Nietzsche's Lutheran father provoked the philosopher's pronouncement 'God is dead'. And so thorough was the rejection of piety in Freud and Voltaire that both even suggested they were foundlings set down in religious families. With James Runcie's background (son of an archbishop of Canterbury), one might have thought that when he turned to crime writing he would opt to defy family shibboleths and write gritty, uncompromising novels about urban Britain, but his continuing series of Grantchester mysteries featuring Canon Sidney Chambers (a linear descendant of **GK Chesterton**'s Father Brown) would have made for a perfectly relaxing read over a cup of Earl Grey for his famous father after a hard day at the coal face struggling with gay and women priests. But if Runcie *fils*' books are resolutely – even defiantly – old-fashioned, that doesn't mean they are not subtly and insidiously pleasurable (if, that is, you prefer **Alexander McCall Smith** to **Ian Rankin**).

Sidney Chambers and the Problem of Evil, the third book in the series, is as entertaining as its predecessors. Once again couched in the form of separate novellas, we are accorded both persuasive scene-setting and a rounded picture of church society; Sidney Chambers' fellow priests in 1960s Cambridgeshire represent a microcosm of the Church of England itself – from an intense biblical scholar to an effete lay reader in suede shoes who is too evangelical for Sidney's taste. Runcie channels a touch of the vitriol to be found in **Anthony Trollope**'s ecclesiastical novels, and throughout the sequence he has created a detailed evocation of the different eras in which the various books are set. In the 1960s, Sidney and his new German wife live in a city with a notionally sedate surface, but we are reminded that political unrest is at large in the world; on the Home Service, Sidney hears that Soviet ships are warily observing US nuclear testing at Christmas Island. Nevertheless, Britain is still very much a Christian country – although the eponymous 'problem of evil' persists.

Sidney, returning from church with his wife, finds a pair of dead doves on their doorstep. Sidney prays for their souls (do birds have souls? Sidney is clearly an unorthodox theologian) but does nothing more – he has bowed to his wife's firm injunction that he takes no further part in the crime-solving activities in the company of his friend Inspector Keating that we have seen in earlier books. But then fellow priests begin to be murdered, and Sidney finds he can no longer be *hors de combat* – he might even be next target on a ruthless killer's list. The other tales here pose equally pleasurable bafflements for Sidney – and the reader. And there are modern touches too: Chesterton would never have tackled repressed homosexuality.

GRANTCHESTER (2014–)

Directors: Harry Bradbeer et al.

The standard-bearer for the return to the gentler, more innocent era of the much-derided 'cosy' is **Alexander McCall Smith**, so it's not surprising to see the creator of Mma Ramotswe evoked in praise of **James Runcie**'s Sidney Chambers in its TV incarnation with James Norton – this is very much an evocation of a more genteel era. Runcie's hero is the vicar of Grantchester, a bachelor with a gentle manner given to solving none-too-upsetting crimes. The structure – on both page and screen – involves narratives set in a classic English village in the 1950s, and the thirtyish Anglican hero appears in a variety of adroitly turned mysteries. As played by the handsome Norton, Chambers is a winning clergyman sleuth, and provided you are not a viewer who prefers red meat in your crime, there is a charm in these artfully fashioned episodes.

Murder in the Caribbean   2018

ROBERT THOROGOOD

If an English winter has you hankering after sultrier climes, try *Murder in the Caribbean* by Robert Thorogood. Thorogood is the creator of *Death in Paradise*, the TV show that combines sunny escapism with relatively unchallenging crime scenarios, and that format is replicated in his novels to beguiling effect. Detective Inspector Richard Poole is in a spot many would envy, the idyllic tropical island of Saint-Marie, but he harbours a wistfulness for such English pleasures as a good cup of tea. When an explosion destroys a boat in the bay, Poole realises that the only clue to tracking down a ruthless murderer is a ruby found at the crime scene. When so much modern crime fare is excoriatingly bleak, there is a place for more comforting fare.

DEATH IN PARADISE (2011–)

Directors: Various

Robert Thorogood has been writing standalone *Death in Paradise* novels based on the first detective, DI Richard Poole, for some years now, and has noted how writing the books differs from writing the scripts for the TV show.

'The first and most obvious difference is that the TV series really is a gang show. Right from the start, from the original idea right through to the finished script, any writer on *Death in Paradise* is helped by the input of a team of writers, plus a script editor, a story producer and all the other execs involved (of which there are many). It means we writers are constantly supported. That entirely natural crippling fear and doubt that we feel in trying to get a story to land is shared among the whole group. Location managers find the perfect setting (and there are plenty of those on Guadeloupe, where we film the TV show); costume and art departments build the scenes and dress the actors; and directors and directors of photography frame the perfect shot and find motivation for the characters. Novel writing is different. You're on your own. Not just for a few days or a couple of weeks. For months at a time. It can be a very, very lonely process, ploughing on week after week gripped by the fear that you'll never make it to the end, or that there's a massive plot hole in the story that you've failed to unearth thus far. But novels don't have budgetary restrictions like the TV show has, or sudden tropical downpours, or hurricanes that shut down production.'

CHAPTER 16

BLOCKBUSTERS
Crime on a grand scale

When my literary editor at the *Independent*, Boyd Tonkin (generally found to be grazing further up the slopes of Mount Parnassus) wrote a lengthy piece about **Dan Brown**, it was clear evidence that (in the words of **Arthur Miller**) 'attention must be paid'. For instance: was the default dismissal of *The Da Vinci Code* author's skills a touch facile? Could 50 million readers be wrong? It must have rankled with Brown that another massively popular thriller writer, **Stieg Larsson**, enjoyed a literary respectability that eluded him – after all, the late Larsson was not a great deal more elegant a writer than his American rival, but he was perceived as more culturally worthy. However, there are people who take the Brown phenomenon seriously – not least rival publishers, eager to supply the reading public's voracious (and continuing) appetite for arm-straining blockbuster thrillers involving the cracking of arcane codes, massively unrealistic villains and globetrotting scenarios. And as the rivals of Dan Brown continue to appear, a new syndrome has blossomed: the Dan Brown-style thriller that delivers all the requisite breathless pace but is decidedly more ambitious in scope and achievement.

The Break Line 2018
JAMES BRABAZON

The notion of what constitutes an accomplished thriller has bifurcated over the years in intriguing new directions, but the best entries finesse established elements, introducing an elasticity into the narratives. In that regard, the much-hyped James Brabazon is undoubtedly one of the most adroit practitioners in the field, as *The Break Line* proves. Max McLean's work for the British government has always been clandestine, but he has recently been under a cloud where his employers are concerned, and they have decided to give him a final task to prove his worth. He is sent to a military research facility for a meeting with an ex-comrade-in-arms – a man who is now incarcerated for his own protection. Max's colleague has had a breakdown during an operation in West Africa, and Max himself is soon dispatched on a dangerous mission to Sierra Leone that will test his own will to the limit. *The Break Line* is an intelligent thriller that delivers a full-throttle exercise in tension.

The Master of Rain 2002
TOM BRADBY

Tom Bradby's sprawling novel sweeps the reader headlong on a high-octane tale of double-dealing and murder in 1920s Shanghai. And, what's more, Bradby never allows his teeming canvas to overwhelm his beleaguered characters, who always remain well realised. Richard Field, Bradby's capable hero, has been seconded to the police force in the turbulent city of Shanghai. He finds a jostling melange of British imperial civil servants, American gunrunners and vicious Chinese gangsters. The grisly case he is landed with involves the mutilated body of a young White Russian woman, and Field discovers that her neighbour, Natasha Medvedev, is somehow crucial to the investigation. But Natasha's only agenda is self-preservation, and Field finds himself – unwisely – falling in love with her. Can he crack the mystery before the next victim dies – particularly as the signs are that it will be Natasha? The book is masterly in its depiction of a beautiful, dirty and corrupt city and a population in thrall to the imperatives of the market: human life, like everything else in Shanghai, has its price. Nearly 500 pages – but an accelerated pace mitigates the length.

The Lost Symbol
DAN BROWN
2009

The Lost Symbol was the follow-up to Dan Brown's much-mocked but phenomenally successful *The Da Vinci Code* (2003). Reviews grimly echoed those of the earlier book (notably my colleague Jake Kerridge's excoriating piece in the *Daily Telegraph*), but sales records were still broken. *The Lost Symbol* has incorporated all the elements that clearly worked for readers in *The Da Vinci Code*: complex, mystifying plot (with the reader set quite as many challenges as the protagonist); breathless, helter-skelter pace (**James Patterson**'s patented technique for keeping readers hooked by ending chapters with a tantalisingly unresolved situation is very much part of Brown's armoury). And, of course, the central character, symbologist Robert Langdon, was back, risking his life to crack a dangerous mystery involving the Freemasons (replacing the controversial trappings of the Catholic Church and homicidal monks of the previous book). And while Brown will never win any prizes for literary elegance, his prose – one has to admit – is always at the service of delivering an involving thriller narrative in colourful locales. Robert Langdon flies to Washington after an urgent invitation to speak at the Capitol. The invitation appears to have come from a friend with copper-bottomed Masonic connections, Peter Solomon. But Langdon has been tricked: Solomon has, in fact, been kidnapped, and a macabre mutilation (echoing the grisly opening of *The Da Vinci Code*) plunges Langdon into a tortuous quest: his friend's severed hand lies in the Capitol building, positioned to point to a George Washington portrait – one that shows the father of his country as a pagan deity. Caveats are pointless here; Dan Brown, at the time comfortably the world's most successful author, is utterly review-proof.

State of Fear
MICHAEL CRICHTON
2004

As far back as his prescient movie *Westworld* (1973), filmmaker and writer Crichton was the finest practitioner – and, some would argue, the virtual creator – of a particular genre of thriller: the science-based novel of adventure. The premise is usually this: take a highly plausible scientific thesis, put it into practice in a cloistered environment... and let things go horribly wrong, with much ensuing bloodshed. *Prey* (2002), concerning micro-robots, is a prime example. The formula worked triumphantly well for many years, and readers always know that a Crichton novel will deliver the requisite amount of intelligent thrills; he may not have been a writer who won literary prizes, but he was one of the most reliable practitioners of popular fiction at work. Even before **Steven Spielberg** filmed the 1990 novel *Jurassic Park* in 1993, Crichton was an 'A-list' author, a writer who married considerable narrative skill with a knack for technology-based plotting, a winning combination that stormed the bestseller lists time after time.

Accusations that Crichton's position on global warming came across as the kind of complacency that led George W Bush to spurn the Kyoto Protocol did absolutely nothing to hurt the sales of *State of Fear*, which built a highly enthralling plot around the author's contentious views – and nor did the allegations made by climate scientists and environmental groups that Crichton was distorting the evidence. There's little doubt that this novel works with some less-than-promising material. Several disparate events around the world are forming a curious pattern: an experiment in a French laboratory causes the death of a physicist; clandestine purchases in a Malaysian jungle are made by a powerful unidentified buyer, with extensive excavation in mind; in Canada, a midget sub is hired for 'research' in the Pacific. As attorney Peter Evans finds that his work for rich businessman George Morton has very dangerous implications, a South Pacific island initiates a million-dollar lawsuit against American interests, while ecology-minded terrorists inaugurate a fantastic scheme: they will create earthquakes and subterranean tremors with a view to persuading the world that global warming is responsible. Ironically, with the most recent incumbent of the White House describing climate change as a Chinese plot to destabilise the US, the novel may have found at least one target reader (if he reads novels).

Guilty Minds
JOSEPH FINDER
2016

Guilty Minds melds ruthlessly orchestrated suspense with economical but sharp characterisation. Nick Heller's special forces training is tested to the full when he is hired to disprove allegations about a murdered prostitute and a Supreme Court judge; Nick has two days to untangle the situation before a Washington gossip website blows open not just the case but the entire justice system. When readers reach the point when Nick is tied to an aluminium chair by a dangerous nemesis, they may start believing that the resolution they have been impatiently waiting for is becoming less and less possible. Precisely, of course, why we have to keep reading... Not vintage Finder, perhaps, but if the modern thriller has a future beyond globetrotting banality, it will be in the hands of writers such as him.

Pendulum
ADAM HAMDY
2016

The talented Adam Hamdy is a British writer and film producer who has worked in venture capital; he is also a mover and shaker behind the London crime fiction festival Capital Crime. His varied work includes the comic book series *The Hunter* (2007–) and the feature film *Pulp* (2012), which became the first film ever to premier on Xbox video platform. Hamdy has worked with film producers on both sides of the Atlantic (including on an adaptation of **David Mitchell**'s 2001 novel *number9dream*) and his debut novel *Battalion* (2010) was a persuasive political techno-thriller that enjoyed enthusiastic reviews. His second novel was *Out of Reach* (2015), but it was his third book, *Pendulum*, that drew most attention for its accelerating suspense and intriguing concepts. The protagonist awakes confused, disorientated and with a noose around his neck, standing on a chair. John Wallace has no idea why he has been targeted and no idea who his attacker is. Nor does he know how he will prevent the inevitable. Then the pendulum of fate swings in his favour; he has one chance to escape,

The Orpheus Descent 2013
TOM HARPER

For quite some time, Tom Harper has been producing elaborate thrillers that marry ironclad narrative skills with finely honed writing; if anyone deserves the sobriquet of the thinking person's **Dan Brown**, it's him. As well as providing outlandish plotting, mysterious artefacts and a desperate search (in this case for archaeologist Lily Barnes, who has vanished on a dig in modern-day southern Italy), Harper takes the reader back 2,500 years to the philosopher Plato's search for an aeons-old mystery written in gold. The legacy of this McGuffin consists of 12 golden tablets now in museums around the world, each supplying the dead with a passage to the afterworld. Harper has the chutzpah to channel other ambitious thrillers – the past/present time frame of **Peter Ackroyd**'s *Hawksmoor* (1985) and the challenging philosophical strain of **Umberto Eco**'s *The Name of the Rose* (1980) – but pulls it all together with admirable panache. Harper is a writer who reminds us that the international thriller can keep both one's pulse and one's grey matter tingling.

I Am Pilgrim 2013
TERRY HAYES

Few books in the blockbuster genre have made such an impact as Terry Hayes' prodigious and eventful epic – nor have many enjoyed such a divided response from readers. That being said, the book was something of a sales phenomenon (dissenting voices notwithstanding) and inspired other publishers to try to follow suit – not least in their endless hopeful suggestions that they had just published 'the new *I Am Pilgrim*'. The protagonist is the leading agent in a US espionage department that is so secret it is unknown to most branches of government. Hayes' hero decides to leave his dangerous profession behind – which, needless to say, is not easy to do. Admirers of the book praised it at the expense of such rivals as **Tom Clancy** and **Robert Ludlum** – but it is clearly a marmite novel, with people either regarding it as unputdownable or clumsily written. The book is 700 pages long, so take a deep breath.

Mississippi Blood 2017
GREG ILES

Like its sprawling widescreen predecessors *Natchez Burning* (2014) and *The Bone Tree* (2015), this prodigious epic is typical Greg Iles fare: colourful, bravura, and always justifying its prodigious length. Former prosecutor Penn Cage (whom we met in the earlier volumes of this trilogy) is a haunted anti-hero dealing with the trauma of his father being on trial for murder. At the same time, a brutal offshoot of the Ku Klux Klan is engineering his destruction due to his incendiary knowledge of the group's secrets. But Penn's incarcerated father also has a secret that will affect his family – and even the history of the South itself. The stakes for Penn could not be higher, and he has everything to lose. Operatic in its reach, this is still essentially a tough crime procedural, with a blistering courtroom drama in the mix. *Mississippi Blood* is Southern Gothic delivered in the most incarnadine of hues.

Star of the North 2018
DB JOHN

The best thrillers offer something more ambitious than simply raising the pulse rate of the reader. In *Star of the North* by DB John, it's geopolitical complexity: the book is set in the dictatorship of North Korea and includes unusual protagonists as well as an unsparing picture of the regime, contrasting the wealth of the elite with the grinding poverty of the disadvantaged. Jenna Williams was born to a Korean mother and an African-American father; she grew up fluent in the North Korean dialect and is now desperate for news of her missing twin, who vanished in South Korea over a decade ago. All this means that she is perfectly placed for CIA recruitment, and is dispatched on a hazardous mission to North Korea to save her sister. There she meets Cho, an ambitious politician in the Ministry of Foreign Affairs who reluctantly agrees to help her, and she has a surprising encounter on a train with the country's youthful leader. John (who co-authored North Korean defector **Hyeonseo Lee**'s memoir *The Girl with Seven Names* (2015)) parlays his knowledge of the country into a grim but intelligent narrative with echoes of **Martin Cruz Smith** and **Robert Harris**, creating a masterly evocation of life under the Kim regime with everyone, rich or poor, living in fear of the all-seeing State Security.

White Crocodile 2015
KT MEDINA

Few crime novels deserve to be called operatic – in the sense of being larger than life, with emotions etched in the most eye-catching of colours – but KT (Kate) Medina's remarkable debut certainly qualifies for the adjective. Painted on the most ambitious of canvases, *White Crocodile* takes the reader into a Cambodia that suggests the fraught psychological territory of **Joseph Conrad**'s Africa in *Heart of Darkness*. In Battambang, not all danger is located in the lethal minefields; young mothers are being abducted. Some are discovered gruesomely mutilated, their abandoned babies by their side. In this superstitious society, people live in fear of the 'White Crocodile', a creature that means death for all who encounter it. In England, Tess Hardy has found some equilibrium in her life after severing relations with her abusive husband Luke. Then she receives a call from Cambodia, where Luke is working as a mine-clearer, and Tess realises that he has changed. But there is to be no reconciliation; a fortnight later, Luke is dead. Despite her better judgement, Tess sets out for the killing fields of Cambodia to find out what happened to him. But, just as in Conrad, the source of evil in a less 'civilised' foreign country is a metaphor for corruption in comfortable England, and a decades-old act of violence at home is to put Tess in peril in the present. And is the white crocodile corporeal rather than mythical?

Medina has the full measure of the sweltering Cambodian locale, and her own experience in the Territorial Army has been incorporated into the novel with great skill. The descriptions of the minefields of Cambodia – along with those who undertake the terrifying job of finding and disarming mines and IEDs – demonstrate the author's personal sympathy for this damaged country, where thousands of individuals are still maimed and killed by these relics of a bloody war; it might be argued that Medina's anger is the backbone of the novel, lifting it out of the crime category into something more complex and ambitious. But, in fact, the real skill of *White Crocodile* lies in its vulnerable but resolute heroine Tess Hardy, the perfect conduit for the reader through a novel that is unyielding in its grip. The myth of the white crocodile is still believed in Cambodia today, and Medina's use of this as the story engine has allowed her to produce both a strongly written thriller and a passionate meditation on the West's exploitative attitude to a benighted country.

Gene 2005
STEL PAVLOU

Stel Pavlou's *Gene* really is something different, although he has not achieved the recognition that once appeared to be his for the asking. As *Decipher* (2001) and his treatment for the movie *The 51st State* (also 2001) resoundingly demonstrated, Pavlou is an author capable of marrying the glossy surface of the (slightly) futuristic thriller with steel-hard plotting. This second novel adds a layer of sophisticated characterisation, as the protagonist struggles to cope with some jaw-dropping revelations about his own past. Detective James North is handed a difficult assignment; he has to deal with a mentally disturbed young man holding a child hostage at the Metropolitan Museum of Art in New York. The hostage taker has been asking for North by name, even though the detective has never met him. When the hostage situation ends badly, North is injected with a preparation that plunges him into a hallucinogenic state, with nightmarish manifestations and fragments of memory that are not his own. As North ransacks the city for his assailant, he finds himself mentally impelled to destroy a man called 'Gene'. And when he does, a bizarre secret about his own past manifests itself – one with a 3,000-year legacy. This involves a Greek warrior who fought in the Trojan Wars and is destined by the gods to be reincarnated many times, forced to confront his nemesis in each lifetime.

Death Games 2017
CHRIS SIMMS

At the time of writing, *Death Games* is the latest in Chris Simms' series featuring Detective Inspector Jon Spicer, a series that began with *Killing the Beasts* in 2005 and has included such powerful and unsettling psychological thrillers as *Cut Adrift* (2010). *Death Games* demonstrates a further refinement of the author's craft, with Spicer once again a durable and multifaceted protagonist. In Manchester, the survivor of a motorway crash escapes from the scene but leaves behind an indication that a terrorist outrage is being planned. Spicer, now a member of Manchester's Counterterrorism Unit, is in bad odour with his bosses; he has been removed from his previous job and demoted to the rank of detective constable. The intuitive Iona Khan has her own problems – such as struggling to be taken seriously in the male-dominated unit. Readers will not be surprised to hear that the duo find themselves obliged to work together, as a very high-profile target is in the sights of the terrorist group. This is Simms on customarily authoritative form and shows that he has not lost an iota his narrative grip.

The Tower 2013

SIMON TOYNE

Simon Toyne has largely been spared cutting comments, even though his books are in the familiar mould of the blockbuster thriller: breathless, picaresque page-turners with plots underpinned by the threat of some cataclysmic event – in *The Tower*, those threats include strange weather phenomena and mass migrations that suggest the End of Days. Toyne must be well aware that there are people who will find such a synopsis off-putting precisely because of *The Da Vinci Code* associations, but he is no doubt hoping to channel the American writer's Midas touch. In fact, Toyne deserves it; he may trade in familiar elements (his Robert Langdon figure is tyro FBI agent Joseph Shepherd), but he delivers his outrageous plot with an intelligent use of language. A catastrophe hits NASA's deep space search programme – it is wiped clean, replaced with a minatory announcement: 'Mankind must look no further.' The warning is greeted with scepticism, but not by the FBI's JJ Shepherd. At the same time, ex-crime reporter Liv Adamsen relocates from the Turkish citadel of Ruin to an oilfield in Syria. The oil development is abandoned, but an oasis forms around her new dwelling – along with a nameless danger. All around are suggestions of Armageddon: a hideous plague is beginning to spread (emanating from the Ruin citadel), and the weather is behaving in a terrifying fashion that cannot be accounted for by global warming. The signs predict that all human endeavour is drawing to a close, unless a handful of determined individuals can avert doomsday.

The pleasures of *The Tower* do not lie in the writing, literate though it is. The author (who worked in television for two decades) knows that sheer narrative gusto is far more valuable than nuance in this sort of book, and everything is presented in primary colours. But that is not a criticism. High-concept thrillers may be ten a penny, but Toyne rises above the competition to deliver something more confident and cinematic than most of his rivals.

The Cartel 2016

DON WINSLOW

Don Winslow is *sui generis*, a writer's writer – but his work is also a gift to all discerning crime readers. Winslow's epic *The Power of the Dog* (2005) is now regarded as something of a high watermark in the genre in terms of its ambition and reach; it was a difficult act to follow, but Winslow pulled it off with the remarkable *The Cartel*, every inch as acerbic and involving as the earlier book. Once again, we are presented with a sprawling, mightily ambitious narrative, but, for all that, there is not a wasted word in this story of power, corruption and justice in the American Drug Enforcement Administration and the Mexican drug cartels.

The Border 2019

DON WINSLOW

Don't be daunted by the imposing length of this epic crime novel, the final instalment in the trilogy that started with *The Power of the Dog* (2005) – Don Winslow justifies every one of its arm-straining 700-odd pages. Veteran cop Art Keller has devoted decades of his life to the war on drugs, bringing down Barrera, the godfather of the Sinaloa Cartel. But Barrera's successors are turning Mexico – a country Keller loves – into a criminal warzone, and Keller's personal battle against the US heroin epidemic is compromised by massive levels of corruption, not least in the American administration. With a dramatis personae that makes Tolstoy look underpopulated, this is Winslow at his sensational best.

CHAPTER 17

COMIC CRIME
Tongue-in-cheek mayhem

The writer **Mike Ripley** once said to me that he felt that the comic crime genre – a field in which Ripley himself possesses no mean expertise – has lost its commercial viability, hence the sparseness of such material in the 21st century. Certainly, writers such as Ripley himself have largely abandoned the genre for other fields; Ripley has moved into historical fiction, while the versatile British writer **Peter Guttridge** has retired his witty detective Nick Madrid in favour of more caustic Brighton-set novels. But there is clearly life in the genre, as the Last Laugh award for the genre annually given out at Bristol's CrimeFest attests. And as further proof, here is a selection of some choice comic crime writing…

Murphy's Revenge   2005

COLIN BATEMAN

We can now call the writer Colin Bateman by his full name again; the brief, ill-advised publicity stunt when he used his surname alone has been happily retired. It's always a gift for a crime writer when his series character enjoys a successful TV incarnation, as Bateman has done with his Murphy books. Or is it? James Nesbitt made the character very much his own on television, but every reader will have their own conception of the character when they read the cleverly written novels. In fact, it's probably best to forget the face of the actor involved and let the author work his particular magic. There is a serious point at the heart of *Murphy's Revenge*: who defines the moral imperatives if it is possible to track down and kill the person who murdered a loved one? A support group for relatives of murder victims counsels empowerment through therapy, but someone is choosing to murder the killers involved. Detective Martin Murphy joins the group undercover, but finds it impossible to remain aloof when his own past is wrenched into the investigation. What makes all of this even more involving than one might expect from the reliable Bateman is the insidious way in which he confronts the reader's own prejudices. Surely the scum who have murdered loved ones deserve no more pity than they gave to their victims? The moral equivocation forced on the unwilling Murphy strengthens Bateman's narrative.

The Burglar on the Prowl   2004

LAWRENCE BLOCK

This 10th appearance of Lawrence Block's sophisticated crook Bernie Rhodenbarr is an exuberant delight. Bernie sells rare first editions for his day job, but spends evenings engaged in larceny. In the course of the series, Block very cleverly pulled off a tricky task (as did **Patricia Highsmith**): making us root for a criminal, via sharp dialogue and some masterful plotting. Sometimes the series is a little hit and miss, but when Block is on top form (as here), he demonstrates why he enjoys such a loyal following as a writer. Bernie's friend Marty has commissioned him to get his hands on some money in the apartment of a plastic surgeon. This money is undeclared, but Bernie isn't exactly suffering any moral qualms in any case. As so often in the past, things go wrong: Bernie makes a mistake by checking out other apartments in the doctor's neighbourhood, only evading capture by hiding under a woman's bed, but then he realises that the woman is being raped by yet another intruder in her flat. His moral code may be flexible when it comes to robbery, but this outrage inspires him to get on the trail of the brutal attacker. Needless to say, everything goes pear-shaped, and soon the body count is rising. While Block's plotting sometimes causes the eyes to widen at its sheer audacity, largely speaking he makes the reader buy into some of the more outrageous developments on offer here.

A Bullet in the Ballet — 1937

CARYL BRAHMS

Caryl Brahms (pseudonym of **Doris Caroline Abrahams**) was prolifically talented as a novelist, critic and arts journalist. Her studies at the Royal Academy of Music in London persuaded her that she was not cut out for life as a musician – a gift, in fact, to the world of books. Her comic novels (sometimes in collaboration with **SJ Simon**) utilising ballet themes built up a considerable following. Her signature book is *A Bullet in the Ballet*; its follow-up, *Casino for Sale* (1938) was published in the US with the more crime-oriented title *Murder à la Stroganoff*. *Envoy on Excursion* (1940) was a tongue-in-cheek espionage thriller.

The Wooden Overcoat — 1951

PAMELA BRANCH

The Asterisk Club is inaugurated in Chelsea to supply a home for wrongfully acquitted murderers. Entrée to the amenities of the club? Simply that prospective members name the club as beneficiary in their wills. But Benji Cann, an upscale tailor, is acquitted of the murder of his lover; complications galore and a rising body count follow. Allowances have to be made for the distinctly non-PC attitudes of the era, but this is still a diverting black comedy, and Pamela Branch merits rediscovery.

The Shooting in the Shop — 2010

SIMON BRETT

Ah, the civilised entertainments of the clubbable Simon Brett! It's a breath of fresh air to pick up one of his witty and civilised essays in the crime genre. To say that Brett has been turning out books like this for years sounds like faint praise; in fact, one is in awe of Brett's consistency over a lengthy period. Perhaps the books sit neatly in the cosy genre, but this is the finest writing in that oft-dismissed genre. The plot of *The Shooting in the Shop* involves a store that is mysteriously burned down, with several suspicious characters in the frame – including a comedy writer who isn't very funny. Unlike Brett. The series, set in the seaside town of Fethering, features Brett's unlikely detective duo of the rather uptight Carole Seddon, a retired divorcee, and her bohemian neighbour Jude.

Furious Old Women   1960
LEO BRUCE

After a career as a literary journalist, Leo Bruce (real name **Rupert Croft-Cooke**) experienced personal catastrophe when he was one of the last people to be arrested for homosexual offences in the UK. His distinctive crime series featuring the ungainly Sergeant Beef, a physically unappealing British policeman (who subsequently becomes a private detective) is essentially a parody of the preternaturally gifted sleuths of the Golden Age in British fiction. Subsequent to his arrest, Bruce began another series, featuring Carolus Deene, crime-solving history teacher at a public school. In *Furious Old Women*, a key book in the series, the self-described 'furious old woman' Mrs Bobbins (a play on the 'angry young men' of the time) asks Deene to look into the death of her sister.

Slaughter's Hound   2012
DECLAN BURKE

Take a deep breath before this one. The acclaim that greeted Declan Burke's adroit *Absolute Zero Cool* (2011) was replicated for *Slaughter's Hound*, which arrived bearing an encomium from no less than Lee Child, as well as a striking jacket that rather cheekily lifts motifs from the designer Saul Bass – but then everyone does that these days. Burke's protagonist, the world-weary Harry Rigby, is witness to a suicide – a suicide that may be part of an Irish national epidemic. And in Harry Rigby's Sligo, life can be very cheap – and Harry is to be reminded of this in the most forceful of terms. Those familiar with Declan Burke's work will know what to expect here: that wry authorial voice, married to a particularly idiosyncratic command of dialogue. In some ways, perhaps, it's the latter that marks Burke out.

Thus Was Adonis Murdered 1981
SARAH CAUDWELL

Daughter of the celebrated journalist Claud Cockburn, Sarah Caudwell had expectations to live up to, coming from a writing family. But her four legal whodunnits in the Hilary Tamar series more than established her reputation. Written over two decades, the books are set in London's Lincoln's Inn and focus on four barristers at the chambers, overseen by the visiting narrator Professor Tamar, who functions as a detective figure – with the sex of the character never established. Complex plotting and sharp humour are the hallmark of the series.

Anarchy and Old Dogs 2007
COLIN COTTERILL

Colin Cotterill's very individual crime series (beginning with *The Coroner's Lunch* in 2004) features Laos's only coroner, Dr Siri Paiboun. In a relatively short time, the books gleaned a devoted legion of readers, as much for the sharp and quirky characterisations as for the colourful evocation of the Laos locales, though the series has faltered of late. In *Anarchy and Old Dogs*, the ageing Siri is, as usual, up to his elbows in double-dealing on the part of officialdom as much as he is involved in the mysteries of the case he is working on. A blind dentist is struck by a logging company truck and killed. It transpires that he was en route to post a letter, but when Siri examines it, he finds that it is impossible to read: the dentist has used invisible ink and has then encrypted the message. But as Siri peels back the layers of confusion surrounding the case, he realises that the stakes are higher than anyone could have imagined.

Love Lies Bleeding 1948
EDMUND CRISPIN

There are many crime readers (and not just those of a certain age) who would rather turn to one of Edmund Crispin's elegant and inventive crime novels than the more gritty offerings of contemporary thriller fiction. His sleuth, Dr Gervase Fen, is one of the great creations of the genre, and *Love Lies Bleeding* is generally felt to be a key outing for the detective. Rehearsals of a play at Castrevenford school are interrupted by high emotion among the cast, and violent deaths further destabilise the status quo. Oxford don Gervase Fen investigates, and confronts a mystifying skein of a missing Shakespearian manuscript, kidnapping and even witchcraft. All of this is handled in prose of quiet and unspectacular skill, always witty and amusing, with a brilliantly created cloistered world at its centre. Plotting was always a speciality of Crispin's, and the authoritative organisation behind this novel is supremely satisfying.

Killing the Emperors 2012

RUTH DUDLEY EDWARDS

The refreshingly unsparing style (in both her life and her writing) of the writer Ruth Dudley Edwards has meant that she is noted as much for her unbuttoned analysis of political and societal issues as she is for her wickedly funny crime writing in which a variety of self-important establishment figures and shibboleths are ruthlessly punctured. *Killing the Emperors* is a typically lacerating Edwards piece in which the mechanics of the crime novel are balanced with a cutting satirical edge; here, she takes on the crazy, corrupt world of conceptual art. Edwards has frequently demonstrated that for her nothing is sacred, and it is this merciless quality that makes her books so mischievously diverting.

Hard Eight 2002

JANET EVANOVICH

Bounty hunting was a relatively new profession in the crime genre when Janet Evanovich made it the career of the protagonist of *One for the Money* in 1994, but it was a choice that was sparked off by several high-profile real-life cases. And with the ever reliable Janet Evanovich, you know you're in safe hands. In the comedy thriller stakes, she has few equals – even if, at times, her splenetic imagination falters and the farcical takes over. Not here, though: *Hard Eight* is vintage Evanovich, firing on all cylinders and throwing out the one-liners in a positively spendthrift fashion. Bombshell bounty hunter Stephanie Plum is back on her Harley – so we're in for another wild ride. Fresh and full of surprises – if a touch self-conscious – Evanovich's adroit thriller is crammed full of more diverting misadventures for Stephanie. As she spirals and tumbles through her customarily frenetic and incendiary world, she can hardly catch her breath, let alone her man

– even if she could decide which one to chase. Like Stephanie, the author grew up in New Jersey and cannily draws on her background for some evocative scene-setting; the comedy and thrills are always anchored in a plausible world. She has won major crime fiction awards for her Stephanie Plum novels: *One for the Money* (1994) bagged a Crime Writers' Association award, as did *Two for the Dough* (1996). It's always good to spend time in the company of the feisty Ms Plum and her ingeniously numbered series.

The Eyre Affair 2001

JASPER FFORDE

After spending several decades in the film business, Jasper Fforde debuted on the *New York Times* bestseller list with *The Eyre Affair* in 2001. His speciality is a strange synthesis of seemingly disparate genres – essentially, the books are police procedurals eccentrically yoking in characters from nursery rhymes and magic. There are those who are utterly addicted to his work, while others find the whimsy distinctly resistible. But there is no denying Fforde's extremely clever and witty writing.

Bryant and May: The Bleeding Heart 2014

CHRISTOPHER FOWLER

Is there anyone else in the crime genre currently writing anything as quirky as Christopher Fowler's Bryant and May series? Fowler eschews all recognisable genres, though the cases for his detective duo have resonances with the darker corners of British Golden Age fiction. The Peculiar Crimes Unit is handed a typically outlandish case here in which two teenagers have seen a corpse apparently stepping out of its grave – with one of them subsequently dying in a hit-and-run accident. Arthur Bryant is stimulated by the bizarreness of the case but is tasked with finding out who has made away with the ravens from the Tower of London – not an insignificant crime, as it is well known that when the ravens leave the Tower, Britain itself will fall. The usual smorgasbord of grotesque incident and eccentric humour is on offer; if you aren't an admirer yet, I would suggest you find out what the fuss is about before any television series clinically removes Fowler's individual tone of voice.

No Laughing Matter 1997
PETER GUTTRIDGE

The tag line for Peter Guttridge's debut comic novel, *No Laughing Matter*, was: 'Comedy is a serious business – some people just die laughing.' And that pretty much sums up the absurdist blend of laugh-out-loud comic incidents with ugly deaths. Nick Madrid – Guttridge's yoga-obsessed journalist protagonist – witnesses the suspicious death of one of the performers at 'Just for Laughs', the biggest comedy festival in the world, where ambitious performers would kill to get that movie or TV deal. Nick turns gumshoe to find out whether or not the death was accidental and is helped in his quest by Bridget Frost, the Bitch of the Broadsheets, whose pushy and tacky exterior conceals – well, a pushy and tacky interior. Madrid and Frost quickly discover that there is no rest for the witty – except when they start getting killed off. As the trail leads first to the mean streets of Edinburgh during the Festival and then to Los Angeles, where the truth lurks among the dark secrets of some of Hollywood's biggest movie stars, Guttridge takes satirical swipes at performers, movie stars, showbiz in general and, of course, journalism, that being one of his varied trades.

Sick Puppy 2000
CARL HIAASEN

It's always fascinating to observe the phenomenon whereby a thriller writer progresses from being the esoteric favourite of a small minority to being a highly influential, much read success on a far grander scale. It happened with **Elmore Leonard**, and it can certainly be said to have happened to the wonderful Carl Hiaasen. This novel sports all the usual Hiaasen fingerprints: Florida setting, lurking environmental issues, quirky, offbeat humour, bizarre but totally plausible characterisation and plotting whose crazy ingenuity leaves the reader reeling. And characters who seem to be unaware that laws exist. It's a tradition that he established in *Tourist Season* (1986). As a thriller writer, Hiaasen is on his own, and if *Sick Puppy* breaks no new ground, admirers will not complain. His protagonist, Palmer Stoat, is worried by a black pick-up truck following him and is convinced that his beloved Range Rover is about to be carjacked. But the man tailing him is bent on vengeance. Twilly Spree is hardly your average criminal: wealthy and pathologically idealistic, he is on a crusade to save Florida land from despoliation. And Stoat's trail of fast-food litter is the curtain-raiser to a weird and wonderful narrative in which this highway encounter leads to a much larger-scale bout of political fisticuffs. From phony big-game hunters to prostitutes who will service only Republicans, the cast of characters is as wonderful as only Hiaasen can create.

Basket Case

2002

CARL HIAASEN

When a whole slew of authors admit to being influenced by Carl Hiaasen, it's clear that his cult status is fully established. But the self-conscious, surrealistic quality of his writing is a hard act to sustain, and although such books as *Skinny Dip* (2004) brilliantly create a world that is very much his own, there is a certain suspense with the appearance of each new Hiaasen title. Can he pull it off again? In the case of *Basket Case*, the answer is a qualified yes, although his delirious plotting is a tad more reined in than usual. Set in the Florida that is the author's customary stamping ground, this outing sports a melange of journalists, rock and roll, and lizards – always count on a nasty reptile somewhere in the Hiaasen mix, as omnipresent as the bears in **John Irving** – and it's as outrageously entertaining as its predecessors. Jack Tagger is the kind of journalist we've encountered many times in the crime novel, given to haplessly screwing himself in both his career and his relationships, and his pathological rubbing people up the wrong way has consigned him to the graveyard of the obits page. He's made a particular enemy of the newspaper's owner, Race Maggad III. But then Jack stumbles on the story of a lifetime: rock star James Stomarti has cashed in his chips in a diving accident, and Jack finds that his sexy starlet widow stands to gain from her husband's death. Jack begins to dig for the truth, but he comes up against not just the politics of his own paper but some pretty dangerous enemies too. The lunacies of the rock world are well conjured – no mean achievement, as this territory is always a snare and delusion for thriller writers who can't resist warmed-over Spinal Tap-style digs at the witless pretensions of this coke-fuelled milieu. *Basket Case* may be less inventive than most Hiaasen, but it's still a heady brew. The real Florida, though, can't be as entertaining as Hiaasen's Dali-esque vision, can it?

Hamlet, Revenge! 1937
MICHAEL INNES

Michael Innes (the pseudonym of **John Innes Mackintosh Stewart**) wrote in a variety of fields, including, towards the end of his life, straightforward adventure thrillers, and was a student of such classic writers as **William Shakespeare** and **Joseph Conrad**. His copper, Inspector John Appleby, appeared in over 30 entertaining books, all of them full of gentle but pointed comedy. A notable entry is *Hamlet, Revenge!*, which takes place backstage with a theatrical company.

The Long Midnight of Barney Thomson 1999
DOUGLAS LINDSAY

After the customary avalanche of rejection slips, Douglas Lindsay's Barney Thomson series got off to a flying start with *The Long Midnight of Barney Thomson*, in which a barber who has killed his employer by accident is suspected of being a serial killer. This is an unusual series; highly unlikely but always amusing adventures, the books are cinematic in the sense of short scenes and cutting. Get past the sometimes impenetrable Glaswegian dialogue, and you'll find these outings are quite unlike anything by any of the author's contemporaries.

Sour Cream with Everything 1966
JOYCE PORTER

The four books featuring Edmund 'Eddie' Brown are quite unlike anything else in espionage fiction in their wry humour; other books by Joyce Porter have a similarly ironic take on crime genres – her policeman Detective Chief Inspector Wilfred Dover appears in complex but comic whodunnits, while her other series character is an upper-class spinster who solves crimes more by luck than detective judgement. In their time, Porter's spy novels acquired a devoted following and enjoyed critical acclaim, but they have not achieved a long-lasting place in crime fiction history, which is something of a shame. Rediscovery may be overdue, now that readers are enjoying **Mick Herron**'s similarly satirical take on the world of espionage.

Aberystwyth Mon Amour 2001

MALCOLM PRYCE

With the witty and scabrous comic thriller *Aberystwyth Mon Amour*, Malcolm Pryce set himself a challenging task: making the sedate Welsh town of Aberystwyth look as fascinating and menacing for his low-rent private eye as the mean streets of **Raymond Chandler**'s Los Angeles. Pryce pulls off the task with considerable aplomb. Schoolboys are disappearing without trace, and Louie Knight, the town's sole private detective, becomes involved when he is called on by the exotic singer Myfanwy Montez. She is the star of Wales' most outrageous nightclub, and is keen for Louie to track down her missing cousin, known as Evans the Boot. Aided by such eccentrics as philosopher-cum-ice cream seller Sospan, Louie is challenged by a plot quite as labyrinthine as any that exercised Philip Marlowe. Surely Lovespoon, Grand Wizard of the Druids and the town's most powerful citizen, had a hand in the disappearances? But nothing is quite as it seems in Pryce's outrageous and irreverent tale, which functions as a canny thriller as much as a wry parody. A good deal of the humour comes from relocating Chandler's sun-baked California locales to a parochial Welsh town, and all the clichés are ruthlessly exploded. But it's the language – which leaps off the page – that really marks Pryce out as a stylist of no mean skill, and his bizarre refraction of Marlowe-speak is cleverly done.

Angel in the House 2005

MIKE RIPLEY

The sharp and witty crime novels of Mike Ripley feature the fast-talking Fitzroy Maclean Angel, the most reluctant private eye in British detective fiction, with the emphasis on entertainment rather than threat. What gives Ripley's books their distinctive individual flavour is the combination of nicely observed detail of character and locale interspersed with moments of chaotic hilarity – although the latter are always within the realms of plausibility (think **Tom Sharpe** with added crime). In *Angel in the House*, the beleaguered sleuth is chafing at the thought of parenthood and is persuaded by his fashion designer wife to join a private detective agency – one, moreover, that has previously employed only women. The plot throws in stolen Botox and Russian sailors selling elderly classic cars, all handled with the edge we expect from Ripley.

A Shot in the Dark — 2018
LYNNE TRUSS

The notion of 'cosy' crime fiction produces derisory chuckles among many hardcore thriller fans who regard the genre as twee and inoffensive, redolent of an earlier era. Such books, the naysayers complain, are closer to Cluedo's Colonel Mustard and Miss Scarlett than to real life. And a similarly dismissive response is often prompted by the comic crime genre, generally regarded by readers as a poor relation of more serious detective novels, despite the highly diverting efforts of such droll writers as Simon Brett and LC Tyler. Might these dual prejudices be overturned? Perhaps it takes a writer of Lynne Truss's wit and intelligence to take on both the cosy and the comic fields, shaking them up to forge something fresh and beguiling. Truss is, of course, most celebrated for her tongue-in-cheek book on grammar, *Eats, Shoots and Leaves* (2003), but she has also made her mark as a novelist and as a radio dramatist; *A Shot in the Dark* is an extension of her successful BBC Radio 4 series featuring the obdurate Inspector Steine. Truss's setting here is Brighton, and the year is 1957. After the discreetly handled scene of mass murder that opens the book (where two rival criminal gangs destroy each other), Inspector Steine maintains that there is no longer any lawbreaking in the town, and he resists any suggestions to the contrary. His life is comfortable – no crime and no criminals (he claims), just a series of undemanding duties. Such local lowlifes as 'Stanley-knife Stanley' hardly register on his radar, and when an energetic and enthusiastic newcomer, Constable Twitten (a name that will mean something only to readers who know the local Brighton vernacular – other character names are rather more obvious), begins to shake things up at the station, Steine is obliged to accept that things are slowly turning nasty. And when Twitten attends a theatrical opening night, he finds himself sitting next to a poisonous theatrical critic who is murdered during the play. The town is plagued with a series of burglaries, and Inspector Steine's saturnine colleague Sergeant Brunswick, a man whose days as a war hero are long behind him, is frustrated by his boss's refusal to confront reality. Brunswick is bumped by Constable Twitten into accepting that the town is starting to look more and more like it does in the crime-ridden book Steine despises, **Graham Greene**'s *Brighton Rock*.

A large cast of strongly drawn characters – including an 'angry young man' dramatist – helps keep things bubbling along, and not only is the whole thing delightfully witty – more early **Evelyn Waugh** than **Agatha Christie** – it also functions very successfully as a novel in the vein of the very genre it is satirising, the police procedural. And, as in *Brighton Rock*, we are given a vivid picture of the town in its pre-chic heyday, with kiss-me-quick hats and candy floss. Twitten, in particular, is a delightful creation; he is the classic copper in conflict with his complacent superior, the latter as much of an obstruction to the pursuit of justice as any of the various criminals involved. Sceptical readers will not only find their prejudices against comic and cosy crime being swept away, but will be eager for more such outings with Twitten and co. Oh, and, needless to say, there is not a single misuse of the English language in the entire book – how could there be from Lynne Truss?

Crooked Herring 2014

LC TYLER

LC (Len) Tyler is one of the most sheerly enjoyable novelists in comic crime territory, and a typically diverting entry is *Crooked Herring*. Ethelred Tressider is handed his strangest case yet when fellow crime writer and literary critic Henry Holiday confesses to having murdered somebody. The problem is that Holiday can't recall where he did it or who he killed. But, for his own peace of mind, he would like Ethelred to find out what has happened. Ethelred is sceptical; Henry is in every respect an unlikely killer – short and addicted to checked waistcoats and yellow bow ties. Then it becomes clear that another writer, Crispin Vynall, with whom Holiday had been drinking on New Year's Eve has vanished. As ever, Ethelred proves to be a less than reliable narrator and Elsie (Ethelred's literary agent and co-sleuth) a less than honest and straightforward assistant. There are plenty of practised liars around and nobody's version of the truth can be entirely trusted. As Ethelred observes at the end: 'That's what we writers do all the time – suspend disbelief for a while and tell a story. Then the curtain falls.'

CHAPTER 18

THROUGH A GLASS DARKLY
Historical crime

To some degree, reading any crime novel is a form of escape into another world – one in which all the moral codes we may hold dear are torn to pieces. But it can also be a temporal escape. If you feel the need to read about dark deeds committed somewhere long ago and far away, historical crime offers the perfect passport. Digging into conspiracies in Ancient Rome? **Lindsey Davis** and **Steven Saylor** will hold your hand. Murder inside the Third Reich? **Robert Harris** and **Philip Kerr** both know the territory. Evil in 19th-century New York? Go to **Caleb Carr**. Medieval bloodshed? The late **Ellis Peters** will put you in the muddy lanes. Mass murder in 18th-century France? **Patrick Süskind**. Victorian England? Try **Abir Mukherjee**, **MJ Carter** or **Kate Griffin**. In fact, there are now so many guides to mayhem in ancient times that we're coming to know the mean streets around the Coliseum in Rome as well as Marlowe's LA. The task facing writers of historical crime is rather similar to that facing science fiction authors: how much of the incidental detail of this unfamiliar society does a writer keep filling in, without slowing down the forward trajectory of the narrative? And – a problem very specific to historical crime – how to persuade the reader that the private investigator (a relatively recent phenomenon) had predecessors spread throughout history? Here's a collection of writers who pull off that sleight of hand (and many others) with panache…

Darkness Falls from the Air   1942
NIGEL BALCHIN

Wartime London: a man – possibly bisexual – agonises over his friendship with the man he knows is sleeping with his wife; a weapons scientist struggles with his own demons – and the bottle. And there is a crucial engagement with bombs…

While his name may now be known to only a select few, cult writer Nigel Balchin was one of the most unorthodox of UK novelists working in the thriller field; his fascinating books touched on subjects of science and society, with strongly etched characters, usually troubled. *Darkness Falls from the Air*, with its London Blitz setting, was both a commercial and critical success. Sammy Rice is a crippled weapons expert drowning his bitterness in alcohol. While its powerfully drawn wartime atmosphere and suspense set pieces (including the defusing of a bomb) are of their time, the hero's alienation and disenchantment render him a very contemporary figure. Balchin's best-known book was *The Small Back Room*, published a year later, principally because it was made into a palm-sweating Michael Powell film in 1949. Later books were also well received, but the double whammy of these two titles is Balchin's greatest achievement.

A Dark Anatomy   2011
ROBIN BLAKE

The distinguished historical crime novelist Robin Blake has a writing identity subtly different from that of his contemporaries – elegant and nuanced. His highly accomplished series features the lawyer Titus Cragg, who makes his first appearance in *A Dark Anatomy*, set in 1740. While holding down his own legal practice, Cragg is also coroner for Preston, tasked with holding inquests into unexpected deaths. His associate Luke Fidelis is a youthful doctor who functions in something like a pathologist's role. Fidelis is rational, experimental and quick-witted, and a man of the Enlightenment, acting as contrast to the more traditional mien of Titus Cragg.

The Syndicate   2018
GUY BOLTON

Despite his youth (33 at the time of writing), Guy Bolton displays a knowledge of – and enthusiasm for – Hollywood and Las Vegas lore of the 1940s which matches that of a vintage novelist. His debut, *The Pictures* (2017), was an incisive noir thriller set in this milieu, and with *The Syndicate* he caught lightning in a bottle a second time. Ex-LAPD cop Jonathan Craine has abandoned Hollywood for a bucolic life on a Californian farm, but when mobster Bugsy Siegel is killed, he is drawn back to Las Vegas by the sinister Meyer Lansky with the task of tracking down those who murdered Siegel. As before, the unravelling of a connection between Hollywood and the criminal world is adroitly done, and the period language never sounds a false note.

Paris in the Dark   2018
ROBERT OLEN BUTLER

Utilising his own considerable experience as a war veteran and journalist, the award-winning Robert Olen Butler displays a mastery of the historical thriller in his felicitous trilogy set during World War I. Butler's 2012 title *The Hot Country* sported echoes of **Arturo Pérez-Reverte**'s colourful, kinetic fare and was the first in an ambitious series featuring doughty American war correspondent Christopher 'Kit' Marlowe Cobb. In this further instalment, as Parisians meet death by dynamite in a campaign of bombings, the German-speaking protagonist Kit seems to be the person to discover who is behind it. But things in a Butler novel are never straightforward. Those who have read earlier books by the author will have little hesitation in picking this one up. Once again, on the surface *Paris in the Dark* appears to be a cocktail of adventure, romance and espionage, but it's soon apparent that the book is not only shot through with a keen intelligence rare in the genre, but it is also couched in lambent prose.

The Infidel Stain   2015
MJ CARTER

MJ (Miranda) Carter's writing career has taken off on surprising tangents: biography (a book on Anthony Blunt), history (*The Three Emperors*), then a header into ripping yarn territory with the deliriously enjoyable *The Strangler Vine* (2014), which fused **Wilkie Collins** with **Sax Rohmer** via **Sir Arthur Conan Doyle**. That book introduced her ill-matched sleuths Jeremiah Blake and William Avery in Victorian India. *The Infidel Stain*, the second outing for the duo, is even more fun, with the same audacious blend of derring-do and elegant writing. Back from India, Blake and Avery find Britain in 1841 a changed place and struggle to readjust, not least to the English cold. But a series of brutal killings in the world of London's yellow press re-energises their faltering association as they track down a killer enjoying the protection of people in high places. Delicious stuff, to be consumed at just a few sittings.

Dead Man's Blues   2016
RAY CELESTIN

The Axeman's Jazz was widely acclaimed as an exceptional debut when it appeared in 2014, and any trepidation that Ray Celestin's sequel *Dead Man's Blues* would not be able to match its predecessor was soon allayed. The same protagonists appear – Pinkerton detectives Michael Talbot and Ida Davis – but the narrative is set some ten years later and the reader is taken to a colourfully drawn Chicago of the late 1920s, the Al Capone era. The large cast of characters even has a part for the iconic trumpeter Louis Armstrong, who turns out to be one of Ida's friends.

The Heretics   2013
RORY CLEMENTS

We live in an era of religious fundamentalists brainwashed into carrying out suicide missions, so Rory Clements' readable *The Heretics* is very pertinent, even with the historical distance created by the fact that the book is set in Tudor England and the target of the relentless Catholic assassins is Queen Elizabeth I. This is the fifth novel by the award-winning author to feature the highly intuitive 'intelligencer' John Shakespeare (the less famous brother of the playwright), and in terms of its comprehensive narrative grip it is easily the equal of its distinguished predecessors.

The Damascened Blade 2003

BARBARA CLEVERLY

There's nothing like a full-on historical crime novel, is there? Particularly one set in the dying days of the Raj, as in the work of **Abir Mukherjee**. But *The Damascened Blade* isn't quite that – even though there are some genuinely pulse-racing moments here as James Lindsay, commander of a British squadron in the beleaguered fort of Gor Khatri on the Afghan border, deals with the bloody death of a native prince and its catastrophic aftermath. British policeman Joe Sandilands becomes involved in this incident when he is seconded from London and spends time with Lindsay, an old army colleague. Barbara Cleverly has a keen psychological insight, possibly gleaned from such late master observers of this territory as **Paul Scott** and **JG Farrell**, and both the British and the indigenous characters are realised with an acuity that is always perfectly matched to the exigencies of a suspense-generating plot (the set pieces are splendidly exciting). The moral dilemmas are by no means as clear-cut as they might have been; needless to say, the book is all the more interesting for its careful parcelling out of issues of conscience and commitment. Sandilands is drawn with complexity and skill, as he encounters the disparate group of visitors to the fort and attempts to identify and execute the murderer within the week he and Lindsay have been given. Of course, all of this would go for nothing if the historical details were not similarly spot-on, and the author has demonstrably done her homework. Nothing is ever forced, but all the requisite indicators of time and place are picked out with genuine authority.

Sherlock Holmes and
the Devil's Promise 2014

DAVID STUART DAVIES

Bearing the soubriquet of the UK's foremost Sherlock Holmes expert can be an onerous task, but the urbane David Stuart Davies has carried it off with aplomb for many years. But his real skill lies in his bracing detective novels, particularly those featuring... Now, what's the name of that detective again? Cocaine addict? Plays the violin? This entry arrived bearing an encomium from Mark Gatiss, one of the custodians of the detective's most recent incarnations, and it is fully justified. *Sherlock Holmes and the Devil's Promise* is delicious and ingenious fun for Holmes admirers.

A Body in the Bath House 2001
LINDSEY DAVIS

The two key practitioners of Roman crime novels, Britain's Lindsey Davis and America's **Steven Saylor**, are not quite the bitter rivals one might expect. Of course, it would be perfectly understandable if they cordially detested each other or that either author could be discomfited by reading glowing reviews of the other's books. After all, we want people ploughing the same field to have it in for each other – it's made great copy ever since Brahms and Wagner, Joan Crawford and Bette Davis, Marvel and DC Comics. But in the case of Davis and Saylor, the truth is more prosaic: both happily acknowledge the skills of their rival across the pond. As a chronicler of bloodshed in the Domus Aurea, Lindsey Davis is in a class of her own, and *A Body in the Bath House* is a splendid outing for her Roman sleuth Marcus Didius Falco. While making improvements to his bath house, Falco, fuming at the shoddy workmanship of his builders, becomes aware of a disgusting smell – and finds that a human corpse is the source. But then he is sent by Emperor Vespasian to the murky Roman colony of Britain to examine why everything is going wrong with the building of a new palace for the British King Togidubnus (spoiler alert: we know it gets built eventually, as it's the Roman palace at Fishbourne, near Chichester, the remains of which can still be seen today). Soon Falco is up to his elbows in murder and deception – par for the course, in fact. This is wonderful stuff, with impeccable historical detail allied to plotting that is always full of elan.

Pandora's Boy 2018
LINDSEY DAVIS

By the first decade of the 21st century, Lindsey Davis had seen off all her rivals – notably **Steven Saylor**, mentioned on page 341 – to become the unassailable market leader in the 'crime in Ancient Rome' genre (though see also **RS/Ruth Downie** on page 343). In *Pandora's Boy*, Davis sidelines her Roman sleuth Falco to focus on his strong-minded daughter Flavia. On the day of her wedding, disaster occurred when her new husband, Tiberius, was hit by lightning. Now, less than ten weeks later, he has disappeared, while a distracted Flavia investigates what may be a poisoning by an illegal love potion. Davis's squalid, vibrant Rome is as pleasurable as ever.

Garden of Beasts 2004
JEFFERY DEAVER

Like so many lawyers, Jeffery Deaver decided to abandon one already lucrative profession for an even more remunerative one – that of the bestselling thriller writer. And Deaver swiftly built up a considerable following for his Lincoln Rhyme crime novels, highly adroit thrillers featuring a quadriplegic investigator assisted by a young policewoman, Amelia Sachs (who faces most of the danger). But while some authors are happy to plough the same furrow for most of their careers, Deaver clearly felt the need to re-energise his batteries by introducing two distinctive new heroes in *The Blue Nowhere* (2001): Frank Bishop (a flawed but ruthlessly effective cop) and his reluctant associate, Wyatt Gillette, a highly talented young computer hacker released from prison to help Frank track down a kind of online Hannibal Lecter. And if that weren't enough, he struck off in yet another direction with *Garden of Beasts*, a period thriller that is among his most accomplished work.

Set in New York in the 1930s, the central character here is hitman Paul Schumann, who is grabbed by the police when a hit goes belly-up. Schumann is offered a choice: travel to Berlin to murder Hitler associate Reinhard Ernst, or be tossed in jail with the key thrown away. There would, of course, be no novel if Schumann didn't take the first option – and his lethal hunt through a brilliantly realised Berlin, in chaos as preparations for the Olympics are under way, delivers the requisite tension – particularly as an implacable German cop is on his tail, not to mention the assembled might of the Third Reich. This particular 'garden of beasts' is not a comfortable place to be – exactly what thriller addicts want, in fact – and Schumann is a strong anti-hero.

Vita Brevis 2017
RUTH DOWNIE

Ruth Downie's anachronistic – but winning – sleuth is Gaius Petreius Ruso, an army doctor in Ancient Rome who, in earlier books, has been dispatched to colonial Britain. Here, Ruso and his partner Tilla (who is both his Watson and the mother of his child) arrive in Rome to discover that the city's splendour is matched by corruption on a massive scale. Ruso's predecessor, Dr Kleitos, has fled the city, leaving behind a barrel bearing both a corpse and the legend 'Be careful who you trust'. Ruso's hard-won reputation is soon under threat, and he realises he must find his missing colleague – urgently.

Those familiar with Downie's work will not be surprised to hear that *Vita Brevis* is crammed with pithy characterisation (notably the intuitive Ruso), mordant humour and beautifully integrated historical detail. Who cares that there were no detectives in Ancient Rome?

Gallows Court 2018
MARTIN EDWARDS

Gallows Court marks an intriguing change of direction for Martin Edwards, former chair of the Crime Writers' Association and a noted expert on the British Golden Age of crime fiction. Here, he pays homage to the legacy of vintage thrillers but introduces an urgency and sense of dark menace that are notably contemporary. In 1930s London, a series of macabre killings have made the streets unsafe for women. But Rachel Savernake is unlike most of her sex: she is the daughter of a famous hanging judge and has already nonplussed Scotland Yard by cracking a case known as the Chorus Girl Murder. Now she is tracking down a new killer – but her methods are extreme, to say the least. Journalist Jacob Flint is convinced that there is much more to her than her deductive abilities – but he has no idea how much. Evocative period detail, twist-packed plotting and a fascinatingly enigmatic anti-heroine.

## Seven for a Secret	2013
LYNDSAY FAYE

'Seven for a secret, never to be told' runs the nursery rhyme, but we can be grateful that the gifted Lyndsay Faye *does* tell us the grim secrets here. This heady narrative of kidnapping on the streets of 19th-century New York centres on the 'blackbirders', slave catchers whose violent trade is sanctioned by the state. The star policeman of New York's recently established force, Timothy Wilde (a character we first encountered in the author's baggy and impressive *The Gods of Gotham* (2012)), takes on the sinister traders and is shocked to find out that he is not quite as inured to the malignity of human behaviour as he believed. Lyndsay Faye is a member of the Baker Street Irregulars and a worshipper at the shrine of **Sir Arthur Conan Doyle** – but it is her own skill at evoking the dark world of the 19th century, crammed with plausible detail, that distinguishes this slice of historical crime writing.

## The Hanging Shed	2011
GORDON FERRIS

The Kilmarnock-born writer's fourth novel became one of the most downloaded books in Britain after being released in electronic form. Ironically, this success via hypermodern means has been granted to what is essentially a traditional piece. The setting is Glasgow in 1946, and the author's depiction of the immediate post-war years has a bristling immediacy. As Ferris has noted, the war years and the rock and roll era of the 1950s have been exhaustively mined by writers, but the mid-1940s remain somewhat underused. Ferris finds much to explore in a period when Britain was undergoing tumultuous change – the Empire passing into history, and the country struggling with an austerity that makes the start of the 21st century look like a cornucopia. Social problems are created by demobbed soldiers struggling to find jobs, while women are beginning to enjoy a taste of independence. Ferris is particularly sharp on the burgeoning crime of the period, including black market enterprise and violent street gangs. Ferris's tough protagonist Douglas Brodie is an ex-policeman; home from the war, his paratrooper's uniform discarded, he finds himself forced to save his childhood friend Shug Donovan from hanging. The latter was in Bomber Command and was shot down over Dresden; when he returns to Glasgow he is unrecognisable – scarred and mutilated – and he turns to heroin. Donovan makes everyone around him uncomfortable, and when a local boy is discovered raped and murdered, the drug-addicted loner is the perfect fit for the crime. But Brodie distrusts the mass of evidence that points to his friend's guilt, and – with the aid of local advocate Samantha Campbell – he begins a daunting odyssey through the dangerous backstreets of the Gorbals, obstructed by both bent coppers and murderous razor gangs.

Ferris is a writer of real authority, immersing the reader in his Celtic nightmare world with a brand of scabrous writing reminiscent of **William McIlvanney**'s *Laidlaw* (1977). If the notion of the sparring male/female duo at the centre of *The Hanging Shed* has a warmed-over quality, everything else here speaks in an original voice.

The Tilted World 2013

TOM FRANKLIN AND BETH ANN FENNELLY

Sometimes a crime writer comes along who shakes the genre so that all the clichés come rattling out like loose nails, leaving something clean and spare. Tom Franklin proved to be such a writer with *Crooked Letter, Crooked Letter* (2009), an atmospheric crime offering set in rural Mississippi. But is Franklin even a crime writer at all? Or is he, like his great predecessor **William Faulkner** (a clear influence), using the trappings of the crime novel for literary ends? So authoritative was the earlier (solo) book that the heart sank when seeing he had enlisted his wife (a poet) as co-writer for this novel, but this unruly tale set against the historic flooding of the Mississippi River in 1927 is even more impressive than *Crooked Letter*. Two incorruptible prohibition-era federal agents are sent to investigate the disappearance of two colleagues who had been closing in on a local bootlegger. Gritty, engrossing fare.

The Bellini Card 2008

JASON GOODWIN

Goodwin's Ottoman detective Yashim quickly established himself as a readers' favourite. Of course, having a eunuch investigator at the centre of your narratives is a fairly sure-fire guarantee that your series will be particularly memorable, but that basic concept has to be underpinned by solid, atmospheric writing – and that is just what Goodwin delivered in *The Janissary Tree* (2006) and *The Snake Stone* (2007). Those books were crammed full of fast-moving narrative incident (including chases and even heady erotic episodes), not to mention elegant plotting and writing – elements that are well to the fore once again in *The Bellini Card*. Here, Yashim travels from sultry Istanbul to the darker city of Venice, employed by the Sultan to track down a lost painting by Bellini. Assisted by his old friend Palewski, the Polish ambassador, Yashim immerses himself in a world of shady dealers, down-at-heel aristocrats and reckless pleasure seekers. Needless to say, the stakes are higher than simply finding a missing painting, and people soon begin to die violently. This is richly entertaining writing, delivered with the intelligence and flair that we have come to expect from Jason Goodwin.

Critique of Criminal Reason   2006

MICHAEL GREGORIO (Michael G Jacob and Daniela De Gregorio)

References to the philosopher **Immanuel Kant** in a thriller? The heavyweight intellectual baggage of Michael Gregorio's ambitious historical novel is there in the title, which might suggest we're in **Umberto Eco**/*Name of the Rose* territory. If Gregorio's achievement is not as prodigious, this is still a sweeping and brilliantly detailed read. The age of Enlightenment: Kant's writings are realigning approaches to reason and science. Prussian magistrate Hanno Stiffeniis will find Kant is to aid him in investigating a series of violent deaths that have terrified the town of Königsberg. But does the hunt for a murderer matter when Napoleon's troops threaten the borders of the state? The premise may owe something to **Hans Hellmut Kirst**'s *The Night of the Generals* (1962) (criminal investigation in a time of war), but Gregorio threads philosophical underpinnings through the dark narrative with genuine assurance.

Kitty Peck and the Music Hall Murders   2013

KATE GRIFFIN

Sporting a notably unusual detective (even in the often eccentrically characterised historical crime genre) – a 17-year-old trapeze artist – Kate Griffin's exuberant debut novel is a lively romp through the seamy yet fascinating world of the East End music halls of 1880s London. Griffin has found the perfect voice for Kitty, the period is sharply conjured, and the eventful plot doesn't let up for a moment. Griffin is a former journalist who worked for Britain's oldest heritage charity SPAB (the Society for the Protection of Ancient Buildings), a job that aligned with her own personal historical interests. Maintaining the promise of that impressive first book is the follow-up, *Kitty Peck and the Child of Ill-Fortune* (2015), with the third book – still keeping up the momentum – being *Kitty Peck and the Daughter of Sorrow* (2017).

The Vanishing Box 2017
ELLY GRIFFITHS

Elly Griffiths' idiosyncratic work has dealt with the collision of the ancient and the modern, and although this novel is set in a well-evoked Brighton of the early 1950s, we see things through Griffiths' very modern sensibility. The death of a flower seller, which is somehow connected with the Hippodrome Variety Theatre, has Detective Inspector Edgar Stephens involved once again with a charismatic man he knew in the war, the magician Max Mephisto, as well as his daughter and co-star Ruby. And Elly Griffiths herself dispenses several acts of prestidigitation, invigorating the format of the police procedural with a piquant mixture of humour, period detail (including the church-baiting nude tableaux of the day that play a key role in the narrative) and truly beguiling characterisation. This is the fourth book in Griffiths' series featuring the unlikely duo, a series that has proved to be as successful as her earlier novels featuring archaeologist Ruth Galloway.

Fatherland 1992
ROBERT HARRIS

Of late, the excellent Robert Harris has moved into other areas of history, but this picture of a crime investigation in a Europe in which Germany won World War II remains his *chef-d'œuvre*. The concept of a victorious Germany is hardly a new one, of course – it has been explored by such writers as **Philip K Dick** – but by adroitly marrying an investigative narrative to this alternative history, Harris created something very special indeed. In April 1964, the drowned body of an old man is discovered, and a routine investigation is initiated by Harris's dogged Berlin copper. But when he discovers that the Gestapo is involved, things become very messy indeed. He finds himself with a case whose tendrils reach right into the heart of the Reich. As Harris demonstrated in subsequent books, political intrigue is one of his specialities (Harris is a political insider), and it's that element that powers the plot here. The trick, of course, is to make the central investigation interesting when the reader is keen to know everything that is different about this world that never happened, and Harris performs this juggling act admirably: information about the victorious Reich is freighted into the plot just at those moments when it is appropriate, not when such details would be extraneous. For a while, Harris struggled to rediscover the form that he displayed in this novel, but he resolutely recaptured it in such later books as *Pompeii* (2003).

FATHERLAND 1994

Director: Christopher Menaul

Most people who bothered to watch it considered this by-the-numbers adaptation of **Robert Harris**'s novel somewhat underwhelming. Rutger Hauer (a talented actor often miscast) and the usually reliable Miranda Richardson are the protagonists involved in cracking a truly sinister plot, but Christopher Menaul's tepid direction largely keeps tension at bay, and the convolutions of Harris's plot are disappointingly smoothed out into something a touch penny-plain. Some sharp small-part playing (by Peter Vaughan, for instance) provides compensation.

The Devil in the Marshalsea 2014

ANTONIA HODGSON

The world of historical crime writing was once a sparsely populated field, back in the days of **Ellis Peters** – but how different it is today! There are so many writers competing for the various prizes in the genre that it has now become essential to be innovative to rise above the rest. This is no problem for Antonia Hodgson, who proves at a stroke with this first novel that she is one of the most impressive practitioners, fully deserving the breathless encomium from **Jeffery Deaver** on the jacket.

Her territory is London in 1727, and her protagonist, Tom Hawkins, has been enjoying the fleshpots of the capital, luxuriating in a world of brothels, coffee houses and gambling dens. But he is about to enter a world grimly familiar to anyone who reads **Charles Dickens**: the debtors' prison of Marshalsea. As painted by Hodgson, this is virtually an entire city within stone walls, with its own ruthless rules and hierarchies. However, there is one certainty here: those who have connections (either family or friends) who provide some remuneration enjoy a degree of comfort denied their fellow debtors. If you are unlucky enough to have no access to such largesse, your future probably consists of disease and death. And escape from the iron fist of the governor and his henchmen is only the remotest of possibilities. Tom Hawkins finds it very difficult to adapt to this brutal universe, not least because of his inability to follow rules. And while the gruesome murder of a fellow debtor, Captain Roberts, spreads fear among the inmates, the captain's widow is out for revenge for the killing. The man immediately in the frame is the mysterious and terrifying Samuel Fleet – and he happens to be the man with whom Tom is sharing a cell. It's up to Tom to discover the real murderer, a quest that may cost him his life. Tom Hawkins is a winning protagonist, and *The Devil in the Marshalsea* really was something new in the world of historical crime fiction. Such is the detail and atmosphere of Hodgson's writing that at times she even rivals Dickens – but with far more crime. Any lovers of the historical crime genre need to keep a weather eye on Antonia Hodgson.

In the Kingdom of Mists 2002

JANE JAKEMAN

Historical detail seamlessly integrated into the plot? This is one area where Jakeman has few equals: there's never a sense that the author is thinking 'Hmmm... time to freight in a tad more background' – the balance is always faultless. *In the Kingdom of Mists* is prime Jakeman and a reminder that her current absence from the scene is to be regretted. The novel is set in

19th-century London, with the impressionist artist Claude Monet figuring prominently in the narrative. The painter is creating his famous views of the Thames, but a series of grisly murders is inspiring fear and dismay, with bodies turning up in the river. Is another bloodthirsty killer wreaking havoc in the fashion of Whitechapel's Saucy Jack? Oliver Craston, on the lower rungs of the diplomatic service, gets involved as his Foreign Office masters become increasingly nervous about the political implications of the killings. So, with Monet and his family staying at the Savoy under supervision, a desperate hunt for a monster gets under way.

Walking the Shadows 2003

DONALD JAMES

With such books as *Monstrum* (1997) and *Vadim* (2000), Donald James proved himself to be a master of the large-scale thriller in which violent action is set against a vibrantly realised period canvas, and *Walking the Shadows* continues in the same exhilarating style. In the village of St Juste in southern France, all is silence and darkness. The village was drowned in World War II, but when a drought drains the reservoir that has taken its place, many secrets come to light. James' protagonist Tom Chapel arrives in St Juste in order to discover why a man from the village left a massive fortune to his daughter in his will. She was subsequently kidnapped and is now in a coma, barely alive. Predictably, Chapel encounters a wall of silence from the local police (when did you last read a thriller in which the local police were helpful?) and he has to travel back in history to uncover some unpalatable facts. Under the sway of the hated Vichy government, resistance fighters were helping Jews leave the country – and Tom Chapel was one of those escapees. But is the betrayer of this organisation, who was responsible for the death of several Jewish women, still alive and prepared to kill to protect his secret?

The Last Templar 1995

MICHAEL JECKS

Michael Jecks is known for his historical accuracy – nothing goes into his books which he knows to be wrong. Even the 14th-century murders and cases investigated in his books come from the Coroners' Rolls and contemporary records; he does not write straight crime novels – the books are intended to be modern-day thrillers that happen to be set in the past.

Cadfael they ain't! Although the characterisation is very important to him, there are two other planks to his stories. Plot, naturally, but also the countryside. It was a canny move to base the main action on Dartmoor, because the author clearly considers that there is nowhere so redolent of the past in Britain as this wild moorland. In his stories, it's fair to say that the countryside is often as important as the people.

Set in the years of the great European famine of 1315–16, *The Last Templar* looks at what happened to some of the men who had served in the great religious army, the Knights Templar, after their destruction by an avaricious French king and grasping pope. The famine caused massive dislocation, and all over Europe bands of men clubbed together to rob, rape and murder. In 1316 in Devon, Simon Puttock, the new bailiff of Lydford Castle, discovers a body in a burned-out house…

Greeks Bearing Gifts 2018

PHILIP KERR

Hollywood's loss was British readers' gain in the case of Philip Kerr, who died in 2018. After the success of his remarkable Berlin Noir trilogy, featuring compromised Nazi-era detective Bernie Gunther, the writer was enticed to California to prepare a series of treatments for films. They were never made, but any fears that Kerr may have lost his novelistic mojo were allayed on his return to the UK: his subsequent outings for Bernie were even more accomplished. In Kerr's penultimate novel, *Greeks Bearing Gifts* (he delivered a final novel in the series – *Metropolis* (2019) – before he died), time has moved on for the saturnine copper. The year is 1957, and an impoverished Bernie, no longer a policeman, takes a new job as a claims adjuster investigating a fire in Athens that has sunk a small ship. When the owner is savagely killed, Bernie is reminded of his chequered past and suspects that the killer is a Nazi war criminal who deported thousands of Greek Jews to Auschwitz. Having worked – reluctantly – for both the SS and Goebbels, Bernie recognises the strategies of his former bosses. For bereft Kerr admirers, this is a vintage draught, as themes of redemption are explored grippingly.

Death in the West Wind 2001
DERYN LAKE

The characters created by Deryn Lake (the pseudonym of **Dinah Lampitt**) don't always behave in a strictly plausible fashion, given their 18th-century setting, but the assiduously researched detail allows us to accept all the murderous shenanigans, however outrageous. *Death in the West Wind* is vintage stuff, with the author on good form. Lake's customary protagonist, apothecary John Rawlings, is enjoying his honeymoon in Devon, but – needless to say – marital bliss is not on the cards for long when the mutilated body of a young girl, Juliana van Guylder, is found on a schooner. Then the young girl's brother Richard vanishes, and Rawlings traces a sinister trail to the Society of Angels, a clandestine group that appears to have something to do with the mystery. But thrown into the mix is a highwayman and even a phantom coach, so Rawlings calls for help from the canny Joe Jago and the Flying Runners, his London colleagues.

Live by Night 2012
DENNIS LEHANE

Lehane's historical novel *The Given Day* (2008) weighed in at over 700 pages, and its successor, *Live by Night*, while leaner and more focused, still has a daunting reach, with a background of the Prohibition era and the vicious gangsters who flourished then. The timespan of the novel is a decade, beginning in 1920s Boston and moving to Tampa and Cuba as we follow the tribulations of Joe Coughlin. Despite his respectable antecedents (he is the son of a Boston captain of police), Joe has embraced a criminal lifestyle and is employed by one of the most ruthless of Boston's bootleggers. The life Joe has chosen is infused with betrayal and violence, and what pangs of conscience he has must be vigorously suppressed. But he struggles with his own bad faith and regret as he realises that the choices his father warned him of can no longer be avoided. What's more, Joe's beautiful, rebellious Cuban wife uses the dirty money from his activities to save women from the streets – even as Joe finesses the very mechanisms that keep these women's lives in such a desolate state.

There are many things to praise here, not least the well-crafted period detail of Lehane's crowded narrative. There is also the author's typically acerbic command of language, a skill that seems to get better from book to book. If there is a problem with *Live by Night*, it is that the characters seem more moved by the demands of the narrative than being individuals with the kind of authentic life Lehane depicts in such books as *Mystic River* (Joe's crises of conscience have far less force than those to be found in the earlier book). Nevertheless, Dennis Lehane admirers will luxuriate in the persuasive storytelling here, and Lehane's grand-scale writing makes most contemporary crime fiction look footling and lacking in ambition.

The False Inspector Dew — 1982

PETER LOVESEY

Aboard the ocean liner *Mauretania*, sailing for New York in 1921, an unassuming dentist, Walter Baranov, nerves himself to chloroform his domineering wife and push her out of a porthole. The idea is that he and his lover Alma, who has stowed away, will then pose as a police inspector and his wife. This, of course, is a refinement of the real-life Dr Crippen case, and with a nice sense of irony Walter becomes 'Dew', borrowing the name of the inspector who arrested Crippen and his mistress at sea. But then a body is recovered from the sea; the victim has been murdered and so the ship's captain invites Walter, the fake policeman, to lead the investigation. He is compelled to make a show of detective work, questioning American millionaires, professional gamblers and wealthy matrons seeking matches for their marriageable daughters. What follows is a series of twists and surprises. *The False Inspector Dew* won the Crime Writers' Association Gold Dagger and was ranked 27th in a *Times* poll of the top 100 crime novels of all time. Acclaim for Lovesey's sophisticated, dazzlingly plotted books, such as *The Detective Wore Silk Drawers* (1970), is universal. Like all the best historical crime, the marriage between seamlessly incorporated period detail and dexterous characterisation is a harmonious one.

The Frost Fair — 2002

EDWARD MARSTON

Keith Miles, writing here as Edward Marston, has made his mark as a playwright and has run his own professional theatre company, but this Renaissance man among crime writers has one real métier: his impeccable series of richly atmospheric crime novels, such as the Domesday series exploring crime in Norman England. *The Frost Fair* (subtitled *A Restoration Mystery*) is perhaps his most accomplished and detailed book: historical crime of the first order. The novel is set in the terrible winter of 1669. London ignores such hardships as a frozen Thames by celebrating Christmas with a traditional 'frost fair' on the river. Amidst the carousing throng is a talented young architect who is escorting the daughter of one of his clients. The architect, Christopher Redmayne, has romantic designs on the delightful Susan, and he's further pleased to encounter his friend Constable Jonathan Bale, who is there with his family. Christopher and Jonathan, while saving a boy from the river, discover a frozen cadaver underneath the ice. The corpse is that of an Italian fencing master, and despite Christopher's best efforts, he finds himself further embroiled in the mystery when his brother Henry is accused of the murder. When so much historical crime seems to be dispatched by rote, it's refreshing to encounter a writer like Marston, who never gives less than his best.

The Somme Stations 2012

ANDREW MARTIN

Anyone who has heard Andrew Martin talk on stage will have noticed that, initially, the writer will appear to be taciturn and uncommunicative, all Yorkshire glumness. But just as the spirits are starting to sink, the real Martin will appear: iconoclastic, opinionated, entertaining and often devastatingly witty. The unsmiling exterior conceals intriguing depths – rather like Martin's period novels featuring the railway detective Jim Stringer, which reveal their treasures with subtlety. *The Necropolis Railway* (2002) inaugurated his winning synthesis of deftly sketched historical detail, intriguing plotting and a passion for steam railways that communicated itself even to non-train lovers (the author has carved out a separate career in TV documentaries, talking about not just the beauty of rolling stock but also the crankier byways of household husbandry). However, Martin has been chafing at the restrictions of the series format, and *The Somme Stations*, while channelling many elements of its predecessors (the low-key Stringer is still at the centre of things) plunges into the horrors of World War I trench combat. Risky territory: is Martin able to invest the crime novel format with such sombre gravitas?

At the time of the Somme, newly enlisted Jim Stringer is shivering in a shell hole as a maelstrom bursts about him. He remembers that even before his team left for France, a member of the unit had been found dead. Stringer and his unit must undertake dangerous nocturnal assignments: driving the trains taking munitions to the front. Death is everywhere, as the trains travel through blasted surrealistic landscapes, and a single-minded military policeman continues to investigate the killing that occurred before the departure for France. Stringer finds himself in the frame for the murder – a death that seems of little importance given the carnage surrounding the soldiers on the trains.

The book's jacket gives no hint that this is crime fiction, suggesting, in fact, a serious novel about war – and, to a large degree, that is what we get. Because Stringer is no larger-than-life figure, he is an apposite still centre for a novel that treats the soul-destroying terrors of trench warfare with a seriousness worthy of more ambitious fiction. Yes, there is still the celebration of trains and railways that invariably characterises the author's work, and the murder mystery plot is dispatched with aplomb. But the real achievement of *The Somme Stations* is the bravura picture the reader is given of men in war – a war receding in time as the last participants die, but that Martin subtly allows to stand in for all conflicts.

The Body in the Boat 2018

AJ MACKENZIE

Marilyn Livingstone and Morgen Witzel, an Anglo-Canadian husband-and-wife team of writers and historians with very different personalities, are skilful practitioners of the period crime novel. In *The Body in the Boat*, smugglers using the English Channel transport something other than their usual cargo: a coffin. Reverend Hardcastle and Mrs Chaytor are drawn into the worlds of high finance and organised crime in this Georgian mystery.

The Ashes of Berlin 2017

LUKE McCALLIN

Oxford-born, Africa-educated Luke McCallin is becoming recognised as one of the most ambitious and accomplished writers in the genre, and this follow-up to *The Man from Berlin* (2014) has a panoramic sweep to match its laser-sharp characterisation. Humane German intelligence officer Captain Gregory Reinhardt has returned to a broken Berlin after the end of the war to serve in the civilian police force, but he finds that divisions and hatreds still reign in the city. A serial killer is on the loose, and one of his victims is the brother of a Nazi scientist. Reinhardt's investigations propel him into the dangerous company of those for whom the war is not over. This is peerless stuff, written with the kind of authority that McCallin has demonstrated in the past, and Reinhardt is a multifaceted protagonist.

The Savage Garden 2007
MARK MILLS

Is your taste for the literary novel of feeling, in which atmospheric evocations of locale and nuanced descriptions of character are couched in delicate prose? Or do you prefer the stronger meat of crime fiction, in which a baffling mystery is cracked while the hero experiences violent pummellings – and, if the writer is feeling generous, graphically described sexual gratification? Actually, there are many of us given to alternating such pleasures – and with Mark Mills, we have an author who can simultaneously slake both appetites. As *The Whaleboat House* (originally published as *Amagansett* in 2004) demonstrated, here was a 'crime' author utilising the kind of writing more often found on the bedside tables of Booker Prize judges. But Mills is also a dab hand at plotting a mystery, and if this book doesn't quite bring off these dual skills with the panache of earlier work, it's still a mesmerising piece. Mills' playfulness is evident in his first chapter – my God, the reader is likely to mutter in dismay, this so *badly* written – what's happened to Mark Mills' talent? But, in fact, we discover that this first chapter is something written by a girlfriend of the hero, Cambridge student Adam Strickland. When he's invited to give his opinion, we already know he'll have to bite his tongue. Adam is a complaisant young man, just about getting by in the Cambridge of 1958, when he's handed an intriguing assignment: he is to visit and write about the garden of the Villa Docci in Tuscany, devised in the 16th century by a widower in memory of his wife. Quickly out of his depth, Adam encounters a series of mysteries: what is the secret of the elderly Signora Docci and her family? What is the truth about the killing that took place at the villa during the German occupation? And is the beautiful Antonella everything she appears to be? All of this is handled with brio by Mills, not least the picture of Italy. So iridescent is the prose that one is prepared to forgive the odd melange of books that jostle behind the narrative: there's **Henry James'** *The Aspern Papers* (reclusive elderly woman and her younger female companion to whom the hero makes love); there's **John Fowles'** *The Magus*, with a seductive young girl leading a mystified protagonist into a secret world (Fowles' *The French Lieutenant's Woman* also springs to mind, with a powerfully erotic coupling halfway through the book); and – considerably lowering the tone of literary allusions – good old **Dan Brown**, with clues to the solution of the mystery rather schematically laid out like cats' eyes in the road. But Mills is a skilful writer and braids these disparate strands into a detailed tapestry.

The Red Hand of Fury   2018

RN MORRIS

Roger Morris has moved on since dragooning **Fyodor Dostoyevsky**'s detective Porfiry Petrovich from *Crime and Punishment* into an excellent series of new cases; in 2012 he began a new sequence, moving his settings forward to 1914 and adopting a new protagonist, Silas Quinn of the Special Crimes Unit at Scotland Yard. Combining rare psychological intensity with an ingeniously twisted plot, *The Red Hand of Fury* – the fourth in the series – exhibits all the hallmarks of the author's best work. As the world descends into the madness of the Great War, Morris's flawed central character is pushed to the edge of sanity. Dark, disturbing and original.

Smoke and Ashes   2018

ABIR MUKHERJEE

The response to the Raj-set novels of Abir Mukherjee has been one of unalloyed praise, not least for the fact that these exuberant narratives are so nuanced in their treatment of that era. Damaged English policeman Sam Wyndham encounters trouble in 1920s India alongside his intuitive Sergeant 'Surrender-not' Banerjee, who may seem to be the Watson to Wyndham's Holmes but is actually the more perceptive of the two.

Smoke and Ashes has Wyndham struggling with the opium addiction he is obliged to keep hidden. Less able this time to rely on Banerjee, he becomes involved with two recent deaths – one of which he stumbles across when he is in a drugged stupor – and in both cases the bodies have been mutilated in ritualistic fashion. But rendering the investigation less important are seismic events connected with the struggle for Indian independence. As in previous books, it is the flamboyant evocation of Calcutta in the 1920s that makes this such a mesmerising read.

The Quincunx   1990
CHARLES PALLISER

As a very clever synthesis of **Charles Dickens** and **Wilkie Collins**, Charles Palliser's labyrinthine magnum opus is carried off with supreme elan, despite the fact that he dismissed it as a postmodern literary experiment. All the tropes of historical mystery developed by the masters of an earlier century are reactivated with great skill, but it's the infusion of a modern sensibility into these dark deeds of the past that makes this arm-straining volume so distinctive. John Huffam and his mother have been leading clandestine lives for as long as he can remember. John's potential inheritance is formidable, but there are many people laying claim to this wealth. The proof of John's right to his estate lies in a missing will – and the search for this in the dark corners of a cathedral town is the engine for a vast, baffling narrative that is often as redolent of **Mervyn Peake** as it is of Dickens – although neither author raked in so many carefully orchestrated suspense sequences. While characterisation is writ large, the naive hero is particularly well honed – but it's the period atmosphere that claims the attention.

Heresy   2011
SJ PARRIS

Heresy shows that SJ Parris (the pseudonym of **Stephanie Merritt**) possesses the quality needed to make a mark in the burgeoning field of historical crime fiction; this is an accomplished premier outing for Giordano Bruno, who is simultaneously a monk, a poet and a highly accomplished sleuth. His investigations as the latter take place in Elizabethan Oxford, where he is a truly memorable figure with his keen mind and anachronistically modern sensibility. Parris has the measure of all the necessary period scene-setting here, while also painting a sharp picture of a society riven by religious intolerance.

Hard Revolution 2004
GEORGE PELECANOS

It's the spring of 1968 and Martin Luther King is attempting to preach his message of non-violent change to young blacks who are seething with impatience. Washington DC is a hotbed of resentment – and Pelecanos's hero Derek Strange is at the start of his police career, not yet the character we've come to know through the author's other books. Then Dr King is assassinated and all hell breaks loose. The fashion in which George Pelecanos counterpoints small-scale crime against national disaster within a brilliantly evoked historical episode is powerfully handled, and he once again proves that no black writer – not even the firebrand **James Baldwin** – could show more single-minded concern for issues affecting black and other ethnic Americans.

A Morbid Taste for Bones 1977
ELLIS PETERS

Edith Pargeter wrote such successful historical mysteries as Ellis Peters before her death in 1995 that, until 2012, her name was used for the Crime Writers' Association's prestigious historical crime fiction prizes. Peters was a writer for five decades and produced nearly 100 books, but it was her Brother Cadfael titles that cemented her achievement in the popular mind. Along with **Umberto Eco**'s William of Baskerville, Peters' herb-growing, intuitive monk, solving medieval crimes in authoritatively rendered historical settings, forged a genre that is still growing in popularity to this day: the mystery set in the past featuring a detective before there really were such people. The Cadfael books were always slim and beautifully turned, and the first, *A Morbid Taste for Bones*, remains the perfect entry point.

At a Benedictine abbey, a young monk has a vision in which he thinks he sees St Winifred in her pre-celestial incarnation as a young girl in a Welsh village. She communicates the fact that she is unhappy with the state of her grave and wishes to be moved to the abbey. For the monks, this is a very fraught enterprise, and they finally agree to travel to Wales to redeem the holy relics. But an influential nobleman who has strongly opposed the monks' plans is killed, and suspicion falls – naturally enough – on the monks, obliging Cadfael to discover the real murderer. This first outing for Cadfael, the ex-crusader living a cloistered life in Shrewsbury, is brilliantly realised. Apart from the impeccable historical detail, Brother Cadfael arises as a fully fledged master detective, deserving the place in the pantheon that he was quickly to acquire.

A MORBID TASTE FOR BONES 1996

Director: Richard Stroud

While certain liberties were taken with Ellis Peters' impeccable plotting, few complained, as the standard of this television adaptation was so high. But while a solid cast was assembled, there is no denying that the success of this film – along with all the others in the popular series – rested squarely on the shoulders of one of Britain's finest classical actors, Derek Jacobi. Brilliantly conveying the hyper-inventive mind behind the benign monkish exterior, Jacobi also cannily suggested the violent crusader past that makes Cadfael such an intriguing character.

Mayhem 2014

SARAH PINBOROUGH

The writer Sarah Pinborough has long been interested in testing the parameters of fiction, a concern that she attacks with relish in this novel. Is it a piece of historical crime fiction? Or is it located within the supernatural genre that the author has also profitably explored? Whatever the answer to this question, the result in *Mayhem* is spellbinding and original – and, what's more, it's a book that manages to find something new in the well-trodden Jack the Ripper territory, although the book is not about Saucy Jack himself, but another murderous figure. A decomposing torso is found within the vaults of New Scotland Yard, and police surgeon Dr Thomas Bond becomes aware that there is another killer plying his bloody trade in London apart from the Ripper. Bond, unhappy in his own skin, becomes dangerously involved when, escaping from his problems in an opium den, he sees another figure who doesn't belong there – a man in a black coat. Who is this sinister figure? This is deliciously inventive stuff, delivered with the narrative nous and sense of atmosphere that lifts *Mayhem* above the raft of many similar novels.

Lying in State 1985
JULIAN RATHBONE

Now largely forgotten, but highly rated by those who do know his work, Rathbone wrote thrillers for nearly 40 years. He attempted on three occasions to write a series, but each time after the third book he declared himself bored with the same character and setting and went off to do something completely different. This makes it difficult to find a pigeon hole to fit him into. The common factor, if there is one, comes from his attachment to the work of **Eric Ambler**. As with Ambler, there is usually a bigger arena in the background: the Cold War, agri-business, genetic modification, nuclear energy, and so on.

Lying in State was inspired by a series of actual events. While exiled in Madrid, Juan Perón taped his memoirs and, on his return to Argentina, he gave them to his actress friend Nini Montiam. Following his death, she found that no one was prepared to pay the sort of money she thought they were worth, and upped the ante by threatening to sell them to an English agent. The complete tapes are reputed to have been dynamite – especially on the subject of Nazi exiles in Argentina including Adolf Eichmann. Rathbone takes this background and imagines the existence of a second set of tapes, even more sensational than the first, and builds a tense narrative around the character of an impoverished Argentinian bookseller who is employed to authenticate them.

The House on Half Moon Street 2018
ALEX REEVE

The rude health of the historical thriller may be attested by noting the impressive debuts that have appeared over the last year or two. *The House on Half Moon Street* is a highly original – if slightly overlong – piece of work, inaugurating a series set in Victorian London. This vision of the 1880s is of a Stygian hue, with the hero, coroner's assistant Leo Stanhope, accused of the murder of his lover Maria and obliged to track down the real killer. The new element here is that Leo was born Charlotte, and the transgender theme is handled with sympathetic understanding. Reeve, however, resists any special pleading regarding his unorthodox protagonist.

Carver's Quest 2013
NICK RENNISON

With *Carver's Quest*, Nick Rennison has produced a book that bristles with an energy and inventiveness that positively leap off the page. But Rennison (a specialist in historical fiction who reviews for *The Sunday Times*) is well aware that many a period-set novel has fallen at the first hurdle because of a faltering evocation of past times, and he is careful never to make a misstep. This outing for amateur archaeologist Adam Carver and his bloody-minded retainer Quint has the ill-matched duo enmeshed in a mystery involving fabled Ancient Greek texts that may point to the treasure chest of Philip II of Macedonia. With a dizzying panoply of incident, Rennison keeps his narrative on the move, and well before the end of the novel, readers may be hoping to spend more time in the company of Carver and Quint.

A Trust Betrayed 2000
CANDACE ROBB

Candace Robb proved in such books as her debut *The Apothecary Rose* (1993) that her medieval Owen Archer investigations are an intriguing development on themes inaugurated by **Ellis Peters**. However, in *A Trust Betrayed*, Robb takes the action back to 1297 and introduces a new series character – Margaret Kerr, wife of a missing merchant husband. The crimes centre on Margaret's family, and through this device Robb is able to deal with often destructive domestic divisions, as well as examining the position of women in past centuries. Robb is particularly sharp on the very different nature of society when no one really possessed 'the big picture' in the modern sense, and the fragmented aspect of society here is conveyed in all its confusion and disorder. *A Trust Betrayed* is set in late 13th-century Scotland, with Margaret Kerr worried that her husband has been swept up in the revolt against the English. When her husband's agent is murdered, Margaret has to travel alone on a variety of very dangerous missions. This is writing of real craftsmanship, full of authoritative detail.

Night Crossing 2004
ROBERT RYAN

Robert Ryan (no relation to the late actor) may have enjoyed great success with his tough, stripped-down modern thrillers written under the name of **Tom Neale**, such as *Steel Rain* (2005), but his real métier emerged in the World War II novels he writes under his own name. The historical detail in these books has a gritty authenticity, despite the fact that the author is too young to remember the period; a recurrent theme – flying – is equally persuasively handled, especially since the author has done his homework and has flown in more than a few bone-rattlers. The third of Ryan's World War II novels, *Night Crossing*, traces the lives of four characters as the war leaves its mark on them: the classical musician Ulrike (who is Jewish), escaping from Berlin to London; the Scotland Yard policeman Cameron Ross; the German U-boat sailor Erich (engaged to Ulrike); and the sinister SS man Schüller. Ryan has few equals in the multiple perspective novel, and the dangerous panoply of this dark period in history is drawn with customary skill.

The Bloody Meadow 2011
WILLIAM RYAN

Life is not easy for an honest policeman in the Soviet Russia of the 1930s. After surviving encounters with corrupt officials in William Ryan's much-acclaimed debut novel *The Holy Thief* (2010), the intuitive Captain Alexei Korolev finds that, rather than being dead or imprisoned – which he is constantly expecting – he wins the day and is acclaimed as a shining example for the Soviet people; he is even decorated. But Alexei is well aware that nothing good in the pre-glasnost Soviet Union is to be trusted – and the dangerous information he has gathered in his activities has left him in a perilous position. If the authorities discover the extent of his investigations, an ice-cold future in a Siberian prison camp beckons. Soviet citizens of this era learned to dread the knock at the door in the dead of night, but when Alexei hears that knock in a snowy Moscow, it is not the catastrophe he expected. NKVD security chief Colonel Rodinov is the nocturnal visitor, asking him to investigate the apparent suicide of a model citizen. Maria Lenskaya has died during the making of a film in the Ukraine, and her death is a matter of great interest to the sinister Ezhov, Commissar for State Security. The film Maria was making, the eponymous *Bloody Meadow*, is still shooting, and when Alexei arrives on the fraught movie set, he soon finds himself once again in danger, with something unsayable – the failure of the Revolution – a key to the mystery.

The Bloody Meadow is every bit as darkly involving as its predecessor, with all the elements that made *The Holy Thief* so successful: razor-sharp plotting, an evocative sense of locale (here, Ukraine, scene of endless battles), and – most winning of all – the human, and vulnerable, Alexei Korolev making a nuisance of himself.

Dissolution 2003

CJ SANSOM

A well-received first novel, *Dissolution* gleaned advance praise from the likes of **PD James** and proved to be a historical crime novel that redefined the genre. It is 1537, Tudor England. Henry VIII has proclaimed himself Supreme Head of the Church. The country is waking up to savage new laws, rigged trials and the greatest network of informers it has ever seen. Under the orders of Thomas Cromwell, a team of commissioners is sent throughout the country to investigate the monasteries. There can be only one outcome: the monasteries are to be dissolved. But on the Sussex coast, at the monastery of Scarnsea, events have spiralled out of control. Cromwell's commissioner, Robin Singleton, has been found dead, his head severed from his body. His horrific murder is accompanied by equally sinister acts of sacrilege – a black cockerel sacrificed on the church altar, and the disappearance of Scarnsea's Great Relic. Matthew Shardlake, lawyer and long-time supporter of reform, has been sent by Cromwell into this atmosphere of treachery and death, accompanied by his loyal assistant Mark. His duty is to uncover the truth behind the dark happenings at Scarnsea. Shardlake's investigation soon forces him to question everything that he hears, and everything that he believes... Historical details are seamlessly wedded to a powerful narrative gift.

Last Seen in Massilia — 2000
STEVEN SAYLOR

Steven Saylor's highly successful series of books chronicling the murky exploits of Roman sleuth Gordianus the Finder are rich with all the requisite authentic historical detail. Wryness is a key Gordianus characteristic; humour is never far away from his observations on any subject, but he's deadly serious when it comes to his work. Steven Saylor studied history and classics at the University of Texas at Austin, but his home (or one of them) is now the college town of Berkeley, where he may often be found doing research in the stacks of the University of California libraries, unravelling the 2,000-year-old crimes of Ancient Rome. The final years of the Roman Republic offer a treasure trove of all the stuff that makes for a rollicking read: there's political intrigue, courtroom drama, sexual scandal, extremes of splendour and squalor, and no shortage of real-life murder mysteries. The greatest challenge for Saylor is to make two things happen simultaneously at the book's climax: to reveal a solution to the mystery plot that makes perfect sense, and to bring the thematic elements of the story to a satisfying resolution.

In *Last Seen in Massilia*, civil war rages, and Gordianus hears via an unnamed source that his son, Meto, is dead. Meto was acting for Caesar, and the very personal task of tracking down his killer leads Gordianus into very dark waters indeed. This is one of the most polished and most immediate volumes in Saylor's excellent series.

Blood and Sugar — 2019
LAURA SHEPHERD-ROBINSON

When historical crime fiction arrives with an encomium from the doyen of the genre, **CJ Sansom**, readers should sit up and take notice. And this debut by a young British writer set the bar high for her peers in 2019. In June 1781, a tortured body is found on a hook at Deptford dock, bearing the brand of a slaver. But shortly afterwards, Captain Harry Corsham – who has made his mark in the recent wars – discovers that his friend, abolitionist Tad Archer, has vanished. Archer possesses information that has the capacity to destroy the British slave trade, and was accordingly a man with many enemies. Corsham is to find that treading in the footsteps of his friend is dangerous work. Laura Shepherd-Robinson arrives as a fully formed talent who has the full measure of her material: lashings of detailed period atmosphere, distinctive individual characters, and the capacity to find modern social relevance in Britain's unenlightened past. A novel of consummate skill.

The Secret Speech 2009

TOM ROB SMITH

To say that Tom Rob Smith's debut novel, *Child 44* (2008), caused something of a sensation in the crime/thriller field would be to understate the case. The youthful Smith began to collect book award nominations by the bushel, before finally bagging the Crime Writers' Association's Ian Fleming Steel Dagger. Here, unarguably, was a novel of authority – despite an annoying stylistic tic, repeated in the follow-up: all speech is always in italics, granting everything an equal overemphasis. *The Secret Speech* is a further dramatic reinvention of the crime fiction genre. It doesn't have the innovative energy of its predecessor (how could it?), but this second outing for the conflicted former state security officer Leo Demidov shows that Smith has the ability to maintain his earlier success. Smith set himself a daunting problem for any successor to *Child 44* – Leo began that book as a poster boy for Stalin's brutal police force, making all the necessary accommodations with himself to enforce the status quo. But then Leo underwent a *crise de conscience*; with his wife arrested and Leo now the quarry, the apparatus he once supported is now trained against him. How to reactivate the dynamic of that first book, when the scales have fallen from Leo's eyes?

Smith's solution is a canny one: he begins with a flashback to 1949, with Leo savagely beating a man over the concealment of music by an 'anti-Soviet' composer. It's a harrowing scene that's hard to read – but Smith is once again able to (finally) enlist our sympathy for the compromised protagonist. The narrative jumps to 1956; Stalin is dead, and the grim regime begins to come apart. It's the time of Khrushchev's epochal revisionist pronouncements (the eponymous 'secret speech' is one of these), in which the horrors of the Stalinist regime are denounced for the first time. Ex-policeman Leo Demidov, his wife Raisa and their daughters are suddenly in the firing line again, this time because of the new perception of the police as criminals; the brutality of the secret policemen is being bloodily paid back to them in reprisals. Leo's family blames him for an involvement in the death of his adopted daughter's parents, but the real threat here comes from an implacable nemesis. Leo's attempts to save his family plunge him into a terrifying odyssey, from the gulags of Siberia to Hungary's violent streets.

Tom Rob Smith has spoken of his admiration for **Joseph Conrad**'s *Lord Jim*, in which the protagonist has to atone for collusion with evil. That book is a template for Leo's ordeal in *The Secret Speech*, and if the comparison seems grandiose, one has to admire Smith's ambition. The moral conflicts just about keep pace with the tension in a narrative packed with a dizzying mass of incident.

The American Boy — 2003

ANDREW TAYLOR

In the period after its publication, barely a week seemed to pass without Andrew Taylor tucking another award under his belt for *The American Boy*. The author had re-read **Edgar Allan Poe**'s *Tales of Mystery and Imagination* and had been struck again by the European cast of Poe's imagination and by the sense of vulnerability, of wounds that had never quite healed. Poe had lived in England from 1815 to 1820, and *The American Boy* invents a secret history of Poe's childhood, concentrating on an episode in 1820 – the last year of his stay in England. Taylor's novel reflects as accurately as possible the manners and mores of the period. He researched how people spoke, thought and acted in late Regency England, from the mansions of Mayfair to the slums of St Giles and Seven Dials, from the leafy village of Stoke Newington to a country estate in Gloucestershire. He studied that curiously inconclusive war between the world's one superpower and a small, pushy little country half a world away: the War of 1812, the last time the British and the Americans fought on opposing sides.

The book coaxes a murder mystery and a love story from scraps of history and the oblique hints in Poe's writings. Most of the book is the narrative of an impoverished schoolmaster, Thomas Shield, who has a chequered past that includes a brief but disastrous military career and a history of mental instability. At the heart of the fictional Shield's story is Wavenhoe's Bank and the families concerned with its fortunes and misfortunes – and especially the women. The collapse of the bank is based on a real-life embezzlement case, which led to the Fauntleroy forgery trial of 1824 and eventually to the gallows. Poe haunts the book, though for much of the time he appears to play a relatively minor role. It's an astonishing, epic achievement. Also look out for Taylor's *Roth Trilogy* (1997–2000), which triumphantly shows that crime novels can deal with serious themes and use innovative literary techniques.

The Bullet Trick 2006
LOUISE WELSH

How important is the distinction between English and Scottish in the world of books? Louise Welsh's *The Bullet Trick* may have been published by the small Scottish publisher Canongate, but was the target market a Celtic one? Just a few paragraphs of Welsh's assured and highly imaginative period novel makes it clear that she would not be happy with just a local constituency – like many Scottish scribes, from **Arthur Conan Doyle** to **Muriel Spark**, Welsh is simply a writer, interested in the whole range of human experience and less concerned with the petty parochialism that both the English and the Scots perennially display. Welsh made a considerable impression with her first novel, *The Cutting Room* (2002), which sold over 200,000 copies. However, everything is thrown into *The Bullet Trick*, a baggy delight of a book: the down-at-heel, sensuous delights of the burlesque scene, sharply realised locales (Glasgow gin joints, seedy Soho nightclubs and Berlin alleys), and a shabby protagonist in Glaswegian conjurer William Wilson. Wilson has been glumly watching his life go into a downward spiral and is desperate for a change. He begins to tentatively believe that his luck may be improving when he is signed up for a series of cabaret jobs in Berlin. The move from Glasgow is coming at a particularly apposite time, as there are several people Wilson would rather not see again. The decadent charms of underworld Berlin initially look like the answer to a prayer, as Wilson plunges into a heady world of sexually available showgirls and persuasive conmen.

To Kill a Tsar — 2010
ANDREW WILLIAMS

Compromised characters with difficult moral choices are at the centre of Andrew William's *To Kill a Tsar*. Set in a strongly realised 19th-century St Petersburg and dealing with the first significant terrorist cell (a subject also tackled by **Joseph Conrad**), this is bravura storytelling.

A Small Death in Lisbon — 1999
ROBERT WILSON

Robert Wilson's considerable reputation grows from book to book, with *A Small Death in Lisbon* one of his subtlest achievements. It is 1941. Europe cowers under the dark clouds of war, and neutral Lisbon is one of the world's tensest cities. Klaus Felsen, a reluctant member of the SS, finds himself drawn into a savage battle in the Portuguese mountains for a vital element, wolfram, that is needed for Hitler's armaments industry. In modern-day Lisbon, Inspector Zé Coelho is an outsider in the cliquish world of the Polícia Judiciária. Investigating the death of a young girl, he suddenly finds himself deep in the events of 50 years ago, with ramifications for the Portuguese Revolution, which is hardly a generation old. Robert Wilson has carved out a niche for himself as a remarkable writer of distinctive, colourful thrillers written in literary style. Here again he echoes his forebears **Graham Greene** and **Eric Ambler** in a complex and powerfully characterised story that builds inexorably to a breathtaking climax.

A Vote for Murder — 2003
DAVID WISHART

The streets of Caesar's Rome are becoming increasingly crowded with the cunning breed of ancient detectives, and it's a wonder that the anachronistic detectives of **Steven Saylor**, **Lindsey Davis** and David Wishart are not stumbling over each other. But who cares? All three authors have produced work of the highest quality, shot through with wit, offbeat characters and highly plausible historical detail. More than his colleagues and rivals, Wishart seems aware that the whole Roman sleuth enterprise is a confidence trick: we know – he infers – that there were no detectives in this era, but such is his narrative skill that we completely buy the concept and enjoy the outrageously entertaining results.

In *A Vote for Murder*, Wishart's canny investigator Marcus Corvinus is having a leisurely holiday with his stepdaughter and generally enjoying a bibulous time, while keeping half an eye on the Machiavellian antics involved in the pending consulate elections. But when one of the two candidates meets a violent death, Corvinus – with no reluctance – summarily ends his vacation and plunges into the murder hunt. Of course, it's too easy to assume that the rival political candidate would be behind the killing, and some labyrinthine plots are ahead before Corvinus cuts the Gordian knot in his usual fashion and brings things to a highly surprising conclusion. The varied denizens of this dangerous world are drawn with great dash, and the one-liners that Wishart specialises in are quite as sharp as anything the author has entertained us with before.

CHAPTER 19

FOREIGN BLOODSHED
Crime in translation

A hotly debated topic among British crime writers and enthusiasts was brought to a controversial climax by the award of the prestigious Crime Writers' Association Gold Dagger in 2005. The recipient? **Arnaldur Indriðason**, for his novel *Silence of the Grave* (2005), originally written in his native Icelandic. 'Shouldn't all entries for this prize be written in English?' was an oft-heard, irritated cry.

All the fuss was unsurprising. Few crime readers on either side of the Atlantic can have failed to notice the avalanche of foreign crime novels flooding into bookshops – most of them greeted with massively enthusiastic reviews. But these much-acclaimed writers (the late **Henning Mankell, Fred Vargas, Karin Fossum** et al.) – were taking readers into fascinatingly unfamiliar new climes for crime – and gleaning applause for the freshness and invention of their approach to the genre (not just because we were reading about bloody murder in Helsinki rather than Manchester). However, these new voices are only the latest literary combatants in a crime fiction war that began quite some time ago with some remarkably talented writers, of which the following selection has to be – of necessity – selective. Also very worthy of note are **Jussi Adler-Olsen, Jakob Arjouni, Sara Blaedel, Sebastian Fitzek, Pascal Garnier, Jorn Lier Horst, Mari Jungstedt, Liza Marklund, Manuel Vázquez Montalbán, Leif GW Persson, Lilja Sigurðardóttir, Teresa Solana** and **Johan Theorin**.

The Winter Queen
2002, Russia

BORIS AKUNIN

Grigori Chkhartishvili, under the pseudonym Boris Akunin (you can see why he uses a pen name), has produced a series of historical thrillers that have been something of a publishing phenomenon in the author's native Russia. The title chosen to be the first published in English, *The Winter Queen* (translated by Andrew Bromfield), served as an excellent entry point for a very accomplished writer, and in a short time Akunin found himself on many reading lists. The books deal with the young and high-minded Moscow policeman Erast Fandorin, a character who changes as the books progress, with his early idealism somewhat under siege from the realities of his job. *The Winter Queen* is set in Tsarist Russia in the late 19th century. After a suicide in a Moscow park, Fandorin begins to unravel a tortuous plot involving seductive women, labyrinthine conspiracies and a sinister figure with designs on global power. The young policeman's quest to untangle a dark mystery takes him to London (as well portrayed as the Moscow of the opening scenes), then back to his own country, where he realises to his dismay that everything he thought he had deduced has taken him in quite the wrong direction. Comparisons have been drawn to both **Fyodor Dostoyevsky** and **Ian Fleming**, but Akunin is his own man, and these light-hearted, pictorial period thrillers have great charm, even if they steer clear of more serious issues and are slighter than initial reviews suggested.

The Night Buffalo
2005, Mexico

GUILLERMO ARRIAGA

Celebrated as the Mexican writer behind the films *Amores Perros* (2000), *21 Grams* (2003) and *The Three Burials of Melquiades Estrada* (2005), Arriaga disdains genre for something much more individual in a brilliant analysis of personal and moral guilt; *The Night Buffalo* (translated by Alan Page) bears comparison with **Patricia Highsmith** at her best, or **Alfred Hitchcock** at his most subtle. A first-person narrative, it draws the reader into the apparently normal everyday life of its narrator, Manuel. But as each page turns, the increasingly dark levels of culpability that are revealed as we follow the tale of a *ménage à trois* which ends in fatality are peeled like layers of an onion. What horrifies is the narrator's inability to see his responsibility for the events that unravel.

The Woman Who Was No More/ She Who Was No More
1954, France

PIERRE BOILEAU AND THOMAS NARCEJAC

The writing team of Boileau and Narcejac enjoyed a spectacularly successful career writing highly efficient thrillers in their native France. The surprise for most readers when reading this taut and ingenious thriller is the gender switch in the narrative from the famous **Henri-Georges Clouzot** film (see below). Ravinel is a killer. His wife Mireille has been drowned in her bath, and, together with his mistress Lucienne, he has dumped her corpse into a river to give the impression of suicide. But if Mireille is dead, how is she writing to him from beyond the grave? Unfortunately, the plot has been plundered so often that the original has lost something of its novelty. It's worth remembering that **Alfred Hitchcock**'s classic 1958 movie masterpiece *Vertigo* was based on Boileau and Narcejac's *D'Entre les Morts/ The Living and the Dead* (1954/1956) – readers should seek out other work by the team, notably such slim and effective thrillers as *The Victims* (1965) and *The Evil Eye* (1959).

LES DIABOLIQUES/THE FIENDS 1955

Director: Henri-Georges Clouzot

As well as being one of the most accomplished crime films in the history of the cinema – one that retains its power to shock even in our jaded age – Clouzot's classic was immensely influential. Its scene of terror in a bathroom, for instance, is a clear influence on *Psycho* (1960): **Alfred Hitchcock** was an admirer of the film and wryly noted that his own techniques were being repurposed by Clouzot. Apart from the impeccable cinematography, it is, of course, the wonderful performances that make the film work so well: the matchless Simone Signoret and the unpleasant Paul Meurisse as the adulterous lovers, and – most of all – Véra Clouzot's incarnation of the cowed wife. Never was nepotism put to better use than Clouzot's casting of his spouse in this role. **Jeremiah Chechik**'s indifferent American remake in 1996 with Sharon Stone quickly sank without trace.

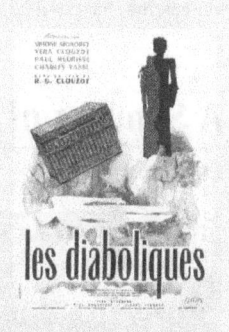

Suburra

2017, Italy

CARLO BONINI AND GIANCARLO DE CATALDO

No ornate use of language is to be found in the caustic and blunt *Suburra*; this massive crime epic is translated by Antony Shugaar in unfinessed fashion – 'Samurai ripped them into shreds. His friend never even fired a shot. Then they shovelled the remains into trash bags and dropped them into the Tiber.' Italy, with its endemic political and religious corruption, is fertile territory for crime fiction. Choosing the Berlusconi era as it entered its long-overdue final phase, Bonini and De Cataldo (journalist and magistrate respectively) set their narrative in Suburra, a run-down and lawless region of Rome. The financial crisis of 2008 has allowed the Mafia to have even greater influence over the police, their own criminal foot soldiers, far-right extremists and a deeply compromised Catholic Church plagued by sex scandals. There's no nuance here, but *Suburra* is a reminder that crime fiction can say as much about a society as many other genres.

SUBURRA

2015

Director: Stefano Sollima

In 2011, a land dispute concerning the seaside town of Ostia near Rome escalates into a conflict between criminals, crooked politicians and the Vatican. Complex and violent, the characterisation here is more rounded than usual in this kind of crime film.

A Summer of Murder

2018, Germany

OLIVER BOTTINI

One of the key pleasures provided by the best thriller writing is the slaking of the desire to travel. But in *A Summer of Murder* (translated by Jamie Bulloch), the second of the Black Forest Investigations by the German writer Oliver Bottini, we are not only transported to the beautiful southwest Kirchzarten region of the Black Forest, we are granted plotting bristling with invention and originality. A burning shed draws the attention of the fire brigade, and a volunteer dies as a hidden weapons cache detonates. Some of the evidence suggests an involvement of German neo-Nazis or arms traders from the former Yugoslavia, but Louise Bonì, who is struggling to readjust to police duties with the Freiburg Kripo after treatment for alcoholism, finds her investigation becoming increasingly intractable with the arrival of the secret service. And by the time she makes a final pulse-racing trip into danger in the depths of the Black Forest, Louise (and the reader) has been party to some difficult truths about her own addictive personality.

Black Water Lilies　　　　　　　　　　　　　　2017, France

MICHEL BUSSI

To say that Michel Bussi's *After the Crash* (2015) made a considerable mark is to understate the case. The highly original premise had critics seeking new adjectives to praise this narrative of the tragic aftermath of a plane crash. *Black Water Lilies* (translated by Shaun Whiteside), however, is a very different kettle of fish, involving a murder in the garden of the French impressionist Claude Monet and is fashioned on a more modest scale. Bussi takes us to Giverny, where tourists flock to see the gardens Monet painted, but reveals another side to this idyllic French village when Jérôme Morval, a man of great passions (for both art and women), is found murdered in the stream that runs through Monet's gardens. Three different women are somehow involved in his death: the attractive village schoolteacher, an ambitious young painter and an elderly widow who surveys the village from the mill near the stream. The three women share a secret. While those expecting something similar to the earlier book may initially be disappointed by the more intimate narrative on offer here, *Black Water Lilies* is quite as accomplished a piece of work as its predecessor, with the details of the slowly unfolding mystery exerting a mesmerising effect.

The Terracotta Dog　　　　　　　　　　　　　　2004, Italy

ANDREA CAMILLERI

As more and more crime in translation began to break through into the mainstream, certain names quickly established themselves as implicit guarantees of quality. One of these names is Andrea Camilleri, and *The*

Terracotta Dog (translated by Stephen Sartarelli) is as good a sampler of the author's work as any. This is a police procedural delivered with all the consummate skill that has always been a speciality of European writers in this field, and it features the author's Inspector Salvo Montalbano, one of the most distinctive Italian coppers on the scene. Montalbano has received an invitation to meet a killer and decides to accept, even though it may be dangerous. In fact, the meeting is a setup and leads to Montalbano finding a clandestine relationship between a whole host of crimes. These involve dirty doings within the Sicilian Mafia and religious institutions (of both the Christian and Muslim variety), and stretch back in a sequence over time involving the American landings in Sicily in World War II.

Earlier, in *The Shape of Water* (2002), Montalbano had already been established as a highly individual protagonist, and Camilleri continues to develop him here not just in his professional dealings (where his laser-sharp mind makes a series of outrageous connections), but within his relationship to the woman in his life, Livia. But while the characterisation here is as adroit as one could wish for, it's the plotting that remains the *chef-d'œuvre* of *The Terracotta Dog*. So popular is the former film director in Italy that his home town changed its name to that featured in many of his books – Porto Empedocle Vigàta – though only temporarily.

INSPECTOR MONTALBANO (1999–)

Directors: Various

This stylish, thoroughly escapist Italian series – featuring **Andrea Camilleri's** Inspector Salvo Montalbano – is a police procedural that is generally light in tone but is delivered with all the quiet skill that has always been a speciality of European filmmakers in this field. The Sicilian copper (charismatically played by Luca Zingaretti) sports a laser-sharp mind and is a gourmet whose attention frequently strays to food. Most of all, we get to see his exotic stamping ground: the beautiful, sleepy territory of Vigàta. And there is the heat – always the heat. As this series shows, Montalbano has a way of finding a clandestine relationship between a host of crimes; these involve dirty doings within the Sicilian Mafia (usually on the periphery) and respectable business institutions as well as more personal cases. But while the characterisation here is as adroit as one could wish, it's the plotting and the locales that remain the key elements.

Involuntary Witness
2010, Italy

GIANRICO CAROFIGLIO

Gianrico Carofiglio is a brave man: an anti-mafia judge in Puglia who has taken on the powerful and lethal corruption that is endemic in Italy. His debut novel (translated by Patrick Creagh) – since followed by other well-received books – begins with the body of a child being discovered in a well at a southern Italian beach resort. A Senegalese peddler is arraigned for sexual assault and murder, but Defence Counsel Guido Guerrieri realises that the truth is more complex. A tangled skein of racism and judicial corruption confronts Guerrieri. Italian crime fiction seems more than ready to take on uncomfortable social issues, and Carofiglio's strong prose makes for irresistible reading.

Frozen Moment
2010, Sweden

CAMILLA CEDER

Camilla Ceder (who lives in Gothenburg) originally studied social science and psychotherapy, disciplines that she puts to intelligent use in her vocation as a writer of psychological crime fiction – although Ceder has not given up the day job, and continues to work in counselling and social work. Her debut novel, *Frozen Moment* (translated by Marlaine Delargy), enjoyed considerable success in Sweden, although the dizzying succession of new Nordic talents made it more difficult for tyro authors to break through in the first decades of the 20th century. Camilla Ceder excels in two particular areas: the first is the adroit evocation of the chilly countryside around Gothenburg in western Sweden, with the mood and atmosphere of the landscape delineated in an almost poetic fashion. But like many of the best Scandinavian writers who have taken up the crime fiction form, she is particularly exercised by the darker psychological impulses of her characters – hardly surprising, given her background. Other issues that engage her in *Frozen Moment* include the decline of rural society, the fragmentation of the family in modern Scandinavia, and the alienation and destruction of lives resulting from the massive spread of recreational drug use. But, if the themes listed above were not challenging enough, she has other fish to fry too, and makes cogent points about the state's role in tackling social dysfunction and breakdown. That's not to say that this debut novel is any kind of sociological tract: Ceder is well aware that readers' paramount concern is powerful storytelling.

A rural town on the Swedish coast. On a frigid winter morning in 2006, Åke Melkersson is making his way to work when his car breaks down. Finding a garage, he discovers to his horror that the garage owner is lying dead on the ground, crushed by a car that has been driven over him again and again. Melkersson calls his neighbour Seja, a reporter, who quickly becomes interested in the murder. Seja gets involved with the enigmatic Inspector Christian Tell, the unconventional copper who is in charge of the investigation, and a sexual charge sparks between them. A second murder occurs, and, to his dismay, Tell finds that Seja has not revealed to him all that she knows – could she be involved in some fashion with the killings? There are a variety of elements to praise here, not least the way in which Ceder has anatomised the psychological patterns of her protagonists, notably Seja, struggling to come to terms with the memories of a difficult and disturbed adolescence.

The Deliverance of Evil 2013, Italy

ROBERTO COSTANTINI

A head of steam built quickly in the UK for Roberto Costantini's epic novel (translated by NS Thompson), despite it being a daunting read. The Tripoli-born writer was touted as an Italian **Stieg Larsson**, with this first book of a trilogy undergoing a title change in English (the Italian title is *You Are Evil*) and featuring a troubled central character, a strong and bitter political strain, and even the imprimatur of Larsson's publishers in the UK. But there the resemblances end. Costantini's detective is Commissario Michele Balistreri, and readers patient enough to stick with the unhurried prose will find a picture of an entire society vitiated by corruption along with one of the most fully realised protagonists in modern crime fiction – if, indeed, this can be called a crime novel. In fact, *The Deliverance of Evil* is actually a state-of-the-nation piece, and the failure and stasis of the compromised hero might be read as a metaphor for Italy's untrustworthy authority figures.

The novel is set in two time periods. In Rome in July 1982 (on the eve of the Italian victory at the World Cup in Spain – success or failure at football is a central image), Elisa Sordi, employed by the real estate company of the Vatican, disappears. The investigator is Commissario

Balistreri. Self-centred and lazy, he invests little in the case, which ends with the body of the young woman being discovered by the Tiber. The crime remains unsolved, but its repercussions spread out over many years. In July 2006, the dead girl's mother takes her own life, and Balistreri once again becomes involved, but he is now a very different man. Although he has been promoted, crippling remorse plagues him, and his self-loathing is hardly alleviated by antidepressants. The long-buried secrets he is to uncover expose the fault lines in his own troubled society; the background of Costantini's protagonist is keenly drawn, from his devotion to Mussolini and the ultra-right to clandestine work for the security forces as Aldo Moro is murdered by the Red Brigades.

With the papacy of Pope Francis drawing attention to the Vatican at the time of publication, Costantini's novel could not have been more timely, although its picture of church power as irredeemably corrupt did not please those hoping for a re-energised Catholic Church (Balistreri himself has been a victim of priestly abuse in the book). Of a daunting length, *The Deliverance of Evil* is not for the casual reader, but those seeking a substantial, ambitious novel drawn on the most sprawling of canvases will find their commitment rewarded.

Romanzo Criminale
2015, Italy

GIANCARLO DE CATALDO

The immense success of Giancarlo De Cataldo's arm-straining, influential novel *Romanzo Criminale* (originally published in 2002), about three close friends who hijack the organised crime scene in Rome, moved into the territory of non-literary phenomenon. The book, complex and heavily peopled, was famously inspired by real-life events. As well as being a forceful crime narrative, it is a chronicle of the 'Years of Lead', the time of socio-political upheaval that extended from the 1960s to the 1980s in Italy, with organised crime and political corruption going hand in hand. From 1960, with the joyriding principals already on their way to becoming ruthless criminals, through the bloody battles of the 1970s (including encounters with terrorists, the Mafia and the security services), the period detail is impeccable, with the stark and shadowy presentation of the characters paying dividends in terms of verisimilitude. This belated English translation by Antony Shugaar is rich and idiomatic.

ROMANZO CRIMINALE: LA SERIE   2008–10

Director: Stefano Sollima

It was inevitable that Giancarlo De Cataldo's novel about three young criminals in Rome would lead to a film adaptation – and, subsequently, a TV series. But the latter was a victim of its own success, with Season 1 finally becoming repetitive. Season 2, however, recaptured the energy of the early days, with its commendable refusal to make any of the self-serving, violent characters sympathetic – or in possession of even minimal moral or humane qualities. As with **Brian De Palma**'s *Scarface* (1983), we are happy to see monstrous, overindulging – but charismatic – characters bring about their own triumph and destruction. In Season 1 we watched the ruthless criminal Libanese take over Rome's underworld, establishing a highly organised gang, and in the second season there is a vicious leadership struggle. The show presents a fascinating picture of corruption in modern Italy involving terrorist atrocities, kidnapping and political double-dealing – even as honest copper Commissioner Scialoja tries to destroy the gang.

The Pledge   1959, Switzerland

FRIEDRICH DÜRRENMATT

One of the most important European writers of the modern age, Friedrich Dürrenmatt is best known for such plays as *The Physicists* (1962), but among his novels this psychologically complex tale of an obsessive detective is a classic of the genre. A little girl is found dead in a Swiss forest, and her murder is similar to several committed years earlier. Inspector Matthäi is put in charge of the investigation but is forced into retirement before tracking down the murderer and becomes adviser to the Jordanian police force. The moment when he must tell the parent of the dead girl the terrible news is highly significant for him: he is forced to make a solemn promise to find the killer. And this – over a very long time period – he feels obliged to do. He takes over a service station near where he assumes the killer must live. And he waits. And waits. As this synopsis conveys, we are by no means in standard police procedural mode here: the psychological state of the relentless pursuer is centre stage in the story and his obsessiveness shades over into something approaching mental illness. As well as steadily building his arresting narrative, Dürrenmatt allows his interest in the mental states of his characters to be paramount.

THE PLEDGE 2001
Director: Sean Penn

When Sean Penn shed the tiresome adolescent antics that characterised his early career, he metamorphosed into one of the finest actors and directors of the modern American cinema. This stunning adaptation of **Friedrich Dürrenmatt**'s novel plays fair by its source material and retains the sense of the passage of time that is so crucial to the narrative. Of course, having Jack Nicholson, one of the most accomplished actors in modern film, as the obsessed detective is the icing on the cake.

The Name of the Rose 1983, Italy
UMBERTO ECO

In the 21st century, it's hard to remember just what impact Eco's remarkable novel had in its day. Certainly, it was literary fiction of an uncommon order. And the success of this book by a celebrated Italian academic and historian of popular culture was something of a Trojan horse for the sales of foreign fiction in translation in both the UK and the US – though the phenomenal sales of this often inaccessible book led to a positive avalanche of far less distinguished historical mysteries. Eco's success outside Italy, of course, was due in no small part to the remarkably sympathetic translation by William Weaver – one of the few occasions when the translator's achievement was loudly celebrated. And despite its dense and allusive prose, Eco's novel was also a classic historical detective story; the name of its monkish sleuth, William of Baskerville, is something of a clue to the book's antecedents. The setting is Italy in the Middle Ages, and as the Franciscan foreigner William cracks an apparently impenetrable mystery in which six monks are found murdered in a variety of ways involving sinister religious sects and ecclesiastical corruption, we are given a picture of religious wars, a detailed history of the monastic orders and a complex and multi-layered vision of the medieval era. William himself is, frankly, something of a cheat: a modern sensibility hides behind the period trappings, but this makes him the perfect conduit for the reader. Even here, though, Eco plays around with this conceit: for all his modernity in some areas, William has a desperately medieval view of women – they are there merely to tempt men from the ways of God.

THE NAME OF THE ROSE   1986

Director: Jean-Jacques Annaud

Sean Connery makes a rather more muscular Franciscan friar than most people will have envisaged when reading **Umberto Eco**'s novel, but any thoughts that William of Baskerville might be a medieval 007 are quickly banished by his charismatic performance. The production design of the film is stunning, and the hiring of the great F Murray Abraham (Salieri in the **Miloš Forman** 1984 film of *Amadeus*) as a sinister inquisitor was a masterstroke. All of the novel's intricate religious discourse is, of course, jettisoned.

Zero   2018, Austria

MARC ELSBERG

Zero (aka *Code Zero*) is nothing if not topical. This novel by Marc Elsberg (translated by Simon Pare) was a sizeable hit in the author's native Austria and other German-speaking territories. The source of menace here is a lifestyle app that promises power and social influence – and comes with massively life-changing results. Journalist Cynthia Bonsant uncovers massive criminality when she investigates the social media platform Freemee, a Facebook-style enterprise that offers to fulfil subscribers' dreams. Cynthia is not the only person concerned about what lies behind the organisation – the shadowy activist Zero, high on the wanted lists of several countries, has exposed the dark underbelly of social media giants' societal control via the manipulation of data. (Elsberg is prescient here; this is all pre-Cambridge Analytica – *Zero* was published in Europe in 2014.) Needless to say, Cynthia is soon in the sights of the sinister forces behind Freemee and its battery of surveillance tools, with the final chapters generating a real head of steam. Elsberg's doughty heroine may be cut from familiar cloth, but this is a thriller with a finger on the zeitgeist.

He Who Fears the Wolf
2003, Norway

KARIN FOSSUM

There is no room for debate: one of the most important female writers of crime fiction at work today not writing in English is the Norwegian Karin Fossum. In many ways, her unprecedented success has opened the floodgates for other foreign writers in translation who have been reinvigorating the field. *Don't Look Back* (2002), featuring her protagonist Inspector Sejer, was a dark piece of interior writing quite different from the standard fare that many readers had become accustomed to, and *He Who Fears the Wolf* (translated by Felicity David) continues Fossum's subtle reinvention of the genre. Her first reviewers in Norway spotted parallels with the British crime writer **Minette Walters**, but **Ruth Rendell** (a favourite writer of Fossum's) is nearer the mark – that is, Rendell in her decidedly non-cosy mode as a cold-eyed examiner of the darker reaches of the soul. In *He Who Fears the Wolf*, a savagely mutilated body is discovered in a secluded village, and the apparent killer is subsequently committed to an asylum. Shortly afterwards, a bank holdup results in a hostage situation – and it's the strange relationship between the criminal and the female hostage that is the crux of the book, brilliantly developed by Fossum, always moving in directions that take the reader by surprise. The idiosyncratic picture of Nordic society – both like and unlike Britain – is one of the key elements in the success of the book (and most of Fossum's work).

Death under a Tuscan Sun
2015, Italy

MICHELE GIUTTARI

The Tuscan countryside is baking under the unrelenting heat, but the atmosphere is particularly noxious in the dank prison cell in which serial killer Daniele de Robertis spends his time plotting revenge against those who betrayed him – if he ever gets out, that is. And then (of course!) de Robertis escapes. Once he is on the loose, an upscale lawyer and his wife are savagely killed at their home, and the police discover a series of gruesome photographs of the bodies of nine women. It's up to Florentine Police Chief Michele Ferrara to capture a murderer and crack open a sinister cult in the teeth of irritation from the crème de la crème of Italian society, none of whom shows the slightest inclination to help in his investigations.

As well as being an accomplished – if sometimes inconsistent – novelist, Michele Giuttari is the genuine article in the crime-solving stakes. Born in Sicily, an ex-inspector of police, he faced down the Cosa Nostra and monitored mafia activity for the Interior Minister in Rome. His crack squad in Tuscany was tasked with reopening the case of the 'Monster of Florence', who murdered 16 people and was a template for **Thomas Harris**'s Hannibal Lecter. Giuttari's discovery that the killer did not appear to work alone unravelled a web of conspiracies, and when the policeman swapped his career for the safer profession of novelist, he had plenty of inspiration for his debut book, *A Florentine Death* (2008) (a bestseller in Italy). His copper borrows his creator's first name, his elegant grey-flecked locks and Sicilian sensibility, as well as a German wife. Five books have followed that impressive debut, not all of which have maintained the initial momentum, but *Death under a Tuscan Sun* (translated by Isabelle Kaufeler) is Giuttari closer to his early form. We have that sense of total authenticity that is the sine qua non of his best work, and the portrayal of the beleaguered police chief and his crew has a saltiness that has sometimes been lacking. And it's this rediscovered vein of characterisation as well as the inexorable page-turning quality that make it clear that Giuttari is out of his literary slough. The gunfire exchanged in the final chapter signals a satisfying conclusion to a complex mystery. Despite the tasteful presentation of the jacket, which suggests literary crime, that's not really Giuttari's fiefdom; this is essentially a straightforward police procedural with nothing particularly elegant about the prose. But that's a matter of category rather than quality, and this is a sultry and atmospheric antidote to the bone-freezing temperatures of the various Scandinavian crime scribes.

The Devotion of Suspect X 2011, Japan
KEIGO HIGASHINO

Can 2 million Japanese readers be wrong? *The Devotion of Suspect X* has not only sold a huge number of copies in its native country; it has also acquired the status of a phenomenon – and even become something of a national obsession. Yasuko is a devoted mother, living with her only child and working in a Tokyo bento shop. She has freed herself from an abusive husband, but her divorce does not mean that she has seen the last of her tormentor. He appears at her door, pleading for reconciliation. This is familiar territory for the weary Yasuko, but her former husband tries to talk to his teenage stepdaughter who wants as little to do with him as his ex-wife. In a rage, he begins to beat her and Yasuko attempts to pull him away, grabbing the cord of a heated table (a common feature of Japanese homes) and strangling him.

This is the startling opening of Keigo Higashino's novel (translated by Alexander O Smith and Elye J Alexander), and the first thing that will strike the reader is the beautifully judged prose, which is cool but involving, functional but poetic. We are hooked even before the author pulls off another coup: after the almost accidental murder, there is a knock at the door and Yasuko's neighbour – a man she has hardly been aware of – enters the room and instantly understands what has happened. Ishigami is a super-intelligent mathematician holding down a dead-end job at a local school. His one source of pride is his devastatingly logical intellect, and he quickly assesses the situation, realising that the mother and daughter were attempting to protect themselves. To the women's – and the reader's – surprise, Ishigami devises a plan: he will help them dispose of the body, on the condition that they put themselves totally in his care. And when the authorities arrive, other idiosyncratic characters are introduced, including Manabu Yukawa, a physicist who is helping the police and was a classmate, and intellectual equal, of the helpful mathematician neighbour. What follows is fascinating, tense and, above all, endlessly surprising.

Anyone who regularly writes about the crime genre is repeatedly asked one question: what's the next trend? And if there were more genre authors in Japan as accomplished as this writer, the answer would be simple: Japanese crime fiction. But Higashino appears to be something of an evolutionary sport who has grown up paying obeisance to no other novelists – and inspiring no imitators as yet. As well as being a minutely detailed picture of life and mores in modern Japan, there is a host of other pleasures crowded into *The Devotion of Suspect X*, including a postmodern take on the conventions of the detective novel.

The Sweetness of Life 2008, Germany
PAULUS HOCHGATTERER

The Sweetness of Life (translated in the UK by Jamie Bulloch) was the Austrian recipient of a European prize for literature, and marked Paulus Hochgatterer out as a writer prepared to employ unorthodox effects. With a cast of troubled individuals in a village in Austria, the author detonated a series of literary incendiary devices following the discovery by a traumatised young girl of the mutilated body of her grandfather. Detective Superintendent Ludwig Kovacs joins sensitive psychiatrist Raffael Horn to open a particularly nasty can of worms. The book encountered some criticism for its dyspeptic vision of Austrian village life, but events in the real world prove that, if anything, Hochgatterer underplayed the horrors that can lurk beneath placid bourgeois surfaces.

The Susan Effect 2017, Denmark
PETER HØEG

The late **Henning Mankell** once told me that the book he most wished he had written was Peter Høeg's *Miss Smilla's Feeling for Snow* (1993) – with the caveat that he would have rewritten the unsatisfactory science fiction ending (his reservations about that book's coda are widely shared). And had the creator of Kurt Wallander lived to read Høeg's *The Susan Effect* (translated by Martin Aitken), there is little doubt that he would once again have wanted to rejig the unlikely climax. Høeg's signature character, Smilla Jaspersen, had an almost supernatural intuitive ability involving weather – hence her deductive instincts – and the author echoes that here by giving the eponymous Susan a similar gift: like Wonder Woman, she is able to compel truth from her listeners. But Susan – who also possesses an Olympian sexual appetite – is responsible for putting her equally odd family in danger when she is called on to investigate a clandestine think tank called the Future Committee and finds herself in territory where the stakes are nothing short of apocalyptic.

Interestingly, *Miss Smilla* was marketed as literary fiction (about, among other things, Denmark's postcolonial legacy) with its crime fiction trappings somewhat incidental, in the same way that the axe murders in *Crime and Punishment* are less important than the study of guilt and redemption. But Høeg is evidently no snob, and he now seems happy to move decisively into this 'less respectable' field. Judged in genre terms, this is an artfully written, exuberant thriller with a mercurial central character. It will please many – or at least those in whom the unlikely climax doesn't inspire a Mankell-like desire to do a rewrite.

Voices

2006, Iceland

ARNALDUR INDRIÐASON

Many felt that Arnaldur Indriðason would be the first foreign-language crime writer to break the stranglehold that **Henning Mankell** maintained on this particular branch of the genre. And this remarkably talented writer was certainly one of those who did just that. British and American readers may have problems pronouncing his name, but they are fully aware of the highly distinctive talents of these Reykjavik-set thrillers. After the remarkable successes of *Jar City* (2004) and *Silence of the Grave* (2005), *Voices* (translated by Bernard Scudder) is another taut and beguiling thriller. Indriðason's detective Erlendur comes across echoes of his difficult past when the doorman at his own hotel is stabbed to death. The manager attempts to keep the murder quiet (it is the festive season) but, of course, Erlendur is obliged to find out what happened. As he works his way through the very bizarre fellow guests who share the hotel with him, he encounters a nest of corruption that gives even this jaundiced detective pause. The particular pleasure of Indriðason's books is the combination of the familiar and unfamiliar – while we have seen similar detectives before, the locales and atmosphere are fresh and surprising for the non-Scandinavian reader.

Photo: Jóhann Páll Valdimarsson

The Shadow Killer 2018, Iceland
ARNALDUR INDRIÐASON

The undisputed king of the Icelandic thriller is enjoying an Indian summer with such books as *The Shadow Killer* (translated by Victoria Cribb). We first met Detective Flóvent (dour in manner, as befits all Nordic sleuths) in *The Shadow District* (2017), and the economical, pared-down style of that book is replicated here. Reykjavik 1941. The body of a travelling salesman is discovered in a basement, murdered by a bullet from a Colt .45, which points to the killer being a member of the Allied occupation forces. The city is in chaos as the British hand over to the Americans, and the relations between servicemen and local women are a headache for the authorities. Flóvent is under intense pressure to solve the case before a pending visit by Winston Churchill; the screws are tightened by the fact that the British appear to be involved in the murder. And there is another disturbing element in the case – medical experiments on Icelandic children a decade earlier. There are echoes here of the earlier baroque flourishes of such Indriðason books as *Jar City* (2004), but he is a more austere writer these days. However, those attuned to the Indriðason style will find that he has not lost an iota of his authority.

The Marseilles Trilogy 2005–07, France
JEAN-CLAUDE IZZO

Total Chaos (2005), *Chourmo* (2006) and *Solea* (2007: all translated by Howard Curtis) comprise the late Jean-Claude Izzo's Marseilles trilogy, which was described by *The Nation* as 'the most lyrical hardboiled writing yet', a contradictory statement with more than a grain of truth in it. Izzo's sequence, featuring ex-cop Fabio Montale, is a provocative and resonant classic of European crime fiction and its publication was the catalyst for the foundation of an entire literary movement, Mediterranean noir, as well as making its author an overnight celebrity. A reissue of the trilogy by Europa features an introduction by a man who is arguably the reigning king of Mediterranean noir, Massimo Carlotto. When his oldest and best friend is murdered, Fabio Montale turns his back on a police force marred by corruption and takes the fight against the local mafia into his own hands. Hard-driven protagonist aside, the real skill of the trilogy lies in the evocation of Marseilles itself, its rich character fully realised.

Rider on the Rain
1999, France

SÉBASTIEN JAPRISOT

The remarkable success achieved by Sébastien Japrisot's highly engaging French crime novels (he was called the '**Graham Greene** of France') has not really been repeated outside his home country. But the fact that two of his best books, *Rider on the Rain* and *Trap for Cinderella* (1964), have enjoyed elegant translations (by Linda Coverdale and Helen Weaver respectively) makes these books even more cherishable. Comparisons made with the earlier novels of **Georges Simenon** are not high-flown: as a storyteller, Japrisot has the same steely grasp. *Trap for Cinderella* has a remarkable premise: the protagonist is detective, murderer, victim and witness all at once. Who is the scarred, amnesiac survivor of a fire that gutted a beach house – perpetrator or target? But *Rider on the Rain* is one of the key Japrisot books. A deserted Riviera bathing resort is the scene of a brutal rape. When an enigmatic American meets the victim, Mellie, he seems to know the full story of that night – and the desperate young woman descends into a whirlpool of fear, while the reader has to figure out if the American is an ally or an enemy. The book – with nary a wasted word – is vintage Japrisot.

RIDER ON THE RAIN
1970

Director: René Clément

Hardly the finest hour for acclaimed veteran director René Clément, this steady adaptation of **Sébastien Japrisot**'s novel was poorly received at the time but now has a certain perverse interest. Marlène Jobert is charismatic as the victim of a rape who kills her attacker, with a miscast Charles Bronson as the stranger whose identity is uncertain. It has its moments.

The Darkness
2018, Iceland

RAGNAR JÓNASSON

Ragnar Jónasson is an Icelandic writer who was familiar to some Brits before a single book of his had appeared in translation. He is a noted Anglophile and translator into Icelandic of the novels of **Agatha Christie**. The wait for his own books was worthwhile, and *The Darkness* (translated by Victoria Cribb), the first in a trilogy, is a very efficient piece of work. Jónasson's protagonist is Reykjavik policewoman Hulda Hermannsdóttir, who is being forced to retire by her unsympathetic boss. Investigating a cold case – the death of a female asylum seeker – Hulda unearths secrets that her own force wants her to sit on. All par for the course in the world of the police procedural, but Jónasson has the full measure of the Nordic noir genre and pushes all the requisite buttons. *The Darkness* was published in Iceland in 2015 under the title *Dimma*, and the series also includes *The Island* (2019) and *The Mist* (2020).

The Minotaur's Head   2012, Poland

MAREK KRAJEWSKI

Sometimes an author arrives sporting an utterly individual style that marks them out from fellow writers; Marek Krajewski is clearly in that august company and discerning readers are discovering that his work marries literary weight with sheer narrative nous. Krajewski's protagonist, Abwehr Captain Eberhard Mock, quickly became an essential travelling companion for many readers of crime in translation when the books began to appear outside the author's native Poland. *The Minotaur's Head* (translated by Danusia Stok) might almost be said to function as a signature book, with all the writer's virtues shiningly in evidence. Breslau 1939. Eberhard Mock is summoned from a New Year's Eve party to a notably blood-boltered crime scene that gives even the hardened detective pause. A young girl who has been suspected of espionage, recently arrived by train from France, is discovered murdered in a hotel room, the skin ripped from her cheek by the teeth of her murderer. In Poland, a series of equally horrific crimes in the same vein have the populace in terror. Mock makes the journey across the border to assist his colleague Commissioner Popielski (with whom he shares a taste for a sybaritic lifestyle and the pleasures of the mind), and this idiosyncratic duo is soon on the trail of a particularly grotesque killer. As in earlier books by Krajewski, it is hard to know what to praise first here: the pithily realised foreign locales, the subtly inflected sense of period or the riveting storytelling. In the final analysis, though, it is probably the luxuriant characterisation of the two slightly eccentric coppers that sounds the most piquant note; their interchanges are one of the particular pleasures of the book.

Babylon Berlin
2016, Germany

VOLKER KUTSCHER

I spoke to Volker Kutscher about his remarkable Weimar Germany novel, which appeared in the UK in a translation by Niall Sellar, asking if he was wary about exploring such a sensitive period of German history. 'Yes, of course,' Kutscher replied. 'There are many traps waiting for you to walk into and many clichés which you can either avoid or use them and play with them – contrary to the reader's expectations. It's important to me that I don't let our contemporary perspective leak into the story. My characters don't know what the future holds. We all know but they didn't. And it's a burning and not easily answered question: why all these things happened in Germany. Why did the Weimar democracy turn into such a barbarous dictatorship? Germany was a civilised country before 1933, Weimar was a well-functioning democracy for at least a few years – why did it fail?'

BABYLON BERLIN
2017

Directors: Tom Tykwer, Hendrik Handloegten and Achim von Borries

Production values were conspicuously lavish in Tom Tykwer's version of **Volker Kutscher**'s ambitious novel, with a remarkable recreation of Weimar Berlin, but characterisation remained relatively unnuanced, despite the best efforts of a talented cast.

The Hidden Child
2011, Sweden

CAMILLA LÄCKBERG

Camilla Läckberg (a celebrity of major proportions in Sweden) was inspired by British crime writers such as **Ruth Rendell**, and comparisons may be drawn between modern Britain and Sweden; there is an implication, for instance, that a lack of joined-up thinking is just as endemic in Swedish policing as it is in the British system.

In *The Hidden Child* (translated by Tiina Nunnally), the novelist Erica Falck is writing a new crime novel but has made a significant discovery: her mother's diary from the war, along with a Nazi medal and a T-shirt stained with blood. She consults a local World War II historian, but then the elderly scholar is brutally murdered in a house he shares with his brother, who is tracking Nazi war criminals. Does the killing have anything to do with the burgeoning neo-Nazi movement in Sweden? And what did the dead man know about the clandestine activities of the country in the war years? There is an alternation between the present and the 1940s in the novel that Läckberg handles with steely skill, as she does the dangerous investigation into dark secrets from Sweden's past.

The Girl in the Spider's Web 2015, Sweden
DAVID LAGERCRANTZ

How much suffering and trauma can an author put one of their characters through before it begins to border on a kind of literary sadism? The multiple rapes, torture sessions and beatings that the late **Stieg Larsson**'s signature character endured in his massively successful Millennium trilogy posed challenges – never, in the event, confronted – for the author. His original plan was a ten-novel sequence, but, in order to maintain the character dynamic and give Lisbeth Salander a revenge motive for all the gruesome violence she visits upon her tormentors, would she be put through more of the repeated abuse of the first three books in each new volume? As Larsson himself is now out of the picture, the same problem has presented itself to his successor, the Swedish writer David Lagercrantz: replay the motifs of the earlier books? Or attempt something fresh? When Larsson's publishers commissioned a fourth book, they turned to Lagercrantz, who had previously delivered an accomplished crime novel built around the death of Alan Turing, *Fall of Man in Wilmslow* (2015). Lagercrantz has toned down the nigh-operatic sexual violence of the original trilogy, but not at the expense of delivering a cleverly written recreation of the world of the earlier books. His assumption of the Larsson reins has been much excoriated by the late writer's partner, Eva Gabrielsson, already at daggers drawn with Larsson's family over the legacy, but *The Girl in the Spider's Web* (translated by George Goulding) often reads uncannily like Larsson's own text – even to the extent that he includes some unwieldy detail concerning minor characters who swiftly vanish from the narrative.

Lisbeth Salander has been working with an eccentric Swedish computer scientist, Balder, whose innovative work concerns artificial intelligence. But Balder is distracted by an astonishing discovery about his mute, damaged son, whose depiction is one of the book's key achievements. Salander has also cracked the US National Security Agency database, and so she has both the security services and a shadowy, murderous group called the Spiders on her trail. Mikael Blomkvist, meanwhile, adrift and beleaguered in a new high-tech media age, is summoned by Balder for a conversation that will never take place. It is, of course, inevitable that Blomkvist and Salander – ex-lovers as well as former colleagues – will meet and will soon be up against the kind of lethal enemies they encountered in the earlier books. As well as forging a persuasive simulacrum of Larsson's style (minus the more outrageous plotting and graphic sexuality), Lagercrantz's real accomplishment here is the subtle development of Salander's character; he allows us access to her complex, alienated world but is careful not to remove her mystery and unknowability. Lisbeth Salander remains (in David Lagercrantz's hands) the most enigmatic and fascinating anti-heroine in fiction, and this is a book that will – largely speaking – please Larsson admirers.

The Black Path
2012, Sweden

ÅSA LARSSON

There is a piece of trickery at the beginning of this novel by Swedish crime queen Åsa Larsson (translated by Marlaine Delargy) that both wrong-foots the reader and imparts some local colour, reminding us that we are reading something set an ocean away from Liverpool or Ohio. A man is sitting fishing on a spring evening in Torneträsk. At this time of year, the residents make the trip to a secluded area where the ice is more than a metre thick, riding snowmobiles and towing their 'arks' behind them. These arks, we learn, are small fishing cabins in which the fishermen sit, warmed by a Calor gas stove, and where they drill a hole in the floor through which they can fish. But the fisherman in *The Black Path* is unlucky. Stepping outside in his underwear to relieve himself, he watches in horror as his ark is whipped away by a storm. He knows he will die unless he finds another ark. Stumbling across a deserted one, he breaks in; he sees a blanket on the bed and pulls it off. And underneath it lies the body of a woman, her eyes frozen into ice. It is at this point that the reader realises that this stunningly described chapter is, in fact, a clever revision of one of the oldest clichés in the crime thriller lexicon: the discovery of the corpse that sets the plot in motion. But those who have read Larsson's *The Savage Altar* (2007) will know that every element of her work, however familiar it may be, is always granted an idiosyncratic new twist. And while many Nordic crime writers are content to have their bloody deeds take place in familiar-seeming urban locales, Larsson is always looking for the more off-kilter setting. Here, we again meet her two protagonists: attorney Rebecka Martinsson, desperate to return to work after a grisly case that has shredded her sanity; and lone wolf policewoman Anna-Maria Mella, who is handed the gruesome murder case. The woman's body has extensive evidence of torture, and there is a puzzling detail: underneath her workout clothes, she is wearing seductive lingerie. What's more, the victim is a key employee in a mining company with a global reach – a murky scenario. Larsson fans will know that her investigative duo is among the most quirky and individual in the field – no easy task in a genre awash with damaged female protagonists – but the author's grasp of all her characters' psychology possesses a keen veracity.

The Millennium Trilogy 2008–09, Sweden

STIEG LARSSON

Not many crime writers can qualify as authentic heroes – but the Swedish writer Stieg Larsson fits the description. Before his untimely death at the age of 50 in 2004, he had produced three remarkable (if controversial) crime novels, and the first of his trilogy, *The Girl with the Dragon Tattoo*, sold more than a million copies in Sweden before it was translated. As a journalist, he was best known for taking on neo-Nazi organisations, and he became one of the world's foremost authorities on right-wing and extremist groups. His battles – which often put him in considerable personal danger – were not

THE MILLENNIUM TRILOGY   2009

Directors: Niels Arden Oplev and Daniel Alfredson

To some degree, the Swedish trilogy of films made from the novels of **Stieg Larsson** were an essential part of a battering ram that pushed the author's astonishing posthumous fame to such giddy heights. The Swedish film company Yellow Bird commissioned and created the original films, enjoying in the process immense commercial and critical acclaim. The company had originally been created by the crime writer **Henning Mankell** and producers Ole Søndberg and Lars Björkman specifically to film the Kurt Wallander novels of Sweden's most celebrated writer at the time – and it showed an unerring grasp of commercial realities by also getting involved in the production of the British series with the actor Kenneth Branagh. But the ambitions of Yellow Bird extended beyond this enterprise, and a film of Stieg Larsson's *The Girl with the Dragon Tattoo* in 2009 did more justice than was expected to the late writer's original concept through a combination of pared-down writing (by **Nikolaj Arcel** and **Rasmus Heisterberg**) and effectively utilitarian directing by Oplev. But perhaps the key factor in the success of the film was the canny casting, with Noomi Rapace proving to be the perfect visual equivalent of Larsson's tattooed and pierced sociopathic anti-heroine Lisbeth Salander. Utilising a Method approach, the dedicated Rapace was able to find a truthfulness and verisimilitude within what is essentially an impossible character (even more so when rendered on film): a woman who is barely able to function on any kind of social level, but shows a variety of nigh-superhuman skills in situations that put her *in extremis*. The casting of Michael Nyqvist as the compromised journo Blomkvist who becomes the unlikely partner and lover of the taciturn heroine was more controversial, but Nyqvist was able to maintain a through line between the resilience and vulnerability of the character. As in the books, the dynamic of Larsson's gender role reversals is rigorously maintained, with Rapace demonstrating the conventionally masculine traits of violence and retribution while Nyqvist is placed in the traditionally feminine role, being rescued from certain torture and death.

A creditable American version followed in 2011, with Daniel Craig as the journalist Blomkvist, Rooney Mara as Lisbeth Salander and the cult director **David Fincher** in charge of the project.

---

just political but personal, and he befriended and supported many people whom he considered to be vulnerable. But Larsson had a separate career from that of crusading journalist – that of a crime novelist, with massive and sweeping state-of-the-nation novels. However, his greatest achievement was to do something most crime writers would kill for in the three books of his Millennium trilogy (two and three were *The Girl Who Played with Fire* and

The Girl Who Kicked the Hornets' Nest – all translated by Steven T Murray under the pseudonym Reg Keeland): Larsson created an entirely new kind of protagonist for the crime novel. His freelance private investigator and computer wizard Lisbeth Salander is a million miles away from the alcoholic coppers with messy private lives who crowded most crime books at the time of her appearance. She is a resentful young girl, using her goth makeup, tattoos and piercings to conceal – and barely, at that – her sociopathic tendencies. But the appearance is deceptive – she has a laser-like intelligence and an ability to assess the depths of the human psyche. Stieg Larsson pairs her with a journalist who has fallen from grace and is redeeming himself by investigating a string of grisly killings from four decades ago. But his surly computer hacker assistant turns out to be more than his equal when the duo takes on the influential Vanger family. *The Girl with the Dragon Tattoo* is an exuberant piece of fiction that defies category, with extremes of sexual violence (Salander is repeatedly abused) that divide readers. Sadly, the author was never able to witness his trilogy's prodigious success in languages beyond the one in which he originally wrote it. (I wrote the first biography of Stieg Larsson, *The Man Who Left Too Soon* in 2010.)

Alex
2013, France

PIERRE LEMAITRE

How easy is it to reinvigorate a shop-worn formula? One way is to shoot each familiar effect full of adrenalin. The other is to inject subtly innovative elements into the detail, subverting the clichés. *Alex* (translated by Frank Wynne) by Pierre Lemaitre is a book that has it both ways: yes, we've had the brutal kidnapping of a young woman before (**Hans Koppel**'s bleak *She's Never Coming Back* (2012) and **Jussi Adler-Olsen**'s *Mercy* (2011), to name but two), but the victimised woman here is very different from her predecessors. And although the details of her kidnapping and incarceration are familiar – as is the desperate police search to find her – Lemaitre has something very surprising up his sleeve. But is this enough to explain the feverish word of mouth that this book achieved?

Alex is an intriguing young woman who is introduced to us in something of a state of flux. She appears to be constantly attempting to change her identity – and her appearance – for reasons that are obscure, but seem more playful than calculated. After a flirtation with a man in a restaurant, she is assaulted and bundled into a white van where she undergoes a savage beating. The scenes of the kidnapping that follow are handled with disturbing force by the writer – however, unlike, say, the Hans Koppel mentioned previously, the effect of these scenes is not dispiriting but relentlessly gripping. The man tasked with Alex's rescue is Commandant Camille Verhœven, and we might be forgiven for thinking 'Here we go again': tormented copper, personal tragedy, uneasy with subordinates. This detective, however, is something new: Verhœven is Napoleon-sized – congenitally stunted – and Lemaitre skilfully communicates the thought processes of a man driven by his nature to prove himself bigger than those around him in everything except height. Familiar elements aside, it is quickly apparent that Lemaitre is worthy of all the fuss. In Frank Wynne's sympathetic translation, various subtle detonations of the crime novel are handled with aplomb, such as an examination of the nature of identity (as represented by the enigmatic Alex). And Alex herself turns out to be the author's ace in the hole, for reasons that will not be revealed here. By page 200 you may believe that you're moving to a pulse-raising conclusion. But you will be wrong; in some senses, the novel has only just started…

Almost Blue

2004, Italy

CARLO LUCARELLI

Italy has become an attractive destination for literary bloody murder, particularly among writers not native to that country. Of the Italians, Carlo Lucarelli has established a considerable reputation as one of the most accomplished – and most disturbing – writers in the field. His first book was *Carta Bianca* (*Carte Blanche*), published in Italy in 1990, which featured his male protagonist Commissario De Luca. But *Almost Blue* (translated by Oonagh Stransky) has at its centre the female inspector Grazia Negro, and the book is firmly in **Thomas Harris** territory: i.e. the tracking down of a ruthless serial killer. The setting is Bologna, and a blind young man, Simone, hears the voice of a murderer on his ham radio set. As Grazia attempts to corner a very dangerous maniac, Simone becomes an essential tool in her armoury. The real coup of the novel – and the one that has brought it much attention – is the three-way split in the narrative: the accelerating momentum of the plot is carried forward by the three voices of young Simone, the policewoman Grazia and the brutal killer himself.

It is, of course, the murderer's sections that are most riveting. Despite the praise the book gleaned outside Italy, there were dissenting voices, but most would agree that Lucarelli is a name to watch.

Firewall
2002, Sweden

HENNING MANKELL

Loud was the wailing and gnashing of teeth when the late Henning Mankell announced that he was retiring his laconic detective Kurt Wallander. Crime devotees had long taken the Scandinavian copper to their hearts, and the news that Wallander's daughter was to take centre stage, working long Ystad nights cracking the mysteries that were her father's speciality, didn't exactly whet the appetite. And when the initial outing of Wallander *fille* didn't match the panache of the earlier books, Mankell fans wore expressions as bleak as the Scandinavian winters. But we still have those early Wallander outings. Mankell's excellent Wallander novels became the standard bearer for foreign crime in translation, and the author has been very lucky in his translators. But even as British and American readers became aware that some of the finest modern crime novels were being produced by this Swedish writer, thanks to such books as *Sidetracked* (1999), Mankell's work still encountered some resistance. Understandable, perhaps, for Mankell is from a country noted for Nordic gloom – like one of the most acclaimed of all filmmakers, Ingmar Bergman – and the lazy-minded are not always prepared to go beyond stereotypes. That's their loss: like his cinematic compatriot (Mankell was, in fact, married to Bergman's daughter), the writer is a man of rare skills.

In *Firewall* (translated by Ebba Segerberg), Wallander is trying to track down the perpetrators of a series of bizarre deaths in very disparate circumstances. The trail leads to the internet, with techno-criminals bent as much on destabilising society as on mere monetary gain. Once again, Wallander has to motivate his recalcitrant team, while also worrying about his uncertain health, and the results – for Mankell fans – are as compulsively readable as one could wish.

Trackers
2011, South Africa

DEON MEYER

Who are the trackers in Deon Meyer's splendid novel? Lemmer, a bodyguard who ensures that the privileged in South Africa are protected from those lower down the social scale? Or Milla, struggling to break free from an abusive marriage? Or private detective Mat Joubert, helping a young woman find her vanished husband? In fact, it is all three – but another tracker is involved: the reader. Meyer, who is not just the finest crime writer in South Africa but one of the best anywhere, hands us our own assignment: which of the three labyrinthine plot strands should we focus on? Can we sort out what is most important in the mass of local detail and socio-political commentary? Those who have read earlier Meyer books such as *Blood Safari* (2009) and *Thirteen Hours* (2010) will know that keen engagement is required for his frequently dense prose, but how fulfilling the rewards are for those seeking crime fiction with real texture and intelligence. With a divided narrative such as this, it is crucial that the central characters in each storyline command our attention equally. Milla, coping with her violent spouse, is at the centre of a major anti-terrorist operation in Cape Town. Ex-cop Joubert is watching his hopes of a smooth leave-taking of private investigation disappear as the search for a missing husband takes him into some very dark areas. And as for the bodyguard Lemmer, his dangerous assignment is to look after two white rhinos smuggled from the brutal regime in Zimbabwe, with fresh memories of his recent encounters with the legacy of the war in Mozambique.

Part of the pleasure here is to watch the steady way in which Deon Meyer orchestrates the structure of his novel with the precision of a Bach fugue. The author (who, despite his impeccable English, writes in Afrikaans – the idiomatic translation is by KL Seegers) presents an unsparing picture of the massive social divisions in post-apartheid South Africa, with the comfortable lifestyle of the rich contrasted with the poverty of the illiterate poor. But perhaps his greatest achievement is the astutely drawn trio of central characters: the conflicted bodyguard, streetwise, but falling for a major deception; the young woman fleeing from a desperately unhappy marriage and discovering something that changes the perception she has of herself; and the ex-cop finding that the incendiary reserves of violence in his personality are nearer to the surface than he thought. *Trackers* is a sprawling, invigorating and socially committed crime novel.

The Frozen Woman

2017, Norway

JON MICHELET

Readers may initially wonder why *The Frozen Woman* by Jon Michelet bagged a big Norwegian prize. But those who persist will realise that the longueurs are intentional, and Michelet's insistence on the reader's patience pays dividends. Winter holds Norway in its grip. Left-leaning lawyer Vilhelm Thygesen finds a frozen corpse in his garden – that of a young woman, victim of a bloody knife attack. The police dismiss the murder as drug-related, but then a member of a biker gang once represented by Thygesen dies in what appears to be accidental circumstances. The common denominator in the two cases – the sixtyish, bolshie lawyer – is suddenly of interest to the police, who have long nurtured a dislike of him. It doesn't hurt that the translation is by the reigning monarch of the art, Don Bartlett.

Night

2019, France

BERNARD MINIER

It's difficult to recommend just one novel by Bernard Minier, so consistently accomplished is his work, but a strong entry point might be *The Frozen Dead*, with its provocative ingredients: an isolated snowbound town, an asylum for the criminally insane and a cop with a fondness for Latin tags. However, Minier's reluctance to repeat himself means that each of his novels sports a distinct and discrete identity; the one thing that they all have in common is their consistent readability and elegant use of language. In the latter, Minier has been fortunate in the translators assigned to him – not least Alison Anderson, who renders *Night* in consummate style.

The novel begins in Norway with a body discovered in a church in the far north. Detective Kirsten Nigaard follows a trail leading to an offshore rig and is soon tracking down a ruthless serial killer, Julian Hirtmann, accompanied by tenacious Toulouse sleuth Martin Servaz. The author's choice of name for his heroine – Kirsten Nigaard – inevitably suggests the influence of Nordic noir, and there are signs that Minier has been sampling that genre. But while there are some frigid Scandinavian fingerprints on the narrative here, the author retains his peculiarly Gallic identity; this may be one of the reasons why the book has been such a success in the author's native country, where 450,000 copies were initially sold.

Arab Jazz
2015, France

KARIM MISKÉ

The themes of murders in Paris, religious fundamentalism and a threat to multiculturalism might have seemed all too topical after the grim events in the French capital in 2017. But Karim Miské's remarkable *Arab Jazz* (translated by Sam Gordon) was, in fact, written five years previously (the original French edition appeared in 2012) and had already earned prestigious French and English awards. Rightly so, as this is a debut of notable assurance, moving between the less salubrious streets of Paris and the synagogues of New York, delivering considerably more than a gripping narrative – although it certainly does the latter. As with so much current crime fiction in translation, Miské tackles serious socio-political issues – the 'added value' that has granted a sometimes frivolous genre a new intellectual clout.

Arab Jazz takes us to a world of bars, second-hand bookshops, kosher sushi and kebabs in a pungently realised 19th arrondissement, where people of different – and antithetical – faiths somehow manage to coexist in a fragile détente. But that coexistence is threatened after a particularly savage murder. Ahmed Taroudant is a sensitive individual who loves poetry and novels; his aim is to lose himself by devouring the whole world in a single, uninterrupted story written by others. But dreaming in his flat, he feels what he thinks is a tear striking him on the end of his nose. He tastes it and discovers to his horror that it is blood dripping from the flat upstairs; it is from the mutilated corpse of his neighbour Laura Vignole. What makes the killing even more disturbing is something discovered alongside her body: raw pork. This religious element makes Ahmed a suspect and things look bad for him, but there are two detectives, Jean Hamelot and Rachel Kupferstein, who are not prepared to take things at face value. As they investigate, they are plunged into a milieu in which drug trafficking and violent religious hatred undermine the very stability of Paris.

This is a vivid, multifaceted picture of an entire community, luminously characterised; the lowlife denizens of Paris have a vitality somewhere between **Émile Zola** and **Elmore Leonard**. Key concerns for Miské are the future of multiculturalism and implacable religious beliefs that allow no dissent from their strict tenets. His own background suggests why this is such a concern for him. Miské was born in Abidjan, Côte d'Ivoire, in 1964 and his mother was a French atheist while his father was a Mauritanian Muslim. The author describes himself as a spiritual atheist, but his mixed parentage has helped him understand the dynamics of integration between antipathetic cultures (he has also made films about the links between Judaism and Islam), and he extends understanding – if not always sympathy – to the varied cast of characters here. And while the book's dispassionate cosmopolitanism is both very French and eccentric – in the manner of, for instance, **Fred Vargas** – the non-judgemental treatment of many of those we encounter suggests not an Olympian detachment but a broad, universal understanding.

What makes the book so provocative is its excoriating critique of religious intolerance, a theme examined with some rigour. The dogged coppers Hamelot and Kupferstein are a memorable duo, quirkily characterised – as is the luckless Ahmed. And as the detectives peel back layers of prejudice and resentment, we are presented with uncomfortable truths about the clash between tolerant secular western society and the belief systems enforced in theocratic countries. *Arab Jazz* is proof that French crime fiction is jostling its way to the top of the noir tree.

All She Was Worth
1996, Japan

MIYUKI MIYABE

Miyuki Miyabe is, along with **Keigo Higashino**, among the most interesting modern Japanese thriller writers, and the most widely translated (here, the translator is Alfred Birnbaum). In *All She Was Worth*, Shunsuke Honma is a widowed Tokyo police inspector with a ten-year-old adopted son. While on leave after being wounded on duty, he is asked by his nephew to look into the disappearance of his fiancée. Ashamed of being so out of touch with his family, Honma agrees and soon finds himself in a nightmarish world of murder and stolen identity. Miyabe explores the world of spiralling debt, loan sharks and the price exacted from Japanese society for its obsessive consumerism. Along the way, she explores the official Japanese mechanisms of social control, as well as changing attitudes to women and money. The nature of reality is also a theme of this and several of Miyabe's other books; this, of course, is another favourite Japanese theme – the best-known example in the West being the mysterious *Rashomon*, both the 1915 story by **Ryunosuke Akutagawa** and the 1950 film by **Akira Kurosawa**. Another of her works available in English is *Shadow Family* (2005), in which she explores the nature of the family and reality in modern Japan, where the cyber world may well have more appeal than the actual one.

Knife
2019, Norway

JO NESBO

Among the most lucrative of crime writers is the Norwegian Jo Nesbo, the breakthrough Nordic noir writer post-**Stieg Larsson** – not least thanks to his memorable alcoholic sleuth Harry Hole in such books as *The Redbreast* (2006). That book was cut to the bone with nary a wasted word, but Nesbo now delivers books such as the 12th Harry Hole, *Knife* (translated by Neil Smith), which weighs in at a hefty 500-odd pages. His previous novel, the similarly arm-straining *Macbeth* (2018), enjoyed a decidedly mixed reception, but *Knife* shows Nesbo back on form (although some will wish that editorial scissors had been wielded more ruthlessly). Harry Hole has fallen off the wagon and wakes after a binge to discover that his wife Rakel has been murdered. The obvious suspect is the ageing rapist and murderer Svein Finne, the first killer Harry ever arrested. This is a police procedural that breaks the bounds of the format with abandon; overcrowded with incident, perhaps, but Nesbo manhandles the reader into contented (if exhausted) submission.

The Queen of the South
2004, Spain

ARTURO PÉREZ-REVERTE

This is a key entry in an impressive array of quite mesmerising novels by Arturo Pérez-Reverte, in which he has refined and enriched a narrative tradition stretching back to his great forebears of the past. He has demonstrated himself to be a master of finely honed storytelling techniques, impatient with the thin gruel we are so often served up today. His historical Captain Alatriste series (1996–2011) is more **Alexandre Dumas** than **Patricia Highsmith**, but a clutch of novels – including *The Flanders Panel* (1994), *The Club Dumas* (1996) and *The Seville Communion* (1998) – explore much the same territory as **Dan Brown**'s *The Da Vinci Code* (2003) and *Angels and Demons* (2000) and roundly trump them in terms of intelligence, credibility and sheer quality of writing. *The Queen of* *the South* has all the panache of its predecessors, but with a new ambition: apart from the trials of his beleaguered heroine, we are given the intriguing insights of her mysterious biographer. Güero Dávila and his lover, the initially docile Teresa Mendoza, are caught up in the drug-smuggling activities of the ruthless Mexican cartels. But when Dávila tries to play both ends against the middle, he ends up dead – and Teresa ends up on the run, fearing for her life. In Spain's sultry and dangerous city of Melilla, she encounters another man engaged in the drugs trade, the dispassionate Galician Santiago Fisterra. He draws her into his activities, and Teresa is soon involved in the hashish trade. It isn't just the impeccable scene-setting of this dangerous Latin world that makes *The Queen of the South* such an impressive read, but the perfectly judged dialogue (of which there is a great deal, ably translated by Andrew Hurley) – Pérez-Reverte is a master of idiom, and everything here rings true. Teresa's central narrative is set against the perceptions of her anonymous narrator, and the result is a fascinating – if perhaps over-ornate – mix.

The Legacy

2017, Iceland

YRSA SIGURÐARDÓTTIR

There may be several pretenders to her crown, but Yrsa Sigurðardóttir remains the queen of Icelandic thrillers – and anyone curious about why simply needs to pick up *The Legacy* (translated by Victoria Cribb), closer in feeling to the macabre work of **Stephen King** than to most Nordic noir. This is the inaugural volume in her Children's House series, but don't be misled by that moniker – this is very much grown-up fare, focusing on a home for traumatised children. A gruesome murder has a sole witness: Margaret, the victim's young daughter. Newly promoted Detective Huldar turns to Freyja, director of the Children's House, for help, but the duo's efforts to keep their young charge safe become increasingly fraught, as an implacable murderer begins to leave a series of coded messages. Some may be daunted by the prodigious length of *The Legacy*, but everything here is storytelling sinew – there is not an ounce of unnecessary fat.

Photo: Lilja Birgisdóttir

Georges Simenon
(1903–89)

Georges Simenon wrote that he had slept with over 10,000 women – and while one may be sceptical of this rather boastful claim, it's fortunate for the world of crime fiction that he found some post-coital periods to write one of the greatest bodies of work in the genre. Belgium-born Simenon was a one-man fiction machine, and his prodigious output included some dark and existential psychological crime novels as well as delicious puzzles featuring his celebrated pipe-smoking sleuth Maigret. More than most, he made a case for the literary crime novel, and such giants as **André Gide** held him in very high esteem. In his early career, Simenon produced a great variety of work, before his trademark *romans policiers* achieved their immense success. *The Strange Case of Peter the Lett* (or *Pietr the Latvian*) in 1931 was the first official Maigret title, and over 70 more books would feature his detective. Like **Ruth Rendell** in Britain, Simenon saved his finest work for the over 100 psychological, non-series titles, such as the marvellous *The Stain on the Snow* (1948). After putting down his crime writing pen in 1973, Simone began his voluminous memoirs – where that jaw-dropping claim of sexual hyperactivity appeared.

The Man Who Watched the Trains Go By

1938 (first English ed.), Belgium/France

GEORGES SIMENON

His readership was worldwide, although the author had no interest in the translations of his work, considering them virtually different books by different authors – even just this one title has had various English-language versions. Those who admire Simenon often venture the opinion that his finest work lies not in his Maigret books but in the more literary psychological thrillers in which the perpetrators or victims of crime are at the centre of the narrative. Of these, *The Man Who Watched the Trains Go By* is generally considered to be one of the best. Shot through with a bleak and evocative atmosphere, the novel's protagonist is the Dutch Kees Popinga, a man secure in his family life until the shipping firm for which he works goes under. This catastrophe effects a terrifying change in Kees: all trappings of normality fall away, and he sinks into a morass of paranoia in which acts of casual violence and even murder become possible. Simenon brings home to the reader just how close to chaos ordinary lives can be, and this lean and tense novel makes for very uncomfortable reading. If this takes your fancy, try Simenon's unique variation on **Patricia Highsmith**'s *Strangers on a Train* (1950), the extraordinary *The Blue Room* (originally published 1964), a chilling demonstration of the unknowable qualities of those we choose to make love to.

The Man Who Went up in Smoke — 1969, Sweden

MAJ SJÖWALL AND PER WAHLÖÖ

It is a cause for real celebration that the complete works of this most celebrated duo of crime writers are now available in English – though this one has been around since the 1960s in a translation by Joan Tate. Their comparative neglect has been remarkable, given that the critical standing of these Swedish writers could not be higher, with most fellow crime writing practitioners rating them as the very best exponents of the police procedural. So if you haven't yet familiarised yourself with the Martin Beck series, now is the time to start. He is, of course, the ultimate copper, gifted with the powers of ratiocination that distinguished his predecessors, but the novels are also powerful human dramas. In *The Man Who Went up in Smoke*, Beck is on an island holiday with his family but is soon called back to work on the case of an unpleasant journalist who has vanished in Budapest. Read this and you will find yourself wanting to collect the other books in the series as quickly as possible.

We Shall Inherit the Wind — 2015, Norway

GUNNAR STAALESEN

Bergen may be a beautiful city, but it has its less salubrious side – and Gunnar Staalesen's volatile detective Varg Veum knows every inch of it. Norwegian master Staalesen is an author who eschews police procedural narratives for noirish private eye pieces such as *We Shall Inherit the Wind* (translated by Don Bartlett), with Veum on the trail of a missing wind farm inspector and encountering the usual battery of hostility and non-cooperation, along with environmental terrorism and religious fanaticism. Staalesen dislikes Scandinavian parochialism in his writing, and he continues to work – bravely, some would say – in a traditional US-style genre, drawing on such writers as the late **Ross Macdonald**. Nevertheless, he is a contemporary writer, and there is some abrasive Scandicrime social commentary here; as Veum says: 'How could so many people who worked all day for the same admirable purpose – to create a better global environment – end up in their own camp, beneath their own flag, with impassable territorial lines?'

River of Shadows

2010, Italy

VALERIO VARESI

Commissario Soneri is investigating what appears to be the suicide of a man in Parma, and he finds a link with a missing bargeman – they were brothers. What's more, the Tonna brothers share an ignominious past: they were both militiamen for the *fascisti* half a century earlier. And, as the River Po recedes, Soneri finds that death in the present has fingers that reach back into Italy's benighted past. Varesi deals with the bitter clash of the partisans and the fascists in the war years, but allows echoes of the iniquities of his country's history to resonate in the present. In a sympathetic translation by Joseph Farrell, *River of Shadows* is a perfect introduction to the worldly Commissario Soneri.

Wash This Blood Clean from my Hand

2007, France

FRED VARGAS

There are those who find Vargas's highly unorthodox detective stories just too outrageously plotted, but aficionados know that this is her special ability: she invariably creates narratives that resemble absolutely nothing else in the genre – and her novels are all the better for it. This example of peculiarly European crime writing starts with an unusual premise: between 1943 and 2003, nine people have been stabbed to death with a curious weapon – a trident. While all the murderers have apparently been brought to justice, there is one bizarre detail: each lost consciousness on the night of the crime and they have absolutely no knowledge of their act. Commissaire Adamsberg has decided to look into this long-running mystery and has settled on the imposing Judge Fulgence as his prime suspect. Soon, of course, history is repeating itself... This is Vargas's weightiest and most ambitious tome, but shot through with that nervy Gallic humour that is her métier – and that is expertly rendered into English by Siân Reynolds.

The Accordionist

2017, France

FRED VARGAS

More European criminality in the distinctly off-kilter *The Accordionist* (translated again by Siân Reynolds) – but then the eccentric literary world of French writer Fred Vargas has quirkiness as a given. The eponymous musician, Clément Vauquer, is the principal suspect when two Parisian women are killed. Clément flees to sanctuary with Marthe, an ex-prostitute and the nearest thing he has known to a mother. Marthe inveigles former investigator Louis Kehlweiler into taking an unorthodox route to unmask the real murderer. Not quite as beguiling as previous entries in the Three Evangelists series, but there is pleasure in the comic interplay between the unconventional sleuths. And – as this is Fred Vargas – a pet toad has a significant role. Some may not respond well, however, to the slight modification of Vargas's characteristic style here.

Six Four

2016, Japan

HIDEO YOKOYAMA

When, oh when are authors and publishers going to take pity on us? With all the omnivorous demands on our attention these days – as we are bombarded with multimedia distractions – do we really have time for modern novels that are the length of *Middlemarch* or *Don Quixote*? There has been little sign of pity on show in recent crime lists, with such books as Hideo Yokoyama's *Six Four* hitting hapless reviewers' doormats with the impact of a small brick. But as this new elephantiasis seems to be the norm, we have at least some consolation with this novel: those who stick with the complexities of *Six Four* (translated by Jonathan Lloyd-Davies) beyond its first hundred or so pages will find themselves comprehensively gripped, and complaints about its considerable extent will melt away – readers may even surprise themselves by talking of the book's 'heavenly length', as Robert Schumann did of Schubert's Ninth.

But just who is the mysterious Hideo Yokoyama? Although not well known in the UK, the author made his mark as an investigative reporter with a Tokyo newspaper before turning to fiction, which he did with great success. Like **Stieg Larsson**, with whom he has been unhelpfully compared, he is a driven workaholic and, like the late Swedish writer, suffered a heart attack after working continuously without breaks for many hours (fortunately, Yokoyama survived). *Six Four*, which may be the author's magnum opus, is ostensibly about a kidnapping, but that is only one detail in a massive, sprawling campus.

For five days in January 1989, the anguished parents of a kidnapped child listen to the abductor's demands on cassette. The case becomes a cause célèbre and has the whole Japanese nation transfixed as the Lindbergh case did in the US. The child, however, is killed and the case is never solved. Fourteen years pass, and the case is reopened, with Press Director Mikami (whose fiefdom is police headquarters) finding himself at the centre of a maelstrom. An old mystery is suddenly re-energised, and what follows is a dense and complex drama that yokes in the police, the media and governmental corruption, laying bare the dark heart of a city. As you may have gathered, this is not a book for the casual reader. Yokoyama demands the closest attention, with a distancing narrative style – much of the plot is recalled after the event. And then there's the multiplicity of names beginning with 'M' (a glossary of characters might have been a useful addition – I kept turning back to find out which character I was reading about). In the final analysis, though, *Six Four*, for all its prolixity, is idiosyncratic and richly worked.

APPENDIX 1
Six key Scandinavian thrillers

Miss Smilla's Feeling for Snow
1992 (1993 in English)

Peter Høeg

The atmospheric literary crime novel that almost single-handedly inaugurated – without trying to – the Scandinavian invasion. *Miss Smilla's Feeling for Snow* mesmerises with its evocative use of Copenhagen locales and weather, so significant for the troubled, intuitive heroine. Most of all, it's the poetic quality of the novel that haunts the reader.

Jar City
2000 (2004 in English)

Arnaldur Indriðason

The talented Indriðason has made a mark with all his Reykjavik-set thrillers, but his debut, *Jar City* (successfully filmed), is his most celebrated. When the body of an old man is found in his apartment, Detective Inspector Erlendur discovers that the murdered man has been accused of rape in the past.

Firewall
1998 (2002 in English)

Henning Mankell

Mankell's Kurt Wallander is one of the great creations of modern crime fiction: overweight, diabetes-ridden and with all the problems of modern society leaving scars on his soul. *Firewall* is one of the writer's unvarnished portraits of modern life, in which society and all its institutions – not least the family – are put under the microscope.

The Redbreast 2000 (2006 in English)
Jo Nesbo

I was credited with (or blamed for) the phrase 'The next Stieg Larsson', proclaimed on Jo Nesbo's book jackets. It wasn't quite what I said, but he's certainly the breakthrough Nordic crime writer post-Larsson, and more quirky and individual than most of his Scandinavian colleagues – not least thanks to Nesbo's wonderfully dyspeptic detective Harry Hole (pronounced 'Hurler'). *The Redbreast*, the best entry point, bristles with a scarifying vision of Nordic fascism.

Woman with Birthmark 1996 (2009 in English)
Håkan Nesser

Where does Håkan Nesser set his novels? It's not important; his crime fiction, located in an unnamed Scandinavian or north European country, is so commandingly written it makes most contemporary crime fare seem rather thin gruel. Nesser's copper, Van Veeteren, was lauded by Colin Dexter as 'destined for a place among the great European detectives'.

The Laughing Policeman 1968 (1970 in English)
Maj Sjöwall and Per Wahlöö

Two writers – a crime writing team – might be said to have started it all. The critical stock of Sjöwall and Wahlöö could not be higher: they are celebrated as the very best exponents of the police procedural. Martin Beck is the ultimate Scandinavian copper, and if you prefer to ignore the subtle Marxist perspective of the books, it is easy to do so.

APPENDIX 2
Top political thrillers

The Manchurian Candidate 1959
Richard Condon

Condon's satirical classic is equally unsparing of US McCarthyism (with an idiot red-baiting senator) and Chinese communist brainwashing. Condon's notion that a hostile communist power could manoeuvre a pliable moron into the White House was dismissed in its day as wildly speculative...

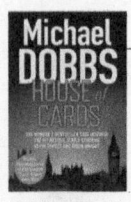

House of Cards 1989
Michael Dobbs

Francis Urquhart – more ruthlessly corrupt than any expenses-massaging real-life MP – is a great literary monster, even sans Ian Richardson or Kevin Spacey.

Advise and Consent 1959
Allen Drury

As relevant as when it was written, with its compromised president, sexual scandals and eternal message that realpolitik is all.

The Ghost 2007
Robert Harris

The dangerous world of a ghost-writer for Britain's former PM (fictional, of course); even without the thriller elements, this is scabrously entertaining.

APPENDIX 3
Five favourites

Despite the deluge of new crime fiction I tackle – willingly – for the fourth estate, here are five books that I try to re-read at intervals

The Mask of Dimitrios 1939
Eric Ambler

Ambler's most famous book gets better with the years. The crime novelist Charles Latimer hears about the evil Dimitrios in Istanbul when looking at the latter's dead body, freshly retrieved from the Bosporus. But then Latimer makes the mistake of trying to find out the truth about the murdered man...

The Big Sleep 1939
Raymond Chandler

A coruscating diamond of a novel: sardonic, fiercely plotted and boasting a matchless cast of characters. The impeccable whip-crack dialogue remains a yardstick for the genre.

The Case-Book of Sherlock Holmes 1927
Arthur Conan Doyle

The stories here show a willingness to take on subjects that must have been uncomfortable to a less tolerant readership than that of today. Dark and destructive secrets lie at the heart of Victorian propriety, and Conan Doyle's dispassionate unearthing of these undercurrents lends a peculiarly subversive charge.

The Ministry of Fear   1943
Graham Greene

London in the Blitz is brilliantly conjured in this dazzling, if dated, piece. Greene claimed a division between his 'entertainments' and his 'literary' work, but the moral issues here are as rigorously handled as anything in his more ambitious novels. Arthur Rowe is pitched into a world of shadowy, murderous figures.

Mystic River   2001
Dennis Lehane

Lehane is in the top ranks of crime novelists, and *Mystic River* is his best work. Childhood friends Sean, Jimmy and Dave have their lives changed when a strange car turns up in their street. Two and a half decades later, Sean is a homicide detective, while Jimmy has become a criminal. And the past is about to erupt into the present...

APPENDIX 4
Addenda: J Kingston Pierce

As the acknowledgements below attest, I've enlisted help from several of my colleagues to ensure that this volume – despite the fact that it isn't an encyclopaedia – might be as comprehensive as possible within the constraints of the word count. And one of my key resources was my friend J Kingston Pierce, the man behind the invaluable Rap Sheet (therapsheet.blogspot.com). His list of inclusions (after seeing an early draft of the contents) proved very useful, and I decided to list below those suggestions of his that I simply didn't have space for; they all most certainly belong in a volume such as this – if only via a brief mention.

Earl Derr Biggers (1884–1933): the creator of Charlie Chan.

Max Allan Collins (1948–): prolific author of the Nathan Heller and Quarry series, and Mickey Spillane's posthumous co-author in continuing the Mike Hammer series.

Peter Corris (1942–2018): the Australian creator of private eye Cliff Hardy.

George Harmon Coxe (1901–84): best known for his two series featuring photojournalists/sleuths Jack 'Flashgun' Casey and Kent Murdock.

Stanley Ellin (1916–86): winner of the Mystery Writers of America's Grand Master award, and author of the much-heralded short story 'The Blessington Method' (1956) and the Edgar award-winning *The Eighth Circle* (1958).

Loren D Estleman (1952–): author of the Amos Walker private eye books.

Luiz Alfredo Garcia Roza (1936–): Brazilian creator of the Inspector Espinosa mysteries, including *The Silence of the Rain* (1996).

Ed Gorman (1941–2016): multiple award-winning writer of the Jack Dwyer and Sam McCain tales.

Anna Katharine Green (1846–1935): an early female American writer of detective fiction and the author, most notably, of *The Leavenworth Case* (1878).

Stephen Greenleaf (1942–): author of the John Marshall Tanner private eye series.

Steve Hamilton (1961–): creator of the Alex McKnight detective novels.

Dorothy B Hughes (1904–93): the author of *In a Lonely Place* (1947) and *Ride the Pink Horse* (1946).

J Robert Janes (1935–): best known for his World War II-set mysteries starring Chief Inspector Jean-Louis St-Cyr of the *Sûreté* and Detektiv Inspektor Hermann Kohler of the Nazi Gestapo, which are often compared with **Philip Kerr**'s Bernie Gunther books.

Stuart M Kaminsky (1934–2009): author of the Toby Peters, Abe Lieberman and Porfiry Petrovich Rostnikov novels.

José Latour (1940–): the Cuban author of *Havana Best Friends* (2002).

Barry Maitland (1941–): author of the Brock and Kolla novels.

James McClure (1939–2006): South African journalist and author, known for writing the Kramer and Zondi novels.

Nicholas Meyer (1944–): author of *The Seven-Per-Cent Solution* (1974), a pastiche of a Sherlock Holmes story.

Magdalen Nabb (1947–2007): author of the Marshal Guarnaccia detective series.

Bill Pronzini (1943–): winner of the Private Eye Writers of America's lifetime achievement award and creator of the long-running Nameless Detective series.

Rex Stout (1886–1975): the creator of Nero Wolfe.

Paco Ignacio Taibo II (1949–): Spanish-Mexican creator of private eye Héctor Belascoarán Shayne.

Ross Thomas (1926–95): the author of such memorable novels as *Missionary Stew* (1983) and *Briarpatch* (1984).

Roderick Thorp (1936–99): author of *The Detective* (1966) and *Nothing Lasts Forever* (1979), the latter of which was adapted as the movie *Die Hard*.

Charles Todd: mother and son authors of the Inspector Ian Rutledge books.

Jonathan Valin (1947–): Shamus award-winning author of the Harry Stoner detective series.

Ben H Winters (1976–): author of *The Last Policeman* (2012) and its two sequels.

APPENDIX 5
Addenda: Craig Sisteron

My New Zealand opposite number and fellow crime fiction maven Craig Sisterson has been described as 'The Kiwi Barry Forshaw' – which I suppose makes me 'The English Craig Sisterson'. I asked him to take a glance at the inclusions in the book before he began to write his own magnum opus, *Southern Cross Crime*, and Craig told me that he'd looked over things with 'a macro view in mind', mulling on 'mile markers': key authors and characters, along with those who had influenced others or done something notable.

To that end, he mentioned the Australian **Fergus Hume** (1859–1932) and his *The Mystery of a Hansom Cab* (1886), the biggest selling detective novel of the 19th century, along with **Mary Fortune** (1833–1911), a prolific Irish-born Australian crime writer who is thought to be the first ever female detective fiction novelist. Craig also mentioned **Émile Gaboriau** (1832–73) and his Monsieur Lecoq stories, considered by some to be the father of the detective novel.

Of more recent writers, he spoke up for **Emma Viskic**, suggesting that she might be included for her deaf private eye Caleb Zelic (the books have already bagged several awards) and **Paul Thomas**'s detective Tito Ihaka, as a rare example of an indigenous detective in a former British colony (New Zealand). In a similar vein, he also mentioned **Shamini Flint**'s Inspector Singh, a portly Sikh detective based in Singapore, and **John Burdett**'s Sonchai Jitpleecheep books, an 'outstanding, highly original series threaded with social issues' set in Bangkok. **Leonardo Padura**'s Cuban Lieutenant Mario Conde sequence also gets the Sisterson nod, as does **Craig Johnson**'s Sheriff Walt Longmire series set in modern-day Wyoming. Also worth a look is **Paul Cleave**'s memorable killer Joe the Carver, who appeared in *The Cleaner* (2006), selling 250,000 copies in its first two months alone in Germany. *The Good Son* by **You-jeong Jeong** (2018), South Korea's award-winning million-selling queen of crime is now available in English, translated by Chi-Young Kim, while other names worthy of mention – according to Craig – are the Argentinians **Claudia Piñeiro** and **Ernesto Mallo**, along with the Brazilian Dominican friar turned political activist **Frei Betto** and Japan's **Natsuo Kirino**.

ACKNOWLEDGEMENTS

The kernel of this book was the earlier (and much shorter) *Rough Guide to Crime Fiction*. On that slimmer version I worked with three invaluable editors (Joe Staines, Andrew Lockett and the indefatigable Andrew Heritage), and my thanks to them and to Craig Sisterson, J Kingston Pierce, Christopher Fowler, Ayo Onatade, Simon Brett, LC Tyler, Mike Ripley, Caroline Stone and Paul Lunde for their input. Ditto my newspaper colleagues Laura Wilson, Marcel Berlins and Jake Kerridge. Not forgetting my publisher Ion Mills – and, for her copyediting, Judith Forshaw.

ABOUT THE AUTHOR

Barry Forshaw is one of the UK's leading experts on crime fiction and film. His books include *Nordic Noir, Italian Cinema, American Noir* and *British Crime Film*. Other work: *Sex and Film, British Gothic Cinema, Euro Noir, Historical Noir, BFI War of the Worlds* and the Keating award-winners *British Crime Writing: An Encyclopedia* and *Brit Noir*. He writes for various newspapers, contributes Blu-ray extras, broadcasts, chairs events and edits *Crime Time* (crimetime.co.uk).

INDEX OF AUTHORS AND DIRECTORS

A

Abbott, Megan, 174, 175
Abella, Alex, 218
Abrahams, Doris Caroline, 325
Ace, Cathy, 137
Ackroyd, Peter, 317
Adair, Gilbert, 302, 303
Adenle, Leye, 155
Adler-Olsen, Jussi, 371, 396
Akunin, Boris, 372
Akutagawa, Ryunosuke, 402
Aldrich, Robert, 50, 55
Alfredson, Daniel, 395
Algren, Nelson, 57, 79, 220
Allain, Marcel, 16
Allingham, Margery, 26, 27, 39
Altman, Robert, 81
Ambler, Eric, 15, 16, 39, 170, 218, 252, 266, 267, 361, 369, 413
Amis, Kingsley, 269
Annaud, Jean-Jaques, 382
Antonioni, Michelangelo, 182, 242
Anwar, Amer, 218
Apollinaire, Guillaume, 16
Apted, Michael, 31, 129
Arcel, Nikolaj, 395
Arden Oplev, Niels, 395

Arjouni, Jakob, 371
Arlidge, MJ, 84
Armitage, George, 134
Arnott, Jake, 235, 236
Arriaga, Guillermo, 372
Asbury, Herbert, 234
Atkinson, Kate, 60

B

Bagley, Desmond, 268, 269
Balchin, Nigel, 337
Baldacci, David, 203
Baldwin, James, 244, 251, 359
Balzac, Honoré de, 12
Banks, Carla, 175
Banks, Iain, 176
Barclay, Linwood, 65, 176, 177
Barnard, Robert, 26
Barton, Fiona, 177
Bateman, Colin, 323
Bauer, Belinda, 203, 204
Beaton, MC, 155, 303
Beckett, Simon, 137
Behm, Marc, 177, 178
Beineix, Jean-Jacques, 51
Bentley, EC, 18
Bergman, Ingmar, 309, 398

Betto, Frei, 417
Beukes, Lauren, 202
Beverly, Bill, 217, 218, 219
Biggers, Earl Derr, 415
Billingham, Mark, 84, 85, 202, 204
Bird, Antonia, 261
Blaedel, Sara, 371
Blair, David, 37
Blake, James Carlos, 219
Blake, Nicholas, 27, 28
Blake, Robin, 337
Blincoe, Nicholas, 245
Block, Lawrence, 324
Boileau, Pierre, 373
Bolton, Guy, 338
Bolton, Sharon, 178
Bonini, Carlo, 374
Booker, Simon, 156
Boorman, John, 242
Bottini, Oliver, 374
Boulting, , John, 27, 223
Brabazon, James, 313
Brackett, Leigh, 49, 53
Bradbeer, Harry, 310
Bradbury, Malcolm, 41, 116
Bradby, Tom, 313
Bradley, Alan, 155
Brahm, John, 35
Brahms, Caryl, 325
Braine, John, 239
Branagh, Kenneth, 32, 395
Branch, Pamela, 325
Brand, Christianna, 28, 29
Brett, Simon, 155, 325, 326, 334, 418
Broadribb, Steph, 60, 138
Brodrick, William, 138, 139
Brookes, Adam, 269, 270
Brookmyre, Christopher, 156, 157
Brown, Dan, 308, 312, 314, 317, 357, 403
Bruce, Leo, 326
Bruen, Ken, 60
Buchan, John, 15, 18, 19, 22, 26, 36, 171, 266, 267
Bukowski, Charles, 219
Bunker, Eddie, 219, 220

Burdett, John, 417
Burke, James Lee, 17, 59, 61, 62, 63, 65, 130, 244, 254
Burke, Declan, 326
Burnett, WR, 44, 45, 236
Burroughs, Edgar Rice, 29, 57, 219
Bussi, Michel, 375
Butler, Robert Olen, 338

C

Cain, James M, 14, 16, 44, 45, 46, 47, 49, 139, 227, 228
Cain, Chelsea, 85
Cameron, Elaine, 23, 363
Camilleri, Andrea, 375, 376
Camus, Albert, 52, 215
Canet, Guillaume, 180
Carofiglio, Gianrico, 377
Carr, Caleb, 30, 40, 336
Carter, Chris, 204, 205
Carter, MJ, 336, 339
Carver, Will, 205
Caton-Jones, Michael, 222
Caudwell, Sarah, 327
Cavanagh, Steve, 140
Ceder, Camilla, 377, 378
Celestin, Ray, 339
Chabrol, Claude, 28
Chandler, Raymond, 16, 17, 18, 30, 43, 44, 47, 48, 49, 53, 54, 55, 59, 65, 70, 74, 75, 76, 78, 80, 81, 92, 103, 139, 189, 221, 231, 244, 273, 302, 303, 333, 413
Charteris, Leslie, 24, 26
Chase, James Hadley, 24, 50, 86
Chechik, Jeremiah, 373
Chesterton, GK, 19, 157, 309, 310
Child, Lee, 85, 86, 138, 254, 326
Childers, Erskine, 15, 21, 22
Chkhartishvili, Grigori, 372
Christie, Agatha, 15, 25, 26, 27, 29, 30, 32, 33, 34, 40, 140, 197, 261, 301, 302, 303, 304, 305, 306, 308, 335, 389
Clancy, Tom, 270, 271, 317
Clark-Platts, Alice, 179

Cleary, Jon, 86, 87
Cleave, Paul, 417
Cleeves, Ann, 87, 88, 132, 303, 304
Clément, René, 213, 389, 408
Clements, Rory, 339
Cleverly, Barbara, 340
Clifford, Francis, 158
Clouzot, Henri-George, 373
Coben, Harlan, 17, 63, 64, 65, 146, 179, 180
Coe, Amanda, 295
Coetzee, JM, 130
Cole, Martina, 88, 161, 164, 220
Collins, Max Allan, 13, 14, 29, 339, 358, 415
Conan Doyle, Arthur, 13, 14, 20, 21, 22, 23, 25, 29, 90, 121, 305, 339, 344, 368, 413
Condon, Richard, 412
Connelly, Micahel, 64, 65
Connolly, John, 206
Conrad, Joseph, 15, 16, 19, 189, 263, 266, 275, 280, 319, 332, 367, 369
Cook, Robert, 194, 231, 247
Coppola, Francis Ford, 241
Cornwell, Patricia, 68, 115, 136, 140, 141, 151, 193, 202
Cornwell, David John Moore, 280
Costantini, Roberto, 378, 379
Cotterill, Colin, 327
Cox, Anthony Berkley, 36
Cox, Michael, 23
Coxe, George Harmon, 415
Crais, Robert, 65, 66, 81
Creasey, John, 26, 198, 229, 256
Crichton, Michael, 245, 314, 315
Crispin, Edmund, 327, 328, 335
Croft-Cooke, Rupert, 326
Crofts, Freeman Wills, 26
Cross, Neil, 181
Crouch, Julia, 293, 294
Crumley, James, 221, 236, 237
Cruz Smith, Martin, 128, 261, 319
Cumming, Charles, 265, 272, 290
Curtiz, Michael, 19

D

d'Arrast, Harry, 24
Dahl, Julia, 60
Daly, Carroll John, 59
Dassin, Jules, 225
Davies, David Stuart, 340
Davis, Lindsey, 336, 341, 342, 369
Davis, Ossie, 250
Day-Lewis, Cecil, 28
De Cataldo, Giancarlo, 374, 379, 380
De Gregorio, Daniela, 346
de Maupassant, Guy, 58, 195
de Muriel, Oscar, 89
De Palma, Brian, 93, 380
Dean, Will, 158
Deaver, Jeffrey, 89, 304, 342, 349
Deighton, Len, 252, 265, 272, 273, 290
DeLillo, 238, 281
Demme, Jonathan, 210
Denham, Reginald, 33
Dexter, Colin, 89, 90, 121, 411
Dhand, AA, 90, 91
Dibdin, Michael, 91, 237
Dick, Philip K, 347
Dickens, Charles, 7, 29, 123, 136, 281, 349, 358
Dickson Carr, John, 26, 30, 43
Dmytryk, Edward, 80
Dobbs, Michael, 412
Dolan, Eva, 245, 294
Donaldson, Roger, 243
Donen, Stanley, 178
Donner, Clive, 36
Dostoyevsky, Fyodor, 7, 14, 16, 40, 44, 79, 128, 174, 262, 357, 372
Doughty, Louise, 116, 295
Downie, RS/Ruth, 342, 343
Drury, Allen, 412
du Maurier, Daphne, 193, 293, 299
Dudley Edwards, Ruth, 328
Duffy, Stella, 66, 67, 255
Dumas, Alexandre, 403
Durbridge, Francis, 33
Dürrenmatt, Friedrich, 380, 381

E

Easton Ellis, Bret, 206
Eastwood, Clint, 53, 72, 111
Eco, Umberto, 317, 346, 359, 381, 382
Edwards, Martin, 343
Edwards, Rachel, 248
Ellin, Stanley, 415
Elliott, Stephan, 178
Ellory, RJ, 207, 208
Ellroy, James, 17, 92, 93, 130, 168, 208, 209, 238, 244, 258
Elsberg, Marc, 382
Eltringham, Billie, 236
Estleman, Loren D, 415
Evanovich, Janet, 60, 328, 329
Ewan, Chris, 93, 94

F

Farrell, JG, 340
Farris Smith, Michael, 230
Faulkner, William, 49, 53, 183, 345
Faulks, Sebastian, 269, 304
Faye, Lyndsay, 344
Fearing, Kenneth, 53
Feldstein, Al, 45
Fellowes, Jessica, 304
Fellowes, Julian, 304
Fennelly, Beth Ann, 345
Ferris, Gordon, 344, 345
Fesperman, Dan, 265, 274, 275
Feuillade, Louis, 16
Fforde, Jasper, 329
Fincher, David, 395
Finder, Joseph, 316, 365
Finn, AJ, 159, 297
Fitzek, Sebastian, 371
Fitzmaurice, George, 24
Fleischer, Richard, 223
Fleming, Ian, 18, 37, 48, 117, 266, 268, 269, 271, 273, 304, 305, 366, 372
Flint, Shamini, 417
Flynn, Gillian, 94, 182, 296
Foley, James, 57
Foley, Lucy, 183

Forbes, Elena, 94
Forbes, Bryan, 223
Ford, Richard, 69, 238
Forman, Miloš, 382
Forster, EM, 291
Forsyth, Frederick, 171, 221, 222, 240, 269
Fortune, Mary, 417
Fossum, Karin, 371, 383
Foster, Norman, 266
Fowler, Christopher, 1, 329, 330, 418
Fowles, John, 184, 357
Francis, Clare, 142
Francis, Dick, 159, 303
Francis, Felix, 160
Franklin, Tom, 345
Frears, Stephen, 57, 81
Freeling, Nicolas, 260
French, Nicci, 183, 184, 191
French, Sean, 183
French, Tana, 185
Friedman, Kinky, 67
Furie, Sidney J, 273
Furst, Alan, 275, 276
Fyfield, Frances, 170, 185, 186

G

Gaboriau, Émile, 417
Gadney, Reg, 95
Gaines, William M, 45, 230, 231
Galbraith, Robert, 68
Gardiner, MG, 186
Gardner, Erle Stanley, 34, 44
Gardner, John, 269
Gardner, Lisa, 95, 96, 143
Garnett, Tay, 46
Garnier, Pascal, 371
Gash, Jonathan, 160
Gatiss, Mark, 23, 341
Genet, Jean, 219
George, Elizabeth, 30, 96
Gerrard, Nicci, 183
Gerritsen, Tess, 85, 143, 144, 163, 202
Gide, André, 405
Gilliat, Sidney, 29

Giuttari, Michele, 383, 384
Glazer, Jonathan, 230
Glynn, Alan, 160, 161
Godard, Jean-Luc, 51, 52
Goddard, Robert, 161, 162
Goodis, David, 51, 52, 53
Goodwin, Jason, 345
Gorman, Ed, 415
Grafton, Sue, 59, 60, 68, 69
Graham, , Caroline, 97
Granik, Debra, 247
Grant, John, 160
Green, Anna Katherine, 416
Greene, Graham, 16, 27, 61, 107, 128, 157, 170, 188, 222, 223, 224, 252, 259, 267, 275, 276, 277, 280, 292, 335, 369, 389, 414
Greengrass, Paul, 282
Greenleaf, Stephen, 416
Greenwald, Maggie, 57
Gregorio, Michael, 346
Grey, Isabelle, 97
Griffin, Kate, 336, 346
Griffiths, Elly, 347
Griffiths, Rebecca, 295, 296
Grimwood, Jack, 248, 277, 278
Grimwood, Jon Courtenay, 248
Grisham, John, 105, 136, 140, 144, 145, 153, 254
Grosbard, Ulu, 220
Guttridge, Peter, 224, 323, 330

H

Hall, Araminta, 296
Hall, James, 134
Hall, MR, 145, 146
Hamdy, Adam, 316
Hamilton, Patrick, 3435, 308
Hamilton, Steve, 416
Hammer, Chris, 162
Hammett, Dashiell, 16, 17, 29, 43, 44, 46, 47, 52, 53, 59, 69, 70, 71, 74, 80, 103, 231, 244
Handloegten, Hendrik, 391
Hannah, Mari, 97,98

Hannah, Sophie, 304, 305
Hansen, Joseph, 72
Hanson, Curtis, 93
Hare, Cyril, 26
Harper, Jane, 186, 187
Harper, Tom, 317
Harris, Thomas, 17, 99, 115, 202, 203, 208, 209, 210, 212, 384, 397
Harris, Robert, 275, 319, 336, 347, 348, 412
Harron, Mary, 207
Harstad, Donald, 98, 99
Harvey, John, 249, 250
Hawkins, Paula, 159, 296, 297, 349
Hawks, Howard, 47, 49, 53
Hayder, Mo, 99, 126, 143, 162, 163
Hayes, Terry, 317
Hegarty, Frances, 185
Heisler, Stuart, 80
Heisterberg, Rasmus, 395
Heller, Joseph, 278
Hellman, Monte, 134
Hemingway, Ernest, 70, 263
Herron, Mick, 122, 265, 278, 279, 333
Hewson, David, 100
Hiaasen, Carl, 17, 134, 330, 331, 332
Higashino, Keigo, 385, 402
Higgins, George V, 146, 147
Higgins, Jack, 279
Highsmith, Patricia, 49, 150, 177, 186, 187, 188, 189, 212, 213, 214, 217, 324, 372, 403, 406
Hilary, Sarah, 100
Hill, Mark, 101
Hill, Reginald, 101, 102, 103
Hill, Susan, 33
Hillerman, Tony, 247
Himes, Chester, 197, 250, 251
Hines, Joanna, 163
Hitchcock, Alfred, 18, 19, 28, 34, 37, 49, 115, 158, 159, 171, 187, 189, 193, 201, 210, 217, 276, 296, 297, 299, 302, 372, 373
Hoag, Tami, 163, 164
Hobbs, Jessica, 295

Hochgatterer, Paulus, 386
Hodges, Mike, 239, 240
Hodgson, Antonia, 348, 349
Høeg, Peter, 386, 387, 410
Homer, 281
Homes, Geoffrey, 54
Hopper, Dennis, 213, 216
Hornung, EW, 24
Horowitz, Anthony, 269, 305
Horst, Jorn Lier, 371
Household, Geoffrey, 18, 35, 36, 222, 289
Housman, AE, 90
Hughes, Dorothy B, 416
Hugo, Victor, 12
Hume, Fergus, 417
Hunter, Cara, 298
Hunter, Evan, 115, 192, 193
Huntington, Lawrence, 42
Hurwitz, Gregg, 146
Huston, John, 38, 46, 49, 57, 71

I

Ibsen, Henrik, 84
Ide, Joe, 14
Iles, Francis, 36
Iles, Greg, 318
Indriðason, Arnaldur, 371, 387, 388, 410
Innes, Michael, 332
Irving, John, 331
Izzo, Jean-Claude, 388

J

Jakeman, Jane, 349
Jakobi, Francesca, 298
Jakubowski, Maxim, 189
James, Donald, 350
James, Henry, 188, 357
James, MR, 172
James, Peter, 105
Janes, J Robert, 416
Japrisot, Sébastien, 389
Jardine, Quintin, 105
Jecks, Michael, 350
Joffe, Rowan, 223

John, DB, 318
Johnson, Craig, 417
Jónasson, Ragnar, 389, 390
Jones, Morgan, 251
Joss, Morag, 190
Joyce, James, 160
Jungstedt, Mari, 371

K

Kaige, Chen, 184
Kaminsky, Stuart M, 416
Kant, Immanuel, 346
Kasdan, Lawrence, 139
Keating, , HRF, 106
Kellerman, Jonathan, 155, 190, 191
Kelly, , Erin, 191
Kemelman, Harry, 246
Kennedy, , Burt, 215
Kent, Christobel, 298
Kernick, Simon, 107, 227
Kerr, ,Philip, 336, 351, 416
Kersh, Gerald, 224, 225
Kesselring, Joseph, 33
Khan, Ausma Zehanat, 251
Khan, Vaseem, 306
King, Stephen, 107, 108, 109, 177, 178, 211, 290, 404
Kipling, Rudyard, 15
Kirino, Natsuo, 417
Kirst, Hans Helmut, 346
Knox, Joseph, 109, 113
Koppel, Hans, 396, 397
Krajewski, Marek, 390
Kubrick, Stanley, 57, 215, 243
Kurosawa, Akira, 53, 165, 235, 402
Kutscher, Volker, 391

L

La Plante, Lynda, 100, 164
Läckberg, Camilla, 391, 392
Lagercrantz, David, 392, 393
Lake, Deryn, 352
Lampitt, Dinah, 352
Lang, Fritz, 36, 52, 159, 277, 297

Lansdale, Joe R, 109, 110
Larsson, Åsa, 392, 393, 394
Larsson, Stieg, 155, 312, 378, 392, 394, 395, 396, 403, 409, 411
Latimer, Jonathan, 53, 267, 413
Lawrence, Diarrmuid, 104
le Carré, John, 16, 146, 252, 265, 267, 272, 273, 275, 278, 279, 280, 281, 283, 290, 292
Le Queux, William, 267
Leather, Stephen, 110
Lee, Hyeonseo, 319
Legh Clowes, St John, 50
Lehane, Dennis, 72, 110, 111, 352, 353, 414
Lemaitre, Pierre, 17, 245, 396, 397
Leon, Donna, 112, 118
Leonard, Elmore, 17, 109, 134, 147, 165, 217, 219, 225, 226, 238, 239, 330, 401
Leone, Sergio, 53, 313
LeRoy, Mervin, 45, 236
Lester, Richard, 178
Lewis, Ted, 227, 239, 240
Lewton, Val, 53
Liman, Doug, 282
Lincoln, John, 73
Lindsay, Douglas, 332
Lindsay, Jeff, 211
Lindsay, Joan, 187
Lindsey, David, 212
Linskey, Howard, 225, 227
Lippman, Laura, 227
Lipska, Anya, 245, 253
Littell, Robert, 73, 281, 282
Locke, Atica, 17, 94, 253, 254, 288
Lodge, David, 41
Lodge, Gytha, 192
Lombino, Salvatore, 115, 193
Losey, Joseph, 54
Lovesey, Peter, 353
Lucarelli, Carlo, 397, 398
Ludlum, Robert, 110, 282, 283, 290, 317
Lumet, Sidney, 32

M

MacBride, Stuart, 112, 113, 192
Macdonald, Ross, 17, 44, 59, 69, 74, 75, 76, 77, 114, 180, 194, 407
MacDonald, John D, 44, 75, 166
MacDonald, Philip, 37, 38
Mackay, Malcolm, 228
Mackenzie, AJ, 355
Madden, John, 90
Mahmood, Imran, 254
Mailer, Norman, 238, 281
Mainwaring, Daniel, 54
Maitland, Barry, 416
Mallo, Ernesto, 417
Mankell, Henning, 245, 371, 386, 387, 395, 398, 410
Margolin, Phillip, 147, 148
Mark, David, 113, 114
Marklund, Liza, 60, 371
Marsh, Ngaio, 26, 39, 40
Marshall, Michael, 192, 245
Marshall, George, 49
Marston, Edward, 353
Martin, Andrew, 354
Marwood, Alex, 177
Masters, Priscilla, 149
Matthews, Jason, 283
Maugham, Somerset, 266
May, Peter, 114
Maylam, Tony, 22
McAuley, Paul, 254, 255
McBain, Ed, 83, 115, 116, 136, 146, 192, 193
McCall Smith, Alexander, 113, 306, 307, 308, 309, 310
McCallin, Luke, 355, 356
McCarry, Charles, 283, 284, 290
McCarthy, Cormac, 62, 71, 202, 219, 236, 237
McClure, James, 416
McCrery, Nigel, 116
McDermid, Val, 1, 17, 98, 113, 116, 117, 136, 148, 149, 150, 199, 308
McGilloway, Brian, 117

McGowan, Claire, 117, 118
McGrath, , Mel/MJ, 193, 247
McIlvanney, William, 118, 345
McKinty, Adrian, 255
McNab, Andy, 284
McPherson, Catriona, 308
McQueen, Steve, 164
Medina, KT, 319, 320
Mencken, HL, 44
Merritt, Stephanie, 358
Meyer, Deon, 399
Meyer, Nicholas, 416
Michelet, Jon, 400
Miles, Keith, 353
Millar, Kenneth, 74
Millar, Margaret, 193, 194
Miller, Arthur, 312
Miller, Claude, 178
Mills, Mark, 356
Mina, Denise, 256, 257
Minghella, Anthony, 213
Minier, Bernard, 400
Minnelli, Vincente, 55
Miské, Karim, 401, 402
Mitchell, David, 316
Mitchell, Dreda Say, 229
Mitchell, Gladys, 26
Miyabe, Miyuki, 402
Moffat, Steven, 23
Montalbán, Manuel Vázquez, 371
Montgomery, Robert, 80
Mooney, Chris, 213, 214
Morris, RN, 357
Mosawi, Anthony, 194
Mosley, Walter, 244, 257
Mukherjee, Abir, 17, 336, 340, 357
Murphy, Margaret, 258
Murphy, Peter, 150

N

Nabb, Magdalen, 416
Nadel, Barbara, 118, 119
Nadelson, Reggie, 76, 77
Narcejac, Thomas, 373
Neale, Tom, 363

Nesbo, Jo, 403, 411
Nesser, Håkan, 290, 411
Neville, Stuart, 258
Newham, Vicky, 119
Noyce, Phillip, 216

O

O'Brien, Martin, 119, 120
O'Donnell, Peter, 284, 285
Odets, Clifford, 53
Orwell, George, 24, 50
Oswald, James, 120

P

Padura, Leonardo, 417
Pakula, Alan J, 154
Palliser, Charles, 358
Paretsky, Sara, 59, 60, 77, 249
Parker, Robert B, 54, 59, 78, 206, 241, 242
Parris, SJ, 358, 359
Parsons, Tony, 120, 121
Patterson, James, 105, 107, 121, 314
Pavlou, Stel, 320
PD James, 17, 31, 102, 104, 148, 167, 199, 214, 244, 364
Peace, David, 255, 259
Peake, Mervyn, 358
Pears, Iain, 167, 168
Peckinpah, Sam, 236, 243
Pelecanos, George, 78, 244, 259, 260, 359
Pembrey, Daniel, 260
Penn, Sean, 381
Penny, Louise, 122
Percy, Edward, 33
Pérez-Reverte, Arturo, 338, 403, 404
Persson, Leif GW, 371
Peters, Elizabeth, 155
Peters, Ellis, 336, 348, 359, 360, 362
Phelps, Sarah, 31
Phillips, Mike, 175
Pinborough, Sarah, 299, 360
Piñeiro, Claudia, 417

Poe, Edgar Allan, 12, 13, 14, 29, 195, 367, 368
Polanski, Roman, 81
Porter, Henry, 265, 285
Porter, Joyce, 332
Poulson, Christine, 150, 152
Powell, , Michael, 201, 337
Priestley, JB, 33
Pronzini, Bill, 416
Proust, Marcel, 196, 302
Pryce, Malcolm, 333
Puzo, Mario, 240, 241
Pym, Barbara, 308

Q

Queen, Ellery, 43, 67
Quinn, Anthony J, 122

R

Rafelson, Bob, 46
RankinIan, 5, 7, 8, 17, 104, 113, 122, 123, 124, 156, 307, 309
Raphael, Frederic, 36
Rathbone, Julian, 23, 361
Raymond, Derek, 194, 229, 230, 231
Raymond, René Brabazon, 50
Reah, Danuta, 175
Redhill, Michael, 195
Reed, Carol, 277
Reeve, Alex, 361
Reichs, Kathy, 136, 151, 152
Reiner, Carl, 81
Reisz, Karel, 263
Rendell, Ruth, 17, 31, 124, 125, 148, 167, 168, 198, 199, 214, 217, 245, 383, 391, 405
Rennison, Nick, 362
Reynolds, Rod, 168
Rhodes, Kate, 125
Richards, Dick, 57, 80
Richardson, Tony, 160
Riches, Marnie, 125
Rickman, Phil, 169
Ridpath, Michael, 169
Ripley, Mike, 39, 79, 323, 333, 334, 418

Ritchie, Guy, 230, 240
Ritt, Martin, 226, 281
Rivette, Jacques, 165
Robb, Candace, 362
Robinson, Peter, 125, 126
Robotham, Michael, 195, 196
Rohmer, Sax, 29, 339
Rosenheim, Andrew, 286
Ross, Herbert, 81
Rowling, JK, 68
Runcie, James, 309, 310
Russell, Craig, 126
Russell, Leigh, 127
Ryan, Chris, 286, 287
Ryan, Robert, 363
Ryan, William, 363

S

Sallis, James, 196, 197
Sampson, Kevin, 230
Sanderson, Mark, 170
Sansom, CJ, 364, 365
Sapper, 15, 29, 266, 267
Sartre, Jean-Paul, 52, 215
Sayers, Dorothy L, 26, 29, 40, 41, 155
Saylor, Steven, 336, 341, 342, 365, 369
Scorsese, Martin, 166, 234
Scott, Manda, 287
Scott, Paul, 340
Seymour, Gerald, 287, 288, 289
Shakespeare, William, 12, 332, 340
Shamsie, Kamila, 251
Sharpe, Tom, 333
Shaw, George Bernard, 19
Shaw, Joseph T, 44
Shaw, William, 127
Shepherd-Robinson, Laura, 365, 366
Sherez, Stav, 1, 128, 245
Siegel, Don, 54
Siegel, James, 171, 172
Sigurðardóttir, Lilja, 371
Sigurðardóttir, Yrsa, 404
Simenon, Georges, 389, 405, 406
Simms, Chris, 320, 321
Simon, SJ, 325

Siodmak, Robert, 52
Sirk, Douglas, 52
Sjöwall, Maj, 406, 411
Slaughter, Karin, 85, 152, 153, 172, 197, 326
Smight, Jack, 76
Smith, Joan, 260
Smith, Tom Rob, 366, 367
Solana, Teresa, 371
Sollima, Stefano, 374, 380
Sonnenfeld, Barry, 239
Sophocles, 11, 12
Souvestre, Pierre, 16
Spark, Muriel, 368
Spiegelman, Peter, 79, 80
Spielberg, Steven, 315
Spillane, Mickey, 17, 54, 55, 415
Staalesen, Gunnar, 74, 406, 407
Stabenow, Dana, 247
Stark, Richard, 225, 241, 242
Starr, Jason, 232
Steinhauer, Olen, 289, 290
Stevenson, Robert Louis, 123
Stewart, John Innes Mackintosh, 332
Stoker, Bram, 12
Stone, Nick, 80, 81, 82
Stone, Robert, 233, 244, 262, 263
Stout, Rex, 416
Strachey, Lytton, 288
Stroud, Richard, 360
Süskind, Patrick, 336
Swanson, Peter, 299, 300

T

Taibo II, Paco Ignacio, 416
Tarantino, Quentin, 58, 165, 219, 226
Tavernier, Bertrand, 57
Taylor, Andrew, 367, 368
Taylor, CL, 197
Taylor, Tate, 297
Tey, Josephine, 41, 42, 172, 173, 290
Theorin, Johan, 371
Thomas, Paul, 417
Thomas, Ralph, 87
Thomas, Ross, 416

Thompson, 44, 56, 57, 215, 216, 242, 243
Thompson, J Lee, 166
Thorogood, Robert, 311
Thorp, Roderick, 416
Timlin, Mark, 59, 232
Todd, Charles, 416
Tourneur, Jacques, 54
Toyne, Simon, 321, 322
Trevor, William, 199
Trollope, Anthony, 310
Truffaut, François, 51, 52, 58
Truss, Lynne, 334, 335
Turow, Scott, 140, 153, 154
Tykwer, Tom, 391
Tyler, Anne, 227
Tyler, LC, 334, 335, 418

U

Unsworth, Cathi, 82
Updike, John, 123, 238
Upfield, Arthur, 246
Upson, Nicola, 42, 172, 173

V

Valin, Jonathan, 416
Van Dine, SS, 29
Vance, Louis Joseph, 24
Varesi, Valerio, 407
Vargas, Fred, 371, 402, 407, 408
Vaughan, Sarah, 300
Vertue, Sue, 23
Veste, Luca, 130, 131
Vine, Barbara, 124, 167, 192, 198
Visconti, Luchino, 46
Viskic, Emma, 417
von Borries, Achim, 391

W

Wahlöö, Per, 406, 411
Waites, Martyn, 131
Walker, Martin, 131
Wallace, Edgar, 29, 316
Walters, Minette, 26, 197, 198, 199, 245, 263, 264, 383
Wambaugh, Joseph, 132

Ward, Sarah, 132
Ward Baker, Roy, 27
Ware, Ruth, 199
Warshow, Robert, 236
Watkins, , Roz, 133
Watson, SJ, 293
Waugh, Evelyn, 335
Webster, Jason, 133
Welles, Orson, 266
Wellman, William, 53
Wells, HG, 19, 20
Welsh, Irvine, 113, 368
Welsh, Louise, 368
Wenders, Wim, 213
Wentworth, Patricia, 26, 291
Westlake, Donald E, 57, 225, 241, 242
Wilder, Billy, 49, 52, 139
Willeford, Charles, 133, 134, 216
Williams, 170
Williams, Alan, 170, 171
Williams, Andrew, 369
Williams, Charles, 216
Williams, Emlyn, 170
Williams, John, 73, 173, 264
Williams, Tennessee, 76
Wilson, Edward, 290
Wilson, Elizabeth, 291
Wilson, Laura, 200, 300, 418
Wilson, Robert, 17, 134, 135, 265, 292, 369
Winkler, Irwin, 225
Winner, Michael, 49, 80
Winslow, Don, 232, 233, 322
Winspear, Jacqueline, 155
Winterbottom, Michael, 57, 215
Winters, Ben H, 416
Wishart, David, 369, 370
Wolfe, Tom, 130
Woodrell, Daniel, 230, 247
Woolrich, Cornell, 16, 44, 51, 58, 200, 201
Wyndham Davies, June, 23

X

Xiaolong, Qiu, 135

Y

Yokoyama, Hideo, 408, 409
Yordan, Philip, 178
Young, Scott, 247

Z

Zinnemann, Fred, 222
Zola, Émile, 14, 15, 128, 401

INDEX OF TITLES

10 Rillington Place, 223
1st to Die, 121
21 Grams, 372
51st State, The, 320
9tail Fox, 248, 249

A

A Bout de Souffle, 51
A is for Alibi, 68
ABC Murders, The, 31, 32
Aberystwyth Mon Amour, 333
Absolute Friends, 265
Absolute Zero Cool, 326
Accidental Agent, The, 286
Accordionist, The, 408
Acid Casuals, 245
Acid Row, 263, 264
Act of Roger Murgatroyd, The, 302
Adam and Eve and Pinch Me, 168
Adventure of the Creeping Man, The, 22
Adventure of the Mazarin Stone, The, 22
Advise and Consent, 412
Afraid to Death, 178
After Dark, My Sweet, 57
After the Armistice Ball, 308
After the Crash, 375
After You Die, 294
Agatha, 31

Agatha Raisin and the Quiche of Death, 303
Alex, 396
All She Was Worth, 402
All the Beautiful Lies, 299
All the Old Knives, 289, 290
Almost Blue, 397
Along Came a Spider, 121
Always Outnumbered, Always Outgunned, 257
Amadeus, 382
Amagansett, 356
Amateur Cracksman, The, 24
Amateur Spy, The, 274
American Boy, The, 367
American Friend, The, 213
American Psycho, 206, 207
American Tabloid, 238
Amerikanische Freund, Der, 213
Amores Perros, 372
Anarchist Detective, The, 133
Anarchy and Old Dogs, 327
Anatomy of a Scandal, 300
And Then There Were None, 31, 33
And Then You Die, 237
Angel in the House, 333
Angel on the Inside, 79
Angels and Demons, 403

Angels of the Flood, 163
Answers from the Grave, 232
Apothecary Rose, The, 362
Apple Tree Yard, 295
Appointment with Death, 33
Arab Jazz, 401, 402
Arabesk, 118, 248
Arsenic and Old Lace, 33
Ash and Bone, 249
Ashes of Berlin, The, 355
Aspern Papers, The, 357
Asphalt Jungle, The, 44, 45, 46
Associate, The, 148
Asta's Book, 167
Avventura, L', 182
Axeman's Jazz, The, 339

B

Babes in the Wood, The, 124
Babylon Berlin, 391
Bad Blood, 117
Bad Chili, 109
Bad Company, 279
Bad Men, 206
Bad Things, 192
Band Wagon, The, 55
Barbouze, 171
Basket Case, 331
Batman, 146
Battalion, 316
Bay of Souls, 263
Be My Enemy, 156, 157
Beast in View, 193
Beast Must Die, The, 27
Beautiful Dead, The, 203, 204
Before I Go to Sleep, 293
Behind her Eyes, 299
Behind the Scenes at the Museum, 60
Bellevue Square, 195
Bellini Card, The, 345, 346
Belshazzar's Daughter, 118
Bête Humaine, La, 15
Big Heat, The, 277
Big Nowhere, The, 92
Big Sleep, The, 47, 48, 49, 80, 413

Big Thaw, The, 98
Billy Straight, 191
Bird in the Hand, A, 303
Birdman, 99, 162
Birds, The, 115, 193
Birdwatcher, The, 127
Bitter, 298
Bitter Fruits, 179
Black Dahlia, The, 92, 93
Black Maps, 79
Black Mask, 16, 24, 43, 44, 45, 49, 59, 69, 70
Black Path, The, 393
Black Sunday, 209
Black Water, 253, 295, 375
Black Water Rising, 253
Blackboard Jungle, The, 115, 193
Blackhouse, The, 114
Blacklands, 203
Blacklist, 77
Bleak House, 7, 136
Bleed a River Deep, 117
Blessington Method, The, 415
Blindsighted, 153
Blood and Sugar, 365
Blood of Victory, 275
Blood Rain, 237
Blood Safari, 399
Bloodline, 116
Bloody London, 76
Bloody Meadow, The, 363, 364
Blow Fly, 141, 142
Blue Dahlia, The, 49
Blue Hammer, The, 74
Blue Light, 257
Blue Monday, 184
Blue Nowhere, The, 89, 342
Blue Room, The, 406
Body Double, 143
Body Heat, 139
Body in the Bath House, A, 341
Body in the Boat, The, 355
Boiling a Frog, 156
Bone Collector, The, 89
Bone Tree, The, 318

Border, The, 322
Bordersnakes, 221, 236
Born Bad, 125
Bourne Identity, The, 282, 283
Bourne Supremacy, The, 282
Bourne Ultimatum, The, 282
Boy Who Followed Ripley, The, 213
Bravo Two Zero, 284
Break Line, The, 313
Break No Bones, 151
Breaking and Entering, 106
Breathless, 51
Briarpatch, 416
Bride Wore Black, The, 58
Bright Young Dead, 304
Brighton Rock, 27, 222, 223, 335
Broken, 88
Broken Ground, 116
Broken Shore, The, 130
Broken Skin, 113
Broker, The, 144, 145
Brothers in Blood, 218
Brothers Karamazov, The, 14
Bruno, Chief of Police, 131, 132
Bryant and May: The Bleeding Heart, 329
Build My Gallows High, 54
Bullet in the Ballet, A, 325
Bullet Trick, The, 368
Burglar on the Prowl, The, 324
Burial, 181
Burning Air, The, 191
Burning Girl, The, 84
Burning Man, The, 148
Burnt-Out Case, A, 277
Business of Dying, The, 107

C

Cahiers du Cinéma, 52
Calendar Girl, 66
Call for the Dead, 280
Calypso, 115
Candyland, 192, 193
Cape Fear, 166
Captains Outrageous, 110
Cardiff Dead, 173, 264
Careless Love, 126
Cari Mora, 209
Carta Bianca, 397
Carte Blanche, 397
Cartel, The, 322
Carver's Quest, 362
Casablanca, 19, 292
Case Histories, 60
Case of the Turning Tide, The, 34
Case-Book of Sherlock Holmes, The, 22, 413
Casino for Sale, 325
Casino Royale, 268, 282
Casual Vacancy, The, 68
Catch-22, 278
Charade, 178
Charlie Chan, 37, 415
Chatham School Affair, The, 180
Child 44, 366
Chill, The, 74
Chinatown, 81
Choice of Enemies, A, 147
Choirboys, The, 132
Chosen Dead, The, 145
Chourmo, 388
City of Bones, 64
City of Dreadful Night, 224
City of Sinners, 91
Class Murder, 127
Cleaner, The, 417
Close to Home, 298
Closed Casket, 305
Club Dumas, The, 403
Clubbable Woman, A, 101
Clubland, 230, 266
Cockfighter, 134
Cold Cold Ground, The, 255
Cold Day for Murder, A, 247
Cold Desert Sky, 168
Cold Earth, 87
Cold Granite, 113
Cold Mind, A, 212
Cold Six Thousand, The, 238
Cold to the Touch, 170

Cold War, The, 131
Collector, The, 184
Coma, 140, 152
Company, The, 281
Company of Strangers, The, 134, 292
Confessions of a Romantic Pornographer, 189
Constant Gardener, The, 252, 265
Cop Hater, 115
Coroner's Lunch, The, 327
Corpse with the Sapphire Eyes, The, 137
Cotton Comes to Harlem, 250
Coup de Torchon, 57
Craftsman, The, 178
Creeping Ivy, 246
Crime and Punishment, 7, 14, 174, 357, 387
Crime SuspenStories, 45
Crisis, 160
Crisis Four, 284
Critique of Criminal Reason, 346
Crooked Herring, 335
Crooked Letter, Crooked Letter, 345
Cross, 60, 61
Cross her Heart, 299
Croupier, 240
Crucifix Killer, The, 204, 205
Cruel Mercy, 113
Cruellest Month, The, 122
Crust on its Uppers, The, 229, 231
Cuckoo's Calling, The, 68
Cut Adrift, 320
Cutting Room, The, 368
Cutting Season, The, 253

D

D'Entre les Morts, 373
Da Vinci Code, The, 312, 314, 321, 403
Dain Curse, The, 71
Damaged, 88
Damascened Blade, The, 340
Damascus Gate, 263
Dandy Gilver and the Proper Treatment of Bloodstains, 308
Dangerous Lady, 88, 220

Dark Anatomy, A, 337
Dark Blood, 112, 113
Dark Devotion, A, 142
Dark Horse, 163, 164
Dark Passage, 51
Dark Pines, 158
Dark Tides, 93
Dark Tunnel, The, 74
Dark Winter, 284
Darkening Stain, A, 134
Darkly Dreaming Dexter, 211
Darkness,, The, 389
Darkness Falls from the Air, 337
Darling, 248
Day of the Dead, 184
Day of the Jackal, The, 171, 221, 222, 240
Dead Calm, 216
Dead Cert, 159, 160
Dead Cold, 122
Dead Gone, 131
Dead I Well May Be, 255
Dead Like You, 105
Dead Man's Blues, 339
Dead Men Don't Wear Plaid, 81
Dead Souls, 123
Deadly Decisions, 151
Dearly Devoted Dexter, 211
Death Can't Take a Joke, 253
Death du Jour, 151
Death Games, 320
Death in Disguise, 97
Death in Holy Orders, 104
Death in Paradise, 311
Death in the West Wind, 352
Death of a Lake, 246
Death of a Red Heroine, 135
Death of Dalziel, The, 101, 103
Death on the Nile, 31
Death under a Tuscan Sun, 383, 384
Deceit, 142
Decipher, 320
Deep Down Dead, 138
Deep Water, 150
Defence, The, 140
Déjà Dead, 151, 152

Deliverance of Evil, The, 378, 379
Deniable Death, A, 288
Derailed, 171
Desperate Journey, 158
Desperation Road, 230
Detective, The, 416
Detective Story, 44
Detective Wore Silk Drawers, The, 353
Deuce, The, 260
Deviant Ways, 213
Devil in a Blue Dress, 257
Devil in the Marshalsea, The, 348, 349
Devil's Dice, The, 133
Devil's Home on Leave, The, 194
Devotion of Suspect X, 385, 386
Dexter, 211
Dexter in the Dark, 211
Diaboliques, Les, 373
Diamond Bikini, The, 216
Diamonds are Forever, 268
Die Hard, 416
Die with Me, 94
Difficult Lives, 197
Dimma, 390
Disordered Minds, 197, 198
Dispossessed, The, 258
Dissolution, 364
Disturbing Ground, 149
Doctor Strange, 23
Dodgers, 218, 219
Dog Soldiers, 262, 263
Doll's House, The, 84
Don Quixote, 409
Don't Look Back, 383
Double Indemnity, 49, 139, 228
Down There, 52
Down to the Woods, 84
Downton Abbey, 304
Dr No, 269
Dracula, 12
Drama City, 259
Drink Before the War, A, 72
Drop, The, 225, 227
Dry, The, 186
Dying to Tell, 161, 162

E

Eagle Has Landed, The, 279
Eats, Shoots and Leaves, 334
Echo Burning, 85, 86
Eighth Circle, The, 415
Eleven Days, 98
Empire State, 285
Empty Hours, The, 115
Entertainer, The, 160
Entertainment Weekly, 182
Envoy on Excursion, 325
Every Dead Thing, 206
Evil Eye, The, 373
Executioners, The, 166
Exile, 256
Eye of the Beholder, The, 177, 178
Eyre Affair, The, 329

F

Fade to Grey, 73
Faithless, 152, 153
Fall, The, 117
Fall of Man in Wilmslow, 392
Fallen Idol, The, 277
Falls, The, 122, 123
False Inspector Dew, The, 353
Fantômas, 16
Farewell, My Lovely, 47, 57, 80
Fatherland, 277, 347, 348
Fear Itself, 286
Fear of Dark Water, A, 126
Fearful Symmetry, 190
Feast Day of Fools, 61, 62
Fiends, The, 373
Fifty-Two Pickup, 165, 225, 226
Fighter, The, 230
Final Country, The, 221
Final Detail, The, 63
Final Venture, 169
Firefly, 285
Firewall, 284, 398, 410
Firm, The, 144
Fistful of Dollars, A, 53
Five Pubs, Two Bars and a Nightclub, 173

Flanders Panel, The, 403
Flesh and Blood, 190, 191, 249
Florentine Death, A, 384
Flower Girls, The, 179
Force of Nature, 186, 187
Foreign Correspondent, The, 276
Forest of Souls, The, 175
Four Blind Mice, 121
Four Serious Songs, 28
Fox Evil, 264
Franchise Affair, The, 41, 42
Free to Trade, 169
French Lieutenant's Woman, The, 357
Fresh Flesh, 67
Friday the Rabbi Slept Late, 246
Friends of Eddie Coyle, The, 147
Friends, Lovers, Chocolate, 307
From Russia with Love, 268
Frost Fair, The, 353, 354
Frozen Dead, The, 400
Frozen Moment, 377
Frozen Woman, The, 400
Funeral Music, 190
Furious Old Women, 326

G

Gagged and Bound, 245, 247
Gallery Whispers, 105
Gallows Court, 343
Gallows View, 125
Galton Case, The, 75
Gangs of New York, The, 234
Gangster as Tragic Hero, The, 236
Garden of Beasts, 342
Gardens of the Dead, 138, 139
Garnethill, 256
Gas Light, 308
Gaudy Night, 40, 41
Gene, 320
Get Carter, 227, 239, 240
Get Shorty, 238, 239
Getaway, The, 57, 242, 243
Ghost, The, 412
Ghost in the Machine, A, 97
Ghost of a Flea, 196

Girl in Berlin, The, 291, 292
Girl in the Spider's Web, The, 392
Girl on the Train, The, 159, 296, 297
Girl who Kicked the Hornets' Nest,
  The, 396
Girl who Played with Fire, The, 395
Girl with Seven Names, The, 319
Girl with the Dragon Tattoo, The, 394,
  395, 396
Girl Zero, 91
Give Me Your Hand, 174, 175
Given Day, The, 352
Glass Key, The, 71, 80
Go West Inspector Ghote, 106
Godfather, The, 240, 241, 277
Godfather Part II, The, 241
Godfather Part III, The, 241
Gods of Gotham, The, 344
Gods of Guilt, The, 64, 65
Goldfinger, 269
Gone Girl, 296
Gone, Baby, Gone, 111
Good Samaritans, 205
Good Sister, The, 251
Good Son, The, 417
Gorky Park, 128, 129, 261, 277
Grantchester, 309, 310
Gravedigger, 72
Greeks Bearing Gifts, 351
Green for Danger, 28, 29
Green Ripper, The, 75
Greenmantle, 15
Grifters, The, 56, 57, 58
Grissom Gang, The, 50
Guilty Minds, 316
Guilty Party, The, 193
Gumshoe, 81

H

Half Broken Things, 190
Hamlet, Revenge!, 332
Hanging Garden, The, 123
Hanging Shed, The, 344, 345
Hangover Square, 34, 35
Harbour Master, The, 260

INDEX OF TITLES

Hard Eight, 328, 329
Hard Feelings, 232
Hard Landing, 110
Hard Revolution, 359
Harper, 76
Havana Best Friends, 416
Hawksmoor, 317
He Died with his Eyes Open, 194, 231
He Who Fears the Wolf, 383
Head Shot, 105
Heart of Darkness, 319
Heartsick, 85
Heat from Another Sun, 212
Heaven's Prisoners, 63
Heed the Thunder, 56
Heirs of Owain Glyndŵr, The, 150
Hell Bay, 125
Hell Hath No Fury, 216
Hell to Pay, 78
Hello Bunny Alice, 200
Help!, 178
Her Husband's Lover, 293, 294
Heresy, 358
Heretics, The, 339
Hidden Child, The, 391
Hidden Man, The, 272
High Citadel, 268
High Commissioner, The, 86, 87
High Sierra, 45
Hill Girl, 216
Hill Street Blues, 65, 192
Hollow Man, The, 31
Holloway Falls, 181
Hollywood Station, 132
Holy Thief, The, 363, 364
Home Fire, 251
Hostage, 65, 66
Hot Country, The, 338
Hot Poppies, 76
Hound of the Baskervilles, The, 20
Hour Game, 203
House of Cards, 412
House of Wolfe, The, 219
House on Half Moon Street, The, 361
How a Gunman Says Goodbye, 228

Human Beast, The, 15
Hunter, The (Hamdy), 316
Hunter, The (Stark), 241
Hunting Party, The, 183

I

I Am Pilgrim, 317
I Was Dora Suarez, 194
I, The Jury, 55
Ice House, The, 198
If He Hollers Let Him Go, 251
In a Dark, Dark Wood, 199
In a Dry Season, 126
In a House of Lies, 124
In a Lonely Place, 416
In the Dark, 298
In the Kingdom of Mists, 349
Incorruptible, 119
Infidel Stain, The, 339
Innocence of Father Brown, The, 157
Innocent Blood, 102
Inspector Calls, An, 33
Instance of the Fingerpost, An, 168
Into the Water, 297
Intrusions, The, 128
Invasion of the Body Snatchers, 54
Invisible, 150
Involuntary Witness, 377
Ipcress File, The, 273
Island, The, 390

J

Jack's Return Home, 227, 239
Jackal, The, 222
Jackie Brown, 165
Jacquot and the Angel, 119, 120
Jacquot and the Waterman, 119
Janissary Tree, The, 345
Jar City, 387, 388, 410
Journey into Fear, 266, 267
Judgement in Stone, A, 167
Judgment of Deke Hunter, The, 147
Julius Caesar, 12
Jump, The, 88
Junky, 57

Jurassic Park, 315

K
Keep Me Alive, 247
Kill Bill, 58
Killer Inside Me, The, 57, 215
Killer on the Road, 208
Killer!, 28
Killing, The, 57
Killing Habit, The, 84, 204
Killing Me Softly, 184
Killing of the Saints, The, 218
Killing the Beasts, 320
Killing the Emperors, 328
Kill-Off, The, 57
Kim, 15
Kingdom of Shadows, 275, 276
Kiss Me Deadly, 55
Kiss Me, Deadly, 54
Kitty Peck and the Child of Ill-Fortune, 347
Kitty Peck and the Daughter of Sorrow, 347
Kitty Peck and the Music Hall Murders, 346
Knife, 403
Knife to the Heart, A, 119
Knots and Crosses, 123
Known Dead, 98

L
LA Confidential, 92, 93, 238
LA Quartet, 92, 238
LA Requiem, 65
LaBrava, 226
Ladies in Retirement, 33
Lady, The, 143
Lady in the Lake, The, 80
Laidlaw, 118, 345
Land of Fire, 286
Land of the Living, 183, 184
Language of Secrets, The, 251, 252
Last Detective, The, 65, 66
Last Don, The, 240
Last Hours, The, 199

Last King of Brighton, The, 224
Last Policeman, The, 416
Last Seen in Massilia, 365
Last Sherlock Holmes Story, The, 91
Last Supper, The, 283
Last Templar, The, 350, 351
Last Temptation, The, 149
Laughing Policeman, The, 411
Lawless, The, 54
Lazybones, 84
Leavenworth Case, The, 416
Legacy, The (La Plante), 164
Legacy, The (Sigurðardóttir), 164
Legends, 282
Levanter, The, 267
Lewis Man, The, 114
Liar Liar, 84
Lifeless, 84, 85
Light of Day, The, 267
Lighthouse, The, 102
Lincoln Lawyer, The, 65
List of Adrian Messenger, The, 37, 38
Listeners, The, 122
Little Caesar, 45, 236
Little Drummer Girl, The, 280
Live and Let Die, 268
Live by Night, 352, 353
Living and the Dead, The, 373
Lock, Stock and Two Smoking Barrels, 230
Lone Wolf, The, 24
Long Firm, The, 235, 236
Long Goodbye, The, 48, 49, 81
Long Midnight of Barney Thomson, The, 332
Long Run South, 171
Long Way Home, 294
Long-Legged Fly, The, 196
Lord Jim, 367
Lost, 195, 196
Lost Symbol, The, 314
Love Lies Bleeding, 327
Loyal Character Dancer, A, 135
Lune dans le Caniveau, La, 51
Lying in State, 361

M

Macbeth, 403
Magpie Murders, 305
Magus, The, 357
Malice Aforethought, 36, 37
Maltese Falcon, The, 46, 47, 49, 52, 69, 71
Man Between, The, 272
Man from Berlin, The, 355
Man Hunt, 36
Man In Black, The, 33
Man in my Basement, The, 257
Man Who Left Too Soon, The, 396
Man Who Murdered Himself, The, 54
Man Who Was Thursday, The, 19
Man Who Watched the Trains Go By, The, 405
Man Who Went up in Smoke, The, 406
Manchurian Candidate, The, 412
Margery Allingham's Mr Campion's Farewell, 39
Mariée Était en Noir, La, 58
Marseilles Trilogy, The, 388
Masculine Ending, A, 260, 261
Mask of Dimitrios, The, 267, 413
Master of Rain, The, 313
Maura's Game, 220
Mayhem, 360
Medea, 146
Medusa, 91
Memory Game, The, 183
Mercy, 212, 396
Metropolis, 351
Mexican Tree Duck, The, 221
Miami Blues, 134
Miami Vice, 65
Middlemarch, 409
Midsomer Murders, 97
Millennium Trilogy, 394, 395
Ministry of Fear, The, 276, 277, 414
Misérables, Les, 12
Miss Smilla's Feeling for Snow, 386, 410
Missionary Stew, 416
Mississippi Blood, 318
Mist, The, 390

Mitford Murders, The, 304
Modern Ghosts, 195
Monogram Murders, The, 304
Monstrum, 350
Moon in the Gutter, The, 51
Moonstone, The, 12
Morbid Taste for Bones, A, 359, 360
Mortelle Randonnée, 178
Moskva, 277, 278
Mousetrap, The, 33
Moving Target, The, 74, 76
Mr Clarinet, 80, 81, 82
Mr Mercedes, 107, 108
Mr Moto, 37
Murder à la Stroganoff, 325
Murder at the Grand Raj Palace, 306
Murder at the Nightwood Bar, 94
Murder Bag, The, 120
Murder in a Cold Climate, 247
Murder in Mesopotamia, 31
Murder in the Caribbean, 311
Murder is Easy, 33
Murder Must Wait, 246
Murder of Quality, A, 280
Murder on the Orient Express, 31, 32
Murder Room, The, 102, 104
Murder, My Sweet, 80
Murder, She Wrote, 40
Murmur of Stones, The, 180
Murphy's Revenge, 323, 324
My Best Friend, 200
My Cousin Rachel, 299
Mysterious Affair of Style, A, 302
Mysterious Mr Quin, The, 34
Mystery of a Hansom Cab, The, 417
Mystery of Edwin Drood, The, 12
Mystic River, 72, 110, 111, 353, 414

N

Name of the Rose, The, 317, 346, 381, 382
Nasty Piece of Work, A, 73
Natchez Burning, 318
Nation, The, 388
Ne le Dis à Personne, 180
Nearest Exit, The, 290

Necessary Death of Lewis Winter, The, 228
Necropolis Railway, The, 354
Neon Rain, The, 62, 63
Never Come Morning, 220
New Tricks, 116
Night, 400
Night and the City, 224, 225
Night Buffalo, The, 372
Night Crossing, 363
Night Heron, 269, 270
Night Must Fall, 263
Night of the Generals, The, 346
Night of the Hunter, The, 166
Nightfall Berlin, 278
Nine Lessons, 172
Nineteen Eighty, 259
Nineteen Eighty Three, 259
Nineteen Seventy Four, 259
Nineteen Seventy Seven, 259
No Beast So Fierce, 219
No Country for Old Men, 202
No Laughing Matter, 330
No Orchids for Miss Blandish, 24, 50, 86
No. 1 Ladies' Detective Agency, The, 306, 307
Nobody Runs Forever, 87
Noise Downstairs, A, 176
North by Northwest, 19, 171
Nothing Lasts Forever, 416
Novel in a Year, A, 295
number9dream, 316

O

Oaken Heart, The, 27
Odessa File, The, 222
Oedipus Rex, 11, 146
Old Boys, 283
Old Religion, The, 131
One Fearful Yellow Eye, 75
One for the Money, 328
One Small Step, 102
Onion Field, The, 132
Ordeal by Innocence, 31
Orpheus Descent, The, 317
Ossessione, 46
Other Daughter, The, 95
Other Woman, The, 200
Our Kind of Cruelty, 296
Out of Reach, 316
Out of the Dark, 247
Out of the Past, 54
Outbreak, 140
Outerbridge Reach, 263
Over the Edge, 190

P

Palace of Treason, 283
Pandora's Boy, 342
Paris in the Dark, 338
Paths of Glory, 57
Patient Fury, A, 132
Peeping Tom, 201
Pendulum, 316
Perfect Husband, The, 95
Perfect Murder, The, 106
Perry Mason, 34
Peter's Pence, 86
Picnic at Hanging Rock, 187
Pictures, The, 338
Pieces of Her, 172
Pieces of Modesty, 284
Pietr the Latvian, 405
Place of Safety, A, 97
Place to Lie, A, 295
Play It Again, Sam, 81
Playing with Fire, 125, 126
Pleasantville, 253
Pledge, The, 380, 381
Plein Soleil, 213
Point Blank, 241, 242
Poison Garden, The, 177
Poison Tree, The, 191
Polar Star, 129, 261
Pompeii, 348
Pop. 1280, 57
Portrait, The, 167, 168
Portrait of a Killer: Jack the Ripper – Case Closed, 141

Postman Always Rings Twice, The, 14, 46, 139
Postmortem, 140, 141
Power of the Dog, The, 233, 322
Prayers for Rain, 72
Predator, The, 169
Presumed Innocent, 153, 154
Prey, 315
Prime Suspect, 164
Prince of Wales, The, 173, 264
Prisoner of Guantánamo, The, 274
Psycho, 373
Public Enemy, The, 228
Pulp, 316
Pulp Fiction, 226
Pulse, 160
Purple Cane Road, 61

Q

Que la Bête Meure, 28
Queen of the South, The, 403, 404
Quest for Anna Klein, The, 271
Question of Guilt, A, 185
Quiet Belief in Angels, A, 207
Quincunx, The, 358
Quite Ugly One Morning, 156

R

Raffles, 24
Raffles and Miss Blandish, 50
Rain Gods, 62
Rashomon, 235, 402
Rasp, The, 37
Rat on Fire, The, 146
Ratking, 91
Rear Window, 34, 159, 200, 201, 296
Rebecca, 293
Red Crystal, 142
Red Dragon, 208, 209, 210
Red Hand of Fury, The, 357
Red Harvest, 52, 70
Red Rabbit, 270, 271
Red Riding Quartet, 255, 259
Red Road, The, 256, 257
Red Sparrow, 283
Red Square, 129
Redbreast, The, 403, 411
Reservoir Dogs, 219
Restoration Mystery, A, 354
Resurrection Men, 124
Reversible Errors, 154
Rich Full Death, A, 91
Riddle of the Sands, The, 15, 22
Ride the Pink Horse, 416
Rider on the Rain, 389
Right as Rain, 78
Right Behind You, 143
Ripley Under Ground, 188
Ripley's Game, 213
River of Shadows, 407
Rogue Male, 18, 35, 36, 222, 289
Romanzo Criminale, 379, 380
Rope, 34
Roth Trilogy, The, 368
Rottweiler, The, 214
Ruin Beach, 125
Rum Punch, 165
Running Blind, 268
Running Hot, 229

S

S is for Silence, 68, 69
Saboteur, 19
Safe House, 93
Safe Houses, 275
Saint, The, 24
Sandrine's Case, 180
Saturday Night and Sunday Morning, 42, 263
Savage Altar, The, 394
Savage Garden, The, 356
Savage Season, 109
Savages, 232, 233
Sawbones, 112
Scaredy Cat, 84
Scarface, 45, 380
Scarlatti Inheritance, The, 282
Scholar of Extortion, The, 95
Scold's Bridle, The, 198
Scrublands, 162

Sculptress, The, 198
Seagull, The, 87
Seance on a Wet Afternoon, 223
Secret Agent, The, 15, 19, 266
Secret Smile, 184
Secret Speech, The, 366, 367
Seeking Sanctuary, 185
Seizure, 140, 141
Série Noire, 58
Seven for a Secret, 344
Seven-Per-Cent Solution, The, 416
Seville Communion, The, 403
Sex Dolls, 76
Sexy Beast, 230
Shadow District, The, 388
Shadow Family, 403
Shadow Killer, The, 388
Shadow Tracer, The, 186
Shaman's Knife, The, 247
Shape of Snakes, The, 199
Shape of Water, The, 376
Sharp Objects, 182
She Lies in Wait, 192
She Who Was No More, 373
She's Never Coming Back, 396
Sherlock, 23
Sherlock Holmes, 23
Sherlock Holmes and the Devil's Promise, 340, 341
Shining Girls, The, 202
Shock SuspenStories, 45
Shoot the Pianist, 51
Shoot the Piano Player, 52
Shooting in the Shop, The, 325, 326
Shot in the Dark, A, 334
Sicilian, The, 240
Sick Puppy, 330
Sick Rose, The, 191
Sideswipe, 133, 134
Sidetracked, 398
Sidney Chambers and the Problem of Evil, 309
Silence of the Grave, 371, 387
Silence of the Lambs, The, 203, 208, 209, 210

Silence of the Rain, The, 415
Silent and the Damned, The, 134
Silent Room, The, 97, 98
Silent Terror, 208
Silent Witness, 116, 137
Sirens, 109
Six Four, 408, 409
Sixth Lamentation, 138
Skin in Darkness, 189
Skinflick, 72
Skinner's Rules, 105
Skinny Dip, 331
Slaughter's Hound, 326
Sleep, 197
Sleeping Cruelty, 164
Sleepyhead, 84
Small Back Room, The, 337
Small Death in Lisbon, A, 134, 292, 369
Smile of a Ghost, The, 169
Smiling Man, The, 109
Smoke and Ashes, 357, 358
Snake Stone, The, 345
Snow Hill, 170
Soft Target, 110
Solea, 388
Someone Else's Skin, 100
Somme Stations, The, 354, 355
Sopranos, The, 239
Sour Cream with Everything, 332
Southern Cross Crime, 417
Spend Game, 160
Split Second, 203
Spoilers, The, 268
Spook Street, 278
Spy by Nature, A, 272
Spy Who Came in From the Cold, The, 252, 272, 279, 280, 281
Spy's Life, A, 285
Stain on the Snow, The, 405
Stamping Butterflies, 248
Stand By, Stand By, 286
Star of the North, 318
Staring at the Light, 186
State of Fear, 314, 315
Steel Rain, 363

INDEX OF TITLES

Steppin' on a Rainbow, 67
Still Life, 122
Stone Cold, 78
Straight Time, 220
Strand, The, 22
Strange Case of Peter the Lett, 405
Strangers on a Train, 49, 187, 188, 189, 406
Strangler Vine, The, 339
Streets of Darkness, 90
Strings of Murder, The, 89
Strong Poison, 41
Suburra, 374
Sudden Arrival of Violence, The, 228
Summer of Murder, A, 374
Sunburn, 227
Sunday Philosophy Club, The, 307
Sunset and Sawdust, 109, 110
Surfeit of Lampreys, 39
Surgeon, The, 143
Susan Effect, The, 386
Suspect, The (Barton), 177
Suspect, The (Robotham), 196
Suspension of Mercy, A, 188
Swag, 225
Sweetheart, 85
Sweetness of Life, The, 386
Syndicate, The, 338

T

Take My Hand, 111
Taken, The, 179
Talented Mr Ripley, The, 188, 212, 213
Tales of Mystery and Imagination, 367
Taste for Death, A, 103
Taste of Honey, A, 160
Tell No Lies, 146
Tell No One, 179, 180
Tell No Tales, 294
Ten Little Niggers, 33
Tenth Man Down, 286
Terracotta Dog, The, 375, 376
Their Little Secret, 84
Then She Was Gone, 130, 131
Thérèse, 14, 15
Thérèse Raquin, 14
Thief in the Night, A, 24
Thin Man, The, 53, 71
Third Man, The, 277
Third Victim, The, 95, 96
Thirteen Hours, 399
Thirty-Nine Steps, The, 15, 18, 36, 171, 266
This Sweet Sickness, 188
Three Burials of Melquiades Estrada, The, 372
Three Coffins, The, 31
Three Emperors, The, 339
Thunderball, 269
Thus Was Adonis Murdered, 327
Ties that Bind, 147
Tiger in the Smoke, The, 26, 27
Tilted World, The, 345
Time is an Ambush, 158
Time to Kill, A, 144
Tinker Tailor Soldier Spy, 252
Tirez sur le Pianiste, 51
To Have and Have Not, 49
To Kill a Tsar, 369
Tokyo, 162, 163
Torment of Others, The, 150
Torn Curtain, 19
Total Chaos, 388
Touch of Evil, 266
Tough Luck, 232
Tourist Season, 330
Tower, The, 321, 322
Trackers, 399
Traitor to Memory, A, 96
Traitor's Kiss, 287, 288
Trap for Cinderella, 389
Treachery of Spies, A, 287
Treatment, The, 99, 162
Trent's Last Case, 18
Trent's Own Case, 18
Trespasser, The, 185
Trust Betrayed, A, 362
Trust No One, 194
Truth, 129, 130
Turn a Blind Eye, 119

Twelve, The, 258
Twenty Thousand Streets Under the Sky, 35
Twilight Hour, The, 291
Two for the Dough, 329
Two O'Clock Boy, 101

U

Under Western Eyes, 15
Undercurrents, 186
Uniform Justice, 112
Unknown Man No. 89, 226
Unquiet Dead, The, 251
Unsuitable Job for a Woman, An, 103

V

Vadim, 350
Vanish in an Instant, 193
Vanishing Box, The, 347
Vertigo, 373
Victims, The, 373
Vita Brevis, 343
Voices, 387
Vote for Murder, A, 369, 370

W

Walkin' the Dog, 257
Walking the Shadows, 350
Wanted, The, 66
War and Peace, 281
Wash This Blood Clean From My Hand, 407
Wasp Factory, The, 176
Way Through the Woods, The, 89, 90
We Shall Inherit the Wind, 406, 407
Weirdo, 82
Westworld, 314
Whaleboat House, The, 356
What Men Say, 261
What We Did, 298
Whatever You Love, 295
When Red Is Black, 135
When the Bough Breaks, 190
Where the Devil Can't Go, 253
Whispers of the Dead, 137
White Crocodile, 319, 320
White Devils, 254
White Heat, 247
White Jazz, 92
Whitehall Mandarin, The, 290
Who'll Stop the Rain, 263
Whole Wide World, 255
Widow, The, 177
Widows, 164
Winter Queen, The, 372
Winter's Bone, 230, 247
Winterland, 160, 161
Wire, The, 260
Without Trace, 156
Witness for the Prosecution, The, 31
Wolf Winter, 142
Wolves Eat Dogs, 261
Woman in Black, The, 33
Woman in the Window, The, 159, 297
Woman in White, The, 12
Woman Who Was No More, The, 373
Woman with Birthmark, 411
Wooden Overcoat, The, 325
Written in Bones, 120
Wrong Girl, The, 300
Wrong Way Home, 97
Wycherly Woman, The, 74

Y

Y is for Yesterday, 68
Yojimbo, 53
You Are Evil, 378
You Don't Know Me, 254
You Only Live Twice, 269

Z

Zero, 382